THE PENGUIN CLASSICS

FOUNDER EDITOR (1944–64): E. V. RIEU

Editor: Betty Radice

PUBLIUS VERGILIUS MARO was born in 70 B.C. near Mantua in Cisalpine Gaul, the north of Italy, where his parents owned a farm. He had a good education and went to perfect it in Rome. He made friends with many important Romans, but being shy and in bad health he preferred a quiet life of study and meditation. He returned to the Mantuan farm, and in 43 B.C. he began to write the *Eclogues*. But in the Civil War his land was confiscated and he went to live mainly in Naples where the emperor Augustus granted him a residence. He completed the *Eclogues* in 37 B.C., the year in which he accompanied Horace to Brindisi. The *Georgics* were finished in 30 B.C., and he devoted the rest of his life to the composition of the *Aeneid*. In his last year he started on a journey to Greece; he fell ill at Megara and returned to Italy, but he died in 19 B.C. on reaching Brindisi.

W. F. JACKSON KNIGHT was reader in classical literature at the University of Exeter from 1942 until he retired in 1961. He graduated from Hertford College, Oxford, where he won an open scholarship in classics, and after serving in the Royal Engineers during the First World War he taught classics for thirteen years before joining the staff of University College, Exeter, in 1936. He was a foundation committee member of the Virgil Society, becoming its President in 1949. In 1945 he was elected a Fellow of the Royal Society of Literature. His publications include *Vergil's Troy* (1932), *Accentual Symmetry in Vergil* (1939), *Roman Vergil* (1944, Penguin edition 1966), *Poetic Inspiration, An Approach to Vergil* (1946), and, posthumously, *Vergil: Epic and Anthropology* (1967), *Many-minded Homer* (1968) and *Elysion* (1970). He died in 1964.

VIRGIL
THE AENEID

TRANSLATED INTO ENGLISH PROSE
WITH AN INTRODUCTION BY
W. F. JACKSON KNIGHT

PENGUIN BOOKS

Penguin Books Ltd, Harmondsworth, Middlesex, England
Penguin Books, 625 Madison Avenue, New York, New York 10022, U.S.A.
Penguin Books Australia Ltd, Ringwood, Victoria, Australia
Penguin Books Canada Ltd, 2801 John Street, Markham, Ontario, Canada L3R 1B4
Penguin Books (N.Z.) Ltd, 182–190 Wairau Road, Auckland 10, New Zealand

—

This translation first published 1956
Reprinted with revisions 1958
Reprinted 1959, 1960, 1962, 1963, 1964, 1965
1966, 1968, 1969, 1970, 1971, 1972, 1973, 1974, 1975, 1976 (twice), 1977, 1978,
1979, 1980

—

—

Set, printed and bound in Great Britain by
Cox & Wyman Ltd, Reading
Set in Monotype Garamond

To

T. J. Haarhoff

CONTENTS

THE AENEID

ACKNOWLEDGEMENTS

SURELY no translation has ever before had the advantage of so much help, spontaneously offered and lavishly given, from so many expert friends. They have done their level best to protect me from my own deficiencies.

My brother, G. Wilson Knight, has read and criticized the whole book at every stage of its production. Mr John D. Christie has read the translation in manuscript, and written a long and thorough criticism which has radically influenced the final version, and indeed dominates many of its pages; he has also read the proofs and given help not confined to the actual translation. The Rev. Father Ivo Thomas, O.P., has subjected the translation to a comprehensive examination in typescript, often disagreeing with my interpretations and enabling me to correct them. Mr John G. Landels has examined a revised typescript-version, attending in particular to accuracy of thought and choice of manuscript readings, and compiling for me the list of textual variations. He and Mrs Landels have together undertaken the glossary of names with explanatory notes, and prepared the maps for the Publisher's skilful Cartographer, whom I would also thank; and they have examined the whole book in proof. From her unique knowledge of Virgilian topography and landscape Dr Bertha Tilly has contributed vital, timely and indispensable help towards making the translation, the glossary of names, and the maps more accurate and up to date. Miss Rosemary Arundel has given the translation a final criticism in typescript with special attention both to accuracy of rendering and felicity of expression. Mr Bernard Vazquez has seen the whole book in proof and made important suggestions; he has also constructed the genealogical table. I am profoundly grateful for so very much help from scholars of high quality and for the advantage which this volume, in spite of all its faults, must surely have gained from their specialized knowledge of Virgilian problems.

Mrs Monica Hyde successfully typed the translation from a scarcely legible manuscript. After many recorrections to the translation, Miss Pamela Ffooks retyped it, freely offering time and care towards its improvement and furnishing valuable advice on English usage. I warmly thank them both for their skill and friendliness.

ACKNOWLEDGEMENTS

I acknowledge a particular debt to Professor Cecil Day Lewis, whose kindness gave me so much pleasure during our time of Virgilian association; and another, the most recent, to Professor Karl Büchner, who with great magnanimity sent me the page-proofs of his monumental article on Virgil in Pauly-Wissowa, *Realencyclopädie der Alterthumswissenschaft*.

There follows a more unusual acknowledgement. It is to Messrs Allen and Unwin Ltd, for publishing a few years ago a handy volume of *Selections from Vergil*, which might possibly help readers whose interest has been awakened by a translation to find for themselves, as they easily can, some of the keen pleasure to be gained from reading at least a little of Virgil's original Latin.

I have to thank many other friends for valuable and sometimes long-sustained help and encouragement, especially Mr Francis Kinchin Smith, Mr A. J. Creedy, Mrs Jean Creedy, Mrs R. Blemell-Pollard, Miss Alison Rashleigh, Miss J. E. Southan, Mr and Mrs Donald Leat, Dr G. C. Bye, and Dr Alan Smith; the order of names is chronological. Without their kindness I might never have dared this attempt.

There is no space to recognize the great number of written and spoken communications on which I have depended in the Introduction and throughout this book. Some have been acknowledged elsewhere and some are obvious. My silence on this occasion does not mean that I am ungrateful.

Two special acknowledgements remain. One of them is to Professor T. J. Haarhoff who has been helping and guiding me for nearly twenty-five years and has always sent me prompt answers to all my frequent enquiries; how authentic his direction has been must be left to appear hereafter. Finally I offer to Dr E. V. Rieu my heartfelt thanks. Recent experience of his sharp-sighted accuracy, his determination and firm will, and his lavish generosity of mind has helped me to understand, at least a little, why he has been able to create this series.

W.F.J.K.

Exeter
May 1956

INTRODUCTION

THE *Aeneid* of Virgil is a gateway between the pagan and the Christian centuries. Virgil, who was born in 70 B.C. and died in 19 B.C., left the poem unfinished at his death. That was eight years after the republican government of old Rome gave place to the rule of emperors, and only a few years before the Christian Era started. Virgil is the Poet of the Gate.

In the beginning, Rome had been a tiny settlement surrounded by enemies, and it had needed a strong will, proud, disciplined, and sustained, to survive at all. Rome did survive and was led on by successive hard-won victories to world dominion.

The early history is obscure, but the process seems to have taken at least five centuries of almost continuous warfare, and during that period the Romans achieved unparalleled success, apparently through unique merits of their own combined with a special share of divine favour and good fortune. The spectacular rise of Rome was a matter for wonder and a certain reverence to the Romans themselves, especially when, in the later years of the republican period, new chances of peace and prosperity, and a new access of scepticism threatened the old habits of loyalty, integrity, and self-sacrifice. People then looked back on their rich moral inheritance and became increasingly interested in the origins of Rome and in the Roman 'myth', which was both life-giving and poetically true. The valour of old Rome did not pass away before it could give to the Christian allegiance the devout and heroic fidelity which had made and saved the little Republic of long ago. Virgil was the supreme poet of this majestic phase of human experience. He distilled and epitomized it. And by the magic of creation he made it glow with a new light which was to brighten all the centuries to come.

Of Virgil's life something is known, but not very much. His full name was Publius Vergilius Maro. He was born near Mantua, in Cisalpine Gaul, as the north of Italy was then called. His parents had a farm there. The young Virgil was given a very good education and went to Rome to perfect it. He seems to have been interested in all subjects, including science. Though he early made friends with many important Romans, among them probably the young Octavius who was afterwards to become Augustus, the first emperor, Virgil preferred a quiet life, away from Rome. He was very shy and his health was always bad. He soon went to live at Naples, and there he spent most of his life, reading and writing. In 19 B.C. he started on a journey to Greece with Augustus. But he became very ill and had to return. He died at Brindisi. Before he died he asked his friends to burn the *Aeneid*. Apparently he was persuaded to change his mind, and agreed to let Varius and Tucca edit and publish it.

The Emperor Augustus had captured Virgil's imagination when they were both young. Virgil could apparently foresee that he would give the Roman World peace and order, as indeed he did. Virgil passionately believed in the restoration of Roman greatness and Italy's prosperity, and such too was the policy of Augustus and his chief minister Maecenas. They were Virgil's patrons, and in some sense and to some extent he wrote his poetry in conformity with their wishes. But Augustus sometimes used cruel methods, which Virgil could not condone, and indeed subtly criticized here and there in his late poetry. It is even possible that the influence of Virgil and his friend, the great lyric poet Horace, actually helped to reform Augustus, who became milder as he grew older.

Virgil left three literary works, all in verse. Some shorter poems were also attributed to him, but he is not now generally believed to be the author of any of them, at least in their present form, except two, both very short, but delightful.

Of the three certainly authentic works, the first is a collection of 'Pastoral Poems', otherwise known as the *Bucolics* or the *Eclogues*. They are ten short pieces, professedly fiction about imaginary goat-herds and other country people, but sometimes mentioning real people, some of them contemporary, or hinting at realities in a highly elusive kind of allegory. The poetry is full of charming thoughts and pictures, and the music of the Latin is lovely beyond description; and underlying it is a deep wisdom.

The next poem is 'Poetry of the Farm', the *Georgics*, in four books, containing advice to farmers about crops, trees, and animals, especially bees, but clothing it in poetic feeling and colour, usually fascinating and sometimes sublime.

The *Aeneid* is the third, last, and longest, of Virgil's poems. It is a legendary narrative, a story about the imagined origin of the Roman nation in times long before the foundation of Rome itself. It is an epic poem. Epic poems form a large class, beginning for us with the Babylonian Epic of Gilgamesh over four thousand years ago and Homer's *Iliad* and *Odyssey* more than a thousand years after it, and appearing at many other times and places, principally in Asia and Europe. An epic poem is hard to define. But perhaps it can be fairly described as a long narrative poem, full of action, which tells us about human life and makes us think about the relation between man and the superhuman powers, having as the chief characters 'heroes', that is, people who are in some way stronger than ordinary mankind but below the divine level. Epics are either oral poems, poems composed among people who are not yet fully used to writing, or, in later phases of culture, written poems which have been developed, directly or indirectly, out of the old tradition of oral poetry.

The *Aeneid*, as any epic should be, is an exciting story extremely well told and full of incident: it can be read as a story and nothing more. However, besides being a story, it is a kind of moving picture carrying allusive, and in a sense symbolic, meanings.

According to legend some of the Romans could trace their descent back to the Trojans of the city of Troy which had been made famous by Homer. The Trojan prince Aeneas was said to have escaped after the capture of the city and sailed with other Trojans to the west coast of Italy, where he and they settled, and where their descendants afterwards founded, or helped to found, the earliest Rome. Virgil rewrote this legend elaborately and made it serve the purpose of his own vision.

When in the *Aeneid* we read of the Greeks sacking Troy, it seems as if no Trojan can escape the final annihilation. The new destiny of the Trojan remnant starts from utter despair, and afterwards too, as they go on their adventurous way, they are sometimes inclined to hopeless despondency. Yet after immense efforts and much endurance they prevailed, and so made possible the future supremacy and grandeur of Rome. The Trojans succeeded not so much through their own strength as through divine help and divine encouragement. The whole story is threaded along a series of divine appearances and admonitions, with their commands, advice, and explanations, and sometimes with their practical assistance.

Aeneas, the leader of the Trojan band, was supposed to be the son of Venus, the Goddess of Love, and of a mortal father, Anchises. Venus protected Aeneas. But Juno, the Queen of the Gods and wife of the supreme god Jupiter, had been the enemy of Troy and she opposed Aeneas fiercely. Jupiter of course had to see both sides of the question, but he and Destiny, working together, helped the

Trojans and endorsed their success. Other gods and goddesses were also involved, favouring or opposing one character or another or one side or the other. In the poem they communicate with mortal men either directly or through dreams, visions, omens, and the words of prophets and clairvoyants. Virgil had no doubt that the affairs of the earthly world are subject to the powers of another world, a world which is normally, but by no means always, invisible, but no less real for that ; and near the middle of the poem he introduces an explanation of a part of his belief.

The belief is vital to the poem. For Virgil was presenting a true poetic picture of the world, showing how human affairs are controlled by human and superhuman qualities and deeds, and in particular how it had happened that Rome grew to greatness after a process which began in weakness and despair. Aeneas himself is more than once ready to abandon hope. But every time he is given some reassurance. And, whatever his faults, for he had many, he would never disregard the voice of Heaven.

The *Aeneid* shows the way things happen in the world. Some of it is strange to us at first sight, but after a little reflection we are likely to agree that everything in it is true to life. We are left to draw our own conclusions, and, if we do, we find important moral facts, not of course preached to us or pressed on us, but emerging from the situations and the results of the action. For example, the *Aeneid* strongly and frequently confirms two important rules of conduct: one principally Greek, 'Avoid excess', and the other principally Roman, 'Be true', that is, loyal to the gods, to the homeland, and to family, friends, and dependants. Virgil regularly calls Aeneas 'Aeneas the True'; and he introduces many examples of thoughtless excess leading to disaster, especially excesses of inordinate affection when someone is carried too far by an exclusive love for some person or thing. When the Trojans, after a storm at sea, came to shore at Carthage in north Africa, Aeneas and Dido the Queen of Carthage fell in love and settled down to live together, forgetting the destiny which required him to go on to Italy. During this part of the story Virgil even stops calling Aeneas 'The True'. Duly, after some months, the divine reproof came and Aeneas obediently sailed away. In fury at this betrayal, Dido cursed him and killed herself. The result of her curse was to be the terrible antagonism between Rome and Carthage which lasted, with intermissions, for a hundred years. Again, at the end of the *Aeneid*, Aeneas, to avenge his friend Pallas, vindictively killed his defeated enemy, Turnus. He let the memory of the friend whom he himself had failed to protect expel every other thought. We are led to wonder whether, if he had not spoilt his victory by this wanton cruelty, the subsequent history of Italy might have been less blood-stained and bitter.

Most great poems are concerned with wickedness, violence, and horror. But often, at least among civilized people, the whole tendency of the same poems is really towards peaceful goodness, humanity, and reconciliation. Virgil's poem pre-eminently has this tendency. Few if any poets have been so tender and sympathetic as Virgil; and for him the ideas of reconciliation and harmony amount almost to an obsession. And for Virgil it is not only by heroic champions in battle that valour is shown, and it is not only on their courage and resolution that a great future may depend.

Aeneas is to win a kingdom in Italy as a Prince of Destiny, and Divine Powers guide and aid him. He is even given by his mother Venus a set of arms and armour made specially for him by Vulcan, the god of fire and metal-working, who had giants, and all the volcanic might of Etna, to serve him. Now Virgil expresses much of his eloquent wisdom in his similes. These are short comparisons of divine and human characters and actions usually with animals or natural forces, but not always. It is worth while to give careful notice to all Virgil's similes, and to compare them with each other. When Vulcan leaps up from his bed to make the arms for Aeneas, Virgil provides a simile for him; and he compares his alacrity to the devoted will-power of some poor mother in a cottage who works all night at her weaving in order to keep her home together and bring up her children. It is as if Virgil had said that nothing is greater than the courageous fidelity and resolute will of a humble housewife, not even the determination of elemental powers commanding volcanic might and dominating empires.

That is how Virgil's poetry works. All the time there are hints in it which can easily be overlooked without spoiling the exciting story, but richly repay attention. To see, perhaps suddenly and unexpectedly, one of Virgil's deeper meanings softly emerging is to benefit from an artistic pleasure as keen and intense as any aesthetic experience can be. And a great many of these experiences may be enjoyed simply by reading the story and not overlooking the obvious.

Perhaps one should be content with that. Or perhaps it is not only fairer to Virgil but also advantageous to us, his readers, if we give some attention to his method of composition, and see how he went to work. The *Aeneid* was created with both mighty inspiration and immense labour.

There is a good and clear example of Virgil's way of working in an early scene where Venus prevents Aeneas from killing the beautiful but sinful Helen. When Aeneas is at the very lowest point of his fortunes, with his city, Troy, captured and burning and apparently nothing whatever left to him except such satisfaction as he might find in punishing the woman who had been the cause of it all, Venus suddenly appears and tells him not to be angry, but to think of good things, not bad things, and to be practical.

According to a rather second-rate, Greek, version of the sack of Troy, which Virgil knew, it was not Aeneas who found Helen and wanted to kill her, but Menelaus. Menelaus was a Greek king and Helen's former husband, from whom she had run away. The Greeks had fought the war in order to recapture her for him. But when at last he found her he was so angry that he wanted to kill her. Just in time, Venus appeared to Menelaus and reminded him that Helen would still make him a good wife and that to kill her would only be a foolish waste. So Menelaus spared Helen. The occurrence, as it is in this older version, is interesting in its way and perhaps amusing; it could be called a satisfactory part of a very plain tale. But it has no depth and no exaltation. Menelaus is naturally annoyed, but he has no high tragic passion. It would certainly have been foolish to fight for Helen throughout a ten-year war, and then not take her back after all. Venus appealed to Menelaus' selfish interest. It was her business to do this, as she was the Goddess of Love and had always favoured the beautiful Helen. But there are no high motives anywhere, no suggestive force, and nothing to make us think.

Genius works differently. This time Virgil had little to do, one or two touches perhaps; but enough. He simply substituted Aeneas for Menelaus. The consequences are startling. The whole scene is raised to the level of the sublime. Aeneas has a strong and not wholly selfish reason for killing Helen. The drama is intense. Venus is his own mother, not merely an irresponsible love-goddess. Her advice to him has a moral depth and a certain universality which are almost Christian. She tells Aeneas not to blame any human culprit, since Troy has fallen through the gods' inclemency; and here Virgil found in old poetry the phrase 'not Helen but Paris is to blame' and simply changed 'but' to 'or', saying 'not Paris or Helen . . .', thus delicately registering his protest against all hate and all revenge. By such subtle means Virgil contrived to charge his story and especially the critical moments in it with a depth of meaning new to poetry and nearer to ultimate truth than any poet had contrived before.

Virgil always worked like this. The whole *Aeneid* shows a coherent system interlaced with such mutually dependent brilliancies of insight. The great poets have a way of making what is seen reveal the unseen; and they seem to do this better if they collect an enormous quantity of observations on life, their own and other people's, and then condense it under strong pressure so that even a few words have a great power of suggestion and persuasion. No doubt they are all the time choosing with precise accuracy what is most important. The result is an allusive and partly symbolic kind of language able to communicate not merely single happenings but the universal truth behind them.

These greater poets also reach back across past time, and represent a view of the world which belongs not to one man or one generation of men but to the men of many succeeding generations or even a whole civilization. The experience which is distilled may be the experience of many centuries; and it may be condensed and focused by a single genius in a single poetic statement. That is what Virgil did to the experience of the Greeks and Romans in the *Aeneid*.

To do this, he needed to read and remember a very great number of books, and let his own phrases, and therefore the form of his own thought, grow out of them. That is how he worked. And it enabled him to keep in touch with many people, present and past, and especially the past poets, and to be friends with them all the time as he wrote. So well did Virgil succeed that he could almost be said to have written about many different things at once. It would be truer to say that he lived in an ideal world of poetry and found his way through it to new heights without ever losing contact with the poetry which had been there before. This poetic thought-world, compiled from countless previous poetic thoughts, Virgil reorganized and co-ordinated anew. That is how he created an allusive, partly symbolic language which could fitly communicate what he had to say about the real world behind appearances.

Virgil was sensitive and sympathetic to all points of view and all kinds of people, even wicked ones. He was not content to give only one side of a question. Indeed, he often needed to express the truth about people or things when the truth itself looked paradoxical or even illogical, and when probably no one but he could have shown the underlying sense. His allusive method, based on very wide reading, helped him to tell the whole truth, that is, 'the truth of art', not 'the trivial truth of fact'. He certainly had a rare gift for hitting off something vividly in a few words, and giving a rich and true impression. But in general he did not mean to be photographic. He was like a portrait painter who can make his picture a far more life-like resemblance by a few inspired brush-strokes, not closely corresponding to anything which ordinary people see in the face to be painted, than ever he could by copying each individual wrinkle. The comparison can be continued. Virgil was like a portrait-painter who, in order to understand his sitter perfectly, looks at him as he is now, and also tries to see him as he was at all the earlier stages of his life with the help of portraits of him already painted by other artists at different times.

Virgil used his books as the painter might use the earlier portraits. He collected as much material as possible but never copied anything exactly and always tried to have more than one influence working at the same time. Homer was one of his main guides; and in the opening lines of the *Aeneid* he used suggestions from the beginnings of both Homer's poems. Reminiscences of Homer can be noticed all through the *Aeneid*; and Homer's works are only two among an immense number which helped to make it. Situations, and even characters, are composed in this way. For example, in Aeneas himself there are echoes not only of the rather different Aeneas who plays a small part in Homer, but also of Homer's Achilles, his Ulysses (or Odysseus), and his Hector, and, in addition to all these, of Hercules, no doubt drawn from various other books, and probably many more characters, besides the real and living Emperor Augustus, who, like other historical characters, 'shimmers through' the story. 'It was ever Virgil's way to merge the actual in the ideal and so to make its reality shine more brightly.' Even Virgil's philosophical ideas are drawn in part from different earlier writers. Lucretius was a very strong influence. Virgil knew his work well and made free use of many hundreds of his phrases in the *Aeneid*, and let them suggest ideas. But since he violently disagreed with the materialistic philosophy of Lucretius, he could not adopt his thought. Indeed, he apparently delighted in turning it upside down, and expressing something far more like the idealistic philosophy of Plato even when the phrases of Lucretius were influencing him.

When in the middle of the *Aeneid* Aeneas is allowed, like Dante in the Divine Comedy, to visit the Spiritual World beyond death, he has to find, pick, and take with him as his passport a 'golden bough'. Certainly, a great number of facts contributed to suggest the idea of this 'bough' to Virgil, but there is little doubt which was the most important. It was a passage in a Greek poem about the different Greek writers, composed not long before Virgil's time, in which the work of Plato is called a 'golden bough, sparkling all round with every virtue'. Virgil characteristically chose this way of saying that moral goodness is necessary for the spiritual discernment which is in its turn necessary for wise and progressive statesmanship.

Virgil worked with care and deliberation. Sometimes he produced an average of only one line a day. He spent about eleven years writing the *Aeneid*, and that was a very short time for so difficult a task, so elaborately conceived, and subject to so many conflicting requirements. He intended, if he had lived, to spend three years revising it. So the poem is imperfect; but what exactly he meant to do to it is not known. There are little misfits and incongruities in the *Aeneid* as we have it, but so there probably are in all long literary works, especially the greatest. The same remark or action may be attributed in one passage to one character and in another to someone else; and sometimes it is hard to see how a period of time, or a distance, squares with what Virgil has said in some other part of the poem. None of these little oversights matter. Possibly Virgil would have corrected at least some of them if he had lived.

There are also things in the poem which, though they may seem odd to us, are nevertheless a necessary part of Virgil's art, and will not even seem strange to us if we remember what sort of art Virgil's was. They may be there simply because Virgil was not content to be photographic, but preferred to tell more of the truth than he could tell by confining himself to plain fact. For example, the Trojans travel in a few quite small ships, but they seem to have with them everything that they need, including elaborate clothing and jewellery for presents to their various hosts, and even sometimes bulls and sheep for sacrifices to their various gods. The reason, put shortly, is that the imagery and symbolic suggestion are on these occasions more important than the ordinary restrictions of possibility; it matters that we should be impressed with the former wealth and power of the Trojans and the nobility and piety which they still had, but it does not matter whether we are convinced that the whole story really happened, which anyhow no one is likely to believe.

Then there is the warfare. Some of the battles seem to belong to no single place or time, but to involve different and incompatible fighting methods and weapons. This is quite in accordance with Virgil's principles of art, and his habitual way of writing of several things, or different stages in the evolution of one thing, at the same time. He could have made all his battles old-fashioned like Homer's battles, or contemporary, like Julius Caesar's. But he preferred to do more than that. It was his way of showing what all war is like, not only one particular battle, which may not be a good example of what usually happens in war.

There are also exaggerations. They are characteristic of epic poems but may surprise readers new to the epic manner. Exaggerations are quite in place in the fairyland of epic. Nor are they childish, but a serious and important symbolic means, used by gifted poets of many places and times, for expressing deep and true meanings. On the whole, Virgil, and Homer still more, were very moderate with their exaggerations. Even Virgil's Turnus, who has a helmet which discharges flames of fire, automatically hotter as the battle grows fiercer, and whose face actually emits sparks when he is in a hurry to fight, is not too fantastic. The flames and sparks are part of the recurring imagery used to express the nature of Turnus. He was a very attractive hero, young, noble, handsome, generous, valiant, and unfortunate, and certainly more attractive than his conqueror, Aeneas. But he had one fault: he was too fiery. And the fire of Turnus was not creative. This Virgil indicates in two similes, one for Turnus and one for Aeneas, and each about water in a bowl or cauldron. For Turnus, the water boils over and sends up steam and smoke. For Aeneas, rays of light are reflected from the surface, and presently, as the water ceases to sway, they become steady. Aeneas, with all his faults, can see the light in the end, but for Turnus the end is darkness. If Virgil had written his psychological analysis of Aeneas and Turnus in a scientific book, the length of it would have been frightening. As it is, a wealth of truth emerges from a few deft images here and there.

Virgil's art was not confined to images, symbolic allusion, and good story-telling. It included many kinds of symmetry and pattern, all subject to the great law of variety. The sun very frequently rises and sets in the *Aeneid.* The various descriptions, though similar, are never exactly the same; and apparently the expression chosen has to symbolize the events and situations which are to follow in the coming day or night. The words themselves throughout the poem are chosen and fitted according to many subtle principles. Their vowels, consonants, and rhythms had to be right in relation not only to the other words in the same line but to the words in other lines in the same passage. Words are chosen because they begin with the right letter, end with the right sound, and otherwise fit the designed patterns of both music and meaning. Lines near together are in elaborate relations of echo and contrast with one another, and a line in one place may significantly echo a line far away in the poem. There are several kinds of rhythm, some governed by long and short syllables, some by stress-accents, and some by vowel sounds; and the rhythms not only form their own and other patterns through interaction together, but also help the meanings. People who know not a word of Latin can enjoy the music of Virgil.

All this must be lost in a prose translation, but a great deal, far more in fact, ought not to be lost; for what counts most of all is the story, the drama, and the meanings which the story and the drama reveal. Therefore it need not be altogether unfair to Virgil's poem to read it in a version which is content to tell in plain prose Virgil's tale.

This, of course, is not easy to arrange. Such a version must not, if it can be avoided, leave out anything which really matters, and it must not add anything which might alter or distort any of Virgil's more important meanings. But, so subtle and elaborate is Virgil's art, and so difficult is his language to understand exactly, that it is hard to be sure that any omission or any expansion will be harmless. Virgil's words are so allusive that no attempt can be made to represent his whole meaning, which, even if it were possible, would only lead to excessive length and hopeless complication. And yet his phrases are so condensed, and his power to say much in little is so striking, that at least some expansion is necessary, and indeed much more than is normally inevitable when poetry, the medium of suggestion, is to be translated into prose, the medium of statement. In translating Virgil, therefore, there are unusually sharp conflicts between the necessity to express enough and the fear of expressing too much, and also between the primary need to keep the narrative clear and fluent and the continuous responsibility for discovering or deciding, as well as possible, what is the exact meaning of the original. In this predicament I cannot hope to have avoided slips, oversights, and perhaps even sheer mistakes. There are probably many of all three. And even when there is nothing really wrong, it may look as if something is wrong, because it is often impossible, at least to me, to be fair to a sentence or paragraph without being unfair to some of the words in it. The whole is more important than the parts; but the parts still have their claims.

In language, Virgil was a master of eloquence in every style. 'Apocalyptic majesty', as it has been well called, and the softest pathos in a still, small voice, are equally characteristic of his Latin. He normally wrote with dignity and a certain formality. But he used informality also: occasionally there is an effective colloquialism and even here and there something like slang. Virgil had some of the caprice which is usually found in very great men. He also had that masterful impatience with conventional and accepted speech which appears to be typical of the greatest poets.

To find the right kind of English for a prose translation of this stupendous poem is not easy. It is perhaps not so hard to see what is wanted; but how to provide it is a very different matter.

Obviously it must be contemporary English, reasonably smooth and free from any serious jolts. To make the story of the *Aeneid* dull, slow-moving, hard to read, or obscure, would probably be the unfairest thing of all both to the reader and to Virgil himself.

But the English used must also be as impersonal as possible, and not closely dated to the middle of the twentieth century. The translator has to avoid, if he can, his own mannerisms of writing and sometimes admit expressions more natural to other writers than to himself. He must also avoid the latest colloquial phrases, and tricks of speech current only among specialized groups of people; it would not do to use technical terms only to be understood by, for example, priests, or sailors, or soldiers. If possible, everything should seem at least fairly natural to people accustomed to the English of fifty years ago or fifty years hence; that, anyway, is the ideal. To tell the tale of Virgil's *Aeneid* plainly, it is necessary to avoid distractions, and among them the distractions which are due to special suggestions belonging to particular times, places, and people.

Clearly, the plan must be not to write a book based on Virgil, nor to compete with Virgil by misguided efforts at ingenuity, but to let Virgil himself pass on what he has to say with as little impediment as possible. Perhaps, if there is a sincere attempt not to interfere with him, some at least of his supreme eloquence may come through. The object is to let it come in spite of the translator, not to force it by efforts to translate the untranslatable.

If so, there will often be a time for leaving well alone, or rather for leaving alone what is not well but is more likely to be made worse than better by further tinkering. Occasionally, but I hope not often, the English will seem slightly odd, for Virgil's Latin is liable to be odd, and English entirely free from oddity may give a wrong impression of Virgil. It would be a serious matter if readers were misled and after reading a translation had a less accurate impression of Virgil than they had before. In Virgil's day Latin was very much alive, and still, especially for the greater poets, experimental; it had not become smooth and predictable, as it is in the poems of Ovid, for example, who wrote soon after Virgil. The translation ought not to make it seem that Virgil's style is like Ovid's. On the other hand, it is prudent to soften some things down. When Virgil seems to be colloquial, or to make a small boy or an old lady talk as a small boy or an old lady would, the change in manner should be represented, but only lightly, since we do not really yet know enough Latin to be sure how far Virgil was going in his change of manner, and it would be a pity to take unnecessary risks. Occasionally an old, traditional rendering, long familiar in schools, has been allowed to live on in the translation, however tired of it some of us may be. That, again, is an instance of playing safe. So are several passages where the English still retains traces of a Latin form of expression – a bad fault to all who like translation to be artistic, and yet sometimes to be preferred to alternatives likely to be even worse.

Virgil's *Aeneid* is certainly the principal secular book of the Western World. For nearly five hundred years, from soon after printing was invented, at least one new printed edition was published annually. Before that time the *Aeneid* was probably the most widely known of all secular books in Europe; certainly no other has continued to be so famous from Roman days to ours. On the whole, the *Aeneid* has usually been considered the best book. It has always been easy to argue that it is the best poem.

Soon after Virgil's death he was worshipped as a divinity. Though he died before the Christian era he found a place in Christian worship and Christian art. He was accepted as 'the Prophet of the Gentiles'. He was believed to have been a magician, and in the Middle Ages one of the books written about his miracles was translated into many languages. He was Dante's 'Sweet Master', and helped to make Chrétien de Troyes, Shakespeare, Milton, Camoens, Pope, Victor Hugo, Tennyson, and so on. Whether any western poet of the first rank has been independent of him I do not know. It is said that the little picture in the first four lines of the Pastoral Poems, a picture of a restful goatherd playing music under a spreading beech tree, found its way into every European literature. Virgil even had something to do with the creation of our modern speech, for the Romance languages, and to some extent others too, regularly use sentences shaped, not according to general Latin practice, but according to Virgil's personal style. There are many difficult questions still being argued at great length to which Virgil has given the best answer so far, all in a few words packed with sharp reasoning. This well-known and genuine, but still mysterious, wisdom of Virgil quickly led to the famous 'Sortes Vergilianae', that is, drawing lots to tell the future by Virgil's help. Countless people, important and unimportant, have made decisions by putting a finger blindly on a page of Virgil opened at random. Charles I, for example, did that before the Battle of Naseby. The practice continues today.

The power of Virgil's poem is like a seed in the ground, forcing upwards into the light; and it is still growing. No one, not even any Roman, has ever understood every detail in the *Aeneid*; and there have been many who, through trying to understand everything, have missed the best that the story has to give. What that best is, is hard to define. But in general people seem to have found much of it, although they have often chosen odd ways to talk about what they have found. There have, of course, been opponents of Virgil. Though he leapt into fame as soon as the Pastoral Poems were published, even in his lifetime books were written against him. But, on the whole, disparagement of his overwhelming reputation has always sooner or later collapsed like the Walls of Jericho.

The history of Virgil's fame from his day to ours leaves us wondering how people found time to attend to anything else. He, 'the chastest and royalest poet', as Dryden called him, deserves admiration and faithful thanks. There may be a feeling that, as a later Roman said, 'Virgil has the strange peculiarity of being invulnerable to criticism and unaffected by praise'; but it is more probable that Virgil, the poet of fidelity, still likes mankind's fidelity to him. And yet it is hard to avoid a certain awe in his exalted presence. There is a good story of a sightseer in one of our famous galleries, who remarked to the attendant: 'I don't know why people make such a fuss about these pictures. I can't see anything in them'. To which the attendant made the sublime reply: 'Excuse me, Sir, the *pictures* are not on trial'.

NOTES

Some short passages in the *Aeneid* are thought to be wrongly included, at least in the places where they are found. Of these passages a few are almost certainly included wrongly, and I have put brackets round them. Others are more doubtful, and I have left them as they are.

Aeneas has a young son who has two names, Ascanius and Iulus. It is as well to be warned at the start that these two names represent the same character.

THE AENEID

BOOK ONE

THE TROJANS REACH CARTHAGE

I am that poet who in times past made the light melody of pastoral poetry. In my next poem I left the woods for the adjacent farmlands, teaching them to obey even the most exacting tillers of the soil; and the farmers liked my work. But now I turn to the terrible strife of Mars.

THIS is a tale of arms and of a man. Fated to be an exile, he was the first to sail from the land of Troy and reach Italy, at its Lavinian shore. He met many tribulations on his way both by land and on the ocean; high Heaven willed it, for Juno was ruthless and could not forget her anger. And he had also to endure great suffering in warfare. But at last he succeeded in founding his city, and installing the gods of his race in the Latin land: and that was the origin of the Latin nation, the Lords of Alba, and the proud battlements of Rome.

I pray for inspiration, to tell how it all began, and how the Queen of Heaven sustained such outrage to her majesty that in her indignation she forced a man famed for his true-heartedness to tread that long path of adventure, and to face so many trials. It is hard to believe Gods in Heaven capable of such rancour.

Once there was an ancient town called Carthage, inhabited by emigrants from Tyre, and confronting Italy, opposite to the mouth of the Tiber but far away. Carthage had wealth and power; and it had skill and ferocity in war. Now Juno is said to have loved Carthage best of all cities in the world, giving even Samos the second place. She kept her weapons and her chariot there; and she had already set her heart on making it a capital city governing all the earth, and spared no effort of fostering care, hoping that Destiny might consent to her desire. She had, however, heard of another breed of men, tracing descent from the blood of Troy, who were one day to overthrow this Tyrian stronghold: for they would breed a warrior nation, haughty, and sovereign over wide realms; and their onset would bring destruction to Africa. Such, she had heard, was the plan of the spinning Fates, and it was this plan that Juno feared. Neither could she forget the Trojan War, when she had battled in the forefront for the Argos which she loved. She remembered the origin of that quarrel and the fierce indignation which it had caused her. The judgement of Paris, with its unjust slight to her beauty, remained indelibly stamped on her mind; and besides she was always jealous of the whole Trojan race, and could not forget how Ganymede had been stolen and honoured.

Such were the causes of Juno's fury. And so it was that the Trojan remnant, whom the Greeks, even pitiless Achilles, could not kill, were tossed in storm over all the ocean; and still she kept them far from Latium, wandering for years at the mercy of fate from sea to sea about the world. Such was the cost in heavy toil of beginning the life of Rome.

The Trojans had put out to sea from Sicily. They were just out of sight of land, the bronze-plated oars churning the salt water to foam, and they were happily hoisting sail when Juno, perpetually nursing her heart's deep wound, spoke to herself:

'I, vanquished? I, to abandon the fight? Lacking even the strength to keep Troy's prince from making Italy? The Fates forbid me, indeed! Yet they never stopped Minerva from gutting the Argives' fleet by fire, and drowning all of them, merely because one man, Ajax son of Oileus, he alone, went mad, and sinned. She borrowed Jupiter's devouring fire, and sped it from the clouds. She shattered the ships, and tore up the surface of ocean with winds. And when Ajax, pierced through the breast by the lightning-flame, was breathing his last, she caught him up in a tornado and impaled him on a pointed rock. Yet I, in my stately precedence, Queen of all the Divine, I, the sister and wife of Jove, have been making war for all these years on a single clan. Will anyone again pay reverence to Juno's majesty, or lay his offering on her altar in humble prayer?'

Debating so with herself in her fiery brain, she went straight to Aeolia where the storm-clouds have their home and mad winds are bursting to be free. In the great spaces of a cavern they wrestle, and hurricanes roar: but Aeolus, the king who rules them, confines them in their prison, disciplined and curbed. They race from door to bolted door, and all the mountain reverberates with the noise of their resentment. But Aeolus, throned securely above them, sceptre in hand, tempers their arrogance and controls their fury. Otherwise they would sweep violently away with them every land, every sea, and the very depths of the sky, and drive them all through space. Foreseeing this, therefore, the Father with whom is all power banished the winds to that dark cavern, and piled above them a mountain mass, appointing a king over them who, under a fixed charter, would know how to hold them confined and also, when so commanded, to give them a free rein. To this King of the Winds Juno now made her submissive appeal.

'To you, my Lord Aeolus, he who is father of all gods and king of all men has given authority to lull the waves or to rouse them with a wind. Now a certain people whom I hate are sailing on the Etruscan Sea, and conveying Troy itself and the vanquished gods of Trojan homes to Italy. Smite fury into your winds. Sink their ships; make the sea close over them. Or drive them apart, pitch out their crews, and scatter them on the deep. I chance to have fourteen sea-nymphs of striking beauty, and Deiopea is the loveliest of them all. I shall assign her to be yours in lawful marriage, and in return for your great goodness to me she shall live out with you all the years to come and make you father of splendid sons.'

Replying, Aeolus spoke thus: 'Highness, your sole task is to decide what your wish is to be; and my only duty is prompt obedience to you. I owe to you all my authority in this little realm of mine, for it was you who won for me Jupiter's favour. I owe to you my place at the feasts of the Immortals; and from you I hold my power over storm-clouds and over storms.'

This said, he swung his trident round where the shell of the cliff was thin, and struck home. The winds formed line, and charged through the outlet which he had made. With tornado blasts they swept the earth. They swooped down on the sea. Winds of the east and the south, and the African Wind with squall after squall, came tearing from their depths, and set the long rollers rolling to the shores. Now men were shouting and tackle shrieking. In a moment the clouds had wrested from Trojan eyes the sky and the light of day: a blackness as of night fell on the ocean. The thunder cracked in heaven's height, and in the air above a continuous lightning flared; wherever the Trojans looked, immediate death stared them in the eyes. Instantly Aeneas felt his limbs give way in a chill of terror, and groaned. Stretching both hands, palm-upward, to the stars, he cried aloud: 'How fortunate were you, thrice fortunate and more, whose luck it was to die under the high walls of Troy before your parents' eyes! Ah, Diomede, most valiant of Greeks, why did your arm not strike me down and give my spirit freedom in death on the battlefields of Ilium, where lie the mighty Sarpedon, and Hector the man-slayer, pierced by Achilles' lance, and where Simois rolls down submerged beneath his stream those countless shields and helms and all those valiant dead!'

Aeneas was still pouring forth his words when a howling blast from the north struck squarely his ship's sail and flung the waves sky-high. Oars broke: the bow sheered away; and she took the sea full on her beam. On came, towering, a piled precipice of water. Some of the crew hung poised on wave-crests; others saw the waves sink before them to disclose, below seething water and sand, the very bottom of the sea. The south wind next caught up three other ships, and flung them spinning onto a large spine of rocks, half-submerged in mid-ocean and far out from Italy, where they are called 'the Altars'. The east wind drove three more away from the open sea onto quicksands in shallow water. To the dismay of their friends, the wind ran them aground and built up over them a mountain of sand. One ship carried the Lycians, under their trusty chief Orontes. As Aeneas watched, a gigantic breaker came crashing from its crest onto the stern. The helmsman was whirled head foremost overboard, and fell face downwards. The ship spun three times round where she lay; then a whirlpool caught her and sucked her under. Some of the crew could be seen, one here one there, swimming in the waste of water. Fragments of wreckage, personal equipment, and precious things saved from Troy floated on the waves. The storm had now prevailed against the two stout ships of Ilioneus and of the valiant Achates, and two others also, one carrying Abas and the other the aged Aletes. Every ship had sprung her timbers; the cracks widened, and the deadly sea streamed in.

But meanwhile Neptune had been made aware by the ocean's roaring commotion, and the currents eddying even in the sea's still depths, that a storm had been unleashed. Gravely provoked, he raised his head from the waves and, looking forth serenely high above the surface, he saw Aeneas' fleet scattered and his Trojans overborne by violent waves and all the sky teeming down. He soon realized the trick played by his spiteful sister Juno. He summoned the Winds of the East and the West before him, and straightway spoke:

'So, Winds, is this the length to which your pride of birth prompts you to go? You actually dare, without my sovereign consent, to throw sky and earth into confusion, and raise these mountainous seas? I will show you. . . .! But no, first I had better set the waves at rest; after that you are going to pay dearly for your offence. Make haste now and withdraw. And give your king a message from me. Dominion over the ocean, sanctioned by the ruthless trident, was allotted not to him but to me. His place is the rock's vast cavern where, Wind of the East, you winds have your home. That is the royal court of Aeolus. There he may vaunt his sovereign pride, so long as he keeps the prison of the winds well barred.'

Speaking thus, and quicker than speech, he made the heaving ocean calm. He routed the gathered clouds and brought back the sun. As he did so, Triton and Cymothoe pressed against the ships, and dislodged them from the cutting rocks; and Neptune aided them, levering with his trident. Great sandbanks reappeared, as, lightly skimming the wave-crests in his chariot, he calmed the sea. It had been like a sudden riot in some great assembly, when, as they will, the meaner folk forget themselves and grow violent, so that firebrands and stones are soon flying, for savage passion quickly finds weapons. But then they may chance to see some man whose character and record command their respect. If so, they will wait in silence, listening keenly. He will speak to them, calming their passions and guiding their energies. So, now, all the uproar of the ocean subsided. Its Lord, Father Neptune, had only to look forth over the sea; then under a cloudless heaven he wheeled his horses, gave them the rein, and let his willing chariot fly.

Thoroughly exhausted, Aeneas and his men made efforts to run for the nearest land within reach. They set course for the coast of Africa. There is a haven there, at the end of a long sound, quite landlocked by an island in the shape of two breakwaters, which parts the waves entering from the open sea and draws them off into long channels. On each shore a frightening headland of rock towers massively into the sky; and the wide expanse of water which they overshadow is noiseless and secure. Beyond the water a curtain of trees with quivering leaves reaches downwards, and behind them is an overhanging forest-clad mountain-side, mysterious and dark. There is a cave directly in front at the foot of the cliffs. Inside it are stalactites and fresh water, and there are seats there, cut in the living rock, for nymphs have their home in the cave. Here a tired ship will never need a cable or an anchor with a fluke to bite and make her fast.

Aeneas, who had reunited only a bare seven ships out of all his fleet, moved up into the sound. The Trojans, yearning to be on dry land again, disembarked and, delighted to feel the sand under them, lay down, all caked with brine, on the beach. Achates struck a spark from a flint, the first thing to be done; he had leaves there to catch the fire, which he fed by putting dry material around it, and he quickly had a flame in the tinder. Others, although utterly weary from their plight, fetched out some grain which they had saved, though it was the worse for sea-water, and utensils for cooking. They prepared to grind the corn on stone and bake bread.

While they did so, Aeneas climbed a rock commanding a wide unbroken view far across the sea, in the hope of sighting some Trojan ships, wind-battered but afloat, the ship perhaps of Antheus, or of Capys or Caicus with her high, blazoned stern. But there was not a ship to be seen. He could see, however, three stags straying on the shore, and behind them in a long line their whole herd, grazing in a valley. Abruptly he stopped; and quickly he gripped a bow and some arrows, swift to fly, which his faithful Achates had been carrying. His first shots brought the leaders to the ground, stags with tall antlers like tree-branches. Next he turned on the herd, and his arrows stampeded them in confusion among the green forest trees. Aeneas only ceased shooting when he had triumphantly laid on the earth seven weighty carcasses, in number equal to the surviving ships. He now made his way back to the haven, and shared the meat among his company; and with it he apportioned the cargo of wine-casks which with a hero's generosity the kindly Acestes had given them on the beach in Sicily as they embarked. He then spoke to them, to console them in their grief:

'Friends of mine, we have long been no strangers to affliction, and you have had worse than this to bear. Now, as before, Providence will bring your suffering to an end. You have sailed right in among the rocks where Scylla's rabid sea-dogs bark. You have faced the Cyclopes, monsters of the stones. You must revive your spirits and dismiss unhappiness and fear; perhaps one day you will enjoy looking back even on what you now endure. We have forced our way through adventures of every kind, risking all again and again; but the way is the way to Latium, where Destiny offers us rest and a home, and where imperial Troy may have the right to live again. Hold hard, therefore. Preserve yourselves for better days.'

Such were the words he spoke, but he was sick at heart, for the cares which he bore were heavy indeed. Yet he concealed his sorrow deep within him, and his face looked confident and cheerful. The Trojans now prepared to deal with the game on which they were soon to feast. Some of them flayed the hides from the ribs, disclosing the meat. Others then cut the meat into steaks, and spitted it, quivering. Others again found places on the beach for cauldrons, and provided the fires to boil them. Then they ate and restored their strength; stretched on the grass, they filled themselves with old wine and rich venison and feasted till their hunger was gone. When the meal was cleared away, they talked long, in sadness for their lost comrades, poised between the hope that they might possibly be living yet, and the fear that they had reached their life's ending and were beyond all human appeal. More than any other, Aeneas the True sighed within himself for the lot of the fiery Orontes and of Amycus, thinking of each one, or again of some terrible fate which Lycus might have met, and then of Gyas and of Cloanthus, his valiant friends.

They had now finished their meal when Jupiter looked down from heaven's height on the sea where the white wings sail, on the lands flat below, on the coasts, and on the nations of the wide world. He stood in the zenith of the sky and his eyes rested on royal Carthage. Then suddenly, as he pondered gravely on the issues involved, Venus addressed him. She was downcast, and tears stood in her glistening eyes as she spoke: 'Disposer, by eternal decrees, of all life human and divine, you whose bolt of thunder is our dread, how can Aeneas, my dear son, and the other Trojans have given you offence so grave? Often has death visited them; and now, because they make for Italy, all the earth is closed to them. Yet your promise was of Romans, leaders of men, who should one day with the rolling of the years be their descendants, with Teucer's blood, strong once more, running in their veins; they were to discipline all the sea and all lands under their law. Father, what thought has been changing your will? As for me, your promise consoled me for the dread havoc of Troy's fall, since I could weigh against her fate the compensation of this new destiny. But now the Trojans, driven on from disaster to disaster, are still being pursued by the same ill fortune. Monarch Supreme, what end to their ordeals will you grant them? After all, Antenor escaped right through the press of Greeks, and contrived to sail safely up to the head of the Adriatic where the

Liburnians hold rule, even reaching the fount of the Timavus, the river through whose nine mouths sea water bursts forth from echoing caverns below, so that ocean's roar is heard on the meadows of the land. And here Antenor actually found a place where Trojans might settle and named his city Padua. He has given its people a Trojan name and hung Trojan weapons on the walls; and there in relief from turmoil he is serenely at peace. Yet we, your own children, having your own permission to climb the very citadel of Heaven, are, all through the anger of One, most monstrously betrayed; our ships are lost, and we are parted far from Italy's coasts. Do you so reward our reverence for you? Is this how you install us in the royalty which is our due?'

The creator of the gods and of human kind smiled on her, with the smile which he wears when he calms the storms and clears the sky. Lightly he kissed his daughter, and then spoke: 'Spare your fears, Cytherean. You have your people's destiny still, and it shall not be disturbed. You shall see your city, see Lavinium's walls, for I have promised them. And you shall exalt to the stars of Heaven your son Aeneas, the great of heart. There is no thought changing my will. But now, because anxiety for him so pricks you, therefore shall I speak of the more distant future, and, turning the scroll of the Fates, awake their secrets. Know, then, that Aeneas shall fight a great war in Italy and overthrow proud peoples. He shall establish for his warriors a way of life and walls for their defence; and he shall live until the third summer looks on his reign in Latium, and he has passed his third winter in camp since his conquest of the Rutulians. But Ascanius, his young son, who is now given a second name Iulus, having been Ilus as long as the sovereignty of Ilium survived, shall complete in royal power each circling month for thirty long years. Active and vigorous, he shall build Alba Longa to be strong, and thither shall he transfer his rule from its old seat, Lavinium. Here, under a dynasty of Hector's kin, the royal power shall live. Here kings shall reign for a period of three hundred years until one day Ilia, a priestess of the royal blood, shall bear twin sons to Mars. Then shall one Romulus, nursed by a wolf and gay in a red-brown wolfskin, inherit the line. He shall build battlements of Mars; and call his people Romans, after his name. To Romans I set no boundary in space or time. I have granted them dominion, and it has no end. Yes, even the furious Juno, who now wearies sea, earth, and heaven with the strain of fear, shall amend her plans, and she and I will foster the nation which wears the toga, the Roman nation, masters of the world. My decree is made. Time in its five-year spans shall slip by till an age shall come when the House of Assaracus shall crush to subjection even Phthia and illustrious Mycenae, and conquer Argos, and hold mastery there. And then shall be born, of proud descent from Troy, one Caesar, to bound his lordship by Ocean's outer stream and his fame by the starry sky, a Julius, bearing a name inherited from Iulus his great ancestor. One day you shall welcome to Heaven with peace in your heart this Julius, coming weighted with the spoils of the Orient; and he also shall be invoked to listen to prayers. Then shall our furious centuries lay down their warring arms, and shall grow kind. Silver-haired Fidelity, Vesta, and Quirine Romulus, with his brother Remus at his side, shall make the laws. And the terrible iron-constricted Gates of War shall shut; and safe within them shall stay the godless and ghastly Lust of Blood, propped on his pitiless piled armoury, and still roaring from gory mouth, but held fast by a hundred chains of bronze knotted behind his back.'

So he prophesied; and he sent Maia's son Mercury down from Heaven. For the land of Africa, and Carthage itself with its newly built defences, were to stand open to receive the Trojans as guests, and Dido must not forbid them her territory through ignorance of the ordained plan. So, oared by his wings, Mercury flew, striking out across the broad sky, and swiftly he was there, standing on the coast of Africa. He obeyed his instructions, and at his divine will the Carthaginians put from them all thoughts of hostility. Especially he inspired their queen with a tolerance for the Trojans and a kindly intent.

Meanwhile Aeneas the True, after a night spent in thought, decided to walk out in the freshness of the dawn to investigate this new country, and to see on what coast the wind had driven him and what creatures lived there, whether men or wild animals, for he had noticed that the land was uncultivated; he could then report precisely to his comrades. He left the ships concealed under the trees' mysterious shade, enclosed by the wooded headlands and overhung by the cliff. He stepped out, accompanied by Achates alone and carrying two hunting-spears with broad iron heads quivering in his hand. Under the trees his mother met him. She had a maiden's countenance and a maiden's guise, and carried a maiden's weapons, like some Spartan girl, or like Harpalyce the Thracian who outruns horses till they tire and outstrips even the winged river Hebrus. Slung ready on her shoulder she carried a bow as a huntress would, and she had let her hair stream in the wind; her tunic's flowing folds were caught up and tied, and her knees were bare. She spoke first: 'Ho there, young Sirs! Do you happen to have seen one of my sisters, wearing a quiver and a cloak of spotted lynx-skin, wandering about here, or shouting hard on the track of some foam-flecked boar? If so, tell me where.'

So said Venus. And her son started to answer her: 'No, I have neither seen nor heard any sister of yours . . . young lady . . . only, how am I to speak of you? You have not the countenance of human kind and your voice has no tones of mortality . . . Goddess! For a goddess surely you must be. Not Apollo's own sister? Or one who is kin to the nymphs? Oh, I entreat your favour, whoever you may be, and some relief in our tribulation. Pray tell us under what skies we stand, and where on the world's shores we have been cast. A violent hurricane with its giant waves has driven us hither, and here we now stray, not knowing where we are or who are the inhabitants. If you tell us, we shall offer many victims to you, to fall dead before your altars.'

And Venus answered: 'I am not one to claim any such honour as that. It is the usual habit of Carthaginian maids to carry a quiver, and to wear these high-laced hunting-boots of dark red. The country which you see is ruled by Phoenicians from Tyre, and Agenor's dynasty reigns in their city. But around them is Africa; and no war can subjugate Africans.

Queen Dido, who directs the counsels of our state, came here from Tyre, wishing to escape her brother. It is a long and intricate tale of wrong; but I shall trace for you the main events of the story.

'Dido was married to Sychaeus, who was the greatest landowner of all the Phoenicians; and to her sorrow she loved him ardently. She had been a maid when her father gave her to him; her union with him was her first marriage. But she had a brother Pygmalion, who then occupied the throne at Tyre; and he was a monster of unmatched wickedness. A murderous quarrel broke out between the princes. Pygmalion was so blind with lust for gold that he lay in wait for Sychaeus at a holy rite, caught him off his guard, and sacrilegiously struck him down with a dagger-thrust. But he forgot to fear the power of his sister's love. For long Pygmalion concealed his deed, giving Dido false reasons for hope, and with many cruel pretences deluding her heart-sick anxiety. Then, while she slept, the actual spectre of Sychaeus, who was yet unburied, raised before her eyes a face weirdly pale. The wraith revealed the brutal deed at the sacrifice, showed the dagger-wounds in his breast, and disclosed the whole wicked secret of the palace. And he pressed her to leave her homeland and flee in haste. To help her on her journey he told her where there lay in the earth a long-buried and forgotten treasure of gold and silver in great weight. Shocked by the vision, Dido began to prepare for flight, and to gather for her company any who savagely hated or sharply feared the evil king. They assembled, hastily seized some ships which happened to be ready for sailing, and loaded them with the gold. The miserly Pygmalion lost his hoard, for it was conveyed over the ocean; and the whole enterprise was led by a woman. So they reached this place, where you can already see the towering battlements of a new city, Carthage, and its citadel even now being built. They bought as much land "as they could enclose within a bull's hide", and this land is still called "The Hide" after that event. But, tell me, who are you? From what country do you come, and whither do you voyage?'

In answer to her questions, Aeneas spoke with a deep sigh

out of his very heart; 'Lady Divine, if I were to start at the beginning and then continue all the chronicle of our ordeals, and if there were the time for you to hear, the star of evening would surely close heaven's gate, and set the day to sleep, before the end. From ancient Troy, if that name has ever chanced to come to your ears, we had been sailing over many strange seas; and then of its own caprice a storm drove us on Africa's coast. I am Aeneas, called the True, and I carry with me in my ships the gods of our home rescued from the foe. Beyond the sky my fame is known; and I quest for Italy, the land where my family first sprang from supreme Jove. Following my allotted destiny, and shown my way by my divine mother, I sailed forth onto the Phrygian Sea with twenty ships. Scarce seven survive, wrested from the easterly wind and from the waves. And here I wander, in want, unknown, about Africa's wilderness, driven first from Asia and now from Europe too.'

But Venus would not listen to more complaints from him, and she interrupted his lament: 'Whoever you are, They who dwell in Heaven can scarcely hate you, I think. You still breathe and live; and you have reached the city of the Tyrians. Continue on this path till you come to the doorway of the queen's palace. For I can tell you that the winds, veering to the north, have reversed their direction, your ships have been driven to safety, and your comrades have returned to you; if not, then my parents made false claims, and the lessons in prophecy which they gave me have been failures. Look at those twelve swans, gaily in line. Jupiter's eagle had swooped down from the heights of air, and was just now pursuing them across the whole breadth of the sky. And yet you can now see some of the swans alighting in their long ranks on the ground and others looking down from air to earth, where some have already settled. As these swans, now whirring their wings in play, have come safely home, while others flock and freely circle, trumpeting, in the zenith, so too some of your ships with their Trojan crews are safe in harbour, while others with bellying sails are drawing near to the haven's mouth. So just continue your walk, and go ahead where the way leads you.'

So Venus spoke, and as she turned away her loveliness shone, a tint of rose glowed on her neck and a scent of Heaven breathed from the divine hair of her head. Her gown trailed down to her feet; her gait alone proved her a goddess. Aeneas recognized his mother, and as she vanished his cry followed swiftly after: 'Ah, you too are cruel! Why again and again deceive your own son with your mocking disguises? Why may I not join hand to hand, hear you in frankness, and speak to you in return?'

As he reproached her thus he stepped out towards the city walls. For her part Venus fenced the two Trojans with a thick mist, enveloping them by her divine power with a mantle of dense cloud, so that no one might notice or touch them, hinder them, or ask them why they had come. And Venus herself departed soaring high in the air to Paphos. Joyously she returned to her own home where stands her temple and its hundred altars ever warm with the incense of Sheba, and where unceasingly a perfume is breathed from garlands of freshly gathered flowers.

Meanwhile the Trojans hurried along their way, guided by the path. They were now climbing a massive hill which overhung the city and commanded a view of the citadel. Aeneas looked wonderingly at the solid structures springing up where there had once been only African huts, and at the gates, the turmoil, and the paved streets. The Tyrians were hurrying about busily, some tracing a line for the walls and manhandling stones up the slopes as they strained to build their citadel, and others siting some building and marking its outline by ploughing a furrow. And they were making choice of laws, of officers of state, and of councillors to command their respect. At one spot they were excavating the harbour, and at another a party was laying out an area for the deep foundations of a theatre; they were also hewing from quarries mighty pillars to stand tall and handsome beside the stage which was still to be built. It was like the work which keeps the bees hard at their tasks about the flowering countryside as the sun shines in the calm of early summer, when they escort their new generation, now full grown, into the open air, or squeeze clear honey into bulging cells, packing them with sweet nectar; or else take over loads brought by their foragers; or sometimes form up to drive a flock of lazy drones from their farmstead. All is a ferment of activity; and the scent of honey rises with the perfume of thyme.

Aeneas looked up at the buildings. 'Ah, fortunate people,' he exclaimed, 'for your city-walls are already rising!' He walked on, miraculously protected by the cloud, right through the multitudes, mingling among the Carthaginians but noticed by none.

In the heart of the city there was a group of trees giving a wealth of shade. Here the Phoenicians, while they were still shaken after their stormy voyage, had dug from the earth a symbol whose discovery Juno in her queenly knowledge had predicted. It was the head of a spirited horse, and it indicated that the nation would have distinction in war and a plentiful livelihood through centuries to come. At this spot Dido the Phoenician was beginning to build a vast and sumptuous temple for Juno; inside it the dedicated offerings were magnificent, and the goddess's powerful presence could be felt. Bronzen were the raised thresholds to which the stairways led; bronze clamped the beams; and of bronze were the doors which made the hinges groan. Here among the trees a strange experience met Aeneas; for the first time his fears were allayed, and for the first time he dared to hope for life and to feel some confidence in spite of his distress. For as, while waiting for the queen, he inspected everything which there was to see under the mighty temple-roof, in wonder at the city's prosperity, the competitive skill of the craftsmen, and the great scale of their tasks, he saw pictured there the Trojan War, with all the battles round Ilium in their correct order, for their fame had already spread over the world. Agamemnon and Menelaus were there, and Priam; there, too, was Achilles, merciless alike to all three. Aeneas stood still, the tears came, and he said: 'O Achates, where in the world is there a country, or any place in it, unreached by our suffering? Look; there is Priam. Even here high merit has its due; there is pity for a world's distress, and a sympathy for short-lived humanity. Dispel all fear. The knowledge of you shown here will help to save you.' So he spoke. It was only a picture, but sighing deeply he let his thoughts feed on it, and his face was wet with a stream of tears. For he seemed to see again the antagonists warring around the defences of Troy, on one side the Greeks in flight before the charge of Troy's manhood, and on another the Trojans in retreat, and the crested and chariot-borne Achilles in pursuit. Still in tears he recognized in another scene the snow-white tents of Rhesus' encampment, betrayed to Diomede during the early hours of sleep and wrecked by him; and Diomede himself, bloody from the great massacre, was shown driving the fiery horses away to the Greek camp before they could taste the grass of Troyland and drink the water of Xanthus. Elsewhere poor young Troilus was pictured in ill-matched combat with Achilles and in flight before him; he had lost his weapons and his horses had bolted; he was on his back trailing from his empty chariot, but still grasping his reins, with his neck and hair dragging over the ground, and his lance pointing back and tracing lines in the dust. Meanwhile ladies of Troy, with hair thrown free, were seen walking in a mournful procession of supplication; they had been beating their breasts with open hands and they were bearing an offering of a robe to the temple of Pallas; but she was not impartial, for she stood with averted face and looked fixedly at the ground. And Achilles was shown again, this time selling back for gold Hector's lifeless body which he had dragged behind his chariot three times round the walls of Ilium. At that last sight of his friend, a lifeless body despoiled of arms, and of the chariot, and Priam holding forth weaponless hands in entreaty, Aeneas sighed a deep and terrible sigh. He also recognized himself hotly engaged among the Greek chieftains. He saw too the fighting ranks from the Orient, led by black Memnon with his divine arms. And battle-mad Penthesilea was there, leading the charge of Amazons carrying their crescent-shields; in the midst of thousands she blazed, showing her breast uncovered with a gold girdle clasped below, a warrior maid daring the shock of combat against men.

As Aeneas the Dardan looked in wonder at these pictures of

Troy, rapt and intent in concentration, for he had eyes only for them, the queen herself, Dido, in all her beauty, walked to the temple in state, closely attended by a numerous, youthful retinue. She was like Diana when she keeps her dancers dancing on the banks of Eurotas or along the slopes of Cynthus, with a thousand mountain-nymphs following in bands on this side and on that; she is taller than all other goddesses, as with her quiver slung from her shoulder she steps on her way, and a joy beyond words steals into Latona's heart. Like her was Dido, and like her she walked happily with the throng around her, intent on hastening the work for her future realm. And then, facing the Goddess's doorway, under her temple-dome, with her armed guards about her, she took her seat in the centre on a raised throne. She was already announcing new laws and statutes to her people and deciding by her own balanced judgement, or by lot, a fair division of the toil demanded of them, when suddenly Aeneas saw, moving towards them and followed by a large crowd, Antheus, Sergestus, and the bold Cloanthus, with other Trojans whom the dark hurricane had scattered over the ocean and carried far away to distant coasts. Amazed at this sight, Aeneas and Achates both stopped, overjoyed, and yet anxious. They were in burning haste to clasp their comrades' hands, but disturbed by the mystery of it all. So they made no sign, but, still shrouded by the soft mist, they watched, hoping to discover how their friends had fared, where they had left their ships moored, and why they had come to Carthage; for representatives from every ship were in the crowd, walking amid the noise to the temple, to plead for a sympathetic hearing.

The Trojans now entered, and were allowed to speak directly with the queen. In calm self-possession Ilioneus, the eldest among them, began: 'Your Majesty, to whom Jupiter has granted the right to build your new city, and assigned the duty of curbing lawless tribes with your justice, we are hapless Trojans, whom the winds have carried over every sea. We now entreat you, fend from our ships the terrible flames, and show mercy to a god-fearing breed of men. And indeed consider our predicament more closely. We can hardly have come to devastate your African home with the sword or to lift your cattle and drive them to the beach; as vanquished men we could never be so arrogant and aggressive. No; but there is a region for which the Greeks use the name Hesperia, the Western Land, an ancient land with might in her arms and in her fertile soil. The inhabitants used to be Oenotrians, but it is said that their descendants have now called the country Italy after one of their leaders. To Italy we were setting our course, when suddenly at the rising of Orion, star of storms, the seas ran high. We were carried onto invisible shoals; the gales were headstrong and drove us through seas where the surge boiled over near forbidding rocks. And we few have drifted hither to your coasts. Now tell us – who dwell here? What motherland is so barbarous that it allows such practices? For we are debarred even from such a welcome as barren sands can offer. Your people have started to assault us, and allow us no foothold on the shore. If you have no respect for mortal men or mortal arms, you should at least remember that there are gods who know right from wrong. Aeneas was our king. No one was ever more just than he, nor any greater in righteousness or in prowess at war. If Destiny preserves him still, and if he does not yet lie among the unpitying Shades, but still draws strength from heaven's air, then there is no fear: nor would you ever regret it if you took the first step to compete with him in the exchange of kindnesses. We also have cities in Sicily, well able to fight; and Acestes is there, a prince of fame from the blood of Troy. And we now desire your permission to beach our storm-damaged ships, and in your forests to shape timbers and strip wood for oars, so that we may sail for Italy and Latium, contented if we may make Italy our destination, and if our king and our comrades are restored to us. If however salvation is denied us, and if you, great and good Chieftain of Trojans, lie deep in the African ocean, and if we can no longer see in Iulus our nation's future, we can yet make for Sicily's narrow sea whence our voyage here began and where a place awaits us, and there take Acestes for our king.' So spoke Ilioneus, and all the other Trojans quickly acclaimed him.

Dido then gave her answer, shortly, with lowered eyes: 'Trojans, cast fear from your thoughts and entertain no anxieties. Life is hard for us, and this is a new kingdom. That is why I am compelled to take such grave precautions; I have to use guards and keep extensive watch on my frontiers. But who can there be who has never heard of Aeneas and his kindred, of Troy's city, and the valour of her men, or of that war's dreadful blaze? We Phoenicians are not so dull of mind, nor is the Sun when he harnesses his horses so remote from our Tyrian city. Whether your choice is for illustrious Hesperia, the land which Saturn ruled, or for the region by Eryx where Acestes would be your king, I shall help you to depart in safety under my protection and give you aid from my possessions. Or would you rather settle here in my realm on an equal footing with me? Count as your own this city which I am erecting. Beach your ships. There will be no question of making a distinction between Trojans and Tyrians. But now I only wish your king, Aeneas himself, might appear, forced hither like you by the same gales. I shall certainly send reliable men along the coast with orders to range far and wide through Africa, in the hope that he has been cast ashore and is lost in some city or some forest.'

Her speech startled Achates the brave, and Aeneas, his chieftain, too. They had long felt eager to break free from the cloud. It was Achates who spoke first, addressing Aeneas: 'Son of the Goddess, what do you now advise? You see that all is safe, and we have even recovered our comrades and our ships. Only one friend is missing, and we ourselves saw him drowned amidst the waves. All else agrees with your mother's prophecy.' Scarcely had he said this when the cloud enveloping them suddenly parted, and melted away into clear air. Aeneas checked his walk, and in the bright light he shone; his face and his shoulders bore a divine beauty, for his mother had imparted a grace to his hair, she had shed on him a rich glow of youth, and set a gay sparkle in his eyes; like the shine which art can give to ivory, or like silver or marble inlaid in yellow gold. Then suddenly, to the surprise of all, he addressed the queen: 'Here am I, in your presence, the one for whom you all look. I am Aeneas the Trojan, rescued from the African sea. Queen, you alone have felt pity for the unutterable ordeals of Troy; and now you would receive us as partners in your city and your home, us, a mere remnant left over by the Greeks, and in desperate need, our strength all drained away by every misfortune of land and sea. To thank you fitly, Dido, is not within our power, or the power of any other survivors of the Dardan race who may still exist dispersed in any part of the vast world. But if Powers of the Beyond take thought for the good, if there exists anywhere any justice at all, or some Intelligence able to know the right, then may your true reward come from them. What joyous world gave you your life? Who were great enough to be parents to one such as you? So long as rivers shall hurry to the sea, so long as shadows shall drift over a mountain's shoulder, and so long as the sky gives pasture to the stars, so long shall live the honour which is your due, your praises, and your name, to whatever land I may be called.' So saying, he reached out with his right hand to his friend Ilioneus and with his left to Serestus, and then to the others, the brave Gyas and the valiant Cloanthus.

At her first sight of Aeneas, Phoenician Dido was awestruck, thinking of the terrible fate which had been his. Then she spoke: 'Son of the Goddess, what is this fortune which has been pursuing you through such fearful perils? What compulsion now flings you on this barbarous shore? Can you truly be that Aeneas whom Venus, the kind life-giver, bore to Dardan Anchises by the waters of Phrygian Simois? Now I myself remember Teucer coming to Sidon, for he had been banished from his own homeland, and wished to win a new realm with aid from Belus my father, who at that time was pillaging Cyprus, the rich island which he had conquered and then held under his sway. Ever since that time I have known of the calamity which befell Troy, and known you, and the Greek princes, by name. Even your enemy, Teucer, gave the Trojans his very highest praise, claiming to be himself descended from the same ancient "Teucrian" stock. Therefore, come, gallant friends, and proceed to my home. A fortune not unlike yours has harassed me, and led me, too, through many tribulations, to rest at long last in this country. My own acquaintance with misfortune has been teaching me to help others who are in distress.' After speaking so to Aeneas she led him into the palace. As she walked she gave orders for temple-offerings in thanks to the Gods. She also remembered to send twenty bulls to Aeneas' friends on the shore with a hundred bristling hogs' backs, a hundred fat lambs with their ewes, and the god's joyous gift of wine. Inside the palace the preparations were regally sumptuous. They were making ready a banquet in the central hall. There was drapery artistically worked in princely purple, a massive array of silver on the tables, and gold plate engraved with the heroic deeds of this people's ancestors, in a long succession of historic events throughout all the generations since their nation's birth.

But Aeneas found that his love for his son would not let his mind rest. He sent Achates swiftly to the ships, with instructions to tell Ascanius the news and to bring him to the walled city, for the loving father's every thought was fixed on Ascanius. Achates was also to fetch presents, things rescued from the fall of Troy; a figured gown stiff with gold lace, and a mantle hemmed with a yellow thistle-pattern, both garments which had graced Argive Helen, fine gifts from her mother Leda which she had carried off from Mycenae when she first started for Troy and her wicked marriage. Aeneas added a sceptre, once borne by Priam's eldest daughter Ilione, a necklace shaped like a row of mulberries, and a double diadem of gold set with jewels.

Achates hastened to obey and was soon on his way to the ship. But meanwhile Venus was pondering new plans and new devices. She decided to make Cupid assume the form and features of the charming Ascanius, and go in place of him; he should give Dido the presents, and as he did so enflame her with a distraction of love, and entwine the fire of it about her very bones. For Venus could not help fearing the uncertainty of a home menaced by Phoenician duplicity; Juno's savage will tormented her, and as night drew on her anxiety returned. Therefore she spoke to her winged son: 'Son, you alone are my strength and all my might is in you. Son, you even scorn the Father's Typhoean thunderbolts. Now I appeal to you, and humbly pray to your divine majesty for aid. You know how your brother Aeneas has travelled storm-tossed on the ocean round every coast solely on account of merciless Juno's persistent hate; you have often sympathized with me in my sorrow. And now Phoenician Dido detains him and talks to him, coaxing him to stay with her. I am anxious about the outcome of any entertainment which Juno sanctions; she will certainly not be slow to act at this critical moment. Therefore I plan to forestall her by a trick of my own and enclose the queen in such a girdle of flames that no act of divine power may divert her from submitting, as I intend, to a fierce love for Aeneas. To enable you to effect this, listen now to my plan. Aeneas his dear father has now sent for the young prince who is my own greatest love; and he is now preparing to go to the Phoenician city with gifts, things saved from the fire of Troy and from the ocean perils. I shall lull him into a profound sleep, and then hide him away in my hallowed precinct high up on Cythera or at Idalium; for otherwise he might learn of the trick or appear suddenly while it is being played. You must just for one night assume his shape as a disguise, and wear his familiar features; after all, he is a boy like you. Then, during the royal entertainment, when the wine is flowing, and Dido in her great happiness clasps you to her, embracing you and planting on you her sweet kisses, you shall breathe into her invisible fire, and poison her, without her knowing.' Cupid obeyed his dear mother's command. He took off the wings from his shoulders, and in great amusement copied Iulus' way of walking. Venus now poured delicious and pervasive sleep into Iulus, and holding him closely and caressingly she carried him by her divine power to Idalium's wooded upland, where soft amaracus guarded him amid flowers and shade, and spread sweetness with the perfume which it breathed.

The obedient Cupid was soon on his way carrying the royal gifts for the Queen of Carthage, and happy in the guidance of Achates. When he arrived, the queen had just composed herself, proudly curtained on her golden seat in the centre.

And here Troy's chieftain Aeneas and all the manhood of Troy forgathered, and took their places on coverlets of purple. Attendants held water for them to wash their hands, passed them bread in baskets, and brought napkins of soft material. Beyond, within the palace, waited fifty serving maids, each at her station, whose office it was to replenish the capacious store-rooms and rekindle the hearth-fire of the home. There were a hundred other maids and a hundred man-servants, all matched for age, to load the food onto the tables and set forth the drink. Many Carthaginians, who had been invited to take their places on the embroidered banquet-seats, entered through the festal doorways. They wondered at the gifts from Aeneas, and at Iulus – the divinity in disguise – now wearing a flush of emotion and speaking in his assumed character. They admired the sceptre and the mantle hemmed with the yellow thistle-pattern. But beyond all the rest the unhappy Phoenician Dido, condemned now to sure destruction, could not satisfy her longing. She gazed, and the fire in her grew; she was affected equally by the boy and by the beautiful gifts. Cupid had been clinging to Aeneas and embracing him with his arms around his neck, expressing great love for his supposed father. Then he crossed to the queen. Dido's eyes and her whole mind were fixed on him, and at times she would fondle him and hold him close to her, for she could not know, poor Dido, how mighty a god was entering her. And then he, remembering the wish of his mother the Cyprian, began gradually to dispel from Dido all thought of Sychaeus; and he assailed that heart of hers so long inactive, and her brain, so unused to these thoughts, with the thrill of a living love.

The banquet came to its first pause, and tables were removed. They set in place great bowls of wine, and filled them to the brim. Loud talk broke out in the palace, and the voices rolled through the hall's great spaces. There were lamps hanging from the gold-panelled ceiling, and a blaze of candles vanquished the darkness. The queen asked for a jewelled drinking-bowl of heavy gold. She filled it with wine of full strength, as the first Belus and all his successors had filled it often before. There was a call for silence in the palace, and she spoke:

'Jupiter, you who are said to have created the laws of hospitality, may it be your wish to make this day a fortunate day for the Phoenicians and for the exiles from Troy, a day to be remembered by our descendants. May Bacchus, giver of joy, and Juno the generous, grant their blessing. Phoenicians, show your good will, and make our gathering festive.' So saying, she poured out a drink-offering onto the table. After the libation she first touched the drink with her own lips, and passed it then to Bitias, with a challenge. He boldly drank all the foaming bowl, soaking himself from the full gold vessel. Other Phoenician lords drank after him. And Iopas of the long hair took his lyre bound with gold, and his music rang. The great master, Atlas, had been his teacher; he sang now of the wandering moon and the labouring sun; of the origin of men and of beasts, of rain, of fire, of Arcturus and the Hyads which foretell the rain, and of the two Bears. His song told why on each winter day the sun so hastens to dip in ocean, and told of the cause which then retards the nights and makes them slow. The Phoenicians cheered and cheered again, and the Trojans applauded with them. And the doomed Dido herself spent the whole night in talk of many kinds, drinking deep of her love. She asked question after question about Priam and Hector; she asked what arms the Son of the Dawn had carried when he came to Troy, and enquired now of the quality of Diomede's horses, and now of the stature of Achilles. Then she said: 'But, come! You must tell me, guest of mine, the whole story from the beginning, of the trap which the Greeks set, the calamity which befell your people, and your own wanderings; for it is now the seventh summer of your roaming over the land and sea throughout the world.'

BOOK TWO

AENEAS' NARRATION – THE SACK OF TROY

THEY fell silent, every one, and each face was turned intently towards him. From high on the dais Aeneas, Troy's Chieftain, began to speak:

'Majesty, too terrible for speech is the pain which you ask me to revive, if I am to tell how the Greeks erased the greatness which was Troy and the Trojan Empire ever to be mourned. I witnessed that tragedy myself, and I took a great part in those events. No one could tell the tale and refrain from tears, not even if he were a Myrmidon or a Dolopian, or some soldier of the unpitying Ulysses. Besides, the moist air of late night falls swiftly from the sky. The stars are setting and they remind us that we too must rest. Still, if you are truly anxious to learn what befell us and to hear a short account of Troy's last agony, even though I shudder at the memory and can hardly face its bitterness, I shall begin.

'The Greek commanders, disappointed by fate and broken by the war as year after year slipped by, built a giant of a wooden horse, making its flanks from a trellis of sawn firwood. The craftsmanship was divinely inspired by Minerva. They pretended that it was an offering to secure their homeward voyage; and such was the rumour which spread. Then they drew lots, and unobserved, locked a party of picked men in its dark interior till the horse's cavernous womb was full of armed soldiers.

'Within sight of Troy is the island of Tenedos. In the days of Priam's Empire it had wealth and power and was well known and famous, but there is nothing there now, except the curve of the bay affording its treacherous anchorage. The Greeks put to sea as far as Tenedos, and hid from sight on its lonely beaches. We thought they had sailed for Mycenae before the wind and gone home. So all the land of Troy relaxed after its years of unhappiness. We flung the gates open and we enjoyed going to look at the unoccupied, deserted space along the shore where the Greek camp had been. Yes, here the Dolopians had their station. And there camped the merciless Achilles. Over there the ships were moored; and this was the usual ground for pitched battle. Some of us looked in awed wonder at that massive horse, the gift for Minerva the never-wed, which was to be our destruction. Thymoetes, perhaps out of treason or perhaps because Troy's fate was already fixed, was the first to make a proposal: we should tow the horse inside the city-walls and leave it standing on our citadel. But others, among them Capys, judged more wisely, for they suspected treachery in anything freely offered by Greeks. They advised us to destroy it by casting it down into the sea or by setting fire to it and burning it; or else to pierce it and tear open the hidden lair within. The rest were divided in keen support of one proposal or the other.

'But there, in front of all, came Laocoon, hastening furiously down from the citadel with a large company in attendance. While still far off he cried: "O my unhappy friends, you must be mad indeed. Do you really believe that your enemies have sailed away? Do you think that a Greek could offer a gift without treachery in it? Do you know Ulysses no better than that? Either some of their men have been shut inside this timber-work and are now hiding in it, or the horse itself is a machine for overcoming our walls, perhaps to pry somehow into our homes or threaten Troy from its height; or it hides some other confusion for us. Trojans, never trust that horse. Whatever it proves to be, I still fear Greeks, even when they offer gifts." As he spoke, he powerfully heaved a great spear at the horse's side, into the firm timber-work of its rounded belly, and there it stood, quivering. At the impact, the echoing spaces of the cavernous womb growled and rang; and if the destined will of Heaven had not been set against us, and our own reason had not been deranged, Laocoon had surely driven home a thrust till the iron tore open the Greek lair. Troy would then have survived till now; and, O proud Citadel of Priam, you would have been standing yet.

'But another figure suddenly appeared, a young stranger, with his arms shackled behind him. Some Trojan shepherds had chanced on him, and now with much shouting they were hurrying him to King Priam. He had in fact waited for them to capture him. His set purpose was to lay Troy open to the Greeks; relying on his own cool nerve, he was ready for either outcome, whether success in his deceptions or certain death. Anxious to look at him, the young Trojans came hastening up and gathered round, outdoing each other in mockery of the captive. You are now to hear how the Greeks tricked us. From this one proof of their perfidy you may understand them all.

'The captive halted confused and defenceless in our midst where all could see him. His frightened eyes glanced round the lines of Trojans. Then he spoke: "Oh, is there anywhere now left on land or sea where I can find refuge? No, there is no hope at all for me in this extreme of misery. Nowhere among the Greeks have I any place; and meanwhile the Trojans are no less hostile and vengefully demand my blood!" This piteous talk changed our mood and checked each violent impulse. We pressed him to tell us his nationality and his errand and to explain why he had dared to face the risks of capture. At last he laid his dread aside, and answered: "Whatever is to happen I shall tell your Majesty the whole story, and it will be true. First, I admit that I am of Greek nationality; my name is Sinon. Fortune may have made of me a man of sorrows, but even her malice can never change me into a man of faithlessness and lies. Now there may perhaps have come to your ears some mention of Palamedes, a king of great military renown, whom, in spite of his innocence and merely because he opposed this war, the Greeks arraigned on a monstrous charge of treason and executed; though now, when he has passed from the light, they mourn him. When I was still very young, my father, who was not rich, sent me here to the war to be aide to Palamedes, for we were close relatives. Now as long as Palamedes remained secure in his royal station and exerted influence among the kings in council, I also enjoyed some distinction and respect. But when, through the jealous deceit of Ulysses, which will be no surprise to you, Palamedes passed from the world of the living, I was crushed, and lived a weary life of obscurity and grief, in lonely bitterness at the fate of my innocent friend. But I must have been mad, for I did not keep this resentment to myself. Indeed, I vowed vengeance upon them, should I ever return after victory to my native Argos and have my chance. By my words I roused against myself a fury of hate; and I was already on the slippery path to destruction, for from then on Ulysses never ceased intimidating me with some new accusation, spreading suggestive hints among our army, and coldly planning to strike me down. Nor did he ever rest until, making Calchas his accomplice – but what use is it for me now to trace the course of this story? You do not want to hear it, and I only waste words, for you naturally class all Greeks together, and it is enough for you that I carry the name of Greek. So it is more than time for you to be taking your vengeance on me. How that would please the man from Ithaca! And what would the sons of Atreus not give in return for it!"

'This of course made us most anxious to question Sinon and press him to explain; we had no idea to what lengths of wickedness Greek cunning could go. He, subtle actor that he was, nervously continued his tale:

'"Several times the Greeks, wearied by so long a war, wanted to abandon it, leave Troyland, and somehow effect a retreat. And how I wish they had done so! But each time as they were starting tempestuous seas checked them and contrary winds filled them with alarm; and more than ever, when this horse now stood complete in its texture of maple-planks, did storm and rain shriek across the sky. In our anxiety, we sent Eurypylus to question Apollo's oracle, and he returned from the shrine with this terrible message: 'Greeks, you shed blood when you sacrificed a maiden to calm the winds for your original voyage to Troy. You must shed blood again to win your return, for only the sacrifice of a Greek life can make your prospect fair.' When these words reached the army, they were terror-stricken, and icy shudders ran down their spines. No one could say on whom the choice of Apollo would fall, and who was to meet his doom. At this moment the Ithacan forced Calchas our prophet to come with him before us all. There was uproar. He openly pressed him to explain the meaning of the god's demand. Many were already predicting that I was to be the victim of this brutal and cunning wickedness, but they awaited the outcome without protest. For ten days Calchas maintained a silent reserve, refusing to let any word of his betray anyone to death by sacrifice. But the loud insistence of the Ithacan prevailed; conniving at last, the prophet broke his silence, and marked me for the altar. The others all approved, for, each having feared that this fate would be his, they were relieved when it fell to some other wretch. The day of horror quickly came. The ritual implements of my sacrifice were made ready, with the usual salted grain and the headbands round my forehead. Well, as I can now admit, I burst from my confinement and made my escape from death. All that night I hid unseen amid the reeds in the mud by the lake, hoping against hope that they would sail. I could no longer believe that I should ever again see the ancient land of my home or my dear children or the father for whom I yearned. Probably the Greeks will now wreak vengeance on all of them for my escape, punishing my crime by killing my helpless family. I now entreat your Majesty, in the name of the High Gods and of all those Powers from whom no truth is hidden, yes, and in the name of any fidelity which may remain inviolate in the world of men, have pity on one whose ordeal has been so terrible, and who has borne what none should have to bear."

'These tears gained him his life, and we even began to feel sorry for him. Priam set the example, giving orders for him to be relieved of the taut ropes and handcuffs. He spoke kindly to him: "Well, whoever you are, there are no Greeks here; forget them quickly and become one of us. Now answer my questions, truthfully and thoroughly. What was their purpose in erecting this massive structure in the shape of a giant horse? Who suggested it and what is it for? What is supposed to be its use either in ritual or as an engine of war?"

'That was all. Sinon, adept in deception and with all the cunning of a Greek, raised his hands, newly freed from the bonds, palm-upwards towards the heavens and spoke: "Bear me now witness, eternal Starfire, Majesty never profaned; bear me witness, altar, and ghastly knives, and holy headbands of the sacrificial victim which I myself have worn. It cannot be sin for me to break obligations which are only sacred among Greeks. It cannot be sin for me to show my hatred for them, and expose to daylight what the Greeks are hiding; for I can incur no guilt under any law of my homeland. If I bring you truth and repay you well, all that I ask of Troy, if she is not broken, is, not to break her faith, but honour her plighted word.

'"From the start of the war the only hope of victory which the Greeks ever had lay in help from Pallas. But there came that night when sacrilegious Diomede and Ulysses, always quick to invent new crimes, crept up to wrest Troy's talisman, the image of Minerva, from your hallowed temple, cut down the sentries guarding the upper citadel, seized the holy figure, and actually touched the virgin headband of our goddess with blood still on their hands. From that night the prospects of the Greeks receded like an ebbing tide and trickled away; their strength was gone; the heart of the goddess set hard against them.

'"Of this she herself gave certain proof by marvels. The image had hardly been set down in the Greek camp when flickering flames shone in its staring eyes, a salt sweat ran down over its limbs, and three times it lunged miraculously from its base, shield in hand, lance quivering. Calchas, under inspiration, advised the Greeks to attempt an immediate escape across the sea, since no Greek attack could now demolish Troy's defences, unless they first went back to Argos to receive again the promise of divine favour which freighted their shapely galleys when they first crossed the sea. So now they have sailed back to their home-city Mycenae only to re-arm, and to re-enlist their divine allies, and they will soon traverse the ocean again, to startle you with their reappearance. Such was the plan which Calchas pieced together for them from the omens. On his advice they erected this effigy of a horse, to make amends for their profanation of Pallas' image and to expiate the burden of their guilt. At the same time he made them build it of this massive size, a giant structure of hard oak planks, and raise it high towards the heavens, to prevent it from being admitted through the gates or hauled over the walls. If it were, it would only guard your people in the shelter of your ancient faith. For if hand of yours damaged the offering to Minerva, a terrible destruction, such as I would to Heaven Calchas himself might suffer, would come on Priam's empire and the Trojans; but if the horse climbed into your city with help from your hands, then Asia would be free to launch an invasion up to the very ramparts of Pelops, and such would then be the destiny awaiting our grandsons."

'So we gave Sinon our trust, tricked by his blasphemy and cunning. His ruse, and his artificial tears, entrapped men whom neither Tydeus' son nor Larissaean Achilles could subdue, for all their ten years of war and their fleet of a thousand keels.

'But now to our distress a far more momentous and frightful experience befell us, and the unexpected shock of it disordered our minds. Laocoon, who had been chosen by lot to be priest of Neptune, happened at this moment to be sacrificing a fine bull at the altar of the cult, when, and I sicken to recall it, two giant arching sea-snakes swam over the calm waters from Tenedos, breasting the sea together and plunging towards the land. Their fore-parts and their blood-red crests towered above the waves; the rest drove through the ocean behind, wreathing monstrous coils, and leaving a wake that roared and foamed. And now, with blazing and blood-shot eyes and tongues which flickered and licked their hissing mouths, they were on the beach. We paled at the sight and scattered; they forged on, straight at Laocoon. First each snake took one of his two little sons, twined round him, tightening, and bit, and devoured the tiny limbs. Next they seized Laocoon, who had armed himself and was hastening to the rescue; they bound him in the giant spirals of their scaly length, twice round his middle, twice round his throat; and still their heads and necks towered above him. His hands strove frantically to wrench the knots apart. Filth and black venom drenched his priestly hands. His shrieks were horrible and filled the sky, like a bull's bellow when an axe has struck awry, and he flings it off his neck and gallops wounded from the altar. The pair of serpents now made their retreat, sliding up to the temple of heartless Minerva high on her citadel, where they vanished near her statue's feet behind the circle of her shield. At this an access of utter panic crept into every trembling heart. Men said that Laocoon had deserved to pay for his wickedness in damaging the sacred woodwork with his lance, when he made his sinful cast at the horse's side. All were loud in their desire for the horse to be towed to its rightful place and prayers of entreaty to be offered to Minerva's might.

'We cut through our walls and threw our defences open. All set to work with zest. Rollers for smooth running were placed under the horse's feet and hempen ropes tied round its neck. That engine of doom, pregnant with armed men, mounted our walls. Boys and unwedded girls sang hymns around it, happy in the hope that the very touch of the ropes would bring them luck. The brute climbed on; then sank menacingly to rest right inside Troy. O Ilium where gods had their home, O my land and ramparts which Trojans held in glorious defence! Four times the horse halted in the gateway, and each time weapons clanged within it. But we remained witless, and blind, and mad; we pressed ahead, and stationed the malignant horror within our consecrated citadel. Cassandra, whom her own god had ruled that no Trojan should believe, let her lips utter once again the truth of what destiny had in store. We, poor fools, spent this our last day decorating with festal greenery every temple in our town.

'Meanwhile the sky circled round, and night fell over the ocean, wrapping in a single darkness the earth, the high heaven, and the treachery of the Greeks. There was no sound from the Trojans, stretched out weary in the embrace of sleep about the fortress-city. By then the whole Greek fleet was sailing from Tenedos with all ships in ordered lines under the friendly secrecy of a hidden moon toward the old landing-place. Suddenly the king's ship displayed a fire signal; and Sinon under the divine protection of an unjust destiny stealthily removed the horse's pinewood bars and released the Greeks from their confinement. The horse stood open, restoring them to the fresh air. Glad to be free, forth from the timber cavity came the two chieftains, Thessandrus and Sthenelus, and then the merciless Ulysses, sliding down a rope dropped from the horse. Next came Acamas and Thoas, Neoptolemus of Peleus' line, and Machaon in the lead; Menelaus, too, and Epeus, the very craftsman who had made the device. They marched on a city buried in a sleep deepened by wine. The sentries were cut down, the gates stood open, they admitted all their comrades, and the forces were joined, as planned.

'It was the hour when divinely given rest first comes to poor human creatures, and creeps over them deliciously. In my sleep I dreamed that Hector stood there before my eyes. He looked most sorrowful, and was weeping plenteous tears. He was filthy with dust and blood, as he had been that day when he was dragged behind the chariot, and his feet were swollen where they had been pierced by the thongs. And, oh, how harrowing was the sight of him: how changed he was from the old Hector, back from battle wearing the spoils of Achilles, or that time when he had just flung Trojan firebrands onto the Greek ships! Now his beard was ragged and his hair clotted with blood, and all those wounds which he had sustained fighting to defend the walls of his homeland could still be seen. I dreamed that I spoke first, weeping and forcing myself to find words for this sad meeting: "Light of the Dardan Land, Troy's surest hope, what held you from us so long? How we have waited for you, Hector! From what bourne do you come? We are weary now, and many of your folk are dead. We and our city have had many adventures, many trials. To think that we may look on you again! But what can have so shamefully disfigured your princely countenance? And why these wounds which I see?" He made no reply and gave no attention to my vain questions, but with a deep, choking sob he said: "Son of the Goddess, make your escape quickly from the fires around you. Your walls are captured, and all Troy from her highest tower is falling; Priam and our dear land have had their day. If any strong arm could have defended our fortress, surely mine would have defended it. But now Troy entrusts to you her sanctities and her Guardians of the Home. Take them with you to face your destiny, and find for them the walled city which one day after ocean-wandering you shall build to be great, like them." As he spoke, with his own hands he fetched out from the inner shrine the holy headbands, Vesta in whom dwells power, and her hearth-fire which burns for ever.

'Confused cries of anguish now began to reach me from inside our city. The house of my father Anchises lay back, secluded behind a screen of trees; but even there the battle-noise grew louder and louder, till the air was thick with its terror. I was startled out of my sleep, and climbing to the highest point of the roof stood listening keenly. It was like fire catching a cornfield when wild winds are blowing, or like the sweep of a mountain torrent in flood, flattening smiling crops for which oxen had toiled, and bringing whole forests down, while some shepherd standing high on a crag of rock hears the roar in helpless wonder. There was no doubt now as to the truth; it was at once clear how the Greeks had outwitted us. Already the fire had vanquished the broad mansion owned by Deiphobus, and down it crashed. Ucalegon's, closest to it, was already ablaze. The wide Straits of Sigeum were lit up by the burning. Shouts arose and trumpets rang. Out of my senses, I grasped my arms; not that I had any plan for battle, but simply a burning desire to muster a band for fighting, and rally with my comrades at some position of defence. Frantic in my fury I had no time for decisions; I only remembered that death in battle is glorious.

'But now appeared Panthus, Othrys' son, who was priest of Apollo's temple on the citadel. He had escaped the Greek missiles and was running wildly to our doorway, leading his little grandson by the hand and carrying his sacred vessels and figures of his defeated gods. "Panthus," I cried, "Which is the point of greatest danger? Where do we take our stand?" I had hardly spoken when with a moan he replied, "The last day has come for our Dardan land. This is the hour which no effort of ours can alter. We Trojans are no more: no more is Ilium; no more the splendour of Teucrian glory. All now belongs to Argos; it is Jupiter's remorseless will. For the Greeks are masters of our city and already it burns. The Horse stands towering within our ramparts, streaming armed men; and Sinon glorying in his triumph stirs the blaze. The main array of the Greeks, all those thousands who came from imperial Mycenae, mass at the open gates. Others have blocked the narrow streets with weapons levelled, and their unsheathed swordpoints, a flickering line of steel, stand instantly ready to kill. Only the foremost sentinels at the gates attempt resistance, and they fight blind."

'These words from Panthus, together with some impulse from above, sent me dashing into the fires and the fight, guided by the roaring, the shouts which rose to heaven, and the dark instinct of revenge. I was joined by Ripheus and the mighty warrior Epytus who came up looming through the moonlight. With them were Hypanis and Dymas, and young Coroebus; and they all stood together at my side. Coroebus was a son of Mygdon, and he had come to Troy as it chanced a few days before, because he hoped to win the hand of Cassandra, whom he loved with a mad and burning love, by an offer of aid to Priam and our nation; and it was disastrous for him that he had not heeded the wild warnings of his princess. Seeing them all shoulder to shoulder, dauntless for battle, I called out to them: "Men, valiant hearts, though valour cannot help us now, if your ardour is set on following the path of daring to the very end – you see for yourselves how our fortune stands. Those gods on whom our power hitherto depended have forsaken their altars and their shrines and are gone forth from us; the city which you would rescue is already ablaze; and it is for us to plunge amid the spears and die. Nothing can save the conquered but the knowledge that they cannot now be saved."

'That gave to their proud hearts the strength of desperation. Like wolves out for prey in a thick mist, forced blindly onwards by hunger's incessant torment and the thought of their cubs left behind and waiting with parched throats for their return, we drove on amid the spears to certain death, taking the way to the centre of Troy and passing directly through the enemy, shadowed by the soft, black wings of the darkness.

'No tongue could describe the carnage of that night and its orgy of death; no tears could match such agonies. An ancient city was falling and the long years of her empire were at an end. Everywhere the dead lay motionless about the streets, in the houses, and on those temple stairs which our tread had reverenced so long. Nor was it only the Trojans who paid the penalty by their blood. Sometimes prowess revived even in the vanquished, and then it was Greeks who fell despite their victory. All was a torment of suffering and fear, with death in a thousand forms.

'The first to meet our band was Androgeos, who appeared with a strong force of Greeks beside him, and carelessly mistook us for some of his own side on the march. He even gave us a friendly hail: "Make haste, my comrades! Why are you late, and idling along like this? Are you only now arriving from the tall ships, when already the centre of Troy is afire and the rest are looting and pillaging?" But he received no assurance in answer; and he had hardly spoken when he realized that he had stumbled right into the enemy. He shrank back at the shock, and checked his words; he was like a man who, as he puts his weight to the ground, finds that he has trodden on a snake lying unseen amid wild brambles, and recoils in sudden fright as it angrily raises the swelling metal-blue of its neck. Just so did Androgeos tremble at the sight of us and try to retreat. But we charged, and our counter-attack enveloped the Greeks, who did not know the ground and were seized by panic. We bore them down; our first enterprise had met with luck. It was now that the high-spirited Coroebus, triumphant at this success, cried, "Friends, let us accept this first hint from Fortune, and win to safety, guided by her smile. We must exchange shields with the Greeks and wear their badges. Who cares whether what we do to an enemy is treachery or valour? The Greeks shall give us the arms which we need." With these words he began equipping himself with Androgeos' plumed helmet and his nobly blazoned shield; and he girded the

Argive sword to his waist. Ripheus, Dymas, and all our company followed his example in high spirits, arming themselves with the newly won spoils of the vanquished. So we strode on, mingling with the Greeks and submitting to alien deities. In the utter darkness we were often plunged into conflict and whenever we fought we despatched many a Greek to the land of the dead. Others scattered and fled to their ships, running to the beaches for safety. Some were even cowardly enough to climb again into the capacious horse and hide as before in its belly.

'Sad to say, even trust in Heaven is forbidden when Heaven itself declines the trust. For there before us Priam's own daughter Cassandra was being dragged from the very shrine of Minerva's temple; her hair was astream, and she could only turn her burning eyes helplessly to heaven, for bonds prevented her from raising her delicate hands in prayer. Coroebus could not bear to see her in this plight. The madness entered him, and he plunged among the Greeks to certain death. Our whole force followed, charging with massed weapons. And now for the first time we were attacked by our own side, and came under a shower of spears from the temple-roof. They had mistaken our Greek crests and the Greek shape of our arms; and so started a tragic massacre. The Greeks roared with indignation at the rescue of the girl. Concentrating from all around, they came on, Ajax the most furious of them all, with Agamemnon, Menelaus, and all the Dolopian army; like winds in conflict when a hurricane bursts, winds of the west and of the south, and the east wind exultant on horses of the dawn, while forests howl, and Nereus, making violent play with his trident amid the foam, stirs the sea to its very floor. We were even confronted again by some of those whom in the darkness we had sent hurrying away in the night-shadows and pursued in flight through all Troy; they were the first to see through our deceptive weapons and shields; and they had noticed that our language was foreign to them. We were quite helpless, and weight of numbers bore us down. Coroebus was the first to fall; he died by the hand of Peneleos beside the altar of the goddess mighty in arms. Ripheus fell also, he, the most just of all Trojans, who never wavered from the right; yet the gods regarded not his righteousness. Hypanis, too, and Dymas died, pierced by their friends; and you, Panthus, even all your holiness and Apollo's own emblem on your brow could not save you in your falling. Ashes of Ilium, O last flame burning all that was dear to me, bear witness that at your setting I never shrank from any risk of combat amid the spears, but earned at Greek hands the death which fate denied me. And now we were forced apart. With me were Iphitus, ageing and slow, and Pelias who was hampered by a wound from Ulysses. Guided by shouts we made direct for Priam's palace. There the ferocity of the fight was intense indeed; all the warring and the slaughter elsewhere in the city were nothing to it. We faced Mars in his full fury. The Greeks were dashing to the building, and thronging round the entrance with their shields locked together over their backs; ladders were already firmly in place against the walls, and the attackers even now putting their weight on the rungs close to the door-lintels. Holding shields on their left arms thrust forward for protection, with their right hands they grasped the roof. To oppose them the Trojans, on the brink of death and knowing that their plight was desperate, sought to defend themselves by tearing up tiles from the roof-tops of houses and even loosening towers to use as missiles. And they sent rolling down on the enemy gold-plated roof-beams, the pride of the ancient Trojans. Some of them, with sword-points bared, blocked the entrances and, closing their ranks, guarded them well. We felt a new surge of courage and determined to aid the palace, bring relief to the defenders and lend fresh vigour to the vanquished.

'There was a secret access to the palace gained through a concealed entrance, a doorway never noticed by passers-by, which communicated between the mansions of King Priam's family. In the days of our empire poor Andromache would often walk this way, unattended, to Hector's people, when she took little Astyanax to see his grandfather. Here I entered, and climbed to the highest point of the sloping roof, from which the unhappy Trojans were busy casting their unavailing missiles. Now there was a tower, built on the roof of another structure high into the air above a precipitous drop, whence we used to look out over all Troyland and see the Greek camp and fleet. We hacked with iron blades all round it where the upper storeys presented loosened joints. We wrenched it free from its high position, and thrust it over. Down it suddenly slid with a roar trailing havoc behind, and crashed on many ranks of the attackers. But others took their places, and their showers of stones and the missiles of every kind never slackened.

'In the front of the entrance-hall, and right in the gateway of the palace, stood Pyrrhus, a figure of armed insolence sparkling in a sheen of bronze; like a snake which after a winter spent hidden below ground, swollen from a fare of poisonous weeds, now emerges into the light, and shedding its slough becomes shiningly fresh and young, then raises its breast tall to the sun, coils a slithering back, and sets flickering a triple tongue. With Pyrrhus were the gigantic Periphas, Automedon the squire and charioteer of Achilles, and all the company from Scyros. Together they moved up to the building and cast firebrands to the roof. Pyrrhus, who was leading, seized an axe and smashed in the stout door, rending the bronze-plated hinge-posts from their sockets; soon he had hacked out a panel and hewn a hole through the door's tough oak, making in it a great gaping window. The interior stood revealed. A long vista of galleries was suddenly exposed, and the private home of King Priam and the kings before him came into view, with armed defenders standing on the entrance-threshold.

'Inside the palace there was sobbing and a confused and pitiful uproar. The building rang from end to end with the anguished cries of women. Shouts rose to the golden stars. Matrons roved in panic about the vast house, clasping the very pillars in their arms and kissing them. Pyrrhus came on, like Achilles himself in his onset. No bolts or bars, no guards could hold off that attack. The door crumbled under the ceaseless battering. The hinge-posts were wrenched off their sockets, and fell outwards. Utmost violence opened a passage. With access forced, and the first guards cut down, the Greek army flooded in and filled all the palace with its men; more fiercely, even, than some foaming river which breaks its banks and leaps over them in a swirling torrent, and defeats every barrier, till the mad piled water charges on the ploughland and sweeps away with it cattle and their stalls over miles of country. My own eyes saw Pyrrhus with the blood-lust in him, and Agamemnon and Menelaus right inside the gate; they saw Hecuba with her hundred princesses, and Priam himself, fouling with his blood the altar-fire which he had hallowed. Those fifty wedding-rooms with all their hope of lineage to be, and those pillars vaunting their trophies and laden with orient gold, crashed down. The Greeks were masters wherever the fire had not yet come.

'You may also want to know how Priam met his end.

'When he saw that Troy was captured and fallen, that his palace gates were wrenched from their place and the enemy inside his very home, old though he was he vainly drew onto shoulders trembling with age his long unused corslet, and girded at his side an ineffectual sword. And he started hurrying into the thick of the foe seeking to meet his death. In the centre of the palace, and bare to the high heavens above, was a large altar, with near by an old bay-tree bending over it and clasping within its shade the sanctities of the home. Close about this altar, in unavailing sanctuary, with their arms round the statues of our gods, sat Hecuba and her daughters, like doves which have swooped to refuge before a lowering storm. Seeing Priam armed as in his prime Hecuba cried: "O my poor husband, why do you arm like this? What dreadful things would you do? Where are you going in this haste? It is not aid like that, nor any armed defence, which is needed now, and so would it be even if my own Hector had still been with us. No, come to us. This altar will protect us all; or else we shall die together." With these words she drew the ancient king to her, and found a place for him at the holy altar.

'But see, one of Priam's sons, Polites, had just escaped from slaughter at the hands of Pyrrhus and now fled, wounded, through the foemen and their spears down the long colonnades and across the empty halls. Pyrrhus was at his heels in hot fury, with his spear threatening another wound, and each moment he was all but clutching him with his hand. At last Polites came within sight of his parents; and there before their faces he fell, and in copious blood his life streamed away. At that, Priam, even with death all round him and no escape, did not refrain, or spare his anger and his words. "You!" he cried, "if in all Heaven there is any righteousness which takes note of utter wrong, may the gods give you fit thanks and reward you with your due for this wickedness, this foul outrage to a father's countenance, in so making me to see my own son's death before my very eyes! Not so did the great Achilles, whom you falsely claim to be your father, treat Priam when he was his foe; he respected faithfully the suppliant's rights, restored Hector's bloodless body for burial, and gave me safe return to my realm." So said the aged king and he cast his spear. Too weak to wound, it was fended away by the bronze shield: it merely clanged against it and stayed hanging from the shield's centre. Pyrrhus answered: "If so, you shall be my messenger to Achilles my father; remember to tell him of my deplorable deeds and how his son disgraced him. Now die!" So speaking he dragged Priam, quaking and sliding in a pool of his own son's blood, right up to the altar. He twined his left hand in Priam's hair. With his right hand he raised his flashing sword, and buried it to the hilt in his side. Priam's destiny ended here, after seeing Troy fired and Troy's walls down; such was the end fated to him who had augustly ruled a great empire of Asian lands and peoples. His tall body was left lying headless on the shore, and by it the head hacked from his shoulders: a corpse without a name.

'Then for the first time a wild horror gripped me. When I saw King Priam breathing out his life with that ghastly wound, I pictured to myself my own dear father, for both were of an age; and I pictured Creusa, left forlorn, and the pillage of my home, and the fate of my little Iulus. I looked back, to see what force I still had by me. But all had forsaken me. Utterly exhausted they had either flung themselves down from the building, leaping to the ground, or sick with despair they had plunged into the fires. So now I survived entirely alone. And it was then that I saw her, Helen the Tyndarid. As I wandered, peering everywhere in the light cast by the bright blaze, there she was, hiding silent in a place apart by Vesta's door and never stirring. She was dreading equally the bitter hate of the Trojans whose citadel had fallen, and the vengeance due to her from the Greeks and from the fury of the husband whom she had deserted. She had proved a curse alike for Troy and for her homeland; and she lurked concealed, a hated thing, at the altar. Out flashed all the fire in me and I was filled with a rage to avenge my home, and wreak punishment, crime for crime. "So!" thought I, "shall she, unharmed, again see Sparta and Mycenae the land of her birth, and enjoy her state as a victorious queen? Shall she look once more on her husband, her home, her parents and her children, and have round her a retinue of Trojan ladies and lords of our land to serve her? This, after Priam has fallen by the sword, Troy blazed in flames, and our Dardan coast again and again sweated with blood? Not so. There may be no great honour in killing a woman; such a victory can bring no fame. But I shall have some credit for having stamped dead a mortal sin, and punished a wrong which cries out for justice; and it will be joy to have glutted my desire for the vengeance of the fire and satisfied the ashes of all that were ever dear to me!"

'Such were my wild words, for madness had mastered my judgement and gained complete control. But even as I spoke, there in front of me, and more clearly visible to my sight than ever before, appeared my gentle mother, shining on me with pure radiance through the dark, revealing all her divinity, and in loveliness and stature even as the Immortals see her. Catching me with her hand she restrained me. And she spoke to me from her lips of rose: "Son, how can any bitterness awake in you such ungovernable fury? Why this blind anger? And how can your love for us have passed so far from your thoughts? Ought you not first to see where you have left Anchises your age-wearied father, and whether your wife Creusa and your son Ascanius still live? Around them everywhere the hordes of Greeks are prowling, and, if my thought for them had not been their defence, they would by now have been caught by the flames or devoured by the pitiless sword. You must not blame the hated beauty of the Spartan Tyndarid, or even Paris. It was the gods who showed no mercy; it is they who are casting Troy down from her splendour and power. Now look! For I shall wrest away all the dank and gloomy mist surrounding you which veils and dulls your mortal vision. You must not fear a mother's command, nor decline to obey her bidding. There, where you see masses of masonry scattered, stones wrenched from stones, and smoke and dust billowing upwards together, there Neptune himself is at work shattering the walls and the foundations dislodged by his mighty trident, and tearing the whole city from its site. Over there stands Juno most furious in the van before the Scaean Gates, and with her sword at her side and violence in her heart she is calling the marching ranks of her friends from the Greek ships. Look round! On the citadel's height sits Tritonian Pallas, light glaring from her garment of cloud and the merciless Gorgon-head on her breast. Even the Supreme Father gives renewed courage, strength and victory to the Greeks, and inspires the gods themselves to fight against the arms of Troy. Son, make your escape and flee. Put an end to the striving. I will be near you everywhere, and set you safe at your father's door." She finished and then vanished into the dense shadows of the night. And there were revealed, oh, shapes of dread, the giant powers of gods not friendly to my Troy.

'And in truth all Ilium was now, visibly before me, settling into the fires, and Neptune's own Troy, uprooted, was overturning; like an ancient rowan-tree high up among the mountains, which, hacked with stroke after stroke of iron axes by farmers vying all round to dislodge it, begins to tremble and continues threatening while the crest shakes and the high boughs sway, till gradually vanquished it gives a final groan, and at last overcome by the wounds and wrenched from its place it trails havoc down the mountain-side. I climbed down from the roof, and with the goddess guiding me won my way between the flames and the foes. The weapons let me through; the fires drew back from me.

'But when I reached the threshold of the ancient building

which was my father's home, he, whom I had been dearly hoping to find and carry, as my first care, high up into the mountains, refused to go on living in exile after Troy had been razed from the earth. "You others", he said, "your blood does not run the slower for the years, and your strength is unimpaired and still has the vitality which nature gave it. It is for you to hurry your escape. As for me, if the Dwellers in Heaven had wished me to live on, they would have saved my home here for me. I have already once seen Troy sacked and once survived our city's capture. That is enough, and more. Ah, say your goodbyes to me as I lie here just as I am. I shall find death in my own way. The enemy will show pity to me: their thoughts will be set on the spoils. As for burial – that will be a small price to pay; suffering as I do under Heaven's hatred, my age has been prolonged to no purpose through the years, ever since He who is Father of Gods and King of Men blasted me with the winds of his thunder-stroke and touched me with its fire." So he spoke, firm in his resolution, and could not be shaken. We on our side, my wife Creusa, Ascanius, and all our household, wept bitterly and told him with entreaties that he, the head of our family, must not dream of dragging all our hopes down with him like this, and so weighting against us still more the doom which bore so heavily upon us. But he still refused, and would not stir from his seat or change his purpose.

'Bitterly disappointed and longing only for death, I was already starting towards my arms again, for what else could I do and what alternative was open? "Were you," I said, "my own father, really expecting me to leave the house and desert you here? Could a father's lips have expressed so shocking a thought? If the Powers Above have willed that out of all this great city nothing shall remain, if your resolve is fixed, and if you mean to add the death of yourself and your kin to the ruin descending on Troy, the door to such a death stands wide open. Pyrrhus will soon be here fresh from the pool of Priam's blood, he who massacres a son before his father's eyes and then slays the father at an altar. But, O my gentle Mother, is it for this that you have been rescuing me and guarding me amid the fires and the weapons, for me to see the enemy inside my very home, and Ascanius and my father, and Creusa at their side, falling like sacrifices in one another's blood? Quick, comrades! Bring me arms. The vanquished are summoned to meet their life's end. Let me go back to the Greeks. Let me return to the battle and fight once more. We shall not all die this day unavenged!"

'Now I was buckling on my sword, slipping my left arm into the shield strap and adjusting my shield. But as I was on the point of leaving the house, there in the doorway was Creusa. She stopped me, clasping my feet and holding out our little son Iulus to his father. "If", she cried, "you go forth to die, take us also, quickly, to face with you whatever may happen. But if what you have seen of the fighting leads you to suppose that there is still any hope for us in resuming battle, your first care should be the defence of our home here. Otherwise, to whom will you leave our little Iulus, your father, and me, whom you once called your wife?"

'Loud was her appeal, and all the house was ringing with her words of anguish, when suddenly a miracle occurred. For there between the faces of the two distressed parents, and between their hands as they held him, the light cap worn by the little boy caught fire, and a bright flame, harmless to the touch, licked his soft hair, and played about his forehead. We moved quickly, trembling in alarm; we shook his hair to quench the flame, and tried to put out the holy fire with water. But my father Anchises raised his eyes to the stars in joy, and stretching his palms towards the sky said, "Jupiter Almighty, if any prayer can change your will, look down on us this once. We make one prayer only, and if our righteousness has earned some favour, give us now your presage, and confirm this sign." Scarcely had the aged prince so spoken, when with a sudden crash came thunder on the left, and a shooting star trailing a firebrand slid from the sky through the dark and darted downwards in brilliant light. Now we saw it glide above the roof of our house, sharply revealing the roads, and then, still burning bright, hide in the forests of Mount Ida. It left a long luminous streak in its wake, and far around a sulphur-smoke was seen to rise. My father was convinced. Raising himself and looking upwards he prayed to our gods and worshipped the holy star: "Ah, there is no reluctance now. I follow, Gods of our Race, and wherever you lead, there shall I be. Save our house; and save my grandson. Yours is this hallowed sign, and in your power Troy rests. And, son, for my part, I give way. I consent to go at your side."

'My father had spoken. But now through the town the roar of the fire came louder to our ears, and the rolling blaze brought its hot blast closer. "Well then, dear Father," I said, "come now, you must let them lift you onto my back. I will hold my shoulders ready for you; this labour of love will be no weight to me. Whatever chances may await us, one common peril and one salvation shall be ours. Iulus must walk beside me, and my wife shall follow at a safe distance in our footsteps. Now you others, my servants, attend to what I say. As you leave the city, there is a hillock with an ancient and deserted shrine of Ceres and by it an aged cypress-tree held in reverence by our forefathers for many years. We shall meet at this point, approaching by different routes. Now you, Father, take up the gods of our ancestral home, our holy symbols. I cannot touch them without sin, until I have washed my hands in a living spring, for coming as I do straight from the fury of war, I have fresh blood still on them." So saying, I bent down and cloaked my neck and shoulders with a red-brown lion's skin. I then took up my load. My little son Iulus twined his fingers in my right hand and kept beside his father with his short steps. Creusa followed behind. So on we went, keeping to the shadows; and now, though up till then I had remained quite unaffected by any weapons or even the sight of Greeks charging towards me, I myself was now ready to be frightened at a breath of wind and started at the slightest sound, so nervous was I, and so fearful alike for the load on my back and the companion at my side.

'I was already near the city gates and thinking that I had come all the way in safety, when suddenly we seemed to hear hurrying steps and my father, looking forward through the darkness cried, "Son, you must run for it. They are drawing near; I can see shining shields and flashes of bronze." Then, in the severe stress of my anxiety and haste, some unkind power robbed me of my wits. For after leaving the streets, which I knew, I lost direction, and I was running over trackless country when – oh, terrible! – my wife Creusa – did she stop running because some bitter fate meant to steal her from me, or did she perhaps stray from the path or just sink down in weariness? We cannot know; but we never saw her again. I had never looked back for her when she was first lost, or given her a thought till we came to the hillock consecrated to the ancient worship of Ceres. There we finally rallied all our company and found that she alone was missing, and that without knowing it her husband, her son, and her friends had lost her for ever.

'I was mad with horror; I upbraided every deity, and cursed the whole human race. In all Troy's overthrow nothing which had happened was so heartrending to me as was this loss. To my comrades I entrusted Ascanius, Anchises, and our Trojan Gods. Leaving them hidden in a winding valley I returned to Troy. I girt on again the gleaming arms. I was resolved to re-enact the whole adventure, and, exposing myself once more to every peril, to retrace my whole course through Troy.

'First I went to the shaded gateway in the city wall through which we had left, watching keenly in the darkness for my tracks and following them back. All the time I had the sense of some menacing presence and the very silence terrified me. I found my way back to our house, just in case she might have walked there, just in case. The Greeks had poured into it and now occupied the whole building. All was over; the wind rolled devouring fire high to the roof; the flames leaped over it and the hot fumes rioted to the sky. I moved on and again visited Priam's palace on the citadel. There in the deserted colonnades under Juno's protection Phoenix and the terrible Ulysses, who had been picked for the duty, kept watch over the plunder. Here the treasures pillaged from all Troy's gutted temples were being piled together, tables for divine feasts, wine-mixing bowls of solid gold, and captured garments. Children and mothers in a long, frightened line waited near. I even risked shouting through the darkness. Again and again I filled the streets with my cries in useless repetition, as in my grief I called out Creusa's name. And then, just as, distracted and with no end in sight, I was continuing my search among the city's buildings, there, directly before my eyes, appeared the very wraith of Creusa, her own mournful shade in her ghostly stature taller than life. I froze, my hair stiffened, and my voice choked in my throat. She spoke to me and her words allayed my distress: "Sweet husband, why do you allow yourself to yield to a pointless grief? What has happened is part of the divine plan. For the law of right and the Supreme Ruler of Olympus on high forbid you to carry Creusa away from Troy on your journey. You have to plough through a great waste of ocean to distant exile. And you shall come to the Western Land where the gentle current of Lydian Tiber flows between rich meadows where men are strong. There happiness and a kingdom are in store for you, with a queen for you to marry. Dispel your tears for the Creusa whom you loved. For I, being of the blood of Dardanus and a daughter to divine Venus, have not to face the arrogance of a Dolopian or Myrmidon home, or to go in slavery to women whose sons are Greeks; the Great Mother of the Gods is keeping me within the boundaries of Troyland. And now, goodbye. And guard the love of the son whom we share." Having spoken so, though I wept and longed to say so much to her, she forsook me and vanished into thin air. Three times I tried to cast my arms about her neck where she had been; but three times the clasp was in vain and the wraith escaped my hands, like airy winds, or the melting of a dream.

'With the passing of the night I returned to my comrades, and was surprised to find their number increased by a great concourse of new arrivals, mothers, husbands, and young men, all pathetically gathered together for banishment. They had come there from everywhere around with a fixed resolution, and their belongings ready, for me to lead them to any land which I might choose beyond the sea. And now the morning star was rising above the slopes near Mount Ida's crest, bringing the day. The Greeks held and blocked every entrance-gate to the city, and no hope of rescue remained. In resignation I lifted my father and moved towards the mountains.'

BOOK THREE

AENEAS' NARRATION CONTINUED – HIS TRAVELS

'THE Powers Above had decreed the overthrow of the Asian empire and Priam's breed of men, though they deserved a better fate. Lordly Ilium had fallen and all Neptune's Troy lay a smoking ruin on the ground. We the exiled survivors were forced by divine command to search the world for a home in some uninhabited land. So we started to build ships below Antandros, the city by the foothills of Phrygian Ida, with no idea where Destiny would take us or where we should be allowed to settle. We gathered our company together. In early summer our chieftain Anchises urged us to embark on our destined voyage. In tears I left my homeland's coast, its havens, and the plains where Troy had stood. I fared out upon the high seas, an exile with my comrades and my son, with the little Gods of our Home and the Great Gods of our race.

'Some distance from Troy is a land owned by Mars with wide plains cultivated by Thracian farmers. Once the fierce King Lycurgus had reigned there, and the country had had from of old close ties of friendship and a family alliance with Troy in the days of her prosperity. To this land I now sailed, and chose a site where the coast bends round to start on walls for our city, which I decided to call Aeneadae after my own name. But Destiny was against my enterprise.

'I was offering sacrifice to Venus the Mother and to other Deities who might favour my undertaking, and also to the Supreme King of all the Dwellers in Heaven. I was just about to sacrifice a handsome bull by the sea-shore. Quite near there happened to be a mound of earth, at the highest part of which were growing thickets of cornel and a dense cluster of spiky myrtle-stems. I went up there and tried to wrench the green growth from the ground to provide a leafy covering for our altar. There I was confronted by a horrible and astounding miracle. For from the first bush which I tried to break off at the roots from its soil, blood oozed in dark drops, fouling the earth with its spots. I felt a cold shudder run through me; my blood seemed to freeze with horror. But I persisted. Anxious to discover the cause of the mystery I tore at the resisting stalk of a second bush. But again dark blood flowed from the bark. So, greatly wondering, I began a prayer to the nymphs of the countryside and Father Mars who rules over Thracian lands, imploring them to divert the omen's dread significance and turn all to good. I tried straining with my knees against the sand and putting more weight into my efforts in a third attempt at the stems. And then – can I dare to utter it, or should my lips be sealed? – a piteous moan came from the base of the mound and I heard a human voice answering me: "Why, Aeneas, must you rend a poor sufferer? I am buried here. Wound me no more, and do not stain your righteous hands with sin. I am no foreigner: I am Trojan-born. And when harm is done to this stalk it is human blood which flows. Ah, make haste to flee these coasts of avarice, this land of savagery! For I am Polydorus. Here death overpowered me in a crop of piercing iron-pointed spears. And so a crop resembling javelins has grown over me."

'At this my mind was crushed by uncertainty and dread. The shock stilled me; my hair stood stiff and my throat was speechless. For when the hapless Priam, realizing that Troy was condemned to a long siege, had begun to lose faith in Trojan arms, he had secretly entrusted Polydorus, and also a heavy store of gold, to the care of the King of Thrace. When Troy's power was indeed broken, and her good fortune dwindled, this king went over to the side of the victorious Agamemnon. And he broke every known law of righteousness. He murdered Polydorus and forcibly seized the gold; no wickedness is beyond a man whom that accursed gold-lust drives. When I was no longer too paralysed to move I chose some of my companions, leaders of Troy, including, of course, my father. I told them about the miracle and asked them what they thought. With one mind they insisted that we should at once leave this wicked land, break off all contact with a place which had desecrated the laws of hospitality, and let the winds bear our ships away. So we gave Polydorus a new burial, piling masses of earth on his barrow, and erecting to the Shades below an altar sad with dark drapery and the dead-black of a cypress. Ladies of Ilium, with hair duly unbound, stood by. We then offered foaming bowls of warm milk and phials of consecrated blood; and so we committed the soul to peace in its grave and lifted our voices in farewell.

'As soon as we could trust the ocean, when winds offered us smiling seas and the whisper of a breeze invited us onto the deep, my comrades crowded to the beach and launched our ships. We sailed forth from the haven, and the land and its cities sank behind us. Now far out to sea there lies Delos, a holy island with people dwelling on it, and well loved by the Nereids' Mother and Aegean Neptune. The Archer-God had found it drifting about the sea from coast to coast; and, since it was his birth-place, in loyalty to his mother, he chained it firmly to high Myconos and Gyaros; and he made it a stable dwelling-place for men, with power to scorn the waves. To Delos I now sailed, and our tired band received a safe and kindly welcome in its harbour. We disembarked and paid reverence to Apollo's city. The king was Anius, who was priest of Apollo as well as king, and wore the holy bay-leaves and ribbons on his brow. He came to meet us and recognized Anchises as an old friend. He shook hands with us, treating us as his guests; and we walked up to the palace. Reverently I entered the temple built of ancient stone and prayed: "Apollo, grant us a home of our own. We are weary. Give us a walled city which shall endure, and a lineage of our blood. Let there be some new citadel for us; henceforth preserve it as a remnant of Troy saved from the Greeks and from merciless Achilles. Who is to be our guide? Where do you bid us go, where settle our home? Be to us a father-god; tell us your will and speak direct to our hearts."

'I had scarcely spoken when of a sudden everything seemed to quake, even the God's entrance-door and his bay-tree; the whole hill on which we stood appeared to move and the shrine seemed to open and the tripod within to speak with a roar. We bowed low and fell to earth. A voice came to our ears: "O much enduring Dardans, the land of your ancestors whence you are sprung shall receive you on your return to her generous bosom. Seek out your ancient mother. And from this land the House of Aeneas, the sons of his sons, and all their descendants shall bear rule over earth's widest bounds." At Apollo's words there was a great outburst of joy and the keenest excitement. We all wondered where was the walled city which he meant when he called the wanderers to return to their ancient mother. Then my father cast his mind back over our early tradition. "Lords of Troy," he said, "hear me, and learn where your hope lies. Great Jove owns an island, Crete, set in the midst of the sea. In it there is a Mount Ida; and it is the cradle of our race. The Cretans live in a hundred great cities and the bosom of the land which they rule is fertile. And it was from Crete, if I remember rightly what I have heard, that our ancestor Teucer originally sailed to Troyland, and there chose a site for his royal capital, for until then no Ilium and no Trojan Citadel had existed there, and the people lived down in the valleys. From Crete came also the Great Mother Cybele with her ritual and her Corybants, who clash their bronze cymbals in the forests of Mount Ida; and from Crete were derived the reverential silence of our worship, and the lion-team harnessed to our Great Lady's chariot. Now, therefore, come! Let us take the path shewn by the divine command. Let us gain the favour of the winds and sail for the realm of Cnossos. With Jupiter's help the voyage need not be long; the third dawn will see our fleet at the Cretan shores." So saying, he consecrated at the altar the proper offerings, a bull for Neptune and another for glorious Apollo, a black sheep for Storm and a white sheep for the genial West Winds.

'A rumour had rapidly spread that Idomeneus the Cretan prince had been banished from his father's kingdom, that the Cretan land was now deserted, and that we should find no enemies but only empty houses standing ready for our use. We left the harbour of Delos and sped over the seas. We threaded our way through currents racing by many shores past Naxos, where bacchanals revel on hill-slopes, past the green Isle of Reeds and the Isle of Olives, and then marble-white Paros and the Cyclades sprinkled about the sea. The shouting mariners vied with each other at their tasks. "On to Crete, the home of our forefathers!" was the cry of my friends as they urged each other on. A wind rose from astern and helped us on our way. And at length we sailed smoothly to the ancient coastlands where the Curetes dwell.

'Passionately I began work on the walls of the city for which we yearned. I called it Pergamea and my people were happy with this name. I told them that they should love their new homes and raise for our protection a high fortress. Our ships were soon nearly all high and dry on the shore, our young people already busy with weddings and work on their new farms, and I myself occupied in deciding on laws and allotting houses, when all at once, falling from some poisoned part of the sky, a heart-breaking pestilence attacked and rotted trees, crops, and men, and the only yield of that season was death. The people either lost their precious lives, or could hardly move, so ill they were. The Dog Star's heat scorched the fields till they were barren. Plants were parched and the diseased crops refused us livelihood. Then my father advised me to retrace the sea-ways to Apollo's oracle at Ortygia, and, with prayers for his indulgence, to ask him what end to our distress he would permit, where he would have us seek aid in our heavy tasks, and whither we should direct our course.

'It was night, and the creatures of the world were held in repose. But as I slept there appeared to me, standing clear before my eyes in a flood of light where the full moon poured in through windows in the walls, the divine and holy figures of our Trojan Gods which I had carried from Troy at the hour of its burning. And they spoke to me and with their words relieved my anxiety: "See, Apollo of his own will sends us to your room, and he now gives you the prophecy which he would have given you at Delian Ortygia had you sailed back there. When the fires had ruined Troyland we followed you and your arms, and in your care we traversed the heaving ocean with the fleet. And we shall exalt your grandsons to the stars and give dominion to your city. So make ready her walls, great walls for your Great Gods, and never shrink from the long effort of your exile. But you have to change your home, for Apollo of Delos never ordered you to settle in Crete, and this is not the coast which he recommended to you. There is another region for which the Greeks use the name Hesperia, the Western Land, an ancient land with might in her arms and in her fertile soil. The inhabitants used to be Oenotrians; but it is said that their descendants have now called the country Italy after one of their leaders. This Italy is our true home. From Italy came Dardanus, and Iasius, another chieftain of our blood, and founder of the Trojan nation. Come, arise! Rejoice, and hand on this message which we bring, a message true beyond doubt, to your aged father. Let him travel in quest of the Land of Italy and the town of Corythus. Jupiter denies you Mount Dicte's fields."

'At such a vision, and at the very voice of our Gods, I was bemused. This could be no dream. I seemed to recognize, there before me, their garlanded hair, and their lips as they spoke. Chill sweat spread over me. I started from my bed, raised upturned hands towards the sky with a prayer, and poured an offering of unwatered wine on the hearth. Then, glad to have performed this duty, I told Anchises exactly what had happened. Gradually he came to realize that two lines of descent from separate ancestors had been confused and that a mistake of his own had led him to misinterpret the old traditions about these lands: "O my son, you who bear the burden of Troy's destiny, nothing like this was ever foreseen by anyone except Cassandra. I remember now that one of her prophecies foretold this destiny for our race and that she often invoked Hesperia and Italy as our future realm, calling them by these names. But who would ever have believed that Trojans would travel to Hesperian shores? And who at that time heeded Cassandra's prophecies? Let us trust Apollo, accept his warning, and follow a better course." So he spoke, and we were all overjoyed to obey his instructions. We moved on from Crete as we had from Thrace, leaving only a few of our number on the island. We set sail and sped on our buoyant timbers across the mighty ocean.

'When our ships were well out on the high seas, with no longer any land in sight but on all sides nothing but water and sky, over our heads there stood an inky-black rain-storm, bringing tempest and gloom, and ruffling the waters to darkness. The winds quickly set the sea-surface rolling and lifted it in great waves. The ships were scattered storm-tossed on the huge waste. Clouds hid the light of day and darkness and rain blotted out the sky; and again and again the clouds tore apart and the lightning blazed. We were driven off our course and wandered blindly amid the waves; even my helmsman Palinurus said that he could not, by looking at the sky, tell night from day, and that in mid-ocean without landmarks he could not plan a course. For three whole days, hard though they were to reckon, and as many starless nights, we wandered in the sightless murk over the ocean. [On one side the nations of Pelops and Malea's roaring rocks hemmed us in and land menaced us no less than the sea; and all the time we were being battered and swamped by the cruel waves.] Only on the fourth day did we at last gain our first sight of a coast rising before us, with distant mountains behind and smoke curling upwards. Our sails fell slack and we rose to our oars. Our oarsmen were quick to put weight into the stroke; they swept the blue surface and thrashed the sea to foam.

'Saved from the ocean I first found haven on the shores of the Strophades, in the wide Ionian sea. They are fixed now, but they are still called by this Greek name, which means the Turning Islands. They had been the home of the dreaded Celaeno and the other Harpies ever since the palace of Phineus was closed against them, and in fear of their pursuers they abandoned the tables where they had previously fed. No monster is more grim than the Harpies; no stroke of divine wrath was ever more cruel, and no wickeder demon ever soared upwards from the waters of Styx. They are birds with girls' countenances, and a disgusting outflow from their bellies. Their hands have talons and their faces are always pallid with hunger.

'Here we made the land and entered a harbour. Before us we saw prosperous herds of cattle ranging over plains, and goats unguarded on the pastures. We attacked them sword in hand, inviting the gods, including Jupiter himself, to share our plunder. Next we built seats of turf along the curving shore and started on a rich feast. But suddenly, with a terrifying swoop down from their hills and loudly flapping wings, the Harpies were upon us. They pillaged our meal, making everything filthy with their unclean touch; their stench was foul and their screams horrible. Then once more we laid out our tables and relighted the altar fire, this time in a deep retreat under an overhanging rock [and enclosed by trees which cast a mysterious shade]. But the noisy flock, which had been hiding out of sight, swooped down on us from a different point, flew round the prey with their clawed feet, and again fouled the food with their lips. I immediately gave my orders to my comrades: they must take up arms for we had to make war on this grotesque tribe. They did exactly as I bade them, concealing their swords here and there in the grass and placing their shields out of sight. Accordingly, when the Harpies swooped clattering down over the curving beach, Misenus from a point of vantage sounded the alarm on his bronze trumpet. At the sound my comrades charged, and attempted a weird battle, seeking to inflict sword-wounds on these sinister, filthy ocean-birds. But they did not feel our blows on their feathers and no wound ever reached the skin on their backs; they fled swiftly, soaring to the sky and leaving behind them the remains of the meal and the revolting traces of their visit. But now one of them, Celaeno herself, perching high on a rock, broke silence and spoke to us like a prophetess of doom: "So, you kindred of Laomedon, so you would go to war to defend your cattle-raiding? You would fight for these slaughtered bullocks? And drive us innocent Harpies from our rightful realm? Attend then to my words and fix them in your thoughts. For I, chief among all Furies, reveal to you a prophecy which Phoebus Apollo made to me, having himself received it from the Father, the Almighty. Italy is the destination of your voyage. You will invite the winds, and to Italy you will go. You will not be forbidden to enter an Italian harbour. But never shall you be granted a city, to gird it with your walls, until first, to punish you for your sin in striking at us, a fearful hunger has forced you to gnaw and devour your very tables." With these words she flew away and darted swiftly back into the wood.

'At this my comrades' blood chilled and froze in sudden dread. Their spirits sank and they advised me to rely for our deliverance not on weapons but on prayers and vows, whether the Harpies were goddesses or only sinister, filthy birds. My father Anchises, standing on the beach, stretched forth his opened hands and called upon the High Powers. He appointed for us the required rites of worship, and prayed: "Gods, forfend this menace and avert all such calamities. Be gracious, and preserve righteous men." Next he commanded us to fling hawsers from moorings and uncoil and ease the sheets. South winds stretched our sails. We fled over foaming waves where the wind, and the helmsman, chose us a course. And now the wave-girt wooded island of Zacynthus came into view, and then Dulichium, Same, and Neritos with its steep stone cliffs. We evaded the rocks of Ithaca where Laertes had reigned, and cursed the land which had given birth to the savage Ulysses. Presently there appeared before us the cloud-capped headland of Leucate, and Apollo's temple on the mainland promontory which seafarers hold in dread. Being weary, we put in to land and cast anchors from the prows. The sterns made a line along the beach. We walked up to the little city.

'So, beyond all our hopes, we had at last won our way to land. We cleansed ourselves ritually in Jupiter's sight and kindled altars whereon to repay our vows. Next we held Trojan games on the shore of Actium, and great was the throng. My comrades stripped themselves and sleek with olive oil engaged in their sports just as on the wrestling-grounds of their old home, happy to think that they had safely escaped their enemies and kept clear of so many Greek cities on their way. Meanwhile the sun in his annual course round the year rolled on. Ice came, the winter's north wind roughened the waves of the sea. I fixed on a door-frontal a shield of hollowed bronze which had once been carried by the mighty Abas, and under it wrote a memorial, "Armour captured from victorious Greeks and dedicated by Aeneas".

Then I gave the order to man the rowing-seats and leave port. My comrades swept the sea-surface, striking it in rivalry. Very soon we saw Phaeacia's airy heights sink behind us, and skirted the shores of Epirus till we approached the harbour of Chaonia and finally reached the hill-city of Buthrotum.

'Here we heard a strange tale, almost beyond belief. Helenus, Priam's son, had been accepted as a king among Greeks. He had succeeded to the throne of Pyrrhus the Aeacid and had married his queen Andromache, who thus became united once more to a husband of her own kin. I was struck with amazement, and in rare curiosity hurried to question Helenus and hear more of this extraordinary outcome. I left the shore and my ships and was walking up from the harbour when I chanced on Andromache herself, sorrowfully pouring a drink offering in a ritual of sacrifice to Hector's ashes. In a wood near her city by a river named after the Simois she was calling on Hector's spirit at his cenotaph of green turf, where she had reverently set up two altars as a place for her mourning. Andromache was aghast to see me approaching, equipped as I was in Trojan style. Unnerved by the shock, suddenly, as she looked, she stiffened; the warmth left her, she could hardly stand, and it was some time before she could find words: "Are you real? Can I believe my eyes? Son of the Goddess, may I know that it is you? Are you a living man? Or, if life's light has passed from you, tell me, where is Hector?" As she spoke she broke into tears and the whole place was loud with her crying. So wild was her grief that I was only able to interrupt with short answers, following at intervals as best they could: "Yes, I am indeed a living man; life goes on for me, but in keenest suffering. Have no doubts; your eyes do not deceive you. But, oh, what has fate done to you since you fell from the high estate of your illustrious marriage? Has fortune smiled on you again, as brightly as Hector's Andromache deserves? Are you still the wife of Pyrrhus?"

'She replied, speaking low and with downcast face: "Ah, happy beyond all others is that daughter of Priam who was sentenced to die by an enemy's grave at the foot of Troy's towering ramparts! She was no captive slave, chosen by lot to gratify a conqueror's lust. I saw my home burnt. I was carried far across the seas to suffer the scornful arrogance of Achilles' young son, and endured all the travail of slavery. However, my husband soon left me, being passionately eager to marry a Spartan named Hermione, the grand-daughter of Leda, and so passed me on to be mate to Helenus, two house-slaves together. Meanwhile, Orestes, who was still being tormented by the Furies for his crime, and whose wife it was that Pyrrhus now planned to steal, burning with jealousy lay in wait for Pyrrhus, caught him off guard, and stabbed him to death at the altar of his home. After Pyrrhus died, part of his realm passed to Helenus in course of law. He chose the names Chaonia and the Chaonian Plain after Chaon in Troyland, and built above the hill-slopes a Fortress of Ilium, a Citadel of Troy. But you, what winds and what destiny have brought you voyaging here? Or perhaps some God forced you to land, in ignorance, upon our shores? What of your little son, Ascanius? Does he still live, and still breathe the strengthening air? You had him with you in Troy.... And can he remember the mother whom he lost? Does he know that Aeneas is his father and Hector was his uncle, and does the knowledge already awake in him the qualities of a man and the spirit of olden time?"

'She was still asking me this torrent of questions, and weeping and moaning with long, vain sobs, when Priam's princely son, Helenus himself, came walking from the city walls with a large retinue. He recognized his kin with joy and led us to the gate, talking to us with many tears at every word. As I walked onwards I recognized this little "Troy", with its citadel built to resemble the old citadel, and a dry water-course called "Xanthus"; and I even saluted the threshold of a "Scaean Gate".

'The other Trojans gladly joined me in sharing the city's friendship. The king received them in a spacious colonnade. In a courtyard a meal on gold plate was set, and from bowls in their hands they poured an offering of the gift of Bacchus.

'And now day followed day, and breezes invited our sails; a south wind was filling and swelling the canvas. Therefore I spoke to Helenus, who had the power of prophecy, and asked him questions: "You, Trojan-born, are Heaven's interpreter. You know the truth of Apollo's power, you know his tripods, his bay-trees at Claros, the stars too and the voices of birds, and the prophetic meanings of their flight. Come, speak to me. My every pious observance has given me fair hope for my voyaging. Every divine message has urged me, with its whole authority, to force my way onwards towards distant lands and sail for Italy, except only Celaeno the Harpy who pronounced against me grim wrath to come and prophesied a monstrous event, a blasphemy even to mention, a famine meaning doom. Therefore, what dangers shall I principally avoid? What will guide me safely through the dread ordeals to come?"

'At this Helenus first formally sacrificed bullocks, and won the gods' indulgence with a prayer. He next relaxed the ribbon round his hallowed head, and in high fervour, so strong was the divine power, he led me by the hand to Phoebus Apollo's door. Then, straightway, by right of priesthood from inspired lips he prophesied: "Son of the Goddess, it is clear and it is certain that you traverse the deep by sanctions from the Greater Powers. So are the lots of destiny drawn by the King of Gods; so does he set events to roll their course; so does he turn the pages of history to come. I shall speak, in my words to you, out of many truths a few only, that you may voyage the more safely over foreign seas and succeed in reaching repose in an Italian harbour. For the rest, either the Fates allow not Helenus to know, or Saturnian Juno forbids his prophesying. First, therefore, you have been ignorantly assuming that Italy is now near enough for you to sail direct to one of its havens. But for you Italy is still far, and lies at the end of a long voyage over uncharted waters and past long coastlands. And you must first strain at the oar in Sicilian waters, your ships must traverse the salt surface of the Italian seas, and you must pass by the Infernal Lakes and Circe's Aeaean Isle before you can settle your city on safe soil. Now I shall give you a sign; store it in your thoughts, and remember. When in an anxious time you shall find lying by a distant river's water under holm-oak trees on the bank a huge white sow, stretched on the ground with her thirty young which she has just farrowed, all white like her, gathered round her teats, that place shall be the site for your city, and there you shall find sure repose from your tribulations. And be not appalled by the fear of gnawing your tables; Destiny will find a way for you, and if you call on him Apollo will be there to aid. But you must avoid the land on this side, along the nearer coastline of Italy, which is closer to us than any other shore washed by our own sea's tide, for there every walled city contains hostile Greeks. One of these cities was founded by Locrians of Narycium. In another is Idomeneus of Crete, whose men-at-arms infest the level lands of the Sallentinians. Elsewhere is little Petelia, the famous town of Philoctetes the chieftain from Meliboea; it seems to rest on its encircling wall. But, when you have passed them all, and your fleet rides in safety on the sea's farther side, then must you erect altars on the beach and repay your vows. When you do so you must be clothed in purple raiment, which shall even veil your hair, lest, while you are at worship and the hallowed fires are burning, some intruder's presence may obscure the divine message. Your comrades as well as yourself must always observe this rule of sacrifice, and your descendants, if they would be pure of conscience, must stay faithful to this rite.

'"Now further, when you have departed thence, the wind will carry you near the coast of Sicily and the barriers of narrow Pelorus will open to show a clear passage. Then you must steer for the land on your port side, sailing in that direction on a long, circuitous course over the open water, and avoiding the shore and the sea to starboard. It is said that the lands here were in the past one unbroken whole, but that some titanic convulsion long since tore them up so that they flew apart, for time's vast antiquity has been sufficient to compass even so mighty a change. And next the sea burst violently between, rent the Italian cities apart from Sicily's coast, and flowed in its narrow mill-race severing the lands and the cities which their new coastlines sundered. Here your way will be blocked by Scylla on the right and on the left by the never-pacified Charybdis, who thrice in a day drinks giant waves down the sheer depth of her engulfing abyss, and then shoots them up again to the sky, as though trying to lash the stars with water. Scylla however hides in a cavern and remains out of sight; but she thrusts out her mouths and sucks ships onto the rocks. Her upper half, as far as the groin, is human in shape as of a maid with a fair breast, but her lower part is a monstrous whale with many dolphin-tails growing from wolves' bellies. It will be wiser not to hasten but rather to take a long and roundabout course, bending back again at Cape Pachynus in Sicily, than to risk setting eyes even once on the hideous Scylla deep in her monstrous cavern, where the rocks are loud with the bark of her sea-blue hounds. And more: so surely as Helenus has second sight, and his prophecy deserves belief, so surely as Apollo inspires him with truth, even so, O Goddess-Born, I will pronounce to you one supreme duty, in itself as peremptory and important as all the rest together, and I would repeat this warning again and again and again. Above all you shall worship mighty Juno's godhead and offer her entreaties; and with your whole will submit your vows to her. And you shall win that mighty Mistress over to you by offerings in supplication; for only so may you leave Sicily behind you and come victoriously to Italy's frontier. Then, having reached Italy, you shall first visit the city of Cumae where lie ghostly lakes amid Avernus' whispering forests. There shall you see a frantic maiden-prophetess who from deep within a cavern of rock foretells the decrees of Destiny. She commits words to writing by making marks on leaves; afterwards she sorts into order all the prophecies which she has written on them, and allows their messages to remain, a closed secret, in her cave. There they stay, all in order and motionless; but if once the hinge-post turns and even a slight wind strikes them, the delicate leaves are disturbed by the door's movement, and the prophetess never afterwards thinks of catching them as they flit within the rock-hollow, or of putting them together again into prophecies. Consultants therefore depart unanswered, and are bitter against the sibyl's oracle. Now, to save you from so costly a loss of time, I warn you that however your comrades chide you, and even though your plan for your voyage urgently invites your sails onto the deep with a following wind to fill your bellying canvas, you must nevertheless visit the prophetess, and with insistent entreaty extort responses from her; you must make her unseal her lips and pronounce her answers herself with her own speech. She will then reveal to you the nations of Italy, the wars which you must fight, and how you may escape or endure each of the ordeals to come. If you court her well, she will give you a fair passage.

'"These, then, are the directions which, in answer to your wish, my lips are permitted to give to you. Therefore go forth, and by your deeds exalt our Troy in grandeur to the skies."

'Having spoken his prophecy, the kindly seer next gave orders for gifts to be conveyed to our ships, heavy objects of gold and wrought ivory. He packed into the holds a large store of silver, cauldrons from Dodona, and a corslet of hooked chain-mail and three-leash golden weave, and a splendid helmet, coned and crested with long hair, both once owned by Pyrrhus. There were special gifts for my father. Helenus also provided us with horses and with guides. He rearmed my company, and gave us more oarsmen to complete our crews.

'While Helenus was so engaged, Anchises had been commanding us to bend sails onto spars, to make sure that we should not be late in using any favouring wind. And now Helenus, Apollo's own spokesman, addressed Anchises with profound respect: "Anchises, counted fit for exalted marriage with Venus herself, Anchises for whom Gods take thought since twice have they saved you from falling Troy, see – Italy's land is before you, sail fast, and make it yours. But first you must voyage right on, coasting along the nearer side of Italy, which lies out there, across the sea, for it is the far side of Italy which Apollo unlocks for you. Go forth in the strength of your son's loyalty, But why do I continue so? The winds are rising. I must not keep them waiting by my talk."

'And Andromache, too, sad indeed now that the moment for parting had come, was no less generous, and did not lag behind in her liberality. She brought for Ascanius figured garments with woof-thread of gold and an embroidered mantle from Troy. As she loaded him with the woven gifts she spoke to him: "Ascanius, dear, do take these gifts as well; they are from me, to remind you of my handiwork, and to be a lasting token that Hector's Andromache always loves you. Take them, the last gifts to you from your own kin, for all that is left to me of my Astyanax is his likeness in you. His eyes, his hands, his face and his movements were just like yours; and he would now have grown to be just your age."

'As I left them, with tears welling, I spoke: "Live, and prosper, for all your adventures are past. We are called ever onwards from destiny to destiny. For you, your rest is won. You have no expanse of sea to plough, no land of Italy, seeming always to recede before you, as your quest. You may look at your copy of the river Xanthus, and at a Troy built by your own hands, with fairer prospects, I hope, and no more fear of danger from the Greeks. And if I ever reach Tiber's estuary, stand beside it on its fields, and see those city-walls which have been promised to my people, then one day in Italy we shall create by our mutual sympathy kindred cities having close ties with Epirus, a Western Land sharing one founder, Dardanus, and one same history with you; and you and we shall be each equally a Troy. May this be a duty for our descendants to inherit!"

'We sailed out to sea close to the nearby Ceraunian headland, whence the passage by water to Italy is the shortest. As we passed, the sun sank, and the mountains were shadowed in darkness. We disembarked, and, drawing lots for turns on watch by the oars, we thankfully stretched ourselves on the kindly earth close by the sea. So we lay scattered about the dry beach and refreshed ourselves. Sleep came to strengthen our tired limbs. But Night, sped by the hours, was not yet nearing the mid point of her cycle when the ever-alert Palinurus left his couch and listened intently for a wind, caring little from what quarter it might come; he checked every constellation which glided solemnly over the voiceless heaven, Arcturus, the Hyads which foretell the rain, and the Two

Bears, and then, as his eyes roved, Orion of the golden sword. Next, seeing that all was calm and the sky serene, he stood on his ship's stern and sounded a sharp call. We struck camp, adventured out on our way, and spread the wings of our sails. And now, when dawn with its first red glow had routed the stars, we could just see hills along a low coastline across the waters. "Italy!" Achates was the first to shout the name. "Italy!" cried my comrades in joyful welcome. Anchises my father standing high on the quarter-deck took a large wine-bowl, wreathed it, filled it with unwatered wine, and invoked our Gods: "Gods of the Earth, Gods of the Sea, Gods who have rule over storms, give us a wind to help our voyage, and may your breath bring us aid."

'Quicker now came the breeze in answer to his prayer. Quite near, a harbour opened ahead of us; and Minerva's Temple, on the height, came into view. My comrades furled their sails and swung our prows towards land. The harbour had been formed into the shape of a bent bow by waves blown from the east. It was hidden by projecting rocks which foamed with salt spray, and from the towered crags its two walls, like drooping arms, ran steeply down. The temple lay back from the shore. And here I saw our first prophetic sign, four shining snow-white horses straying and cropping the grass on the plain. My father Anchises exclaimed, "War, O Stranger Land, is the message which you bring us; horses are equipped for war, and it is war that these animals threaten. Yet there are times when these same four-foot creatures are trained for harnessing in a team and are yoked in harmony and bridled in contentment." And he added, "So there is also a hope of peace." Then we offered prayers to the holy might of weapon-clashing Minerva who was the first to welcome our exultant band. We stood before the altars, our heads veiled with Phrygian cloth; and in due form kindled the sacrifice to Argive Juno which Helenus had warned us to remember as the most momentous of his commands. We did not wait; having duly performed our vows we immediately swung to the wind our yard-arms and our sails; and so we left those fields, not trusting any place where men of Greek stock dwelt. Our next sight was Tarentum on its gulf, a city visited, if the tale is true, by Hercules; and opposite to it towered Lacinian Juno's temple. Yes, and there stood Caulonia's fortress, and there Scylaceum, where ships founder. And now far off, and rising from the sea, Sicilian Etna was visible, and we heard in the distance the ocean's mighty waves crashing on rocks, and loud and fitful sounds audible alongshore. Sea-water spurted from the depths, and sand swirled in the boiling surge. My father Anchises cried, "This must surely be the dreaded Charybdis; those terrifying rocks, there, are the crags of which Helenus warned us. Tear yourselves free. Jump to your oars, and keep together." My comrades did as they were commanded. Palinurus was the first to wrench his roaring prow to port and out to sea; then all our company made after him with oars and sails. We were lifted towards the sky on a heaving swell, but again the waves drew off, and all at once we were settling deep down, and sinking towards Hades. Three times the crags shouted the echo of the sea back at us as we lay wallowing low between arching rocks. Three times we looked through foam spewed from the sea and saw the sky through a screen of spray. But meanwhile both wind and sunlight had deserted us. We were tired, and, not knowing our way, we gently drifted to the coast of the Cyclopes.

'The harbour there is spacious enough, and calm, for no winds reach it, but close by Etna thunders and its affrighting showers fall. Sometimes it ejects up to high heaven a cloud of utter black, bursting forth in a tornado of pitchy smoke with white-hot lava, and shoots tongues of flame to lick the stars. Sometimes the mountain tears out the rocks which are its entrails and hurls them upwards. Loud is the roar each time the pit in its depth boils over, and condenses this molten stone and hoists it high in the air. The story is told that huge Enceladus, whom the bolt of thunder charred, lies crushed under Etna's mass and that the enormous volcano stands there above him, breathing flames from its bursting furnaces; and, each time that Enceladus tires and turns over, all Sicily quakes and growls and veils the sky with smoke. All that night we hid in the forest subjected to fantastic experiences without seeing what caused the noise. There were no blazing constellations, no height of heaven bright with a starry glow, but only mists in a muffled sky and the moon wrapped in murk at deadest night.

'And now the morrow was arising with a first gleam in the east, and already the sunrise had parted the moist shadows from high heaven, when suddenly there emerged from the forest a grotesque stranger, pitifully unkempt and gaunt with starvation. He stretched his hands in entreaty to us on the shore. We looked at him with curiosity. His dirt was fearful, his beard untended, and his garment hooked together with thorns. But in all else he was a Greek, who had once gone on the expedition to Troy wearing his father's arms. When he saw before him Dardan dress and Trojan weapons, he checked his walk, stood for a moment frozen in terror, and then dashed headlong to the beach with tears and entreaties: "I implore you, Trojans, by the stars, by the High Gods, by the shining air which is our breath, carry me away, take me to any land which you choose; that is all I wish. I know that I was a member of the Greek expedition. I confess that I made war on Trojan homes. For that, if the dreadful wrong caused by my crime deserves it, scatter me in fragments over the waves and drown me in the wastes of sea. If I must die, death by a human hand will be happiness."

'With this cry, he clasped my knees and clung to them grovelling. We encouraged him to tell us who he was and of what breed, and to recount his sufferings at the hands of fortune. After a little pause my father Anchises gave his hand to the young stranger, increasing his confidence by this willing gesture, so that at last he laid his dread aside and spoke:

'"I come from Ithaca, which was my home, and I was a comrade of the ill-fated Ulysses. My name is Achaemenides and my father was Adamastus. He was a poor man; and how I wish we had stayed as we were! But I parted from him, and I sailed for Troy. I was left here in the Cyclops' monstrous cave by my comrades, who forgot me in their pressing anxiety to escape through that horrible entrance. The interior of the dwelling is dark and enormous, and filthy too from those bloody meals. The Cyclops is a giant, towering high enough to hit the sky; oh, Gods, fend such a horror far from the world of men! He is an offence to our eyes, and not to be addressed in human converse by any man. He feeds on the inner parts and dark blood of his poor victims. I myself have seen him grasp two of our number in that huge hand, and, still lying prone in the centre of his cave, smash them on a rock; I have seen all the passage-way splashed and swimming with gore. I have seen him chew their limbs, all dripping and blackened with clotting blood, and their joints quiver, still warm, as his jaws closed. But he suffered for his deed. Ulysses could not let such savagery pass; and in this grim crisis our Ithacan proved true to himself. For no sooner was the Cyclops replete with his eating and sunk in a drunken sleep, stretched vast across his cave with his neck bent and vomiting, as he slept, morsels of food, thick wine, and blood mixed together with other filth, when we, with a prayer to the High Powers, drew lots for our tasks. Together, we all dashed in to surround him. With a sharp instrument we pierced the huge single eye set deep below his frowning forehead and as big as an Argive shield or Apollo's sun; and gleefully we avenged the ghosts of our comrades. But you, you poor strangers, you must hasten to escape. Rend your hawsers from the shore. There are a hundred other appalling Cyclopes, just like this Polyphemus who pens and milks his woolly flock in his spacious cave, and just as large, living everywhere on the coastland along this curving shore and straying high up into the mountains. For the third time now the moon is filling her horns with light, and for so long have I been dragging out my days in the woods and the wilderness where only beasts have their haunts and lairs, observing these fearful Cyclopes from a rock on which I used to stand and ready to start trembling at every sound of their feet and voices. I have been living on meagre fare from the boughs; stony cornel-berries and grasses torn up from their roots have been my food. And, though I was always on the look-out, never till now have I caught sight of any ships sailing to this coast. When I saw yours, I decided to trust myself entirely to them, whatever they might be, for surely nothing could matter if once I escaped from the appalling race of Cyclopes. Rather than face them I would let you end my life by any means you choose."

'He had scarcely finished when we saw Polyphemus himself, massive and monstrous, walking down from the mountain-heights with his flock about him, which he was shepherding as usual to the sea-shore, a horrible and hideous ogre of a giant with his eyesight gone. He carried a pine-trunk cut short, to guide his hand and steady his steps; the fleecy ewes which went with him were his sole joy and now his only consolation. And then he waded out into the sea until he reached deep water. Groaning and grinding his teeth he washed off the blood which flowed where his gouged eye had been. He walked on now far out from land, but still the waves never wetted his towering thighs. In alarm we took on board the suppliant, who had earned his rescue; we cut our cables in silence, and hastened to escape beyond the Cyclops' reach. We bent to it and competing with each other churned the sea-surface with our oars. The Cyclops suspected something and turned his footsteps towards the sounds. But since he had no way of aiming a cast at us, nor, if he pursued, was he tall enough to wade in the waves of the Ionian Sea, he raised a tremendous shout. At that shout every ripple of the ocean trembled, far inland the country of Italy took fright, and even Etna bellowed from the depths of its winding subterranean caverns. And now the whole tribe of Cyclopes was aroused. They dashed to the harbour from forest and mountain height, and thronged the shore. We could see them standing there, that brotherhood of Etna, helpless for all their grim eyes and heads towering to the sky; a horrifying assembly, like so many oak-trees growing in Jupiter's forest on mountain-crests and lifting heads high in air; or like a group of cypress-conifers in Diana's stately grove. Our sharp terror urged us to shake our sheets free and stretch our sails to the following winds in headlong flight, regardless of its direction. But Helenus had given a very different counsel, not to steer between Scylla and Charybdis, since the passage between them came within a narrow margin of disaster on either hand.

So we decided to trim our canvas and put back. But then a north wind suddenly arose, blowing over the narrow headland of Pelorus. We sailed carefully past the river Pantagia's harbour-mouth, formed of natural rock, past Megara's bay, and low-lying Thapsus. Achaemenides gave me information about these places, recalling in the reverse order his memories of the shores which he had passed in his wanderings as a shipmate of the luckless Ulysses.

'Plemmyrium, with its flooding waves, called Ortygia by earlier men, lies stretched in front of the Sicanian Bay. A story tells how Alpheus the river of Elis forced his unseen way below the sea to mingle with Sicilian waters at the mouth of Arethusa's stream. There, in obedience to the command, we paid reverence to the High Powers. Next we passed beyond Helorus, the marsh-city of rich soil. After that we sailed by the projecting rocks and reefs of Pachynus. Then into view came Camarina, which according to the oracle "might never be moved", and after it Gela's plains and Gela itself, cruel city called after the name of a laughing river. Next the steep Acragas, once a breeding ground for horses of highest mettle, displayed before us its mighty ramparts. The winds were kindly; I left leafy Selinus behind and picked my way by Lilybaeum through the difficult shallows with their hidden rocks. At last I found a harbour at Drepanum, but there was no joy for me on that shore. For here, after all the persecution of the ocean-storms, O bitterness! I lost my father, lost Anchises, my solace in every adventure and every care. Yes, here, in my weary plight, you, best of fathers, forsook me, after I had brought you so far and through so many dire perils in vain. Even Helenus the seer never foretold this grief to me among all his many dread warnings, nor did foul Celaeno. This blow was my last anguish. For I had reached the destination of my voyage; and I was sailing from Sicily when Providence drove me onto your coast.'

So did Troy's chieftain Aeneas recall his tale of divine destiny and describe his voyaging, with each face turned intently towards him. At last he ceased; here he fell silent, his story at an end.

BOOK FOUR

THE TRAGEDY OF DIDO

BUT meanwhile Queen Dido, gnawed by love's invisible fire, had long suffered from the deep wound draining her life-blood. Again and again the thought of her hero's valour and the high nobility of his descent came forcibly back to her, and his countenance and his words stayed imprinted on her mind; the distress allowed her no peace and no rest. And now the next day's dawn was cleansing the world with Apollo's light and had parted the moist shadows in high heaven, when Dido spoke distractedly to the sister whose heart was one with hers: 'Anna, Sister Anna, why am I poised frightened between fitful sleep and waking? What do you think of this new guest who has joined us in our home? He has a rare presence, and valiant indeed are his heart and his arms. I can well believe, and I have a right to believe, that his parentage is divine. An ignoble spirit is always revealed by fear. But – what torments from destiny and what horrors of war, endured to the bitterest end, were in his story! If I had not been irrevocably resolved never again to desire a union in wedlock with any man, since the time when death's treachery cheated me of my first love, and if all thought of the marriage-rite and the bridal-room had not become utter weariness to me, possibly this might have been the one temptation to which I could have fallen. Yes, Anna, I shall tell you my secret. Ever since the tragic death of my husband Sychaeus, whose sprinkled blood, which my own brother shed, desecrated our home, no one but this stranger ever made an impression on me, or stirred my heart to wavering. I can discern the old fire coming near again. But I could pray that the earth should yawn deep to engulf me, or the Father Almighty blast me to the Shades with a stroke of his thunder, deep down to those pallid Shades in darkest Erebos, before ever I violate my honour or break its laws. For he who first united me with him took all love out of my life; and so it is he who should keep it close to his heart and guard it even in the grave.' She had spoken her thoughts; and the tears welled, and wetted the fold of her garment which she held to her eyes.

Anna answered her: 'Sister mine, whom I love more than life itself, will you live alone sorrowing and pining through all your youth, and never know the love of children and all that Venus gives? Do you really believe that this matters to ashes, to a ghost in a grave? Granted that in the past no African nor, before we came here, any Tyrian suitor could ever tempt you from your grief, for you scorned Iarbas and other chieftains, sons of this land so fertile in victorious fame; must you therefore now resist a love which appeals to you? Besides, you should remember who are the owners of the land in which is your settlement. You are hemmed in on one side of you by the cities of the unconquerable Gaetulians, by Numidians who know no curb, and by the forbidding quicksands, the Syrtes, and on the other by a waterless desert and the ferocious raiders from Barca. And I need not speak of the danger of war from Tyre, where your brother continues his threats. Now it is my belief that, when these Trojan ships kept course for Carthage before the wind, the gods themselves sealed their approval and Juno herself gave her support. And, Dido, only imagine, if you make this splendid marriage, what a great future lies in store for our city and our realm! With a Trojan army marching at our side, think what deeds of prowess will exalt the fame of Carthage! You have only to pray to the gods for their blessing and ensure their favour by sacrifice; and then entertain your guest freely, weaving pretexts for keeping him here, while his ships are still damaged, and winter and Orion the rain-bringer spend their fury on the ocean under a forbidding sky.'

By speaking so Anna set Dido's heart, already kindled, ablaze with a new access of love, gave new hope to tempt her wavering intention, and broke down her scruples. Their first act was to visit the shrines and pray to the gods for their indulgence at each altar in turn, formally sacrificing selected sheep to Ceres the Mistress of Increase, to Phoebus, to Father

Bacchus the Freedom-Giver, and above all to Juno, for the tie of marriage lies in her care. Lovely Dido herself would take the bowl in her right hand and pour the wine between the horns of a pure white cow, or she would pace in the ritual dance near the gods' reeking altars before the eyes of their statues. She would present more victims to start the day of service anew, and peer with parted lips into the open breasts of sheep for the message of their still breathing vitals. But how pitifully weak is the prescience of seers! There lay no help for her infatuation in temples or in prayers; for all the time the flame ate into her melting marrow, and deep in her heart the wound was silently alive. Poor Dido was afire, and roamed distraught all over her city; like a doe caught off her guard and pierced by an arrow from some armed shepherd, who from the distance had chased her amid Cretan woods and without knowing it had left in her his winged barb; so that she traverses in her flight forests and mountain tracks on Dicte, with the deadly reed fast in her flesh. Sometimes Dido would take Aeneas where her walls were being built, letting him see the great resources of Phoenicia and how far the construction of her city had progressed. And she would begin to speak her thoughts, but always check herself with the words half-spoken. At day's decline she would want the banqueting to begin again as before; she would insist beyond all reason on hearing yet once more the tale of Troy's anguish, and again she would hang breathless on the speaker's words. Afterwards, when they had parted, as the moon in her turn quenched her light to darkness and the setting stars counselled sleep, Dido mourned, lonely in the empty banqueting-hall, and threw herself on the couch which he had left. He was away now, out of sight and hearing, but she still saw him and still heard his voice. Sometimes she held Ascanius close to her, under the spell of his resemblance to his father, and trying hard to escape from the love which she dared not tell. Meanwhile the partly built towers had ceased to rise. No more did young soldiers practise arms. The construction of harbours and impregnable battlements came to a stop. Work hung suspended on gigantic, menacing walls, and the sky-high cranes were still.

Now no sooner had Saturn's daughter, Jupiter's dear wife, seen that Dido was in the firm grip of her affliction and that no thought of her reputation any longer resisted her passion, than she approached Venus with a suggestion: 'Well, you and that boy of yours certainly have fine fruits of victory to show, and great is the glory which you have won. Your distinction is indeed high and deserves to be famous, now that you two divinities have managed to trick one woman into defeat. At the same time I am not wholly unaware that you only view the peaceful homes of tall Carthage with suspicion because you fear the strength of my city's defences. But how far do you mean to go? What need is there to continue so fierce a rivalry? Surely it is better for us to collaborate in arranging a permanent peace, sealed by a marriage-compact. You have gained the object on which you had set your heart. Dido has drunk the maddening poison into her very bones; she is ablaze with love. Let us therefore share this nation between us, each having equal authority in its government. Let Dido be free to become a Phrygian's slave-wife and to hand over her Tyrians into your power as the dowry.'

But Venus realized that Juno's words did not express her true purpose and that her real intention was to divert to Africa those who were meant by Destiny to hold rule in Italy. So this is how she replied: 'Ah, who indeed would be so mad as to refuse such an offer, at the cost of being matched against you in war? Provided, of course, that the plan which you describe will, when put in practice, be crowned with success. But I am subject to the Fates, whose design is obscure to me. Would Jupiter wish the Tyrians and the emigrants from Troy to own a city in common, and would he approve of a treaty between them, or any blending of populations? Now you are his wife; there is nothing wrong in your exploring his intentions by a direct request. So go forward; I shall follow.'

Queenly Juno had a reply to make: 'That task will be my responsibility. But now let me briefly explain how we may achieve our immediate purpose. Listen. As soon as tomorrow's sun rises at the dawning to unveil the earth with his rays, Aeneas and the hapless Dido mean to go hunting in a forest together. While the beaters are hurrying to stretch their encircling cordons across the mountain-tracks, I shall set over them a black cloud charged with mingled rain and hail, release a downpour on the royal pair, and awake all the sky with thunder. Their retinue will scatter and vanish in a darkness as of night, and Dido and Troy's chieftain will both take shelter in the same cave. I shall be there, and if I may be sure of your compliance, I shall assign her to him to be his own, and unite them in secure marriage. This shall be their lawful wedding.' To this proposal the Cytherean raised no objection. She nodded her assent, with a smile at so ingenious a deception.

Meanwhile Aurora arose and left the ocean. When her rays appeared, a select company issued from the city-gates. Out came the wide-meshed nets, the small stop-nets, and the hunting spears with their broad iron heads; and out dashed Massylian riders, and a pack of keen-scented hounds. The queen still lingered in her own room, while the noblest among the Carthaginians awaited her at the doors. Her spirited horse, caparisoned in a splendour of purple and gold, pawed the ground and champed a foaming bit. At last she came, stepping forth with a numerous suite around her and clad in a Sidonian mantle with an embroidered hem. Golden was her quiver and the clasp which knotted her hair, and golden was the brooch which fastened the purple tunic at her neck. Up came the Trojan party, too, including the delighted Iulus. As the two processions met, Aeneas, by far the most handsome of them all, passed across to Dido's side. He was like Apollo when in winter he leaves Lycia and the river Xanthus and visits his mother's isle Delos to start the dancing anew, while around his altar, Cretans, Dryopians and tattooed Agathyrsans mingle and cheer; Apollo himself paces on the slopes of Cynthus, with his clattering bow and arrows slung from his shoulder and his flowing hair pressed into neatness by a soft wreath of leaves and held by a band of gold. Aeneas walked as alertly as he; and a grace like Apollo's shone from his noble face.

When the hunters had reached a pathless tract high in the hills, they started a flock of wild goats which came galloping down the slopes from a rocky crest straight in front of them; and, farther round, a herd of stags massed their ranks in a cloud of dust and fled away from the hill-country and across the open moors. Deep in the valley below, the young Ascanius was keenly enjoying his ride on a spirited horse, outstripping now these and now those at full gallop; but how he longed to see appearing among all these harmless creatures a boar, mouth a-foam, or a golden-brown lion, prowling down from the hills!

Soon a confused rumbling sound started in the sky. Then came the rain-clouds and showers mixed with hail. The hunters all scattered in alarm about the fields searching for shelter – the Tyrian retinue, the band of young Trojans, and the Dardan boy who was grandson of Venus. Torrents came streaming from the hills. Dido and Troy's chieftain found their way to the same cavern. Primaeval Earth and Juno, Mistress of the Marriage, gave their sign. The sky connived at the union; the lightning flared; on their mountain-peak nymphs raised their cry. On that day were sown the seeds of suffering and death. Henceforward Dido cared no more for appearances or her good name, and ceased to take any thought for secrecy in her love. She called it a marriage; she used this word to screen her sin.

At once Rumour raced through Africa's great cities. Rumour is of all pests the swiftest. In her freedom of movement lies her power, and she gathers new strength from her going. She begins as a small and timorous creature; but then she grows till she towers into the air, and though she walks on the ground, she hides her head in the clouds. Men say that Earth, Mother of All, brought her to birth when provoked to anger against the gods; she is her last child, younger sister to Coeus and Enceladus. Rumour is fleet of foot, and swift are her wings; she is a vast, fearful monster, with a watchful eye miraculously set under every feather which grows on her, and for every one of them a tongue in a mouth which is loud of speech, and an ear ever alert. By night she flies hissing through the dark in the space between earth and sky, and never droops her eyelids in contented sleep. In the daylight she keeps watch, sometimes perched on the roof-top of a house and sometimes on the tall towers of a palace. And she strikes dread throughout great cities, for she is as retentive of news which is false and wicked as she is ready to tell what is true.

Now, in great joy, she spread various talk among the peoples of Africa, repeating alike facts and fictions; how there had arrived one Aeneas, descended from the blood of Troy, and how the beautiful Dido had deigned to unite herself to him; and how they were now spending all the long winter together in comfort and self-indulgence, caught in the snare of shameful passion, with never a thought of their royal duty. Such was the talk which this foul goddess everywhere inserted into the conversations of men. Next she turned her quick steps towards King Iarbas, spoke to him, set his thoughts on fire, and heaped fuel on his fury.

Jupiter Ammon had ravished an African nymph and Iarbas was his son by her. To this Jupiter he had erected a hundred vast temples and a hundred altars about his broad realm; he had consecrated in them wakeful temple-fires and courses of priests to keep unbroken vigils for the gods. The precincts reeked always with blood of sacrifice, and the temple-gates were ever decked with flowers of many hues. It is said that Iarbas, bitterly angry at what he now heard, and frantic in his helplessness, stood before an altar with the divine presences about him, raised hands in supplication, and prayed long prayers to Jupiter: 'O Jupiter Almighty, to whom now the Moorish nation, banqueting on divans of rich-coloured weave, pours Bacchic offering in your honour, do you see what is done? Or, when you cast your spinning thunderbolt, Father, is our dread of you vain? Are those fires which affright us in the clouds blind fires, and is there no meaning behind their mingled and muttering growl? For a woman, a vagrant, who has built a small city on my territory, renting a coastal strip to cultivate under conditions of tenure dictated by me, has rejected my marriage-suit, and accepted Aeneas as her master and joint ruler. So now this second Paris, wearing a Phrygian bonnet to tie up his chin and cover his oily hair, and attended by a train of she-men, is to become the owner of what he has stolen. Meanwhile, here I am bringing my offerings to temples which I take to be yours, though apparently the belief on which I act is quite mistaken.'

Such were the words of his prayer, and as he prayed he touched the altar. The Almighty heard, and turned his eyes on the queen's city and on these lovers who had forgotten their nobler fame. He then spoke to Mercury, and entrusted him with this commission: 'Up, son of mine, go on your way. Call to you the western winds. Glide on your wings! Speak to the Dardan prince who is now lingering in Tyrian Carthage with never a thought for those other cities which are his by destiny. Go swiftly through the air and take my words to him. It was never for this that the most beautiful goddess, his mother, twice rescued him from his Greek foes. This is not the man she led us to think that he would prove to be. No, he was to guide an Italy which is to be a breeding-ground of leadership and clamorous with noise of war, transmit a lineage from proud Teucer's blood, and subject the whole earth to the rule of law. And even if the glory of this great destiny is powerless to kindle his ardour, and if he will exert no effort to win fame for himself, will he withhold from his son Ascanius the Fortress of Rome? What does he mean to do? What can he gain by lingering among a people who are his foes, without a care for his own descendants, the Italians of the future, and for the lands destined to bear Lavinia's name? He must set sail. That is what I have to say, and that is to be my message to him.'

He finished, and Mercury prepared to obey his exalted Father's command. First he laced on his feet those golden sandals with wings to carry him high at the speed of the winds' swift blast over ocean and over land alike. Then he took his wand; the wand with which he calls the pale souls forth from the Nether World and sends others down to grim Tartarus, gives sleep, and takes sleep away, and unseals eyes at death. So shepherding the winds before him with his wand, he swam through the murk of the clouds. And now as he flew he discerned the crest and steep flanks of Atlas the enduring, who supports the sky upon his head. His pine-clad crown is perpetually girt by blackest mist and beaten by wind and rain, his shoulders swathed in a mantle of snow, his aged chin a cascade of torrents, and his wild and shaggy beard frozen stiff with ice. Here Cyllenian Mercury first stopped, poised on balancing wings. And from here he plunged with all his weight to the waves; like a sea-bird flying low close to the sea's surface round shores and rocks where fish are found. So did the Cyllenian fly between earth and sky to the sandy shore of Africa, cutting through the winds from the Mountain Atlas, his mother's sire.

As soon as his winged feet had carried him as far as the hut-villages of Africa, he saw Aeneas engaged on the foundations of the citadel and the construction of new dwellings. He had a sword starred with golden-brown jasper, and wore a cloak of bright Tyrian purple draped from his shoulders, a present from a wealthy giver, Dido herself, who had made it, picking out the warp-thread with a line of gold. Mercury immediately delivered his message: 'What, are you siting foundations for proud Carthage and building here a noble city? A model husband! For shame! You forget your destiny and that other kingdom which is to be yours. He who reigns over all the gods, he who sways all the earth and the sky by the power of his will, has himself sent me down to you from glittering Olympus. It is he who commanded me to carry this message to you swiftly through the air. What do you mean to do? What can you gain by living at wasteful leisure in African lands? If the glory of your great destiny is powerless to kindle your ardour, and if you will exert no effort to win fame for yourself, at least think of Ascanius, now growing up, and all that you hope from him as your heir, destined to rule in an Italy which shall become the Italy of Rome.' With this stern rebuke, and even while he was still speaking, Mercury vanished from mortal vision and melted from sight into thin air.

Aeneas was struck dumb by the vision. He was out of his wits, his hair bristled with a shiver of fear, and his voice was checked in his throat. Already he was ardently wishing to flee from the land of his love and be gone; so violent had been the shock of this peremptory warning from the gods. But what could he do? How could he dare to speak to the infatuated queen, and win her round? What would be the best opening for him to choose? Rapidly he turned it over in his mind, inclining now to one plan and now to another, and hurriedly considering all the different aspects and possibilities. As he pondered, one policy seemed preferable to every other. He called to him Mnestheus, Sergestus, and the gallant Serestus: they were to fit out the fleet, make ready all their tackle, and muster their comrades on the shore, without giving any explanations, and concealing the reason for the change of plan. Meanwhile he would see Dido, for in her ignorance and goodness of heart she would never suspect that so deep a love could possibly be broken. So he would try to find the right approach and the least painful moment to speak, and discover a tactful way out of their predicament.

His men obeyed with pleasure and alacrity and began carrying out their orders. But no one can deceive a lover. The queen divined the intended deceit in advance. Before she was told, her intuition discerned what would happen and her fears were alive to every possible danger, real or unreal. In this nervous state the news came to her, brought, once more, by unholy Rumour, that the fleet was being equipped in preparation for a voyage. Furious, and quite unable to face the truth, she ran in excited riot about Carthage, like a Bacchanal uplifted to frenzy as the emblems of Bacchus are shaken and the cry of his name is heard, when every second year the thrill of the festival pricks her and Mount Cithaeron calls her with shouting in the night. At last Dido accosted Aeneas, speaking first, and denounced him:

'Traitor, did you actually believe that you could disguise so wicked a deed and leave my country without a word? And can nothing hold you, not our love, nor our once plighted hands, nor even the cruel death that must await your Dido? Are you so unfeeling that you labour at your fleet under a wintry sky, in haste to traverse the high seas in the teeth of the northerly gales? Why, had you not now been searching for a home which you have never seen in some alien land, and had ancient Troy itself been still standing, would you have been planning to sail even there over such tempestuous seas? Is it from me that you are trying to escape? Oh, by the tears which I shed, by your own plighted hand, for I have left myself, poor fool, no other appeal, and by our union, by the true marriage which it was to be, oh, if I was ever kind to you, or if anything about me made you happy, please, please, if it is not too late to beg you, have pity for the ruin of a home, and change your mind. It was because of you that I earned the hate of Africa's tribes and the lords of the Numidians, and the hostility of my own Tyrians also; and it was because of you that I let my honour die, the fair fame which used to be mine, and my only hope of immortality. In whose hands are you leaving me to face my death, my – Guest? I used to call you Husband, but the word has shrunk to Guest. What does the future hold for me now? My brother Pygmalion coming to demolish my walls, or this Gaetulian Iarbas, marrying me by capture? At least, if I had a son of yours conceived before you left, some tiny Aeneas to play about my hall and bring you back to me if only in his likeness, I might not then have felt so utterly entrapped and forsaken.'

She finished. He, remembering Jupiter's warning, held his eyes steady, and strained to master the agony within him. At last he spoke, shortly: 'Your Majesty, I shall never deny that I am in your debt for all those many acts of kindness which you may well recount to me. And for as long as I have consciousness and breath of life controls my movement, I shall never tire, Elissa, of your memory. Now I shall speak briefly of the facts. I had no thought of hiding my present departure under any deceit. Do not imagine that. Nor have I ever made any marriage-rite my pretext, for I never had such a compact with you. If my destiny had allowed me to guide my life as I myself would have chosen, and solve my problems according to my own preference, I should have made the city of Troy, with its loved remembrances of my own folk, my first care; and, with Priam's tall citadel still standing, I should have refounded Troy's fortress to be strong once more after her defeat. But in fact Apollo at Grynium, where he gives his divination in Lycia by the lots, has insistently commanded me to make my way to Italy's noble land. Italy must be my love and my homeland now. If you, a Phoenician, are faithful to your Carthaginian fortress here, content to look on no other city but this city in far-away Africa, what is the objection if Trojans settle in Italy? It is no sin, if we, like you, look for a kingdom in a foreign country. Each time the night shrouds the earth in its moist shadows, each time the fiery stars arise, the anxious wraith of my father Anchises warns me in sleep, and I am afraid. My son Ascanius also serves as a warning to me; I think of his dear self, and of the wrong which I do him in defrauding him of his Italian kingdom, where Fate has given him his lands. And now Jove himself has sent the Spokesman of the Gods – this I swear to you by my son's life and by my father – who flew swiftly through the air, and delivered the command to me. With my own eyes I saw the divine messenger in clearest light entering the city gate, and heard his voice with my own ears. Cease, therefore, to upset yourself, and me also, with these protests. It is not by my own choice that I voyage onward to Italy.'

Throughout this declaration Dido had remained standing, turned away from Aeneas but glaring at him over her shoulder with eyes which roved about his whole figure in a voiceless stare. Then her fury broke: 'Traitor, no goddess was ever your mother, nor was it Dardanus who founded your line. No, your parent was Mount Caucasus, rugged, rocky, and hard, and tigers of Hyrcania nursed you.... For what need have I of concealment now? Why hold myself in check any longer, as if there could be anything worse to come?... Has he spared a sigh or a look in response to my weeping, or has he once softened, or shed a tear of pity for one who loved him? Depth beyond depth of iniquity! Neither Supreme Juno, nor the Father who is Saturn's son, can possibly look with the impartial eyes of justice on what is happening now. No faith is left sure in the wide world. I welcomed him, a shipwrecked beggar, and like a fool I allowed him to share my royal place. I saved his comrades from death and gave him back his lost fleet.... The Furies have me now, they burn, they drive...! So, now, it seems, he has his orders from Apollo's own Lycian oracle, and next even the Spokesman of the Gods is sent by

Jove himself to deliver through the air to him the same ghastly command! So I am to believe that the High Powers exercise their minds about such a matter and let concern for it disturb their calm! Oh, I am not holding you. I do not dispute your words. Go, quest for Italy before the winds; sail over the waves in search of your kingdom. But I still believe that, if there is any power for righteousness in Heaven, you will drink to the dregs the cup of punishment amid sea-rocks, and as you suffer cry "Dido" again and again. Though far, yet I shall be near, haunting you with flames of blackest pitch. And when death's chill has parted my body from its breath, wherever you go my spectre will be there. You will have your punishment, you villain. And I shall hear; the news will reach me deep in the world of death.' She did not finish, but at these words broke off sharply. She hurried in her misery away and hid from sight, leaving Aeneas anxious and hesitant, and longing to say much more to her. Dido fainted, and fell; and her maids took her up, carried her to her marble bedroom, and laid her on her bed.

Meanwhile Aeneas the True longed to allay her grief and dispel her sufferings with kind words. Yet he remained obedient to the divine command, and with many a sigh, for he was shaken to the depths by the strength of his love, returned to his ships. Vigorously indeed the Trojans set to work. They were soon launching their tall galleys all along the beach, and the freshly tarred keels were again afloat. Men carried rough oars with the leaves still on them, and tough timbers as yet unworked, from the forest, so keen were they to be gone. They could all be seen on the move hurrying from every quarter of the city, looking like ants, which, planning for the winter ahead, pillage some large heap of barley for storing in their homes, and march in a long black line across a plain, conveying their plunder on a narrow trail over the grass; some press shoulders against a massive grain of corn, forcing it onwards; others bring up the rear and punish stragglers; and the whole track is a ferment of activity. What must have been Dido's thoughts when she saw all this movement, and how bitterly must she have sighed as she looked from her commanding citadel, and discerned the lively bustle along the shore and all the turmoil of loud confusion on the sea? Ah, merciless Love, is there any length to which you cannot force the human heart to go? For Love now drove Dido to have recourse to tears again, and again to try what entreaties might do, subjecting pride to passion in a last appeal, in case she had still left some way unexplored, and was going to a needless death.

'Anna,' she said, 'you see the hurrying all over the beach. From all sides they have gathered there. Already their canvas invites the wind, and the mariners have been gaily setting garlands on the sterns of their ships. Perhaps I might have foreseen this terrible grief. Perhaps too, Anna, I shall have strength to endure it. But nevertheless do carry out this one task for your poor sister. For that traitor was never really attentive to anyone but you; you alone had his full confidence, and only you ever knew just how and when to approach this hard man tactfully. So go now, sister, and speak in humble appeal to our haughty enemy. I am not one who conspired with the Greeks at Aulis to exterminate the Trojan people – I sent no fleet against the fortress of Troy – I never tore up Anchises' grave to disturb his ashes and his spirit. So why should his pitiless ears refuse to listen to my plea? And where is he going in such haste? As one last gift to his unhappy love, he might at least make his own flight easier simply by awaiting a favourable wind. I do not now beg him to restore our honoured marriage as it was before he betrayed it, or ask him to forgo his splendid Latium where he hopes to reign. I ask only the time of inaction, to give my mad mood a breathing-space and a rest, until my fortune can teach me submission and the art of grief. This is my last plea for indulgence, and you must bear with me as a sister. And when he has granted it to me I shall repay the debt, with the interest, in death.'

Such was Dido's entreaty; and her poor, unhappy sister carried the tearful messages between them. But all these appeals left Aeneas quite unmoved. He was deaf to every plea, for destiny barred the way and a divine influence checked his inclination to listen kindly. He stood firm like a strong oak-tree toughened by the years when northern winds from the Alps vie together to tear it from the soil, with their blasts striking on it now this side and now that; creaking, the trunk shakes, and leaves from on high strew the ground; yet still the tree grips among the rocks below, for its roots stretch as far down towards the abyss as its crest reaches up to airs of heaven. Like that tree, the hero was battered this side and that by their insistent pleas, and deeply his brave heart grieved. But his will remained unshaken. The tears rolled down, but without effect.

It was final. Dido was lost; and she saw with horror the fate starkly confronting her. Her one prayer was now for death. The sight of heaven's vault was only weariness to her. And, as if to steel her will to fulfil her design and to part from the light of day, as she laid her offerings on the altars where incense burned, she saw a dreadful sight; for the holy waters turned to black and the poured wine by some sinister transformation was changed into blood. She told no one, not even her sister, what she had seen. And furthermore there was in her palace a marble chapel, sacred to her first husband, which she venerated with utmost love, keeping it decorated with snowy fleeces and festal greenery. Now from this chapel when night held the world in darkness she thought that she distinctly heard cries, as of her husband calling to her. And often on a rooftop a lonely owl would sound her deathly lamentation, drawing out her notes into a long wail. Then many presages of ancient seers shocked her to panic by their dread warnings. She would have nightmares of a furious Aeneas pursuing her, and driving her wild with fear, and of being left utterly alone, and travelling companionless a long road, searching for Tyrian friends in a deserted land. She was in the state of Pentheus, when, with mind deranged, he saw the Furies advancing in ranks, two suns appearing in the sky, and two cities of Thebes; or of Agamemnon's tormented son Orestes on the theatre-stage, seeking to escape a mother armed with firebrands and black snakes, while the avenging Spirits of the Curse wait at the door.

So agony prevailed; and Dido was possessed by demon-powers. Having made her decision for death, she first worked out, all by herself, the time and the means. Then, with a calm and hopeful expression to conceal her plan, she accosted her distressed sister and spoke to her: 'Sister, Anna, congratulate me! For I have found the way which will either give him back to me or release me from loving him. Close to Ocean's margin and the setting of the sun lies the land of Aethiopia on the edge of the world, where giant Atlas holds, turning, on his shoulders the pole of the heavens, inset with blazing stars. I have been told of a Massylian priestess living in that land. She guards the Temple of the Hesperides; it was she who fed the dragon, sprinkling honey-drops and poppy-seed, bringer of sleep, and it was she who kept watch over the holy boughs on the tree. She professes by her spells to give freedom to the hearts of any whom she chooses, but to inflict cruel agonies on others. She can stay the current of a river, and reverse the movement of stars. She can evoke the spirits in the night-time; yes, and as you will see, make the earth bellow underfoot, and the rowan-trees march down from their hills. Dear Anna, I swear to you by the gods, I swear by you and your own sweet life that it is against my will that I arm myself with magic. Now, build me a tall funeral pyre. Build it in the centre of our home under the open sky but out of view. Lay on it the arms of the false man, which he left hanging from a wall in our bridal room, and all the garments which he wore, besides; and you must also place on it the bridal bed which was my ruin. I choose to destroy whatever can remind me of one who must never be mentioned. Besides, such is the advice of the priestess.' After saying this she fell silent, and her face suddenly paled. It never occurred to Anna that her sister was using this strange rite to veil her own impending death. She could not herself imagine so violent a passion, and had no fear of anything worse happening now than had happened when Sychaeus died. So she made the preparations, as Dido had asked.

Presently the pyre had been built with logs of holm-oak and pine. It was vast, rising to a great height, and it stood in the centre of the building. The queen had festooned the hall with flower-chains, and wreathed the pyre with the greenery of death. On it was the bed, and there she placed a sword which Aeneas had left, with garments which he had worn, and a portrait of him, knowing all the time what was to be.

Around it were altars. The priestess, hair astream, told in a voice like thunder the names of her thrice-hundred gods, told Erebos and the Void, and Hecate of three forms, who is Diana the maiden of the triple countenance. She had sprinkled water, supposed to be from the fount of Avernus. Herbs, reaped with bronzen sickles by moonlight and bursting with a black poisonous milk, were gathered there, and with them a love-charm ripped from the brow of a baby foal before the mother could take it. Close to the high altar stood Dido, holding the sacred meal and lifting pure hands above, with garment girt back and one foot unsandalled. And, soon to die, she called on the gods and the stars which know fate's secrets to hear her. And she added a prayer to any Power there may be, some Power watchful and fair, with a thought for lovers whose love is not matched well.

It was night, and tired creatures all over the world were enjoying kindly sleep. Forests and fierce seas were at rest, as the circling constellations glided in their midnight course. Every field, all the farm-animals, and the colourful birds were silent, all that lived across miles of glassy mere and in the wild country's ragged brakes, lying still under the quiet night in a sleep which smoothed each care away from hearts which had forgotten life's toil. But not so the Phoenician queen. Her accursed spirit could not relax into sleeping, or welcome darkness into her eyes or brain. Instead, her torment redoubled; her love came back again and again, and heaved in ocean-tides of rage. And she began yet once more to pursue her thoughts, communing with herself in her heart: 'There! What is there for me to do? Risk mockery by returning to my former suitors, sound their feelings, and plead humbly with some Numidian to marry me, though time after time I have scorned to think of one of them as a husband? Or instead should I sail with the Trojan fleet and submit to Trojan orders however harsh? Am I so sure that they are pleased with the aid and relief which I gave them, that they remember, and that their gratefulness for what I did then is still alive? But indeed, even granted that I wished it, would they let me come, and welcome me to their ships? They are arrogant, and hate me.

Lost fool, can you not see? Can you even now not realize how treacherous Laomedon's nation can be? Besides, if I sail with these mariners, who are so triumphant now at their departure, do I go alone, or do I take with me all my Tyrian friends, thronging round me when I go to join the Trojans? If so, how can I order them to spread their sails to the winds and force them to voyage once more out onto the ocean? It was all that I could do to uproot them from their former city, Sidon. No. You have deserved death and you must die. Only the blade can save you from the agony.... O Anna, I have been mad; but it was you who first laid on me this load of suffering, for you gave way to my tears, and set me at the mercy of my foe. If only I could have been allowed to pass my life free from reproach as the wild animals do, without any wedding, and in no danger of anguish like mine.... And the vow which I made to the ashes of Sychaeus is broken too.' Such were the terrible words of grief which burst from Dido's heart.

Meanwhile Aeneas, who had now settled his plans for sailing and completed his preparations, was lying asleep on his ship's stern. As he slept he again had a vision of the god, who returned in countenance as before and was like Mercury in every feature, in his voice and complexion, his blond hair, and limbs with the grace of youth. As Aeneas gazed, Mercury repeated his warning: 'Son of the Goddess, can you, with so great a disaster impending, remain asleep, and not discern the dangers which wait ready to break about your head? Fool! Can you not hear the breath of the favouring west winds? She plans in her thought a fearful and treacherous wrong. In her a violent rage surges and surges again, and she is resolved to die. Will you not hasten away while it is not too late for hastening? You will soon see a confusion of wreckage on the sea, the cruel glare of firebrands burning bright, and the whole shore ablaze, if dawn finds you still lingering here. Ho! Come, have done with delays. Women were ever things of many changing moods.' So he spoke, and then melted into the black darkness.

Aeneas was shocked indeed by the sudden apparition. He leapt up and gave his comrades the alarm: 'Hasten, men!

Awake! Take your places for rowing. Quick, unfurl your sails! For, see! Again a god has descended from high heaven, and again he stings us into haste. We must hack through our twisted hawsers, and flee. We follow you, holy Deity, whoever you may truly be, and we joyfully obey your command, as before. Be with us and graciously aid us. Bring us favours from the stars of heaven.' With the words he quickly unsheathed his sword and struck the cables with the flashing blade. One ardour seized them all. They heaved and they hurried. Not one remained on shore. The water was hidden beneath the fleet. They bent to it, churned the foam, and swept the blue surface of the sea.

By now Aurora, rising, had left the saffron bed of Tithonus and was sprinkling her fresh light on the world. From her watch-tower the queen saw the white gleam of dawn, and saw the fleet moving forward with sails square to the wind. She realized that the shore and the harbour were empty, without a single oarsman. At the sight, she struck her beautiful breast, three times struck it and then a fourth, she tore her golden hair, and she cried aloud: 'Ah, Jupiter! Is this stranger to make a mock of my realm, and calmly go? Fetch weapons! Come on, every one in Carthage! Pursue! You there, rush to the dockyards and launch your ships! Quick! Bring some firebrands, hand out arms. Put your weight to the oars! . . . Oh, what am I saying? Where am I? Oh, poor, poor Dido, what mad folly is distorting your mind? Is it only now that his wicked deeds strike home to you? Why did you not think of that before you relinquished to him your sovereignty? See his faithfulness to his plighted word! And yet they say that he carries with him the gods of his ancestral home, and bowed his shoulders to bear his old and feeble father! Could I not have seized him, torn him limb from limb, and scattered the pieces on the waves? And put his comrades to the sword – yes, and killed Ascanius and served him up to be his father's meal? Ah, but the fortune of such a fight was never certain. Uncertain, then. But whom had I to fear, having, in any event, to die? I might have taken firebrands into their camp and set all their ships' decks blazing. I could have quenched the life of son, of father, and of all their line. And then, to crown all, I could have flung myself to death. Sun, whose cleansing beams survey the whole world and all its works! Juno, who share with me the secret of my agony and could tell its truth! Hecate, honoured at every city's three-cross-ways by wavering holloas in the night! Terrible Spirits of Avenging Curse! Angels of Death awaiting Elissa! All of you, hear me now. Direct the force of your divine will, as you must, on the evil here, and listen to my prayer. If that wicked being must sail surely to land and come to harbour, because such is the fixed and destined ending required by Jupiter's own ordinances, yet let him afterwards suffer affliction in war through the arms of a daring foe, let him be banished from his own territory, and torn from the embraces of Iulus, imploring aid as he sees his innocent friends die, and then, after surrendering to a humiliating peace, may he not live to enjoy his kingdom in days of happiness; but may he lie fallen before his time, unburied on a lonely strand. That is my prayer and my last cry, and it comes from me with my life-blood streaming. From then onwards shall you, my Phoenicians, torment with acts of pursuing hate all his descendants to come, each member of his line. This service shall be your offering to my shade. Neither love nor compact shall there be between the nations. And from my dead bones may some Avenger arise to persecute with fire and sword those settlers from Troy, soon or in after-time, whenever the strength is given! Let your shores oppose their shores, your waves their waves, your arms their arms. That is my imprecation. Let them fight, they, and their sons' sons, for ever!'

Such was her curse. And now she turned to consider every course of action, for she wanted, as quickly as might be, to break off her living in day's hated light. She spoke shortly to Barce, who had been Sychaeus' old nurse – her own nurse, dark ashes now, had been left in the ancient homeland – : 'Nurse, dear, ask Anna my sister to come to me here. And tell her she should hasten to sprinkle river-water over her, and bring with her the victims and all else that is needed for the atonement which I have been commanded to make. Let her come, prepared as I say; and you yourself should wreathe your brow with a ribbon of piety. It is my intention to complete certain rites to Stygian Jupiter, which I have formally prepared and begun, and to put an end to my sorrow by committing to the flames the pyre which holds the Trojan's life.' So she spoke. Barce, with all an old woman's interest, quickened her pace.

But Dido, in trembling haste and frantic at her desperate design, burst through the doorway into the inner room. Her eyes were reddened and rolling, her cheeks quivered under a flush, and she was pale with the pallor of imminent death. In a mad dash she climbed the high funeral pile, and unsheathed the Trojan sword, a gift never meant for such a use as this. Her sight rested on the garments which had come from Troy, and on the bed with its memories. She paused a little for tears and for a thought; and she cast herself down on the bed, and there spoke her last words: 'Sweet relics, sweet so long as God and Destiny allowed, now receive my life-breath, and set me free from this suffering. I have lived my life and finished the course which Fortune allotted me. Now my wraith shall pass in state to the world below. I have established a noble city. I have lived to see my own ramparts built. I have avenged my husband and punished the brother who was our foe. Happy, all too happy, should I have been, if only the Dardan ships had never reached my coast!' With this cry she buried her face in the bed, and continued: 'I shall die, and die unavenged; but die I shall. Yes, yes; this is the way I like to go into the dark. And may the heartless Trojan, far out on the deep, drink in the sight of my fire and take with him the evil omen of my death.'

There she ended. And even while she still spoke she had fallen upon the blade. Soon her attendants saw her with blood foaming about the sword and the stains of it on her hands. A cry rose to the palace-roof. Carthage was striken by the shock and Rumour ran riot in the town. Lamentation and sobbing and women's wailing rang through the houses, and high heaven echoed with the loud mourning; as if some enemy had broken through and all Carthage, or ancient Tyre, were falling, with the flames rolling madly up over dwellings of gods and men. Her sister heard, and the breath left her. Marring her cheeks with her finger-nails and bruising her breast with her clenched hands, she dashed in frightened haste through the crowds, found Dido at the very point of death, and cried out to her: 'O Sister, so this was the truth? You planned to deceive me! Was this what your pyre, your altars, and the fires were to mean for me? How shall I begin reproaching you for forsaking me so? Did you scorn your own sister and not want her with you when you died? You should have asked me to share your fate, and then one same hour, one agony of the blade, might have taken us both. To think that with my own hands I even built the pyre, and cried loud upon our ancestral gods, only to be cruelly separated from you as you lay in death! Sister, you have destroyed my life with your own, and the lives of our people and Sidon's nobility, and your whole city too. Come, let me see your wounds – I must wash them clean with water, and gather with my own lips any last hovering breath.' While speaking she had climbed to the top of the steps and clasped her sister, who was still just breathing, to her breast, and fondled her, sobbing, and trying to stanch the dark blood with her dress. Dido attempted to raise her heavy eyes again, but failed; and the deep wound in her breast, where the sword stood planted, breathed loud. Three times she rose, supporting herself on her elbows, but each time she rolled back onto the bed. With roaming eyes she looked to high heaven for the daylight, and found it, and gave a sigh.

But Juno who has all power took pity on the long anguish of her difficult death, and sent Iris down from Olympus to release the wrestling spirit from the twined limbs. For since she perished neither by destiny nor by a death deserved, but tragically, before her day, in the mad heat of a sudden passion, Proserpine had not yet taken a golden lock from her head, to assign her life to Stygian Orcus. So therefore Iris, saffron-winged, sparkling like dew and trailing a thousand colours as she caught the light of the sun, flew down across the sky. She hovered over Dido's head: 'By command I take this lock as an offering to Pluto; and I release you from the body which was yours.' Speaking so, she held out a hand and cut the lock. At once, all the warmth fell away, and the life passed into the moving air.

BOOK FIVE

THE FUNERAL GAMES

AENEAS and his fleet were now far out to sea. He set course resolutely and ploughed through waves ruffled to black by a northerly wind. As he sailed he looked back to walled Carthage, now aglow with tragic Dido's flames. Why that terrible blaze had been kindled was obscure. But the Trojans knew how bitter are the agonies when intense love is outraged, and the extremity to which a woman in distraction will go; and the knowledge started a train of thought sombre with presentiment.

When their ships were well out on the high seas, with no longer any land in sight but on all sides nothing but water and sky, an inky squall gathered above the prince's head, bringing night and storm, and the waves shuddered in the darkness. Even Palinurus, his helmsman, cried from his station high on the stern, 'Why should these heavy clouds envelop the sky? Ah, Father Neptune, what are you planning?' With these words he at once gave orders to shorten sail and make all fast, and to press stoutly on the oars; and he set the canvas aslant to the wind. Then he spoke to Aeneas: 'Aeneas of heroic heart, not even if Jupiter himself gave his promise and his guarantee would I expect to reach Italy under such a sky. The wind has backed and blows on our beam. It is rising out of the western dark to a roar; and the murk is concentrated into thick cloud. We have not the strength to strain against this wind, and no efforts of ours will avail. So, since Fortune has the better of us, let us obey and change our course to steer where she calls us. In any case, if I correctly observed the constellations on our way, and am now plotting our return course by them without mistake, I think that the friendly coastline of Eryx your brother and Sicily's havens are not far off.' Aeneas the True answered: 'I too have for some time been noticing that this is what the winds require of us and I see that you have been striving against them in vain. Trim your sails for a change of course. And certainly I could like no land better, nor prefer any other as a refuge for my tired ships, than the land which guards Dardan Acestes for me and which clasps to its breast the bones of my father Anchises.' Such was his answer. They steered for harbour and a following west wind stretched their sails. The fleet sped swiftly over the depths, and at length, with joy, they turned inshore towards the familiar strand.

Acestes, looking from a distant mountain-crest, had observed their arrival with wonder and recognized that the ships were the ships of friends. He came to meet them, looking wild in his African bear-skin and with his cluster of javelins. Acestes was born by a Trojan mother to the River-God Crimisus, who was her husband. He had not forgotten his parentage, and was clearly delighted to find that his fellow Trojans had returned. He gave them a joyous welcome with his rustic treasures and cheered his tired friends with generous kindliness.

When at earliest dawn the morrow's brightness had put the stars to flight, Aeneas called his companions together from all along the beach to an assembly. He spoke to them from a piled bank of earth: 'Noble sons of Dardanus, descended from the exalted blood of gods, the cycle of a year is being now completed, and a whole twelvemonth has passed since we committed to the earth the bones which are the relics of my now sainted father, and consecrated the altars of our sorrowing. Indeed, if I am not mistaken, since the gods have so decreed, the day is at hand which I shall ever count bitter and ever count revered. If I had been spending it in exile by the Syrtes in Africa, or been overtaken by its arrival while sailing on the Argive Sea, or even while in the very city of Mycenae, I should still have been discharging my vows on this anniversary, formally conducting our yearly rite, and piling appropriate offerings on the altar. But, in the event, we have fared better; we stand here, beside the very ashes of my father's bones. We have come to land and entered this friendly harbour, and for my part I see in this the intention and the will of the gods. Come then, let us all celebrate the joyful duty.

Let us pray to the winds. And when one day I have established my city and founded its temples, may my father be pleased that I offer him this worship every year. Acestes, himself a son of Troy, is giving you cattle, two head in number for each of your ships. Let us invite to our feast the gods of our homes, our own gods, and those others whom our host Acestes reveres. Afterwards, when the ninth dawn has lifted high for mortal creatures her life-giving day, unveiling the world with her rays, I shall arrange for my Trojans a race for their ships; next, let there come forward any who is a fast runner, or any whose strength emboldens him to step forth because he excels with javelin or light arrows, or has the confidence to engage in battle wearing the raw boxing-hide; let all be present and await the award of whatever prizes they earn. Keep holy silence, all, and wreathe your brows with greenery.'

Having spoken so, Aeneas graced his forehead with his mother's myrtle. Helymus, Acestes ripe in years, and the young Ascanius did so too, and the rest of the Trojan manhood followed their example.

Aeneas left the assembly and moved off to the barrow. He went with many thousands, so large was the concourse which accompanied him, and he walked in their midst. In formal libation he poured on the earth two bowls of unwatered wine, two of fresh milk, and two of hallowed blood. Then he scattered some bright flowers, and said:

'Father, my Father Sanctified, hail to you once again. Hail, ashes now; since it was for this only that I saved you. Hail, Father's spirit, spectre, shadow; hail! It was not granted to me to have you at my side as I quested for Italy's boundaries where fate has given us lands, or for Ausonian Tiber, whereever that river may be.'

He had just finished, when a gigantic snake crept, slippery, from the base of the mound, trailing seven huge loops, and seven arching coils, encircling the tomb in kindly embrace, and sliding over the altars. His back blazed with blue markings and his scales with a gleam of gold, like a rainbow catching the light of the sun and flinging a thousand colours on the clouds; and Aeneas was amazed at the sight. The snake crept with all his long trailing length between the bowls and smooth polished vessels. Last, he tasted the fare; and harmlessly moved back to the base of the tomb. He had consumed the offering on the high altar, and he departed.

Now Aeneas, his zeal sharpened by this occurrence, started once more the ritual which in filial duty he was performing. He was uncertain whether to regard the snake as the guardian power of that place or as his father's familiar spirit. He formally sacrificed a pair of two-year sheep, of pigs the same number, and two black-skinned bullocks. He poured wine from the bowls. And he called on the soul of the great Anchises and on his spirit, released from Acheron for the rite. His comrades also, each according to his resources, eagerly brought offerings, piling them on the altars, and sacrificing bullocks. Some set cauldrons in rows. They carried burning coals to the spits, and, reclining on the grass, roasted the meat.

The awaited day arrived. In fine weather Phaethon's horses were now already bringing the ninth dawn. Neighbouring folk had heard the news and that, together with Acestes' fame, had aroused their interest, and so they filled the shore with their gay gathering, all wanting to see Aeneas and his men, and some of them ready to compete in the games. Gifts were first exposed to view in the centre of the ground. There were sacrificial tripods, green garlands, palms to be the victors' prizes, weapons, garments dyed in purple, and talents of silver and gold. Next a trumpet sounded from the crest of a hillock, signalling that the games had begun.

For the first event, four ships mounting heavy oars and equally matched were selected from the whole fleet. Mnestheus commanded the fast Pristis with its vigorous crew; he was to become the Italian Mnestheus and his name originated the family name of Memmius. Gyas was captain of the vast and massive Chimaera; she was as large as a city and forced onwards by Dardan manhood seated in three tiers, with oars rising in three banks. Sergestus, from whom the family of the Sergii takes its name, sailed in the mighty Centaur; and Cloanthus, who gave an origin to you, Roman Cluentius, in the bright-blue Scylla.

Some distance out in the sea was a rock, off a surf-beaten shore. Sometimes it was submerged, and battered by swelling waves, when north-west winds of winter hide the stars. But in calm weather it was quiet. There was level ground on it, raised above a motionless sea, and it was a favourite place for gulls to stand and sun themselves. On this rock the chieftain Aeneas erected a turning-post of green holm-oak, to be a steering-mark for the crews and let them know where to begin the long, circling course for rounding the rock. The captains next drew lots for places. And now they stood on their quarter-decks and the light from the splendour of their purple and gold shone far. The crews donned wreaths of poplar-leaves and smeared their bare shoulders with oil until they glistened. They took their places on the thwarts, and with arms stretched and braced at the oars intently awaited the call. Their hearts beat fast with the strain of nervous excitement and their eager thirst for glory. At last the trumpet rang out clear. Immediately all leapt forward from their places on the starting-line. Seamen's shouts hit the sky as they drew back their arms, and the waters were churned to foam. They clove furrows in unison; wrenched by the oars and cut by the trident-stems, the sea-surface split open. Never with such a headlong pace did any chariots in pair-horse competition stream from their starting-cage and tear racing along the course. Never so did any charioteers shake rippling leather reins on uncurbed teams, or so bend forward to the lash. All the forest-land roared with the applause of onlookers and supporters urging on their favourites. The shouting beat against the surrounding hills and came echoing back; the cries were held, rolling round, about the low ground by the bay. Amid the noise and confusion Gyas had slipped away ahead of the others and was gliding along in undisturbed water. Cloanthus, next, followed him closely. His oarsmanship was better, but his pine-timbers were heavy and slow, and held him back. Behind them, after an equal gap, the Pristis and the Centaur vied closely to win a lead. Now Pristis has it; now the vast Centaur passes her and goes ahead; now both sweep on together, bows level, furrowing the salt sea with long keels.

They were already approaching the rock and about to reach the turning-post, when Gyas, who was leading at this halfway point of the course, and for the time victorious, shouted to his helmsman Menoetes: 'Where are you going, so far off course to starboard? Steer straight this way. Hug the shore. Let oar-tips graze the rocks to port. Leave the high seas to others!' But Menoetes, fearing hidden rocks, swung his prow towards the open sea. With another shout Gyas again strove to call him back: 'Menoetes! Where are you going, right off course? Steer for those rocks!' Then he looked behind and saw Cloanthus pressing on his stern and in the inside position. Cloanthus was risking a course to port inside Gyas' ship and shaving the roaring rocks. He passed the leader and went ahead, left the turning-post behind him and rode on in safe waters. At that, the anger of Gyas blazed forth in violence, as if out of his very bones. There were tears on his cheeks. With no thought of his own honour or his crew's safety, he thrust the too cautious Menoetes headlong from the poop's height into the sea. Then he moved over to the tiller; he would steer the ship himself and keep full control. So he cheered on his men, swung his helm, and steered close to the rock. Meanwhile Menoetes, moving heavily, for he was no longer young and was water-logged in his sodden clothes, at last managed to reach the surface from the depths, climbed up onto the rock, and sank back on dry land. The Trojans had laughed at him as he fell and again as he swam, and they laughed at him yet again as he choked the salt waters from his chest.

And now hope was joyously reawakened in the last two competitors, Sergestus and Mnestheus, who since Gyas had encountered this delay, saw a chance of passing him. Sergestus took the open sea-room first, in front of Mnestheus, and drew near the rock. However, he was leading not by a whole keel's length but by a part only, for the Pristis pressed him, moving alongside in keen competition. Meanwhile Mnestheus walked down his ship among the crew, encouraging them: 'Rise to the oars! In! Out! You who were once the comrades of Hector! You whom I chose to be mine at Troy's last fated hour! Show us now the strength and spirit which you showed in past perils, in the Gulf of African Syrtes, on the Ionian Sea, and amid Malea's vengeful waves. I am not aiming at first place now. I, Mnestheus, am not striving for complete victory; and yet, I wish...! But, Neptune, let those on whom your choice falls be the winners, whoever they are. Only may we be ashamed at the very thought of coming in last! Men, achieve just so much of victory and prevent that terrible reproach!' The crew bent to it with supreme efforts. The bronze-plated ship quivered under their powerful strokes. The sea slipped past from under them. Sharp panting convulsed their limbs and parched mouths; sweat flowed in streams from them all.

A mere accident brought the brave crew the honour for which they longed. For Sergestus, wild with excitement, forced his bow close up to the rocks on the inside of Mnestheus, and forging on with insufficient sea-room by ill luck ran aground on a jutting reef. The rock-crag shuddered. Oars, strained against the sharp edges, snapped noisily; the prow, driven ashore, hung poised. At this check the crew leapt up and shouted loudly. Then they unshipped iron-headed poles and sharp-pointed boat-hooks and rescued broken oars in the water. But Mnestheus was now exultant and all the more energetic for the improvement in his position. He made for the home waters ahead, with his oars pulling in rapid rhythm, and also with winds now behind him in answer to his prayer; and so he swiftly sped across open sea towards land. He came in like a dove which has been suddenly startled from some cavern where she has her nest and her beloved chicks, hidden in honeycombed lava-rock; and, flying off to the meadows in alarm, leaves her home with a noisy clap of wings in her fright; but is presently seen gliding through still air, skimming her way in clear light without any movement of her swift pinions. So sped Mnestheus with the Pristis, cutting the water on the last stage as the momentum carried the flying ship onwards. He left behind him Sergestus, struggling first on the projecting rock and then in the shoal-water, and all the time calling in vain for help and trying to find how to row with broken oars. Next he drew level with Gyas and his vast, massive Chimaera, which being deprived of her helmsman now lost her lead.

So only Cloanthus, alone and nearing the finish, was left. Mnestheus tore after him, pressing him, and straining with every ounce of strength. Now, of course, the shouting redoubled. The watchers all in high excitement urged on the pursuer and the sky rang with their outbursts. The one crew were bitterly fearing that they might not, after all, retain a glory which they had counted their own as surely as if their honour was already won, and would willingly have accepted fame at the cost of life itself. The other crew were strengthened by the taste of success, and confidence gave them power. Indeed, both crews might perhaps have shared the prize with prows finishing level, if Cloanthus had not uttered a passionate prayer, and, stretching both palms towards the ocean, called on the gods to accept his vows: 'Gods who are sovereign over the ocean, Gods on whose sea-surface I sail, if you answer my prayer I shall joyfully station at an altar on this coast a bull of glistening white for you, and I shall cast the entrails as offerings to the salt waves and pour out streams of clear wine.' Thus he prayed. And deep below the waves all the dancing band of Phorcus, all the Nereids, and maiden Panopea, heard; and old Father Portunus himself thrust onwards the moving ship with his own large hands. And so she sped to the land, swifter than the south wind, swifter than a flying arrow, and passed from sight within the spacious harbour.

So Anchises' son following the custom called all together. His herald's loud voice declared Cloanthus the victor, and Aeneas set a wreath of green bay-leaves on his brow. He then presented prizes to be distributed among the crews according to their own choice, three bullocks for each ship, wine, and the fine possession of a large-size silver talent. There were also special awards for the captains. To the winner he gave a cloak embroidered with gold and edged with a double key-pattern of Meliboean purple; and on it was woven a design showing Ganymede the young prince of leafy Mount Ida, starting the fleet stags, casting his javelins, and looking just as if he was breathless in eager pursuit; and then seized and carried aloft in hooked talons by the bird which is armour-bearer to Jupiter, and which had swooped from Mount Ida to capture him; there were the aged tutors, vainly stretching their hands towards the sky, and watch-dogs too, barking after the prince and spending their fury on the air. Then Aeneas presented to the next in order, who by his prowess held second place, a cuirass of smoothly hooking links and three-leashed gold. This he had stripped off Demoleos when he had vanquished him beside the swift Simois beneath tall Ilium, and he gave it now to a warrior to wear as his pride and his protection in battle. His two retainers, Phegeus and Sagaris, scarcely managed to carry that many-ply cuirass on straining shoulders; yet once Demoleos had run while wearing it, as he pursued Trojans in straggling flight. For the third prize, Aeneas presented a pair of bronze cauldrons and two bowls fashioned all in silver with figures in high relief.

They had all received their presentations and were moving off with scarlet ribbons on their brows in exultation at their rich prizes, when, having barely, and with much ingenuity, extricated himself from the cruel rock, Sergestus, with some of his oars gone and one whole tier out of action, brought his ship in with no acclaim but only mockery. She was like a snake, caught as they often are on the bank beside a road, either run over by a bronze wheel, or torn with a stone angrily flung by some traveller and left mangled and only half-alive; trying in vain to escape, it twists in long spasms, for in a part of itself it has life yet, and, though the rest of it, maimed by the wound, drags helplessly, and it can only writhe in knots and fold back on itself, its eyes still blaze and the hissing neck is still held high. Such was the state of the ship's oarage, and it slowed her movement; but she spread her canvas in spite of all and under full sail moved up to the harbour-mouth. And Aeneas, glad that Sergestus had saved his ship and brought his crew home, presented him with the prize which he had offered. He gave him a Cretan slave-girl, named Pholoe, clever at Minerva's tasks and nursing twin baby boys.

Having concluded this event, Aeneas the True hurried away to a place with level turf, enclosed all round by woods which grew on curving hill-slopes forming an amphitheatre for the racing-track in the valley below. Hither the prince walked with many thousands about him, and took his own seat on a platform raised in the centre of the gathering. From the platform he issued invitation and offered prizes to any one of high spirit who might possibly wish to compete in speed of foot. A number of Trojans, and with them some Sicilians, came forward from every part of the ground. Among the first were Nisus and Euryalus; Euryalus was very young, fresh, and strikingly handsome, and Nisus was selflessly devoted to his young friend. Next after them came Diores, sprung from the blood royal of Priam's exalted line, and after him Salius an Acarnanian and Patron, an Arcadian from Tegea's stock. Then came two Sicilians from woodland homes, Helymus and Panopes, young comrades of the old Acestes; and many others besides, whose shadowy names are no longer remembered. Standing in their midst, Aeneas now addressed them: 'Listen attentively to my words, which will please and interest you. Of all your number not one will depart without some gift from me. I shall present to each of you, to keep for your own, two shining Cretan arrow-heads of polished iron and a double-axe of chased silver; these rewards shall be the same for all. The first three to finish will in addition have their brows wreathed with the pale olive, and will be given special prizes. He who comes first is to have, as winner, a horse with splendid trappings, the second is to receive a quiver won from the Amazons and full of Thracian arrows, with a broad belt of gold, buckled and fastened by a clasp made of a polished gem, from which it is slung; and the third will depart the happy owner of this Argive helmet.'

When he had finished speaking the runners took their places. At the sound of the signal they were off, leaving the starting-line and tearing over the course. They looked like a cloud as they streamed forward. Each fixed his eyes on the point where he would finish. From the start Nisus quickly took the leading place, flashing ahead far in front of all the rest, swifter than the winds, swifter than a thunderbolt's wings. Next to him, but at a long interval, Salius pursued; and, after an intervening space, Euryalus ran third. After Euryalus came Helymus; and, close behind, sped Diores, always with a foot grazing the heel of Helymus and a shoulder thrusting forward towards him. If the course ahead of him had been longer, he would have slipped ahead and passed him, robbing him of a victory which he thought certain. And now they were almost at the end of the race and nearing the winning post, and were just about to reach home, exhausted, when the unfortunate Nisus slid on some slippery blood which as it happened had spilt on the ground where some bullocks had been sacrificed, wetting the surface of the green turf. Here the young runner, who was already triumphant in his confidence of victory, pressed a foot on the treacherous soil, failed to keep a foothold, tottered, and fell face-downwards in the mixture of mud and dirt and sanctified blood.

But, even at such a moment as that, Nisus was not one to forget Euryalus and their friendship. He raised himself up on the slippery patch directly in Salius' way. Salius fell with a somersault to find himself lying on the caked sand. Euryalus flashed ahead. He was now, thanks to his friend's kind action, in the lead, and indeed the winner, for he flew home to the accompaniment of loud applause and admiration. Helymus came in close after him, and then, for the third prize, Diores. At this Salius shouted his protests to the elders in the front rows and all who were sitting in the vast amphitheatre, insisting that he had been robbed of his honour by a foul, and must have it back. But the claim of Euryalus was supported by the sympathy which he evoked with his appealing tears and his manly strength just beginning to flower and the more attractive because of his beauty. Diores helped too by making a loud counter-claim on his own behalf. As it was he had qualified for a prize, but, if the honour of first place were bestowed on Salius, he would lose his place as the last on the list of prize-winners. So Aeneas, as president of the games, said to them: 'Young friends, the presentations due to you remain securely yours. No one can disturb the order of the prize-list. But I may be allowed to show my sympathy to a friend in a misfortune which he did nothing to deserve.' With these words he gave Salius a gigantic African lion's skin, weighed down by its shaggy mane and gold-plated claws. At this Nisus asked: 'If you are so sympathetic to runners who fall, and if an unsuccessful entrant receives so handsome a prize, what will you give to me in fair recognition of my deserts? For I, so far as merit went, earned the winner's wreath, except that I was involved in the same bad luck as Salius.' As he said this he showed them the mud which had soiled his face, legs, and arms. Their good and kindly chieftain smiled at him and sent for a shield, of Didymaon's craftsmanship, which Greeks had once taken down from Neptune's hallowed lintel. He presented this choice gift to the noble young athlete.

The racing was now finished and the prize-giving completed. Aeneas next said, 'Now let anyone who has a valorous heart and a quick resource come forward, ready to box with fists gloved in hide.' As he spoke he set out a pair of awards for boxing: for the victor a bullock arrayed in head-ribbons and with gold-plated horns, and a sword and a splendid helmet to console the vanquished. There was no waiting. The monstrously strong Dares immediately looked up and amid much murmuring rose to his feet. Dares, and Dares alone, had always had the courage to face Paris in fight; and, by the barrow of peerless Hector, he had shattered the victorious giant Butes, who claimed descent from Bebrycian Amycus, and stretched him, dying, on the yellow sand. Such was the Dares who now raised his towering head for a first bout, displayed his broad shoulders, and sparred with his right and his left, lashing the air with his blows. All that was now wanted was an antagonist. But not one of all that great host dared to tie boxing-leathers on his hands and come within Dares' reach. Dares therefore, supposing that no one now meant to enter for the prize, walked jauntily up to Aeneas, stood in front of the platform, and with no further delay seized the bullock's horn with his left hand, saying, 'Son of the Goddess, since no one ventures to face the risk of battle, how long have I to stand here? What is the proper time for me to be kept waiting? Tell me, then, to lead the prize away.'

All the Dardanids shouted at once, demanding that the offered prize should be duly given him. At this the grave Acestes spoke reproachfully to Entellus, who was sitting nearest to him on a bank of luxuriant green turf: 'Entellus, was it for nothing that you were once the most valiant of heroes? Will you patiently allow this splendid prize to be taken from your grasp without a fight? What of Eryx? Will anyone believe our boast that he was our divine teacher? And what of your own fame which is spread over all Sicily, and the prizes hanging in your house?' To this Entellus at once replied: 'Neither my love of glory nor my honour has failed. Fear has not crushed my pride. My age is the reason. Age has made my movement slow, my blood is without warmth and fire, and my bodily strength is spent and cold. If I had again that youth which once was mine, and which your shameless braggart there still has, and trusts so exultantly, I should never have needed the bribe of a noble bullock to make me come forward, not I; I care not for prizes.' With these words of explanation he immediately flung on the ground a monstrously heavy pair of boxing-leathers which Eryx himself had always used, binding his arms with their tough hide whenever he set his hand to boxing.

All were astounded, so huge must have been those seven oxen whose immense skins they now saw, stiff with the lead and iron sewn into them. But Dares himself was the most impressed. He stood aghast, and then shrinking back declined the bout. Anchises' heroic-hearted son was trying the weight of the leathers and handling, this way and that, the endless coiling thongs. Then with great emotion the elder champion spoke to Aeneas: 'Ah, but imagine yourself seeing the actual boxing-leathers used by Hercules, and indeed the grim fight which he fought, here on this very shore! And it was your own brother Eryx who once wore these thongs which you see here before you, still stained with blood and fragments of brain. With them Eryx stood and faced the mighty Alcides; and I had them in my own regular use as long as my blood, richer than it is now, gave me strength, and before old age jealously sprinkled both temples with grey. If however you, Dares of Troy, cannot face these my weapons, and if Aeneas the True, with the approval of my supporter Acestes, so decides, let us make the terms of our contest equal. You need not face the hide which Eryx used. So calm your fears. And you shall take your Trojan leathers off your hands.'

So saying he flung back from his shoulders his double-folded cloak, and bared the great joints of his limbs and his thick-boned legs and arms. Gigantic, he took his stand in the centre of the ring. At this Anchises' son, presiding, held high two matching pairs of boxing-leathers, and next entwined the hands of both contestants with these weapons of equal weight. Each at once took position, alert, on tip-toe with eagerness, undismayed, and with arms raised in the air. Holding their heads high and well out of the reach of blows, they began to spar in interplay of fist with fist, warming to the fight. Dares could rely on his youth, and his foot-work was better. Entellus had the strength of his limbs and his massive bulk, but his knees were slow-moving and unsteady; he shook, and a painful panting convulsed his vast frame. Often the boxers would strike dangerous blows at each other but miss; often a punch would smack against the hollow of a flank or land on a chest with a loud thump. Hands flickered fast round ears and forehead. Crack! sounded a jaw under a violent stroke. Entellus stood solidly, never moving but keeping his weight on the same spot, merely swaying and using his watchful eyes to evade the blows. Dares was like a general who, when attacking some tall city with assault-ramps, or remaining under arms to beleaguer a mountain-fortress, tries one approach after another, expertly exploring the whole position, and pressing and always varying his attack, but all to no purpose.

But now Entellus, rising to strike, lifted his right arm high and thrust it out. Dares, who was quick, saw the threat from above him, swayed rapidly, sidestepped nimbly and drew away from the punch. Entellus wasted his strength on the air and fell, without even having been struck, to earth, a heavy man heavily falling by his own immense weight, as sometimes on Erymanthus or mighty Ida a hollow pine, torn up by its roots, will fall. The Trojans and the youth of Sicily too leapt to their feet in their enthusiasm and the shouting rose to the sky. Acestes was the first to move. He hurried up, and in spite of his own age he lifted his friend, in pity, from the ground. Yet the heroic Entellus, as active and as fearless as ever in spite of his fall, returned to the fight all the fiercer, with a new force kindled by rage. His shame, together with his confidence in his own valour, set his strength on fire. Blazing with fury the giant pursued Dares in headlong flight all over the field, redoubling his strokes now with his right and now with his left. There was no pause, no respite. The heroic Entellus battered Dares and sent him spinning. With both hands he showered volleys of blows, thick as the hailstones which storm-clouds send rattling on the roofs. But at last their chieftain Aeneas put an end to his fury. Having decided that Entellus must cease this show of vindictive savagery he stopped the fight and rescued the exhausted Dares, soothing him with kind words: 'Poor Dares, why did you allow this insanity to possess you? Could you not understand that this is strength of a different order and that the Powers have turned against you? You must submit to the divine will.' Thus he spoke, and by his command parted the fighters. Faithful comrades conducted Dares to the ships, dragging his knees in pain, with his head lolling from side to side, and continually spitting out of his mouth thick gore and teeth amid the blood. Others, summoned to come forward in his place, received the helmet and sword on his behalf, leaving to Entellus the palm-leaves and the bullock.

At this the victor, in exuberant arrogance of spirit at having won the beast, said: 'Son of the Goddess and all you other Trojans, you are now to learn what strength I must have had in me when I was young, and what was the manner of death from which Dares, whom you now have safe among you, was reprieved.' With these words he took his stand right in front of the bullock which was waiting near at hand to be bestowed as the prize for boxing. He drew back his right arm, he poised the hard boxing-leather aiming immediately between its horns, and he raised himself high for the blow. Then he smashed the leather into the skull, bursting the brains out.

The ox was felled; it collapsed, quivering but lifeless, on the ground. Entellus added an eloquent prayer from the heart: 'Eryx, I pay to you, in place of the life of Dares, a nobler spirit. After this victory I lay down the leathers, and lay aside my skill.'

Aeneas forthwith invited any who wished to compete with the swift flight of the arrow. He named the prizes; and then with his hands' great strength he erected a mast borrowed from the ship of Serestus, and to it he attached a fluttering dove by a cord passed through the mast-head, as a target for their arrow-points. Competitors assembled and dropped their lots into a bronze helmet held ready to receive them. The first to leap out, before any of the others, was the lot of Hippocoon, Hyrtacus' son. There were cheers of approval. Mnestheus, who had lately been successful in the ship-race and still wore the green olive round his forehead, came next. Third came Eurytion; he was the brother of the illustrious Pandarus, the Pandarus who years before, when commanded to wreck the famous truce, had been the first to strike, speeding an arrow into the thick of the Greeks. Acestes himself, manfully venturing on a trial more fitted for youth, came last, for his lot lay at the bottom of the helmet. So now the competitors, each using all the tough strength at his command, took arrows from quivers and bent their bows into a curve. The young Hippocoon's bowstring gave its sharp twang first and his arrow cut the air swiftly asunder as it flew across the sky. It went straight to the mast, struck it, and remained fixed in the timber. The mast quivered and the bird was frightened and fluttered in its alarm; and loud was the cheering on every side. After Hippocoon, Mnestheus eagerly took his stand, aiming upwards with bow drawn back, and eyes and arrow straining along the same line. But luck failed him and he did not succeed in hitting the bird herself with the iron arrow-head, though he cut the knotted linen-bond with which the foot of the tethered dove had been tied to the masthead; and she flew in haste away into dark clouds towards the quarter of the south wind. But now Eurytion, who had long been standing with his bow held ready and an arrow presented, prayed to his brother to hear him; and all in a flash he took aim at the dove which was now flying happily with beating wings in a free sky, and pierced her as she flew, outlined against a dark cloud. She dropped, dead, leaving her life in the high air amid the stars and in her fall bringing home again the arrow which had pierced her through.

Only Acestes now remained, and he had already lost the palm. Yet none the less he aimed an arrow high into the air, proving that an elder might have skill yet, and could make a strong bow twang. And then a sudden miracle, destined to prove of terrible presage, was presented to their eyes; as afterwards the momentous outcome of it revealed, though when the prophets gave their alarming interpretation of this sign their warning came too late. For the reed shaft of Acestes, as it flew amid floating clouds, caught fire; it marked its trail with flames, burned away, and vanished into airy winds, like the shooting stars which often become detached from the sky and dart across it, drawing their tresses after them. Awe-struck, the men of Sicily and of Troy stood rooted and sent up a prayer to the holy gods. But their exalted prince Aeneas accepted the omen. He embraced Acestes, who was himself delighted at the sign, and lavished on him fine prizes, saying: 'Take them, Father. For the supreme Olympian King had surely ordained, when he sent this potent sign, that you must carry away especial honours. Here is a gift for you which belonged to the aged Anchises himself. It is a bowl for mixing wine, with engraved figures, given to my father long since by Cisseus of Thrace as a right generous gift to take to his home, in remembrance of the giver and for a pledge of his affection.' As he spoke the words he wreathed Acestes' brow with green bay-leaves and declared him the winner of the first prize and vanquisher of all the rest. The good-hearted Eurytion, although he was the only competitor who had hit the dove and had brought her down from the high heavens, was yet not at all envious of the preference in honour shown to another. The next to step forward for his prize was he who had broken the cord, and the last, he who had pierced the mast with his winged reed.

Now before the dispersal at the end of this competition, Aeneas, as President, had called Epytides to him. Epytides was tutor to the boy Iulus, and his close friend. Aeneas whispered into his ear: 'Please,' said he, 'go along now, and, if Ascanius has ready with him his regiment of boys and has prepared the horses for the Ride, tell him that he should now parade his squadrons in honour of his grandfather, and appear before us in arms.'

Aeneas then commanded all the spectators who were crowding the arena to leave it, explaining that the whole ground must now be kept clear. Then, in straight ranks before their fathers' gaze, the boys advanced glittering on bridled chargers, and as they passed were greeted with loud and admiring applause from the manhood of both Sicily and Troy. All the boys wore their hair bound in traditional style by a clipped wreath. Each carried two cornel-wood spearshafts headed with iron, and some also wore polished quivers, slung from their shoulders. Pliant circlets of twisted gold passed round their necks and over their chests. There were three mounted troops and three troop-leaders in the evolutions; and two sections of six boys followed each leader, for so was the regiment divided in equal commands; and all were shining-bright. One band of the young cavaliers was led in proud progress by a little Priam, the illustrious son of Polites, whose name recalled his grandfather and who was destined to give new strength to the men of Italy. He rode a piebald Thracian horse whose fore-pasterns as he trod showed all white and whose head, held high, displayed a white forehead. The second leader was Atys, from whom the Latin Atii trace their descent, a small boy, loved by Iulus with a boy's affection. And last, fair to see above all others, came Iulus himself, mounted on a horse from Sidon which Dido in sweet simplicity had given to him for a remembrance of the giver and a pledge of her love. The other young riders all rode Sicilian horses belonging to Acestes of Sicily, their elder friend. The Trojans welcomed the boys with applause, which they nervously accepted, and found great pleasure in looking at them and seeing the likeness to their forbears in their features.

The riders now moved in gay procession past the whole seated gathering in full view of their kindred. Next, Epytides in a carrying voice shouted a long command to the parade and cracked his whip. They were ready. They first galloped apart in equal detachments, then in half-sections of three broke ranks and deployed their band as in a dance; and then, at another order, they turned about and charged with lances couched. Next they entered upon other figures too, and reversed these figures, with rank facing rank across a space between; and they rode right and left in intertwining circles. And they began a pretence of armed battle, sometimes exposing their backs in flight and sometimes turning their spear-points for attack. Then they made peace again and rode along in an even line. They say that once upon a time the Labyrinth in mountainous Crete contained a path, twining between walls which barred the view, with a treacherous uncertainty in its thousand ways, so that its baffling plan, which none might master and none retrace, would foil the trail of any guiding clues. By just such a course the sons of the Trojans knotted their paths, weaving in play their fleeing and their fighting, like dolphins that swim through the salt sea-water, cutting the Carpathian or African straits and playing as they cross the waves. Much later, when he was girding Alba Longa with her walls, Ascanius inaugurated a revival of this Trojan Ride with its mock-battle, and taught the early Latins to celebrate it just as he had celebrated it in his youth with the other Trojan boys. The Albans taught it to their sons. From them, by succession, Rome in her grandeur inherited it and preserved the ancestral rite. And to this day the boys are called 'A Troy' and their regiment 'Trojan'.

Here ended the Games held in honour of Aeneas' sainted father.

It was at this moment that fortune first veered, and turned treacherously against the Trojans. While they were paying due rites to the barrow in the various games, Juno, Saturn's Daughter, sent Iris down from the sky to the Trojan fleet, giving to her a breath of wind to aid her going; for her old resentment was not sated yet, and she had many plans in view.

The maiden Iris hurried on her way, along her rainbow with its thousand colours, and observed by none flew down her swift path. At the sight of the vast gathering she passed along the shore, noticing that the harbour was deserted and the fleet left unguarded. But some way off, on a lonely beach, were Trojan ladies sitting apart and weeping for the lost Anchises, and through their tears they looked out over the ocean deeps. How tired they were; grim was the thought of still more sea-passages, awaiting them across that vast expanse. They were all weary of suffering the worst that ocean could do to them and were one in their appeal for a city of their own. So Iris, an experienced mischief-maker, darted into their midst. Laying aside the aspect and garments of a goddess, she became Beroe, the aged wife of Tmarian Doryclus, a lady of an illustrious house, who had once had sons, and a famous name. In this guise Iris joined the group of Trojan mothers, and spoke: 'It is sad for you that no Greek hand dragged you to death in war under the tall battlements of your home! A nation invariably unlucky! I wonder how fortune means eventually to destroy you. It is now the close of the seventh summer since Troy's overthrow and all this time we have been travelling on our long journey, swept onwards over the sea-ways from land to land, past every frowning rock and under every star, tossed at the mercy of the rolling waves, in quest of an Italy which ever recedes. But here we have the territory of Eryx, a brother's land, and Acestes as our host. Why not lay foundations here, and let the citizens, who are ready waiting for it, have their city? O Fatherland, Gods of our Homes rescued in vain from the foe, will "Troy Walls" henceforward signify nothing? Shall I never again in any place see rivers called Xanthus and Simois, to remind me of Hector? Rather than that, come! Help me to burn the ships which bring us our ill luck. For I have dreamed in sleep that Cassandra's ghost handed blazing brands to me, and said, "Look here for your Troy; here is a home for you." Now is the time to act, for so momentous a presage cannot be contradicted. See, there! Four altars to Neptune! Neptune himself furnishes us with burning brands, and courage too.' Saying this she took the lead; fiercely she snatched a menacing flame, and, straining, swung her right hand high, brandished the torch, and flung it.

The Ilian ladies were startled and aghast. But now the eldest of their number, Pyrgo, who had been the royal nurse to all Priam's sons, cried: 'Mothers, you have no Beroe here, no lady of Rhoeteum, no widow of Doryclus. Observe those marks of divine beauty, those burning eyes; her commanding mien, her countenance, her walk, her voice's tone! Why, I myself parted from Beroe not long ago; I left her ill, and bitter at the thought that she alone was missing the rich and splendid ceremonial, and could not take her share in paying due honour to Anchises.' So Pyrgo spoke out. At first the ladies were in doubt; and they were still looking at the ships uncertainly with jealous eyes, torn between their pathetic desire to remain where they were, on the land, and the call of the empire to be, when the goddess soared through the sky on poised wings and cut a giant rainbow as she sped outlined against the clouds. Her departure intensified the shock already caused by the mysterious occurrence. Madness seized them. Screaming, they seized fire from indoor hearths, and some of them pillaged altars for flames and cast leaves, brushwood, and burning brands. The Fire-God rioted unchecked along benches and oars and sterns of painted fir-wood.

It was Eumelus who brought the news that the ships were on fire to the barrow of Anchises and the amphitheatre where the onlookers sat in their rows. Even there they could see for themselves the floating cloud of pitch-black ashes and smoke. Ascanius himself, who was still happily leading his trotting cavalry, now, without giving his breathless guardians a chance to restrain him, galloped excitedly to the naval camp, which was already in a turmoil. He shouted, 'Oh, why this sudden fit of madness? You poor ladies of Troy, whatever can you be meaning to do? It is no enemy, no hostile Greek camp that you are burning, but your own hopes for the future. Look, it is I, your Ascanius!' And he flung his empty helmet down at his feet – the same helmet that he had worn when he was acting in play the pretence of warfare. And at that moment Aeneas too came up in haste, his Trojans marching with him. In fear the ladies scattered here and there about the shore, furtively making for the woods and any rock caves which they might find. They were already disgusted at what they had done and ashamed to be seen in the light of day. They were now themselves again, and knew who were truly their friends, for Juno's power was expelled from their hearts.

But this did not make the blazing conflagration relax its indomitable power, for within the moist timbers the caulking was now alive and vomited a heavy smoke; the lazy heat devoured the keels, and the peril crept in, seeping through to all the hulls; and all their heroic efforts, and the rivers of water which they poured, were of no avail. Then Aeneas the True rent the garment off his shoulders, stretched forth the palms of his hands, and called on the gods for aid: 'Jupiter Almighty, if you do not yet look on every Trojan with hatred, and if your loving-kindness, shown of old, can still take note of humanity's suffering, permit our fleet, even now, to escape the flames, O Father, and wrest Troy's slender hope from death. Else, if I so deserve, cast the remnant left of us down to death by your own angry bolt; overwhelm me, by your own hand, here.' Scarcely had he said his prayer when rain poured down; a blackening tempest raged unchecked; and at the thundering of it earth's high places and her very plains began to quake. From the whole sky came the downpour, a drenching murk, black and dense before the southerly winds. The ships were soon full of water from above and the charred timbers were soaked till all the heat was quenched, and all the vessels, with a loss of only four, were saved from destruction.

Even then Aeneas, Chieftain of Troy, shaken by the bitter blow, pondered his heavy responsibilities, turning over the alternatives and looking at them from every point of view; he wondered whether he should forget his destiny and settle in Sicilian lands, or strike out for the coast of Italy. But at this very moment old Nautes gave him reassurance. None but Nautes had ever been taught prophecy by Tritonian Pallas; and she made him famous for his great skill, since on any occasion when grave signs of Heaven's wrath appeared, his answer was ready, and he could explain what they foreshadowed and what sequence of future events had been fixed by Destiny. Nautes now began to speak to Aeneas: 'Son of the Goddess, we should accept the lead which Destiny offers us, whether to go forward or no, and choose our way accordingly. Whatever is to befall, it is always our own power of endurance which must give us control over our fortune. You have Acestes, a Dardan, and of divine descent. Take him into your confidence, as he would himself wish, and make your plans in partnership with him. Entrust to his care all those of us whose ships are lost and all who are wearied beyond recovery by our great enterprise and the strain of your vocation. Choose all who are of advanced age, mothers who are exhausted by the voyaging, and any in your company who may be frail and fearful of risk. Allow the weary to own a walled city here in Sicily, and if Acestes agrees to the use of his name, they shall call the city Acesta.'

Such was the advice from his older friend. But the proposals set his thoughts on fire, and as never before were they distracted by every kind of anxiety. And now black Night had driven high in the heavens on her chariot and occupied the vault of sky. Then straightway, down from that sky came the shape of Aeneas' own father, Anchises, appearing suddenly and seeming to speak to him: 'Son, dearer once than life itself to me, as long as life was mine, Son, who bear the heavy burden of Troy's destiny, I come here by command of Jupiter who drove the fire back from the fleet and from high heaven has had compassion on you at last. Obey the excellent counsel which old Nautes has just given you; it is the noblest way. Convey to your destination in Italy an elect band, the most valiant-hearted of your manhood. When you come to Latium you will have to defeat in war a hardy nation, wild in its ways. But before that you must take your path to Pluto's infernal world, traverse the deep Avernus, and there, my son, seek a meeting with me. For I am confined in no cruel Hell and in no shades of gloom, but instead I dwell in Elysium among the happy gatherings of the True. A holy Sibyl shall guide you there after much blood has flowed from black beasts in sacrifice; and you shall learn then all your future descendants and what manner of walled city is granted to you. And now good-bye. Night with her damp mists is swinging round beyond the half-way of her course; the sun is rising and I can feel the fierce touch of his panting horses' breath.' He finished; and he fled, as smoke flees, into airy wind. Aeneas cried: 'Where do you go in this haste, so soon? Where dart away? Whom are you hurrying to escape? And who denies you to my embrace?' As he spoke he stirred the sleeping ashes till their fires awoke, and paid reverence in prayer to the God of the Homes in Troy's citadel, and to the inner shrine of Vesta the silver-haired, offering in piety salt grain and a filled censer.

Then, immediately, he summoned his comrades, Acestes first. He expounded to them Jupiter's command, his dear father's instructions, and the decision which he had reached in his own mind. There was no opposition to the plan, and Acestes accepted the command which Aeneas gave him. They transferred the older ladies to the new city and in it settled those among the company who so desired, hearts that felt no need for high renown. The remainder repaired rowing-benches, replaced in the hulls timbers which flames had charred, and refitted oars and tackle; they were few in number, but of vital valour for war. Meanwhile Aeneas ploughed a furrow to mark the city's circuit and allotted homes within it. He ordained that in one place there should be an 'Ilium' and in another a 'Troy'. Trojan Acestes, who welcomed the thought of this kingdom, designated a place of assembly, appointed his council, and prescribed their code. Next, on the crest of Eryx and high towards the stars, they founded a home for Idalian Venus; and they adjoined to it a grove, a broad tract of sanctity, with a priest appointed for Anchises' Tomb.

And now, when the whole allied company had feasted for nine days, and honours had been paid to the altars, kindly winds having smoothed the seas, a lively breeze from the south began to blow, inviting them out onto the deep once more. Loud was the weeping along the winding foreshore; all day and all night they clung together, lingering and embracing one another; even the mothers, and men who had lately thought the aspect of the sea too wild and its power too dreadful to face, now wished to go and endure every utmost ordeal on the path of exile. Aeneas spoke gently to them in friendliness and consolation, commending them with tears to their kinsman Acestes. Then he ordered a sacrifice of three calves to Eryx and to the Storms a lamb; and, now that the time had come, he gave the order to cast off the moorings. And he took his stand in front of them all high on his ship's stern, his head wreathed with trimmed olive-leaves and his offering-bowl in his hand; and he cast the meat into the salt waves and poured translucent wine. A wind arose astern and went with them on their way. His comrades swept the sea-surface, striking it in rivalry.

But meanwhile Venus, tormented by anxiety, was in talk with Neptune and releasing a torrent of complaint straight from her heart: 'O Neptune, Juno's oppressive anger and her insatiable will are forcing me to employ every resource and to use every entreaty, however humble. No lapse of time, and no honour duly paid to her, can mollify her. Neither the Fates nor Jupiter's own command can break her opposition. She never rests. It is not enough for her that she has devoured Troy from out the heart of Phrygia by her acts of wicked hate and dragged her through successive punishments of every kind. No, for she persecutes even the remnant left after the death of Troy – Troy's very ashes and bones. Only she can know why her fury is so insane; but you yourself are my witness for the mighty force which she lately aroused so suddenly in those African waves. She confounded all the seas and the whole sky together, daring to intervene within your realm, though her reliance on the winds of Aeolus proved vain. And now she has even started our Trojan mothers on a path of crime, and foully gutted our vessels, so that we have been forced to leave those of our comrades, whose ships have been lost, in a strange land. But, I pray you, if I do not go too far in making such a request, and if the Fates are not to deny us our walled city, consent to allow the remnant to sail safely over your waves for the rest of their voyage and reach Laurentine Tiber.'

Then Saturn's son, master over the ocean deeps, answered her: 'It is indeed right, Cytherean, that you should trust my realm of sea, from which you draw your own origin. And further I myself have earned your trust, for often have I subdued those wild, mad onsets from sea and sky. Nor has my care for your Aeneas on land been any less. I call Xanthus and Simois to witness for me. When Achilles, who was pursuing rank on rank of breathless Trojans, ramming them close up against their wall and casting them down to death in their thousands, so that the rivers were congested and groaned, and Xanthus could find no course to roll on his way to the sea, then did I rescue Aeneas, who had faced Peleus' valiant son but was unfairly matched with him both in strength and in divine aid, by wrapping him in a cloak of mist; I rescued him even though Troy was a city forsworn, and I myself desired to overthrow her walls, which my own hands had built, from their very foundations. I remain constant and of this mind still. Therefore dispel your fear. Aeneas shall reach the harbour by Avernus which you have chosen as his destination, and you will mourn one Trojan only lost at sea, one life given to the depths for many.' By these reassurances he calmed the goddess's thoughts and gave her happiness. Then Father Neptune yoked his fiery horses with harness of gold, inserted the bits in their foaming mouths, and let all the reins flow freely through his hands. Lightly over the surface in the sea-blue chariot he flew. The waves subsided, the expanse of heaving waters was laid smooth below the thundering axle, and the stormclouds fled from the wilderness of sky. And his retinue in their many shapes were there, monstrous sea-beasts, the aged troop of Glaucus, Palaemon Ino's son, swift Tritons and all the host of Phorcus, Thetis on the left, and Melite, the maid Panopea, Nesaea, Spio, Thalia, and Cymodoce.

So now there was no suspense, but only a sweet joyfulness thrilling through the heart of Aeneas the Chieftain. He commanded every mast to be erected quickly and yard-arms to be spread with sails. Together they made sheets fast and in unison let out their canvas now on the port and now on the starboard side; and together they swung, and swung about, the yards aloft. And airs which were perfect for their need bore their fleet along.

Out in front of all the others Palinurus led the close convoy and gave it its direction, for the rest had been ordered to set their course by him. By now Night with her moist air had nearly reached her point of turning in the sky, and the crews, who lay stretched on their hard seats beneath their oars, were relaxed in sweet repose, when the God of Sleep, slipping lightly down from heaven's stars, parted the misty dark and dispelled the shadows. And Palinurus, to you he went, though you had no sin, and he came carrying to you a sombre dream. Disguised as Phorbas, he took his seat high on the stern, and softly flowed his words: 'Son of Iasus, Palinurus, the sea bears the fleet onwards without your aid, full square comes the breath of the breeze and the time for rest has come. Lay your head down; steal from their toil those tired eyes. Just for a little time let me take over your duties from you.' Scarcely raising his eyes, Palinurus answered him: 'Do you ask me, of all men, to be misled by the countenance of the salt sea's calm and of waves at rest? Would you have me put faith in such a demon? For see, am I, who have been deluded so often by a clear sky's treachery, to entrust Aeneas to deceitful winds?' So he spoke, and, clinging fast to the tiller, he never for a moment released his hold, and kept his gaze fixed on the stars above. But suddenly the god took a branch, dripping with Lethe's dew and drowsy from the force of death's river. And he shook it above both temples of Palinurus, and, resist as he would, released his swimming eyes. Scarcely had the unwanted repose begun to creep along his members and relax them, when Sleep bowed over him and flung him overboard into the transparent waves, still holding the tiller and also a part of the stern, which he had wrenched away with it; and he fell headlong, calling again and again on his friends in vain. The god soared lightly on his wings and he flew up into the air. And the fleet ran safely on, just as before, forging ahead with no fear, for so Father Neptune had promised. Soon it had sailed on so far that it was drawing close to the Sirens' Rocks which once were hard to pass and whitened by the bones of many men. Far out were heard the growl and roar of the stones where the salt surf beat unceasingly. Here the Chieftain discovered that his ship was wallowing adrift, for her steersman was lost. Therefore he steered her himself through the midnight waves with many a sigh, for he was deeply shocked by the disaster to his friend: 'Ah, Palinurus, you were too trustful of the calm sky and sea. So you will lie, a shroudless form, on an unknown strand.'

BOOK SIX

THE VISIT TO THE UNDERWORLD

So spoke Aeneas, weeping. Then he gave his fleet the rein and at last came smoothly to Euboean Cumae's coast. They turned their prows to face the sea; soon anchors were making the ships secure by the grip of their teeth and the rounded sterns fringed the beach. A party of young Trojans eagerly darted ashore onto the Western Land. Some searched for the seeds of flame which lie embedded in the veins of flint. Others penetrated the forests and raided the tangled shelters of the wild creatures, signalling when they found a water-stream. But Aeneas the True made his way to the fastness where Apollo rules enthroned on high, and to the vast cavern beyond, which is the awful Sibyl's own secluded place; here the prophetic Delian God breathes into her the spirit's visionary might, revealing things to come. They were already drawing near to Diana's Wood, and to the golden temple there.

Daedalus, for this is the story, when he was in flight from the tyranny of Minos, adventured his life in the sky on swooping wings, and glided away towards the chill north by tracks unknown. At last he hovered lightly above the Euboean stronghold. In these lands he first found refuge, and straightway he consecrated his oarage of wings to Phoebus Apollo, for whom he founded a gigantic temple. On the temple-gate he pictured the death of Androgeos, and, lower down, the Athenians obeying the ghastly command to surrender seven of their stalwart sons as annual reparation; and there was the urn from which the lots had just been drawn. The island on which Cnossos stands, rising high above the sea, balanced the scene on the other leaf of the gate. There he had depicted the Bull's brutal passion, and Pasiphae's secret union with him; and there in the midst, as a warning against wicked love, their hybrid offspring, child of two breeds, the Minotaur. Here was the Cretan building in all its elaboration, with the wandering track which might not be unravelled. But Daedalus himself, who because her love was strong had taken pity on the Princess Ariadne, guided the sightless footsteps by means of a thread and unlocked the building's treacherous, winding ways. And, O Icarus! – you too would have a prominent place in this splendid sculpture, but for the power of grief; for Daedalus had twice tried to express your fate in the goldwork, but each time his hands, a father's hands, had dropped. The Trojans would certainly have read on, scanning every message there, if Achates, who had been sent on ahead, had not just then returned, and with him Deiphobe, daughter of Glaucus and priestess of Phoebus and Diana. Deiphobe spoke to the prince: 'This is no time for such sight-seeing. Better were it now to sacrifice seven bullocks from a never-yoked herd and seven rightly chosen two-year sheep.' Thus she addressed Aeneas. With no delay the Trojans offered the commanded sacrifice. The Sibyl as priestess then invited them into the temple on the height.

There is a cleft in the flank of the Euboean Rock forming a vast cavern. A hundred mouthways and a hundred broad tunnels lead into it, and through them the Sibyl's answer comes forth in a hundred rushing streams of sound. They had reached the threshold when the maid cried: 'The time to ask your fate has come. Look, the God! The God is here!' As she spoke the words, there, before the double doors, suddenly her countenance and her colour changed and her hair fell in disarray. Her breast heaved and her bursting heart was wild and mad; she appeared taller and spoke in no mortal tones, for the God was nearer and the breath of his power was upon her. 'Aeneas, O man of Troy,' she cried, 'are you still an idle laggard at your vows and prayers? For till you pray the cavern's mighty doors will never feel the shock and yawn open.' She spoke, and then fell silent. The Trojans felt an icy shudder run down their hard spines. And passionately their king prayed from his heart: 'Phoebus, you have always pitied Troy in her grievous suffering. It was you who guided the hands of Paris when he aimed his Dardan arrow to strike

Achilles the Aeacid. It was you who led me forth to sail over all those seas which thrust against the vast continents and to force a way even to nations of the remote Massylians and lands screened by the Syrtes. Now at the last we have gained a foothold on Italy's elusive shores. From now on, let Troy's old ill-fortune pursue us no farther. And you too, all Gods and Goddesses, who were jealous of Ilium and the too brilliant grandeur of our Dardan land, may now, with no violation of divine justice, spare the nation which held the fortress of Troy. And you, most holy Prophetess, who foreknow the future, since I ask no empire which my destiny cannot rightly claim, permit my Trojans, and their vagrant deities, the Powers and Patrons of Troy tossed with us in storm, to find in Latium a home. There I shall inaugurate a temple all of marble for Apollo and Trivia with festal days called by Apollo's name; and for you yourself, benign Lady, there shall also be in my realm a noble shrine where I shall store your oracular lots, with the prophetic secrets which you communicate to my people; and I shall choose and consecrate priests for your service. Only, pray, do not commit your prophecies to leaves, for they might fly in disorder as playthings for the grasping winds; I beg of you to chant in words of your own.' He set an end to his lips' utterance.

Meanwhile the prophetess, who had not yet submitted to Apollo, ran furious riot in the cave, as if in hope of casting the God's power from her brain. Yet all the more did he torment her frantic countenance, overmastering her wild thoughts, and crushed her and shaped her to his will. So at last, of their own accord, the hundred tremendous orifices in the shrine swung open, and they carried through the air the answer which the prophetess gave: 'You who have passed safely through every peril on the sea, but have to face still graver risk on land, your Dardans shall come within Lavinium's realm – concerning that you need have no fear – but they will regret their coming. I see war and all the horrors of war. I see Tiber streaming and foaming with blood. You will find there a Simois and a Xanthus and a camp of Greeks; a new Achilles, again a goddess's son, already breathes in

Latium; Juno, the Trojans' affliction, will never be far; and meanwhile you, in helpless plight, will go humbly begging every nation and every city in Italy for aid. Again, as before, the cause of dire calamity for Trojans will be a wedding with a foreign bride from the family of a host. Yet must you not yield to affliction, but reply to it by going forth the more daringly along the way which your fortune permits you. The first path to preservation which will open before you will start, where you least expect, from a Greek city.'

Such were the words of mystery and dread which the Cumaean Sibyl spoke from her shrine; the cavern made her voice a roar as she uttered truth wrapped in obscurity. Such was Apollo's control as he shook his rein till she raved and twisted the goad which he held to her brain. As soon as the frenzy passed and the mad mouth was still, Aeneas with heroic words began to speak: 'Maid, no aspect of tribulation which is new to me or unforeseen can rise before me, for I have traced my way through all that may happen in the anticipation of my inward thought. But I make one prayer to you. Since it is said that here is the Entrance Gate of the Infernal King and near here the marsh in the darkness where Acheron's stream bends round, may I be granted this blessing, to be allowed to come within sight of my dear father face to face; may you fling wide the holy gates and explain the way to me. On these very shoulders I rescued him, passing through the flames and a thousand pursuing javelins, and saved him from the thick of the foe. He went with me on my journey from sea to sea about the world and with me endured every threat of ocean and sky, a task beyond his frail body's powers and ill-suited to a man's declining years. And he it was who charged and entreated me to visit you and stand in supplication at your gates. Lady benign, I implore you to have pity on father and son; for all things are within your power, and not without reason did Hecate appoint you to be mistress over the Forest of Avernus. If Orpheus could win back the wraith of his bride by trust in the music of his stringed Thracian lyre, if Pollux could redeem his brother by dying alternately with him, and so often passing and repassing along death's road, and if the great Theseus too, and Hercules – but what need to mention them? I also am descended from highest Jove.'

So he prayed, with his hands on the altar, and while he still prayed, the prophetess began to answer: 'Seed of the Blood Divine, man of Troy, Anchises' son, the descent to Avernus is not hard. Throughout every night and every day black Pluto's door stands wide open. But to retrace the steps and escape back to upper airs, that is the task and that is the toil. Some few, sons of gods, have been given the power because either they were loved by Jupiter in fair favour or were exalted by their own brilliant heroism above the world of men. Along the whole way stand clustering forests, and pitch-black Cocytus coils and slides all round. Yet if indeed so passionate and so strong is your heart's desire twice to float on the lake of Styx, and twice to see the dark of Hell, and if you choose to give yourself up to this mad adventure, hear what tasks must first be completed. Hiding in a tree's thick shade there is a bough, and it is golden, with both leaves and pliant stem of gold. It is dedicated as sacred to Juno of the Lower World. All the forest gives it protection, and it is enclosed by shadows within a valley of little light. Yet permission for descending to earth's hidden world is never granted to any who has not first gathered the golden-haired produce from its tree, for beautiful Proserpine has directed that this must be brought to her as her especial offering. Each time the bough is torn from its place another never fails to appear, golden like the first, and its stem grows leaves also of gold. So therefore you must lift up your eyes and seek to discern this bough, find it as it is required of you, and pick it boldly. Then, if it is indeed you whom the Fates are calling, it will come willingly and easily; if not, by no strength will you master it, nor even hack it away with a hard blade of steel. But now, furthermore, while you are lingering at my door in quest of oracles, the body of your friend – alas! though you know it not – is lying lifeless, and defiling all your fleet with the taint of death. Bring him first to the home which is his due and lay him to rest in a tomb. Lead forth black sheep, which are to be your first offering for atonement. Only if you do so shall you look on the Forests of Styx, the land which is pathless to the living.' She spoke, pressed shut her lips, and was silent.

Aeneas left the cave, walking onwards sad-faced with downcast eyes, and pondering to himself the uncertain outcome. The ever-faithful Achates walked beside him, keeping step in sympathy with him. Conversing together they exchanged many speculations, trying to guess who was the lifeless friend meant by the prophetess whose body they were to bury. And then, suddenly, they came to the spot, and they saw, where the sea had left the beach dry, lifeless and dead by an unmerited death, the Aeolid Misenus, who had been excellent beyond all others in stirring hearts with his trumpet of bronze and kindling the blaze of battle with his music. Misenus had been a comrade of illustrious Hector, and at Hector's side he would face the fray, recognized everywhere by his trumpet and his spear. Then, after Achilles had despoiled Hector of his life, this most valiant hero joined Dardan Aeneas and became his comrade, serving no lesser cause. But later he fell into utter folly. He played on a horn of hollow shell till the waves echoed, and challenged the gods themselves to compete with him in music. But Triton in jealousy entrapped his mortal rival and drowned him – if we can believe in such a deed – where the water foams among the rocks.

So all the Trojans assembled, and in loud voices raised the cry, Aeneas the True above them all. Without a moment's delay and weeping still they hastened on with the duties which the Sibyl had commanded them to perform. Their task was to pile tree-trunks for an altar-pyre, raised high towards the heavens. They penetrated into an ancient forest of tall trees where only wild animals lived, and soon spruce-trees were falling, the holm-oak rang under the strokes of the axes, ashen beams and the hard oaks good for splitting were rent apart by wedges, and they rolled down giant rowan-trees from the hills.

In all this Aeneas, carrying tools like the rest, took the lead in cheering his comrades on. But he continually gazed up into that endless forest and pondered his problem to himself, communing with his own despondent heart; and, as he pondered, he chanced to say a prayer: 'If only that "golden bough" would reveal itself to me somewhere in all this mighty forest! For the prophetess was right about you, poor Misenus; it was all only too true.' Scarcely had he said it when a pair of doves chanced to come flying from the sky directly before his very eyes, and settled on the green turf. Then did Aeneas, great hero, recognize his own mother's birds, and with joy he prayed: 'O you, be my guides if there is indeed some way! Direct your course through the air to the glade where the bough of blessings shadows a rich soil below. And, Mother Divine, fail me not at this critical time!' So he spoke, and then checked his steps, watching to see what message the birds might send and where they would next decide to go. The doves, now feeding, now flying on, went ahead just so far as the eyes of any who followed could keep them in view. They flew up to the gateway-jaws of pungent Avernus. Here they soared swiftly, skimming through the clear air, found the perch of their desire, and settled on a pair of adjacent tree-tops; and there, through the branches, shone the contrasting gleam of gold. Like the mistletoe, which, though never seeded from the tree on which it grows, encircles a round trunk with saffron-coloured berries, and is always green with young leaves amid the forest even in winter's cold, so looked the leafy gold in the shadowy holm-oak tree, and so tinkled the metal-foil in a gentle wind. Aeneas snatched it down at once. It resisted, but avidly he broke it off, and carried it to the home of the prophetic Sibyl.

Meanwhile on the shore the Trojans were weeping as bitterly as ever for Misenus as they paid the last dues to his ashes, which had no power to thank them now. Their first act was to build a vast pyre of tough sawn timber, with pine-brands added to make it blaze. Then they draped the sides with dark green leaves and erected in front of it funeral cypresses. And on it they laid the glittering arms, and graced it with their splendour. One party prepared warm water in cauldrons seething with the heat from flames, and washed and anointed the cold body of their friend. The lament was raised. And when all the tears were shed they laid the remains on a funeral couch and cast over them bright-coloured raiment, his favourite garments. Some of the Trojans bowed themselves to the sombre service of raising the great bier. Then, averting their faces according to their ancestral rite, they applied a torch to the base of the pyre and held it there. All the heaped mass blazed away, with the offerings of incense and food, and the mixing-bowls with their stream of olive-oil. . . . When at last the cinders fell in and the flame sank to rest, they washed in wine the thirsty ashes of the remains. Corynaeus collected the bones and enclosed them in an urn of bronze; he next purified his friends, carrying clean water round them thrice and sprinkling it in a spray of dew from the bough of a fertile olive-tree; and then he pronounced the last words. And, where the pyre had been, Aeneas the True built a barrow of massive size, on which he set the implements which Misenus had used, his oar and his trumpet. The barrow is at the foot of a mountain towering to the sky, which is still called Misenus after him and preserves his name eternally as the centuries pass.

This done, Aeneas hurried to discharge the Sibyl's commands. There was a deep rugged cave, stupendous and yawning wide, protected by a lake of black water and the glooming forest. Over this lake no birds could wing a straight course without harm, so poisonous the breath which streamed up from those black jaws and rose to the vault of sky; and that is why the Greeks named this placed 'Aornos, the Birdless'. Here the Priestess set in place four bullocks black of hide. That was her first act. Next she poured wine over their foreheads, clipped the bristles growing between their horns, and laid them, as the first taste of the offering, on the sacrificial fire; and as she did so she cried loud to Hecate, the mighty in Heaven and mighty in Hell. Others applied the knife to the victims' throats and caught the warm blood in bowls. Aeneas took his sword and smote a lamb with fleece black as soot in offering to the Mother of the Eumenides and her Great Sister, and a barren cow for Proserpine herself. Now he began the nocturnal altar-rite to the King of Styx. He laid whole carcasses of bulls on the flames and poured rich olive oil on the glowing entrails. And, behold, soon before the first gleam of the rising sun, the ground bellowed beneath their feet, the slopes of the forest-clad mountains began to move, and there appeared shapes like hounds howling and just visible through the shadows; the Goddess was coming and was very near. 'Stand clear!' cried the Priestess, 'all you who are unhallowed: stand clear! Be gone from all the Grove. But you, Aeneas, whip blade from scabbard and step forth on your way. It is now that you need courage and a stout heart.' Saying no more she plunged frantically down into the opened cavern, and strode onwards. With dauntless pace Aeneas followed where she led.

Gods whose dominion is over the Souls, Shades without sound, Void, and you, Burning River, and you, broad Spaces voiceless beneath the Night, may I remain sinless in telling what has been told to me, and, by your divine assent, reveal truth sunk in depths of earth and gloom.

They were walking in the darkness, with the shadows round them and night's loneliness above them, through Pluto's substanceless Empire, and past its homes where there is no life within; as men walk through a wood under a fitful moon's ungenerous light when Jupiter has hidden the sky in shade and a black night has stolen the colour from the world. In front of the very Entrance Hall, in the very Jaws of Hades, Grief and Resentful Care have laid their beds. Shapes terrible of aspect have their dwelling there, pallid Diseases, Old Age forlorn, Fear, Hunger, the Counsellor of Evil, ugly Poverty, Death, and Pain. Next is the Sleep who is close kin to Death, and Joy of Sinning and, by the threshold in front, Death's harbinger, War. And the iron chambers of the Furies are there, and Strife the insane, with a bloody ribbon binding her snaky hair.

In the centre is a giant and shady elm-tree, spreading branches like arms, full of years. False Dreams, so it is often said, take the tree for their home and cling everywhere beneath its leaves. There are besides many monstrous hybrid beasts, Centaurs stabled at the gate, Scyllas half-human, Briareus the hundredfold, Lerna's Beast with its horrifying hiss, and the

Chimaera, weaponed with flames; next Gorgons, Harpies, and the shadowy shape of the three-bodied Geryon. At sight of them Aeneas, struck by a sudden dread, drew his sword and presented its bare edge to any creature which might approach. And had not his companion, from her better knowledge, warned him that they were bodiless, airy, lives flitting behind an empty figment of a form, he would have charged, and to no purpose hacked through mere shadows with his blade.

From this place starts the road which leads to Tartarean Acheron. There in mud and murk seethes the Abyss, enormous and engulfing, choking forth all its sludge into Cocytus. Here there is a warden of the crossing, who watches over the river-water. He is the dreaded Charon: a ragged figure, filthy, repulsive, with white hair copious and unkempt covering his chin, eyes which are stark points of flame, and a dirty garment knotted and hanging from his shoulders. Charon punts his boat with his pole or trims the sails, and so he ferries every soul on his dusky coracle, for though he is old he is a god, and a god's old age is tough and green. Here all the concourse of souls was hastening to the bank, mothers and strong men, high-hearted heroes whose tasks in the body's life were done, boys, unmarried girls, and young sons laid on pyres before their parents' eyes. As numerous were they as the leaves of the forest which fall at the first chill of autumn and float down, or as the birds which flock from ocean-deeps to the shore when the cold of the year sends them in rout across the sea, and sets them free to fly to sunshine lands. The souls stood begging to be the first to make the crossing, and stretched their arms out in longing for the farther shore. But the surly boatman accepted now these and now those, and forced others back, not allowing them near the river-side.

Distressed by this commotion, Aeneas was perplexed indeed. 'Tell me, Maid,' he said, 'What is the meaning of this gathering at the river? What do the souls desire? And how is it decided who are to retreat from the bank and who are to be conveyed over the leaden passage by the sweep of oars?' The long-lived Priestess shortly answered him: 'Man sired by Anchises and of descent most surely divine, you see before you the deep pools of Cocytus and the marsh of Styx, by whose dread power the Gods bind their oaths, and dare not break them. All this multitude which you see are the resourceless, who had no burial. The warden over there is Charon, and these who are ferried over the waves are the buried. It is forbidden to convey them past the banks of dread and over the snarling current before their bones have found rest in a due burial place; instead they must roam here flitting about the river banks for a hundred years, and not until then are they accepted and find their way home to the pools which are now their heart's desire.' Anchises' son checked his steps and halted, brooding deeply, and pitying them from his heart for their unkind lot. And he saw among them there Leucaspis, and Orontes the admiral of his Lycian ships, both mournful, since they had been denied the ritual honours of the dead; for while sailing with Aeneas from Troyland over stormy seas the south wind had overwhelmed them, wrapping in a shroud of waters the ship and the crew.

There, also, wandered the helmsman Palinurus who had lately fallen from his ship's stern during the voyage from Africa as he watched the constellations, and had been flung overboard amid the waves. So dark were the shadows that Aeneas could at first scarcely recognize his sad figure; then, knowing him, he spoke first to him: 'Which god was it, Palinurus, who stole you from us and drowned you in open sea? Tell me. For this is the only time that an oracle of Apollo, whom I never before found to be a deceiver, has misled me. He prophesied that you would come unscathed from the sea and would reach Italy's bounds. Yet is this how he fulfils his promise?' But Palinurus answered: 'Son of Anchises, O my Chieftain, the oracle in Apollo's shrine never deceived you, neither did any god drown me in the ocean. The tiller to which I clung, appointed to be its guardian as I steered our course, I wrenched by accident most violently from its place and I fell headlong, and dragged it with me. I swear by those harsh seas that no fear which gripped me on my own behalf was so strong as that other fear, that your ship, robbed of her steering gear and wrested from her helmsman's hand, might founder, for the waves were rising high. For three nights of storm the south wind bore me, lashed furiously by the water over boundless seas. On the fourth day, buoyed lightly on the crest of a wave, I could just discern Italy and had started swimming slowly towards land; I had all but succeeded in reaching it, and was trying, still weighted down by my sodden clothing, to grasp a jagged point of rock with hooked fingers, when, alas, some savage tribesmen, ignorantly thinking me a rich prize, set upon me with their knives. And now I belong to the waves, and winds roll me to and fro along the shore. So therefore I entreat you, you the Unvanquished, by Heaven's joyous light and the airs you breathe, by your father, by your hopes for Iulus now growing to manhood, rescue me from my plight. Either cast soil upon me yourself, for so you can if you find your way back to Velia's harbour; or else, if any way there be or if your Goddess Mother can show you how, since it is not, I know, without divine sanction that you now prepare to traverse the mighty rivers and float on the Stygian marsh, then give your poor friend your hand and take me with you to cross the waves, that at least in death I may rest at a place of calm.' He had said his say when the Prophetess began her answer: 'Palinurus, how dare you harbour this impertinent desire? Shall you, before burial, look on waters of Styx, the Furies' merciless river? Shall you approach the bank before your time? Cease to imagine that divine decrees can be changed by prayers. But hear what I say, and remember; it may comfort you in your hard plight. For all who dwell near, in many a city far and wide, shall be constrained by wondrous signs from Heaven to make atonement to your relics. They shall erect a tomb, and to the tomb shall send annual offerings; and that place shall bear the name of Palinurus for ever.' His cares were banished by her words and in a little while the pain was driven from his mournful heart. The thought of giving his name to the place brought him joy.

So therefore they proceeded with the journey as before, and as they approached the river the Boatman, who, while still afloat on the Styx, had seen them in the distance walking through the silent wood and turning their steps towards the bank, spoke first and spoke in reproof: 'Whoever you are who stride in arms towards my river, come, say why you approach. Check your pace; speak now, from where you are. This is the land of the Shades, of Sleep and of Drowsy Night. It is sin to carry any who still live on board the boat of Styx. I even regretted that I ever admitted Hercules to the lake when he came here, and Theseus too and Pirithous, though they were Sons of Gods and of unvanquished might. Hercules came to steal by force Hell's own watchdog from under the King's very throne, and enchain him; he dragged him forth, too, trembling. Theseus and Pirithous had undertaken to abduct Pluto's mistress from her own wedding-chamber.' In reply Apollo's prophetess answered briefly: 'We have no such treacherous intent. These arms threaten no violence. Forgo your alarm. Your monstrous guardian at the gate may fiercely howl in his den to all eternity, affrighting the ghosts till they turn pale. Proserpine may stay in fidelity behind her uncle's door. Trojan Aeneas, illustrious for his true righteousness and for his feats of arms, travels in quest of his father down to Erebos' deep shades. But if the sight of fidelity so strong has no power to move you, you must yet recognize this branch.' And she showed the branch which had been hidden in her garment. The storm of anger in Charon's heart subsided and he said no more to them. He looked in awe at the holy offering, the Wand of Destiny, which it was long since he had seen. He turned the blue stern of the boat towards them and came near the bank. Next he hustled away the souls who sat side by side on the long benches, opened up the gangways, and immediately admitted Aeneas, in all his bulk, to the hull. Groaning under the weight the stitched coracle let in much marsh-water through its leaks. They crossed the river; and Charon eventually disembarked both the priestess and the hero, unharmed, on ugly slime amid grey reeds.

Through that part of the kingdom gigantic Cerberus sends echoing howls from his three throats. The monster lay in his cavern ahead of them. But the Priestess, seeing that the snakes of his mane were beginning to bristle, threw before him a morsel which she had charged with drowsiness from honey and drugged corn. Opening wide his three throats, the dog, being mad with hunger, seized the offered food; and relaxing his giant back he sprawled all his length across the floor of the cave. Now that the guardian was unconscious, Aeneas dashed to reach the cave-entrance and swiftly escaped clear of the bank and the waves which allow no return.

Immediately cries were heard. These were the loud wailing of infant souls weeping at the very entrance-way; never had they had their share of life's sweetness, for the dark day had stolen them from their mothers' breasts and plunged them to a death before their time. Next to them are those who had been condemned to die on a false accusation. But here their places are always justly assigned by a jury chosen by lot; for Minos, as president of the court, shakes the urn, convenes a gathering of the silent, and gives a hearing to the accounts of lives lived and charges made. Beyond these souls, in the next places, dwell the sorrowful who, though without guilt, gained death for themselves by their own hand, flinging their lives away in utter loathing for the light. How willingly they would now endure all the poverty, and every harsh tribulation, in the bright air above! But Divine Law bars their way back, the unlovely marsh holds them bound behind its doleful waters, and the nine encircling coils of Styx confine them. Not far thence are displayed the Fields of Mourning, as they name them, and they stretch in every direction. Here there are secluded paths and a surrounding myrtle-wood which hides all those who have pined and wilted under the harsh cruelties of love. Even in death their sorrows never leave them. In this region Aeneas could see Phaedra and Procris; and Eriphyle, grieving and showing the wounds dealt her by her brutal son, and Evadne, and Pasiphae; and with them went Laodamia, and Caeneus who had in youth for a time been male but is now a woman, having been destined again to revert to her original shape.

Among them was Phoenician Dido, who was roaming in the broad wood with her wound still fresh upon her. Troy's hero found himself near to her and as soon as he recognized her dimly through the shadows, like one who early in the month sees or thinks that he sees the moon rising through the clouds, his tears fell and he spoke to her in the sweet accents of love: 'O Dido, unhappy Dido, was the news, then, true which was brought to me, that you had perished, had taken the sword, and trodden the path to its end? Ah, could I have been the cause of your death? By the stars, by the High Gods I swear, I swear by any truth there may be in the depths of earth, that it was not by my own will, your Majesty, that I departed from your shores; but rather was I imperiously forced by that same divine direction which compels me now to pass through the shadows in this world of crumbling decay under deepest night; and I could not know that my leaving you would have caused you so terrible a grief. Stay your step and withdraw not from my sight. Whom do you seek to escape? My speaking to you now is the last indulgence which fate can give me.' By such words Aeneas tried to soften her, and invited tears. But in her the anger blazed and grimly she glared, holding her gaze averted and fixed on the ground; she was no more moved by what Aeneas had begun to say than if she had been hard flint or a standing block of Parian marble. At length she flung herself away, and, in hatred still, fled back into the shadows offered by the wood, where Sychaeus, her husband in former days, had sympathy for her distress and matched his love to hers. Aeneas was shocked by her unjust fate; and as she went long gazed after her with tearful eyes and pity for her in his heart.

After this he set all his strength to the journey assigned to him. They were now nearing the most distant and secluded fields thronged by those glorious in war. Here Tydeus, here Parthenopaeus of illustrious arms, and here the pallid wraith of Adrastus all met him, and Dardanids too, who had fallen in war and had been lamented grievously in the world above. Bitterly he sighed as he saw all the long line of them: Glaucus, Medon, Thersilochus, Antenor's three sons, Polyboetes consecrated to Ceres, and Idaeus, still holding his chariot and his arms. The souls gathered crowding round Aeneas on his right hand and on his left. They were not contented with a single view; they liked to hold him in conversation, to walk close beside him, and to hear from him why he had come. But the Greek chieftains, and the massed ranks whom Agamemnon had led, trembled in violent panic at the sight of their foe with his armour glittering amid the shadows. Some turned to flee as before they had fled to their ships, while others raised a whispering voice; but their attempt at a battle-cry left their mouths idly gaping.

And now Aeneas saw Priam's son Deiphobus, mutilated in every part of his body. Brutally torn were his face and both his hands; his head had been ravaged at each side where his ears had been shorn off, and the nostrils had been cut close with a hideous wound. Though at first he could scarcely recognize him as he cowered in an attempt to hide his frightful punishment, Aeneas addressed him in the tones which Deiphobus knew well: 'Deiphobus of the mighty arms, descended from Teucer's exalted blood, who had the will to inflict on you so savage a revenge? To whom was given such power over you? Report told me that on that last night you sank down on a piled confusion of the slain, for you were exhausted by your endless slaughtering of Greeks. Then, for my own part, I erected a cenotaph to you on the Rhoetean shore and thrice called loud on your shade. Your name and your arms now mark your place. But you yourself, friend of mine, I could not see, to lay you, at my departure, in soil of home.'

To this Priam's son replied: 'You, Friend, have left nothing undone; you have paid every due owed to Deiphobus himself and even to his dead body's shade. It was my own destiny and the murderous wickedness of Spartan Helen which have sunk me in this depth of affliction; it was she who left upon me these remembrances of her. You know how we passed that last night in a delusion of joy; we cannot but remember, only too well. When the Horse of Fate came leaping over our tall citadel's defence, bringing a teeming load of armed infantry in its womb, she, pretending that it was a ritual dance, was leading a band of Trojan women round the city, celebrating with wild cries the rites of Bacchus, and in their midst she herself held high a huge torch, sending thus an invitation to the Greeks from our own citadel's crest. I was then in my disastrous marriage-room, exhausted by anxieties and lying in a heavy sleep; a sweet, profound rest, very like the calm of a peaceful death, weighed me down. Meanwhile that admirable wife removed every weapon from our home, having first even stolen my own trusty sword from under my pillow. Then she threw open the doors and called Menelaus inside the house. Of course she thought that she was doing her old lover a great favour, which might well efface all memory of her past sins. But why prolong the tale? They burst into our marriage-room and beside them was the Aeolid Ulysses, ready as ever to incite to crime. O Gods, as surely as the lips with which I pray for vengeance are sinless, requite the Greeks themselves with horrors such as these! But come, tell me, in your turn, what adventures have brought you, while still living, to this place. Were you forced hither after losing your way on the ocean or did some warning from the gods direct you? If not, what fortune has been pressing on you, that you should visit the sunless homes of gloom in this land of dark confusion?'

But during this exchange of speech Aurora in her rosy chariot had already passed the zenith on her wandering course across the sky; and they might perhaps have let all the time allowed to them pass in such talk, had not the Sibyl, still at his side, addressed Aeneas with a curt warning: 'Night falls, Aeneas; yet we waste the hours in weeping. It is here that the way splits into two paths; one track, on the right, goes straight to mighty Pluto's battlements and by it we make our journey to Elysium; and the other, to the left, brings evil men to godless Tartarus, and, with never a pause, exacts their punishment.' Deiphobus replied: 'Reverend Priestess, be not angry. I shall depart, take my place with the souls once more, and give myself back again to the gloom. Go on your way, you, the glory of our Troy, and meet a happier fate than mine.' He said no more, but as he spoke turned on his heel.

Aeneas looked round and suddenly saw at the foot of a rock on his left some broad battlements encircled by three ring-walls, and a river sweeping round with a current of white-hot flames and boulders that spun and roared; this was Tartarean

Phlegethon, the Burning River of Hell. Opposite stood a gigantic gate with columns of solid adamant, such that no human force, nor even warring Gods of Heaven, could uproot them. An iron tower also rose high into the air; and there sat Tisiphone, with bloody robe girt up, the never-sleeping guardian of the entrance-court by night and day. From within groans were clearly heard. There was a sound of savage flogging and the clanking of iron chains being dragged. Aeneas stopped, listening in terror to the noise and the shouting: 'Maid, tell me straitly, what forms of wickedness are here? And by what tortures are these sinners being scourged? Why does so terrible a lamentation rise into the air?'

Then the Prophetess began thus to speak: 'Famed leader of Trojans, it is forbidden that any man who is pure in heart should set foot on the threshold of wrong. But when Hecate gave me authority over the Forest of Avernus, she conducted me through all Hell and explained the divine punishments to me. Rhadamanthus of Cnossos bears rule here, and his rule is most pitiless. He gives hearing to every work of deceit, and censures each fault. He compels every sinner to acknowledge each act of atonement which he has incurred in the world above, but whose performance he has postponed, blissful in imagined concealment, until death when it was too late. Then at once avenging Tisiphone, armed with her scourge, leaps on the guilty and whips them before her. High over them her left hand threatens them with hideous snakes, while she calls to her ferocious sisters to come in their hordes. See, the sacred gates are opening at last. They creak on their hinges, with horror in the sound. Now can you see what manner of Guardian has her seat in the entrance court, what awful shape watches the gateway? Inside, more savage still, a monstrous hydra, with fifty black throats a-gape, has her seat. And finally there is Tartarus, yawning steeply downwards to the dark twice as far as is our upward view to Olympus in the air of heaven. Here those ancient Sons of Earth, Titans of youthful strength, cast down by a thunder-stroke, are writhing in the lowest depth. And here I saw the two sons of Aloeus, giants in stature, who had assaulted the vast heaven in an attempt to tear it down with their own hands and thrust Jupiter from his empire on high. Here too I saw Salmoneus, who had imitated Jupiter's crashing flames from Olympus, and now paid his cruel penalty. Driving four horses and brandishing a torch, he had ridden triumphantly through the centre of Elis' city with Greek nations about him, and claimed the honours which only gods may claim. Mad fool, to mimic by a clatter of bronze and the beat of horn-hooved horses the storm-clouds and the bolt which may be copied by none! Then the Almighty Father flung his own missile from amid thick clouds – no mere torch did he use, nor any smoky gleam from a brand of pine – and with mighty cyclone-blast he drove Salmoneus headlong down. Yes, and Tityos too could be seen. He was foster-son of the All-Parent Earth; his body stretches over nine whole acres, and an enormous vulture crops with hooked beak his never-dying liver, tearing entrails with their rich yield of pain, groping for food within, and never leaving the deep wound in the breast; and the tissues are ever reborn and are never given repose. Need I speak of the Lapithae, of Ixion and of Pirithous? And of Phlegyas over whom there impends a black flint-rock which seems at every moment about to slip and already to be falling? For Tantalus there gleam golden supports upholding high banqueting-seats, and before the sinner's eyes is laid a royal and sumptuous feast; but close to it reclines the most terrible of all Furies who allows no hand to touch the fare, but leaps up, torch on high, and shouts like thunder. Here dwell those who hated their brothers while life was theirs or struck a parent or entangled a dependant in deceit, or, having found riches, gloated over them alone, setting none aside for their kindred, and of these there are many indeed; and then others who were killed for adultery or took part in an unrighteous war, shamelessly betraying their liege-lords; all these are imprisoned within, awaiting their penalty. Seek not to be told what is their punishment, nor in what calamitous plight they are engulfed. Some roll a huge boulder. Others hang, stretched out and bound, on the spokes of a wheel. Hopeless sits Theseus, and so will sit for ever. Phlegyas in extreme of misery cries loud through the gloom appeals of warning to all mankind: "Be warned, learn righteousness; and learn to scorn no god." And here is one who sold his homeland for gold and burdened her with despotism; here is one who, in return for bribes, posted new laws and cancelled them again; and another who forced a way to a forbidden marriage in his own daughter's chamber. All have dared a monstrous sin and achieved the sin they dared. Even had I a hundred tongues, a hundred mouths and a voice of iron, I yet could not include every shape of crime or list every punishment's name.'

Having spoken so, Apollo's ancient prophetess then added: 'But come now, hasten your walk to fulfil your chosen duty. Let us move faster. I see the battlements which were forged in the furnaces of the Cyclopes, and in the archway opposite to us the door at which authority commands us to dedicate our offering.' This said, they kept pace together along the dimly lighted way, quickly crossed the space between and came near to the door. Swiftly Aeneas gained the entrance, sprinkled himself with fresh water, and set the branch upright on the threshold before him.

When this was done their duty to the Goddess was fully discharged. And now they arrived at the Land of Joy, the pleasant green places in the Fortunate Woods, where are the Homes of the Blest. Here an ampler air clothes the plains with brilliant light, and always they see a sun and stars which are theirs alone. Of these bright spirits, some were taking exercise at games together on the grass of a field of play, or wrestling on yellow sand. Others were treading a rhythmic dance and as they danced they sang. And there too was Orpheus the Thracian seer attired in his trailing gown, who answered their rhythm on seven intervals of notes, striking out the melody now with fingers and now, over again, with an ivory quill. Here was Teucer's ancient dynasty, that family of noble beauty, high-hearted heroes born in happier years, Ilus, Assaracus and Dardanus, the Founder of Troy. Aeneas looked in wonder at their arms and chariots resting idle there before him. Their spears stood planted in the ground; their horses were grazing free about the plain. For the same pleasure in chariots and arms which they knew during life, and the same old interest in tending glossy horses, remain with them still after they have been laid to repose in earth. And, lo, Aeneas saw others to his right and to his left about the grass, feasting and singing a joyful hymn of praise in their choir; they were in the midst of a wood of scented bay-trees whence the full-flowing river Eridanus goes rolling through forest-land to the upper world. Here dwells a band who sustained wounds while fighting for their homelands, others who while life was theirs were priests without sin, or faithful seers whose speech never brought Apollo shame; some who had given life an added graciousness by inventions of skill, and some who had made others remember them by being kind. All of them wore snow-white ribbons encircling their brows. And they all thronged round and the Sibyl spoke to them and in particular to Musaeus, who was in the centre of a very large gathering, towering by head and shoulders above the rest, and all looked up to him: 'Tell us, Souls in Bliss, and especially you, most gentle Poet, in which district is Anchises, and in which part of it may he be found? For it is to find him that we have come, crossing the great rivers of Erebos.' The hero answered her quickly in a few words: 'No one has a fixed home. We live in shady woods and lie here on soft river-banks, or dwell in meadows which the streamlets keep ever fresh. But if the wish in your hearts so inclines, climb this slope and I shall set you on an easy pathway.' As he spoke he stepped ahead, and, from the higher ground on which they stood, showed them glittering lands below. So they descended from the heights.

Now Anchises, the father, was passing under a thoughtful, devoted survey certain souls who were then penned deep in a green vale but destined to ascend to the Upper Light. For it chanced that he was reviewing the whole company of his line, his own dear grandsons to be, and the destiny and fortune which would be theirs, their characters and their deeds. But seeing Aeneas hastening over the grass towards him, he stretched out both hands to him in his delight. Tears started down his cheeks; and a cry broke from him: 'You have come at last! Your father knew that you would be true. So your faithfulness has overcome the hard journey? May I really look on your face, Son, and hear the tones which I know so well, and talk with you? I did in fact expect from my reckoning that so it would be, for I computed the required passage of time. And my calculation did not deceive me. But to think of all the lands and the vast seas which you had to traverse, and all the perils of your storm-tossed journey, before I could welcome you at last! How I feared too that the royal power of Africa might do some hurt to you!' Aeneas answered: 'Father, it was ever the vision of yourself, so often mournfully appearing to me, which compelled me to make my way to the threshold of this world. My fleet lies moored on the Etruscan brine. Father, oh let me, let me, clasp your hand! Do not slip from my embrace!' As he spoke his face grew wet with the stream of tears. Three times he tried to cast his arms about his father's neck; but three times the clasp was vain and the wraith escaped his hands, like airy winds or the melting of a dream.

And now Aeneas saw at the far end of the valley, apart, a bushy wood loud with a forest's rustling sounds; and saw too Lethe's river, where it flows before the Homes of Peace. About this river, like bees in a meadow on a fine summer day settling on flowers of every kind, when lilies gleaming white are sprinkled everywhere and all the fields are noisy with the hum, the souls of countless tribes and nations were flitting. Aeneas was startled by the sudden sight, and in his bewilderment wished to hear his doubts explained, and find what might this river be which he saw before him, and who they were who crowded its banks with this numerous array. His father Anchises gave answer: 'They are souls who are destined to live in the body a second time, and at Lethe's wave they are drinking the waters which abolish care and give enduring release from memory. I have long desired to tell you of them and point them out to you in person for you to see; I wished to detail them to you, these descendants of my line, that you might rejoice with me the more in having found Italy.' 'Oh, Father, am I therefore to believe that of these souls some go, soaring hence, up to the world beneath our sky and return once more into dreary matter? Why should the poor souls so perversely desire the light of our day?' 'I shall tell you, indeed, and I shall not leave you in suspense, my son.' Anchises took up his tale and revealed each truth in due order.

'Now, first. The sky and the lands, the watery plains, the moon's gleaming face, the Titanic Sun and the stars are all strengthened by Spirit working within them, and by Mind, which is blended into all the vast universe and pervades every part of it, enlivening the whole mass. From Spirit and Mind are created men and the beasts; and from Spirit and Mind the flying things, and the strange creatures which ocean beneath its marbled surface brings into being, all have their lives. The strength in their seeds is the strength of fire and their origin is of Heaven; in so far as they are not hampered by the body's evil, nor their perceptions dazed by their members which are of the earth, and the parts of them which are imbued with death. The body is the cause of fear and of desire, of sorrow and of joy, and is the reason why, enclosed within the darkness of their windowless prison, they cannot look with wide eyes at free air. And indeed, even when on their last day the light of life departs, all evil and all the ills of the body still do not entirely pass from the sad soul, for it cannot but be that many engrafted faults have long been mysteriously hardening within, growing inveterate. Accordingly, souls are ceaselessly schooled by retribution, and pay in punishment for their old offences. Some are hung, stretched and helpless, for the winds to blow on them. From others the pervasive wickedness is washed away deep in an enormous gulf, or it is burnt out of them by fire. Each of us finds the world of death fitted to himself. Then afterwards we are released to go free about wide Elysium, and we few possess the Fields of Joy, until length of days, as time's cycle is completed, has removed the hardened corruption, and leaves, without taint now, a perception pure and bright, a spark of elemental fire. Now when these souls have trodden the full circle of a thousand years, God calls all of them forth in long procession to Lethe River, and this he does so that when they again visit the sky's vault they may be without memory, and a wish to re-enter bodily life may dawn.'

Anchises finished; and now he led his son and the Sibyl with him into the midst of the great gathering of souls who were all busy in conversation. He next found a place on rising ground, from which he could see them in their long line straight before him, take note of every one, and recognize all their countenances as they came: 'Come, I shall now explain to you your whole destiny. I shall make clear by my words what glory shall in time to come fall to the progeny of Dardanus, and what manner of men will be your descendants of Italian birth, souls of renown now awaiting life who shall succeed to our name. The young warrior whom you see there, leaning on an unpointed spear, stands in his allotted place nearest to the world's day, and he is to be the first to rise into the upper air having an Italian strain in his blood. He has the Alban name of Silvius, and he is your son, to be born after your passing; your queen Lavinia will rear him in the forests, and he will be king and sire of kings, and founder of our dynasty which shall rule from Alba Longa. The nearest to him, there, is Procas, the pride of the Trojan race; and next Capys and Numitor, and Aeneas Silvius, who will revive your own name and be a prince exalted alike in his righteousness and his arms, if in fact he shall ever succeed to the Alban throne. What men they are! See! What strength they display, and how they wear the oak-leaves of the Civic Crown shading their brows! High on the mountains shall they build Nomentum, Gabii, Fidenae's city and Collatia's fortress, and Pometii also, the guard-post of Inuus, Bola and Cora, which are all now nameless places, but whose names shall be famous one day.

'Yes, and Romulus, son of Mars, shall join his grandfather and walk with him. He will be of the blood of Assaracus; the mother who will rear him is to be Ilia. Do you see how on his head the twin crests stand, and how his Father already marks him for the exalted life above with his own emblem? See, my son! It will be through his inauguration that Rome shall become illustrious, and extend her authority to the breadth of the earth and her spirit to the height of Olympus. She shall build her single wall round seven citadels, and she shall be blessed in her manhood's increase; like the Mother of Berecyntus, who rides in her chariot through Phrygian cities wearing her towered crown, happy in the divine family which she has borne, and caressing her hundred grandsons, who are all dwellers in Heaven and have homes on high. Now turn the twin gaze of your eyes this way, and look at that family, your own true Romans. For there is Caesar, and all the line of Iulus, who are destined to reach the brilliant height of Heaven. And there in very truth is he whom you have often heard prophesied, Augustus Caesar, son of the Deified, and founder of golden centuries once more in Latium, in those same lands where once Saturn reigned; he shall extend our dominion beyond the Garamantians and the Indians in a region which lies outside the path of the constellations, outside the track of the year and of the sun, where Atlas the Heaven-Bearer holds on his shoulders the turning sphere, inset with blazing stars. Even now, before he comes to them, the Caspian kingdom and the land round Lake Maeotis tremble at prophecies of his coming, and the sevenfold mouth of the Nile knows confusion and alarm. Yes, not even Hercules ever traversed so much of the earth, not even when he shot the bronze-footed hind, brought peace to the woods of Erymanthus, and made Lerna tremble at his bow; nor Bacchus himself when he drove his tigers from Nysa's high crest and in triumph guided their yoke with reins of vine. Can we now hesitate to assert our valour by our deeds? Can any fear now prevent us from taking our stand on Italy's soil?

'But who is that, apart, wearing the emblem of an olive-spray, and carrying implements of worship? I recognize his hair and white-bearded chin. He is Numa, that King of Rome who will give to our city its first foundation on law; from little Cures and its barren soil he will have been called to a great dominion. He will be succeeded by Tullus who will shatter the peace of his fatherland and rouse to arms again men who have grown content with ease, and have lost the habit of marching in ranks of triumph. Ancus follows him closely; he is self-assertive and even now takes too much pleasure in the breeze of popular favour. Do you wish also to see Tarquin's dynasty and the arrogant soul of Brutus the avenger, and see the rods of office won back again? Brutus will be the first to be invested with a consul's authority and the ruthless axes; and, for resuming war anew, he, their father, shall hale his own sons to execution in liberty's glorious name. Pitiful, he! However later generations may account his deed, the victory will be with patriotism and limitless passion for fame. But look, also, at the Decii and the Drusi in the distance, at Torquatus ferocious in the use of the axe, and Camillus, rescuer of the standards.

'And then those other souls whom you see there, in the glitter of matching armour – they are in harmony now, and in harmony will they remain so long as the dark weighs on them here – ; but, oh, the dreadful war, and the bitterness of battle and of carnage which in mutual conflict they will begin if ever they come to the light of the living! One, Caesar, the father of the bride, shall march from the fortress of Monoecus down over the Alpine mass, and her husband Pompey shall stand marshalled with the East to confront him. Ah, sons of mine, never inure your spirits to so wicked a war, never turn the stout strength of your homeland on her own vitals! And you, who are of my own blood and trace your descent from Olympus, you should be first in clemency, you should first fling your weapons from your hands!

'Over there is one Mummius who shall triumph over Corinth and drive his chariot to the towering Capitol in glorious victory after the slaying of Greeks. And another, there, Aemilius Paulus, shall uproot Argos and Mycenae, Agamemnon's own city, and kill Perseus the Aeacid himself, the descendant of Achilles the mighty in arms; so he shall avenge his Trojan ancestors and Trojan Minerva's desecrated shrine. And who would leave you without a word, great Cato, or, Cossus, you? Or Gracchus and his family, or the two of Scipio's line, those paired thunderbolts of war who are Africa's annihilation? Or Fabricius with the power of his poverty? Or, Regulus Serranus, you, sowing your furrow with seed? Where would you hasten me to go when I am weary, you of the Fabii? Yes, you are Fabius the greatest of them, Maximus, the only Roman who can give us back success by inactivity. Others, for so I can well believe, shall hammer forth more delicately a breathing likeness out of bronze, coax living faces from the marble, plead causes with more skill, plot with their gauge the movements in the sky, and tell the rising of the constellations. But you, Roman, must remember that you have to guide the nations by your authority, for this is to be your skill, to graft tradition onto peace, to shew mercy to the conquered, and to wage war until the haughty are brought low.'

So spoke the father, Anchises. While they still wondered, he spoke again: 'Look how Marcellus, wearing the Supreme Spoils, strides conspicuous, a conqueror towering above all other warriors! He shall set the strength of Rome free again when it is disordered by the Great Rising, and in mounted combat bring down Carthaginians, and Gauls renewing warfare; and for the third time he shall dedicate to Father Quirinus the Captured Arms.'

But at this, seeing that there was another who walked beside him, a man young, very handsome and clad in shining armour, but with face and eyes downcast and little joy on his brow, Aeneas asked: 'Father, who is that who thus walks beside Marcellus as he goes? Is it a son or some other from the long line of descendants? What a noble presence he has and how loud the acclaim of those who attend on them! But the night flits black about his head and shadows him with gloom.' Anchises, Aeneas' father, began to answer him with welling tears: 'Oh, Son, seek not to know the terrible sorrow of your family. Fate will allow the world merely to see him, no more, and thereafter allow him to live there no longer. Powers Above, you judged that the Roman stock would be too mighty should your gift to them remain their own. Bitter indeed shall be the lamentation raised by brave men about the Field of Mars, beside his own splendid city. Tiber, as you glide past the newly made tomb, what a cortège shall you see! No other boy of our Ilian clan shall uplift the hopes of his Latin ancestors so high, and in none of her sons shall the future land of Romulus take such pride. O righteousness, and old-time faithfulness, O hand unconquerable in war! None could have safely encountered him in arms, whether marching on foot against the foe or mounted and pricking spurs into a foam-flecked charger's flanks. Piteous boy, if somehow you can break through your harsh destiny, you also shall be a Marcellus. . . . Give lilies from full hands! I too shall scatter scarlet flowers, that at least in the gift of these I may be generous to my grandson's soul, and perform an ineffectual duty.'

So did they wander everywhere about that land, in the broad plain's bright haze, reviewing all things there. And now Anchises had conducted his son to see each sight and kindled his imagination with a passion for the glory to be. He next foretold to him the wars which must be fought in the nearer future, with an account of the Laurentine nations and the city of Latinus, showing how he might avoid or endure each trial.

There are twin Gates of Sleep, of which one is said to be of horn, allowing an easy exit for shadows which are true. The other is all of shining white ivory, perfectly made; but the Spirits send visions which are false in the light of day. And Anchises having said his say now escorted his son and the Sibyl with him on their way, and let him depart through the Gate of Ivory. Aeneas took a direct path along the shore to his ships and rejoined his comrades. Next he coasted along to Caieta's harbour. Anchors were cast from prows. Sterns stood along the beach.

BOOK SEVEN

WAR IN LATIUM

YOU, Caieta, Aeneas' old nurse, have in your death enriched the shores of Italy with another legend to last for ever. To this day our reverence for you guards your resting-place, and your buried bones mark the spot with your name in our great Western Land, if in that there is any glory. So Aeneas the True correctly paid the demands of her funeral, and firmly he built her burial-mound. Afterwards, when the ocean's depth had peace, he left harbour and sailed steadily on his way. Favouring breezes blew onwards into the night, and a radiant moon blessed their voyage; the sea sparkled under her quivering beam. They next coasted, close in, past the land of Circe, the wealthy daughter of the Sun, who never lets her secluded grove cease ringing to her music, and who keeps the scented cedarwood burning in her proud palace to illumine the night as her singing shuttle flashes through the gossamer warp. From the palace was clearly heard the angry growl of lions, chafing under their confinement and roaring with the late night above them; and heard too was the fury of bristled boars and bears penned like sheep, and howls from the shadowy shapes of large wolves, all transformed by the pitiless goddess's potent herbs from human shape and now wearing the countenances and skins of beasts. But to save the righteous Trojans from sailing into harbour and suffering this magical change, and even prevent them from drawing near to the uncanny shore, Neptune filled their canvas with favouring winds, carried them past the seething shallows, and gave them swift escape.

And now rays of light were beginning to redden the sea, and Aurora, saffron in her chariot of rose, was already shining forth from high heaven, when the winds dropped, and suddenly every breath of air was stilled, so that the oars strained in shining and languid water. Just then Aeneas, still far out from the land, saw a mighty forest, through which the

Tiber flowed pleasantly, with rapid eddies and yellow from the quantities of sand, to burst forth into the sea. Birds of many kinds, whose home was the river's channel or the banks, caressed the air with their song around and above, as they flew about the forest. Aeneas signalled his comrades to change course and turn their prows to land. And happily he moved up into the shady river.

Erato, visit me now, for I am to disclose the names of the kings in ancient Latium, the stages of its past, and the existing state of the country when this stranger-army first brought ships to land on the coast of Italy; and I shall recall how the first fighting began. Goddess, instruct me, for I am your poet. I shall tell of a ghastly war and of pitched battles; I shall tell of princes whose proud spirit drove them to their deaths, of an army from Etruria, and of all Italy mustered under arms. A graver sequence of events opens before me, and I now begin a grander enterprise.

King Latinus had been ruling over the cities and the farms in serenity for many years of peace, and he was now growing old. We learn that he was a son of Faunus and a Laurentine nymph Marica. Picus had been Faunus' father, and he could claim Saturn himself as his grandfather; Saturn therefore was the original founder of his line. But by a divine decree Latinus had no son and no male heir, for his male issue had been taken from him in the dawn of early youth. Only one daughter remained with him in his house and the whole future of the splendid palace depended on her. She was now ripe for a husband, for the passing years had brought her to the age for marriage. Many from the breadth of Latium and from all the rest of Italy sought her; among them, and far the most handsome of them all, was Turnus, whose claim was strengthened by the high ability of his grandsires and their forbears, and by the devoted affection of the royal consort who was in haste to see him united with her daughter. But certain presages from Heaven, various and menacing, barred the way.

There was in the centre of the palace, within the high-roofed innermost part, a leafy laurus-tree, sacred and guarded in awe for many years. It is said that the chieftain Latinus had found it when he was beginning to build his citadel, had consecrated it to Phoebus, and had named his settlers Laurentines after it. Suddenly, to the astonishment of them all, a dense cloud of bees, riding through clear air and loudly humming, beset the top of this laurus-tree, and, interweaving their feet together, hung there in a swarm from a green-leaved bough. Straightway a prophet proclaimed, 'I discern that a foreign warrior is soon to arrive; I see his army marching from the same direction as the bees towards that place where they now are, and exerting lordship from our citadel's crest.' And again, while the maid Lavinia was standing at her father's side as he kindled the altar with unblemished pine-brands, her long hair, the horror of it! was seen to catch the flame and all her finery to burn away in crackling fire. Her royally tired locks and her splendid, jewelled crown were alight; and wrapped in the smoke of the deep red glare she scattered sparks of Vulcan all about the palace. This shocking sight was indeed counted a visible miracle. The prophets announced that she would be renowned for her glorious destiny, but that for the nation this sign portended a terrible war.

Alarmed at these miracles, Latinus visited the oracle of his father, the fate-predicting Faunus. He sought a response from the forest below Albunea's spring, where Albunea's wood, among all woods supreme, echoes to a holy spring, and breathes forth a malevolent sulphur-vapour in the shade. From this oracle the nations of Italy and all Oenotria seek answers in their uncertainties. There does a priest first bring his offerings, and then, lying on the skins of the sacrificed sheep spread on the ground beneath the silence of night, invites a sleep. In it he sees many floating, mysterious images, and hears voices of many a kind; he profits from converse with gods, and can speak with spirits deep down in Avernus. To this place Father Latinus himself now came in person to ask an oracle. He made formal arrangement for the sacrifice of a hundred fleecy two-year sheep, and he lay down couched on the wool of their piled skins. Suddenly from deep in the forest came the loud response: 'Son of mine, do not seek to join your daughter in any Latin union. Put no trust in any wedding which lies ready to hand. Strangers shall arrive here, to become your kin by marriage, and these strangers shall exalt our name to the stars by mingling their blood with ours; descendants of their breed shall see all the world at their feet, guided and swayed by their will, wherever the sun passes on his returning way, looking on Ocean in the east and in the west.' Now Latinus, having received this reply with its warnings from his father Faunus in the silence of the night, did not keep it to himself, as an untold secret. Instead, Rumour had already flown with the news of it far and wide about the Italian cities, when the warriors from Troy moored their fleet to the grass-banked riverside.

Aeneas, with his principal captains and the fair Iulus, settled down under the branches of a tall tree. They laid out a meal; and since Jupiter in Heaven inspired them to do so, they set on the grass, instead of tables and plates for the food, some meal cakes, and on this flooring provided by Ceres they piled fruits of the countryside. Now it happened that, having finished the rest of the food, they were forced, because they were still hungry and there was nothing else to eat, to turn to the thin cereal platters, boldly snap them in their fingers and jaws, and bite this round-shaped crust of destiny, showing no mercy to the quartered scones. 'Hullo,' said Iulus, jokingly, 'we are even munching our tables!' That was all that he said. His remark, as soon as heard, was the first sign that their trials were ending, and his father instantly seized on his words as he spoke them, and stopped him, in awe at the divine meaning in the remark. And quickly he prayed: 'Hail, Land which fate has reserved for us! Hail, Gods of Trojan Homes, who never fail us! It is here that your homes are now to be. This is your Fatherland. For, as I now remember, my father left me in possession of just such a secret of destiny as this: "Son, when, after you have sailed to an unknown shore, your food is exhausted and hunger forces you to eat your tables, remember then, however weary you are, to expect a home at last; therefore, waste no time in finding a site for your first buildings and starting to labour at their defences." This must be the hunger which he meant, a hunger due to befall us at the last, and fix the limit of our calamities. Come, then, and with the first light of the sun let us in good heart explore the country and find out what land it is, who are its inhabitants, and where is their defended city. We must all go by different ways from the harbour. Meanwhile, offer bowls of wine to Jupiter, call on my father Anchises in your prayer, and set more wine on the tables.' Having spoken so, he next wreathed his forehead with a leafy spray, and offered prayer to the spirit of the place, to Earth who is of all deities the first, to the Nymphs, and to the rivers which as yet they did not know; and then he called on Night and the Stars of Night which were now rising, Jupiter of Ida, the Phrygian Mother in her due place, and both his own parents, one in Heaven and the other in the world below. Immediately the Father Almighty thundered thrice from a clear sky above them, and displayed from the high air a cloud burning with rays of golden light, set quivering by his own hand. The rumour now rapidly spread along the Trojan lines that the day had come for them to found the promised city-walls. In rivalry together they hurried to begin the feast anew. Happy at the powerful sign, they set out their mixing-bowls and wreathed the wines.

When the morrow dawned, cleansing the earth with its torch's first light, the Trojans scattered to search out the city, territory and seaboard of this people; here they found the pools of Numicus' spring, here the river Tiber, and here the dwellings of brave Latin men. The son of Anchises now selected a hundred ambassadors from every rank, and commanded them to go, all wearing Minerva's olive-sprays, to the majestic battlements of the king, to carry presents to him and ask his friendship for the Trojans. Having received their orders they obeyed at once and strode swiftly on their way. Aeneas meanwhile dug a low trench to mark a wall-circuit and started active work on the site, building their first home near the sea-shore, and making it like a camp, with a surrounding earthwork and palisade.

The young Trojans had now completed their journey, and looking upwards they could see high towers and other buildings where the Latins dwelt. They drew near to the walls.

Before the city, boys, and men in the grace of early manhood, were exercising on horseback, learning in clouds of dust to control chariots, bending taut bows, and sending tough-shafted javelins spinning from their shoulders, or offering a challenge to a foot-race or a boxing-bout, when a messenger who had ridden ahead brought to the ears of the aged king the news that tall strangers, wearing unfamiliar dress, had arrived. The king commanded them to be summoned within the palace. And he took his seat in the centre, on his ancestral throne.

The palace of Laurentine Picus was a majestic building, with its great height supported on a hundred columns, and standing on the highest ground in the city; it was a place of dread, set in clustering trees and charged with traditional awe. Here, if he would have a prosperous reign, every king must on his accession receive the sceptre and lift up the rods of office. The palace was a temple and was used by the Latins as their senate-house, and it was also the hall for their holy feasts, when by custom the elders sacrificed a ram and in unbroken lines took their places at table.

There too, near the entrance court, stood statues made of ancient cedar-wood representing ancestors of old in sequence: Italus, Father Sabinus, planter of the vine, guarding in effigy a bent sickle, aged Saturn, Janus with his two faces, and other kings from the beginning, and heroes too who had received battle-wounds fighting for their homelands. There were hanging also on hallowed pillars many weapons, chariots which had been captured, axes with curved edges, crests from helmets, huge bars from gates, spear-heads, shields and rams wrenched off ships. Picus himself, the Horse-Tamer, was figured sitting there, attired in a short toga of State and holding the Quirine Augury-Staff and in his left hand the Sacred Shield. Golden Circe had been wedded to him; and she, overpowered by passion, had struck him with her wand and changed him by her drugs so that he became a bird, with colour-speckled wings.

Such was the temple of the gods within which Latinus was now seated on his ancestral throne. And he summoned the

Trojans into his hall of state. They entered; he spoke first, and serenely addressed them:

'Tell us, Dardans, since we had heard of you before ever you turned hither your course upon the ocean, and we already know both your city and your nation, what is your purpose? What reason or what need has carried you over all the blue ways of the sea to Italy's shore? Whether it is because you mistook your course, or because you were driven by storms – adversities of the kind which mariners often have to face on the deep – that you have entered between our river's banks and are now in port here, you must not hesitate to accept our hospitality and understand who the Latins are; for they are Saturn's kin who need no bond of law to keep them just, but are just by their own free will and hold to the way of their ancient God. Besides, I can remember that Auruncan elders used to tell a story, now perhaps dimmed by the lapse of time, how Dardanus himself had started from Italy's shore when he made his long voyage all the way to the Thracian Samos, which is now called Samothrace, and to the cities beneath Phrygian Ida, having journeyed there from his Etruscan home, Corythus. And now he has been received and enthroned in a golden palace of the star-glittering sky, and his altar lengthens the roll of deities.'

He finished and Ilioneus, following him, spoke thus in answer: 'O King, peerless son of Faunus, we did not approach your land because we had been driven towards it by the waves or forced here by a blackening storm. No star and no coastline set us on a false course. It is with willing hearts, and by design, that all our company has travelled to this city, being exiles from an empire which was once the mightiest ever seen by the sun in all his journeying from the uttermost edge of the sky. Jupiter founded our line, and he is the ancestor in whom our Dardan manhood takes pride. Our king is himself of Jupiter's most exalted kin; it is he, Aeneas of Troy, who has sent us to your gates. How fearful was the hurricane which streamed from merciless Mycenae and swept over Ida's plains, and how destiny impelled the continents of Europe and Asia to meet together in shock, all men have heard, even they who dwell far distant from us at the world's end where the River of Ocean circles back, and those too who live remote in the zone stretching, central of the five, beneath a pitiless sun. We who, after that cataclysm, have sailed over so many vast seas, now ask only a modest home for the gods of our race, a strip of shore which can harm no one, and air and water, which are free for all to share. We shall bring no shame on your kingdom. Indeed, your Latin fame will gain in strength. Our gratitude for a deed so kind will never fade, and Italians will not regret that they received Trojans with open arms. This I swear to you by the destiny of Aeneas and by his strong right hand, whose strength is known to all who have tested it either in friendship or in armed warfare. Many nations and many races have sought alliance with us and have wished to unite us with them. For you must not scorn us because by our own free choice our hands hold forth to you the wool-tied ribbons which plead for peace, and we come before you with words of entreaty. Oracles from gods have commanded and compelled us to find your land and no other, for in it Dardanus was born, and to it we are recalled by Apollo who presses us onwards by his peremptory decrees towards Etruscan Tiber and the holy spring-water of Numicus. Aeneas offers to you, besides, certain small gifts from his former wealth; they are relics which he saved from blazing Troy. Here is a vessel of gold which was used by his father Anchises for drink-offerings at the altars. Here is a sceptre, and here a holy tiara, and here are garments worked by Trojan ladies, which were all used by Priam when, as custom required, he was prescribing laws to his assembled nations.'

Latinus, listening to this speech from Ilioneus, gazed steadily at the ground, remaining motionless in his place, but for the thoughtful movement of his eyes. The embroidered purple and even Priam's sceptre affected him, a king himself, less than his absorption in his daughter's wedding and the marriage-union. He was pondering the oracle of old Faunus deep down in his heart: Aeneas must actually be that bridegroom for his daughter who, according to Destiny's promise, was to arrive from a foreign home; it must be he who was summoned to reign with him in equal sanction of authority; and he must be that prince whose descendants would prove to be men of supreme valour, and by their strength win all the earth for their own. Presently he spoke in happiness: 'May the gods further the enterprise opening before us in direct fulfilment of their prophecy. Trojan, your desire shall be granted. And I readily accept your gifts. So long as Latinus is king, none of you shall want for the rich soil's increase or miss even all the wealth of Troy. Only Aeneas should come to us in person if his desire to be with us is so strong, and if he is in such haste to join us in guest-friendship and to be called our ally. We are already friends, and so he should hardly be frightened to look us in the face; for me, the bargain is incomplete till I have shaken hands with your prince. You shall now carry back my answer in a message to him. I have a daughter whom I am not allowed to unite with any man of my race; that is forbidden by responses from my own father's oracle and by many a heavenly sign, which all predict that the people to whom she will be joined in marriage are to come from foreign lands. That is what the future holds for Latium. The new kindred shall add their strain to ours, and exalt our race to the stars. It is my belief, and, if my intuition comes near to divining the truth, it is also according to my wish, that it is Aeneas to whom Fate is pointing.'

After this candid speech the Latin chieftain chose some horses from all the royal stable, where three hundred well-groomed steeds had their high-roofed stalls. He ordered one of them to be immediately led forth for each Trojan in order of precedence, all wing-footed, each with a saddle-cloth of embroidered purple and a gold poitrel hanging from his chest; they even wore gold armour, and of a deep gold, matching the ornaments, were the bits which they champed between their teeth. As Aeneas was not there, Latinus chose a chariot and a pair of yoke-horses to be led forth for him; they were of Heaven's breed, and the breath from their nostrils was fire; they came of the blood of those bastard horses which the cunning Circe had bred by slyly crossing a stranger-mare with stallions which she had stolen from her father, the Sun.

Such were the gifts, and such was the message from Latinus with which the men of Aeneas returned on horseback, holding themselves high, and bringing home the agreement of peace.

Yet, see! Jupiter's ferocious queen was returning from Argos, city of Inachus, and riding the air on her course, when looking out of the sky all the way from Pachynus in Sicily she saw before her in the distance the now jubilant Aeneas, with his Dardan fleet. She noticed that they were already at work on their buildings, that they had forsaken their ships, and were confidently settling on land. She stiffened, pierced by sharp pain; and tossing her head she spoke a torrent of heartfelt words: 'Ah, hated, hated breed of Troy, with your Phrygian destiny opposing my own! Was there any hope that they might fall in death on Sigean plains? Could they stay in the trap when it closed? Could even Troy in flames burn up the Trojans? No; they found a way straight through the battle, straight through the fires. Must I, then, conclude that my divine power is at last exhausted and prostrate, or that I have had my fill of hating, and found my rest? Why, when the Trojans were flung from their homes, I even condescended to pursue them with my fury over the waves, and I was always there to meet them, mere exiles, at every turn in their wanderings about the ocean. All the strength of sky and sea has been spent against the Trojans. But what use to me were the Syrtes or Scylla or cavernous Charybdis? They now have their desire, and are finding refuge in Tiber's channel, beyond all fear of the ocean and all thought of me. Yet Mars had the power to destroy the monstrous race of Lapiths. The Father of Gods himself gave over ancient Calydon to Diana's spite. And had any sin of Lapiths or of Calydon deserved such a heavy fate? But, meanwhile, I, Jupiter's high queen, after forcing myself in my failure to shrink from no humiliation, after leaving no means untried, I am vanquished, and by Aeneas. Well, if my own divine strength is too slight, then I am not one to refrain from asking aid from any power, anywhere. If I cannot change the will of Heaven, I shall release Hell. I shall not be allowed, I grant it, to bar Aeneas from his throne in Latium, and Lavinia, by unalterable destiny, will still be his bride. Yet I may prolong the process, and cause delay in events so momentous; yes, and tear up by the roots the nations of both the kings. That is the price which they will have to pay in their subjects' blood before the bride's father and her lord can unite. Maid, your dowry shall be blood, Trojan and Rutulian blood. War's Goddess awaits you to be mistress of your wedding. It is not only Hecuba, in her dream, who was brought to bed of a firebrand and bore a son who would start a blaze of marriage havoc. No; the childbirth of Venus herself is the same. She has borne a second Paris and another brand of death against Troy's defences as they rise again.'

Having spoken so, she swooped, a sight of terror, down to the earth. From the Infernal Dark, where the Dread Sisters have their place, she summoned the creatress of grief, Allecto, who dearly loves war's horrors, outbursting wrath, treachery, and recriminations with all their harms. She is a monster, hated even by her own father Pluto, and by her own Tartarean sisters, so many are the countenances which she assumes, so ferocious are her aspects, and such a cluster of countless black snakes sprouts from her head. Juno now spoke to Allecto, and with these words whetted her hate:

'Maid, Daughter of the Dark, do a service for me, and grant me your efforts in a task after your own heart, to prevent my worship and my renown from suffering injury and taking the second place, and to make it impossible for the men of Aeneas to solicit Latinus for intermarriage, or beset Italian territory. You know well how to set brothers, united in love, at armed conflict one against the other. You can wreck homes by hate and bring scourges and firebrands of death within their walls. You have a thousand types of mischief, a thousand artful ways of doing harm. Bestir your fertile brain. Shatter the pact of peace which they have made, and sow in recriminations the seeds of war. In one breath let their manhood want, demand, and grasp their arms.'

Straightway Allecto, charged with her Gorgon-poisons, travelled to the tall palace of the Laurentine ruler in Latium. And there she lay in wait noiselessly at the entrance to the rooms of Queen Amata. Amata was already in a feverish turmoil with a woman's thoughts of anxiety at the arrival of the Trojans and rage for the wedding planned for Turnus. Tearing from her metal-blue hair one snake, the evil goddess flung it at Amata and sent it creeping into her bosom and then deep into her heart, so that by this magic she should fall violently mad, and throw all the palace into confusion. The serpent slid between her garments and her smooth breast, it coiled about her though she felt no touch of it, and without her knowledge breathed viper's life-breath into her, driving her insane. The monstrous snake became the twisted gold about her neck, became the ends of her long headband; it twined in her hair and roved slithering over her limbs. Then, as the taint in the venomous liquid began to ooze under her skin and spread stealing into her senses and plaiting the fire round her bones, but still before the heart in her breast had fully drunk in the flame, she spoke, quite softly and as a mother well might speak, weeping many tears over her daughter and the Phrygian wedding which had been planned:

'Father! Is Lavinia indeed being given for marriage to Trojans, to exiles? Have you no pity for your own daughter or even for yourself? And none for her mother either, whom, with the first northerly wind, this treacherous pirate will leave forlorn, stealing the maiden away and bound for the high seas? Yet was it not so that the Shepherd from Phrygia made his way into the heart of Lacedaemon and then carried off Leda's Helen to the cities of Troyland? What of your sworn promise? What of your old-time care for your own people, and your hand plighted to your own kinsman Turnus again and again? If the suitor who is to intermarry with the Latins has to be found in some foreign nation, if this is immutable and if the command of your father Faunus leaves you no choice, then for my part I count as foreign any land which is not our land and not subject to our sceptre, and I believe that such is the meaning of the gods themselves. And besides, if the family of Turnus were to be traced right back to its origin, Inachus and Acrisius are his forefathers and Mycenae itself is his mother-city.'

By pleading so she sought to persuade Latinus, but in vain; she could see that he stood firm in his opposition. And as the serpent's poison trickled deep within her and spread all over her with its power to drive mad, the unhappy lady gave way; goaded by the horrible magic, blindly she ran in a reckless frenzy about the city; ran as wildly as a top will run under twisting lashes in wide circles round some large empty room, kept spinning by boys who, concentrated on their game, whip it and force it to travel in circular courses, and then, bending mystified over the twirling boxwood, stare in youthful wonderment and give it new leases of life with their blows. So was the queen driven, as wildly as any top, on her course through city-streets under the scornful eyes of the inhabitants. She even went out into the forests in her flight, pretending that the power of Bacchus was upon her, and so venturing on a still graver, wilder sin; and she hid her daughter amid leaf-clad mountains, to prevent the marriage-ceremony and to rob the Trojans of their wedding. 'Ho, Bacchus!' she shouted, and, 'None but you,' she shrieked, 'deserves the maiden! For see, she assumes your soft-leaved wand in honour of you, around you she dances, and to you she has hallowed a growing lock of her hair.' The news flew fast; and every mother's heart now blazed with this same hysterical passion to look for a new dwelling-place. Quickly they forsook their homes, with necks bare and hair left free to the winds. Others, dressed in fawn-skins and carrying spear-shafts of vine, filled the sky with quavering holloas. In the centre of them was Amata, who feverishly held high a blazing pine-brand and, turning all about her her reddened eyes, sang the wedding-song for her daughter and Turnus. Suddenly she roared like a beast: 'Mothers of Latium! Hey! Hear me, each one of you, wherever you may be! If you still have any sympathy for poor Amata in your faithful hearts, or any prick of conscience for a mother's claims, untie the bands around your hair and take to the wild rites with me!'

So fared it with the queen, as Allecto goaded her now this way, now that, and drove her by the Bacchic power amid the forests and the wilderness where only the beasts had their homes. And now the grim goddess, seeing that insanity was afoot and that the edge which she had given it was keen enough, since she had already contrived to overturn the plan, and the home, of Latinus, straightway rose on dusky wing, towards the walled city of Turnus, the hot-headed Rutulian. This city is said to have been founded by Danae for settlers from Argos after she had been driven ashore by a violent southerly gale. Long ago our ancestors named the city Ardea; and Ardea still retains her great name but not her old prosperity. Here, at this moment, in the darkest midnight hour, Turnus lay sound asleep within the high-roofed palace. Allecto put off her ferocious aspect and the maddening form of her bodily parts. She changed her shape and put on an old woman's looks; she ploughed unsightly wrinkles on her brow, assumed white hair, wound a ribbon around, and lastly entwined an olive-spray in her locks. She was now Calybe, Juno's aged servant, who guarded her temple; and so she appeared before the young prince with these words: 'Turnus! Will you passively see all your efforts wasted and lost, and allow a sceptre which is yours by right to be made over to these Dardan settlers? The king refuses you your bride. He has transferred the dowry which you had earned with your blood, and a foreigner is fetched in to inherit the throne. Go on now! Thanklessly expose yourself to every danger and be mocked for your pains! Away, and cut down Etruria's ranks and shield the Latins with the peace which you have won! Yes! The Saturnian Queen, the Almighty, has herself commanded me to say this openly to you while you lie in night's kindly peace. Therefore, come! Take heart! Prepare your men to arm, and move out of the gates for action. You are to burn their brightly painted ships, and with them these Phrygian chiefs also who lie in port on our noble river. This is the peremptory command of the Gods in Heaven. And if King Latinus himself does not by his own admission authorize the marriage and acquiesce in your demands, let him know the cost and, in the last issue, let him test the might of Turnus in arms.'

At this the young prince opened his lips to speak in his turn and make mock of her prophecy: 'The news that this fleet has sailed into Tiber's waters has not, as you suppose, escaped my ears. Do not invent these grave fears to alarm me. And besides, Juno too is royal and does not forget me. But your great age, exhausted and decayed, and past the fertile time for truth, makes you restless and anxious all to no purpose, and deludes you with imaginary dread when you prophesy of warring kings. Your responsibility is to watch over the temples of the gods and their statues. It is for men to wage war and make peace; for that task is theirs.'

Stung by such an answer, Allecto exploded into blazing anger. And even as he spoke the young prince found his limbs suddenly possessed by a trembling, and his eyes became fixed in a stare; so countless were the snakes which uttered the Fury's hiss, and so horrifying was the apparition which stood revealed. Then she bent down on him eyes which were beams of flame, and while he still wavered, trying to continue his reply, she thrust him back, stiffened a pair of serpents from her hair, cracked her whip, and spoke again, out of her now raving lips: 'See who I am, whose great age, exhausted and decayed and past the fertile time for truth, deludes me with imaginary dread when I prophesy of warring kings! Look now at this. I come from the Dread Sisters' station; and in my hand I bear war and death.' With the words she cast a brand of fire at the young prince, and she planted her torch in his breast, where it smoked in a murky glare.

Turnus' sleep was shattered by an overmastering terror. Sweat burst out all over him, drenching his limbs to the bone. Out of his wits, he roared for weapons and hunted for them by his bedside and all through the house. In him there rioted the bloodthirsty lust of the blade, the accursed lunacy of war, and, above all, anger; as when a loudly crackling fire of brushwood is piled up high below the ribs of a seething cauldron, where water leaps as it boils, until it can no longer contain itself, but the flood within riots in vapour, dark steam soars into the air, and the water itself foams upward to the top and overflows.

So therefore Turnus gave command to his young captains

to march to King Latinus, for he had violated the peace. He ordered the preparation of arms, saying that they must defend Italy and force the enemy back from the frontiers, and claiming that, when he joined the fight, he would be a match for both Trojans and Latins together. Having given his orders he called on the gods to hear his vows. And now his Rutulians vied together cheering each other on to battle. The appeal of Turnus was strong, for some were captivated by his attractive grace and his youth, some by his royal ancestors, and others by the glorious exploits of his brave right arm.

While Turnus was inspiring his Rutulians with the spirit to dare, Allecto darted away on her Stygian wings to deal with the Trojans. Choosing a fresh device, she observed the place on the coastline where the handsome Iulus was trapping and hunting wild beasts. The Maid from Hell now possessed his hounds with a sudden fit of madness. She touched their nostrils with a familiar scent to send them in hot-foot pursuit of a stag. This proved to be the principal cause which started the tribulations to come, kindling the spirit of the country-folk for war. For the stag which they chased was a beautiful creature with giant antlers, which had been taken from its mother before it was weaned, and was now kept as a pet by the young sons of Tyrrhus and by their father, who was the master whom the king's herds followed and who held in trust the wardenship of his extensive lands. Their sister Silvia had trained him to obey her, tending him with every care, wreathing his horns with soft garlands to decorate him, and grooming him, wild creature though he had been, and bathing him in pure water. Though he was tame to her touch and regular at the master's table, he would roam at large in the woods, and find his way back by himself, however late the night, to the entrance which he knew so well.

Now, as Iulus hunted, his hounds hot on the scent started this very stag which chanced, during a lonely ramble, to be floating downstream in the river and taking relief from the heat in the shadow of its green banks. Iulus joined in the chase, aflame with a passion for this special glory. Bending his bow he aimed a pointed arrow. His hands, guided by some deity, never lost their aim, and the arrow, with a loud hiss as it sped, passed through the stag's belly and through his flanks. Wounded, the four-foot creature at once fled back to his familiar home and crept moaning into his stall. He was all stained with blood; and as if entreating help he filled the whole house with his plaints. The boys' sister, Silvia, acted first; striking her hands on her arms she cried for aid and rallied the hardy country-folk. They appeared with surprising rapidity – for the furious fiend was there, hiding silently in the woods –, one of them armed with a charred wooden stake, and another with a bulging, knotted bludgeon, as anger made a weapon of the first object which each grasping hand could find. And Tyrrhus called out his levies. He happened to be splitting an oak in four, and had just forced the wedges in. Panting with savage rage, he seized an axe.

This done, the unrelenting goddess, having judged from her vantage point the moment for further harm, flew to the high summit of the stables and from the top of them sounded the Herdsmen's Call. And on her curved horn she exerted her voice in a blast from Hell; immediately all the woodlands quaked at it and the forest-deeps rang again. Far away Diana's Lake heard it; Nar River, white from its sulphurous water, and Lake Veline's springs heard it too; and trembling mothers clasped their sons to their breasts. The call startled into quick movement the dogged country-folk. At once to the sinister clarion's summons they rallied from all around, snatching up weapons as they came. On their side the Trojans opened their camp and sent out a stream of fighting men to aid Ascanius. All arrayed their ranks for battle. It was no longer an affair of hard cudgels or stakes, charred to a point, in peasant conflict. Now they sought decisions by their two-edged blades. War's standing crop stretched afar, iron-grey with the shudder of drawn steel. Bronze gleamed under the sun's reflection, and flashed light upwards against dark clouds; as when at a wind's first breath waves begin to whiten, and gradually the sea rises and builds them higher, until at last it leaps from all its depths to the sky.

Quickly the young Almo, the eldest of Tyrrhus' sons, was

brought to the ground by a whistling arrow as he stood before the front line; the wounding shaft stayed fast below his throat, choking the moist path of his voice and the slender life-passage with a flow of blood. And around him fell many warriors, including Galaesus, an older man who was killed as he sought to intercede for peace; he had been the most strictly righteous of all the Italians in the old days, and their richest land-owner, for five were the flocks of bleating sheep and five the herds of cattle which were daily driven back to his home, and a hundred were the ploughs which turned his soil.

Such were the events now occurring over the plains, and Mars favoured neither side. Meanwhile the goddess Allecto, who now had in her hands the success which she had promised, since she had drawn first blood in the war and had caused deaths in the first clash of the fighting, forsook the Western Land. She rode across the airs of the sky, and in arrogant triumph spoke to Juno: 'Behold, you have your quarrel, and it has been securely ratified by horrors of war. Now, see if you can join them in friendship together again and make them agree to peace! I have already sprinkled Italian blood on Trojans. But, if I can be assured of your consent, I shall do much more than that; I shall spread rumours and so involve the neighbouring cities also in the war, enflaming their spirit with a passion for the lunacy of Mars, and I shall have them marching with aid from every part of the land. So shall I scatter fighting all over the countryside.' Then Juno gave her answer: 'The alarm and the treachery are ample. Motives for a war are established, and armed battle, hand to hand, proceeds; chance first handed them their weapons, and now newly shed blood has stained those arms. Let such be the wedding-rite and such the marriage which Venus' admirable son and King Latinus are to celebrate. But the Supreme Father who reigns over highest Olympus would not wish such as you to stray too freely in the upper air under heaven. Withdraw. If a chance of any further mischief offers, I myself shall direct.' Such were the words which Saturn's daughter used to her. The Fury raised her wings, whirring with the hiss of her snakes. And she set forth for her home by Cocytus, leaving the steeps of sky. There is, at the foot of high mountains in the centre of Italy, a place which is well known and recalled in story throughout many lands. The place is the Gorge of Ampsanctus. Dark it is with dense foliage, and wooded cliffs press on it from either side; in the middle a crashing torrent, with a swirling crest of foam, roars amid rocks. There they point out a frightening cavern, with outlets which are pitiless Pluto's breathing-vents, and a mighty abyss opening noisome jaws where Acheron breaks through. Into them the Fury with her hated power plunged, relieving the world and sky of her presence.

Meanwhile, Saturn's daughter in queenly control was putting the finishing touch to the war. All the herdsmen, in full numbers, crowded into the city from the battle, carrying home the slain, the boy Almo and Galaesus with his face disfigured, saying prayers to their gods and appealing to Latinus. Turnus was there, and while the fiery denunciations of the bloodshed were at their height, he redoubled the alarm by protesting that the Trojans had been invited to share the royal power, that a Phrygian strain was to blend with the Latin blood, and that he was being thrust away from the door. Next, from all sides there gathered the relatives of those women, who under the shock of Bacchus, had gone prancing in frenzied bands about the trackless forests, and supported by Amata's great prestige they too clamoured incessantly for an appeal to Mars. Doomed already, the whole nation was insistent for a wicked war, led by some malign Power to defy Heaven's warning and the Gods' destined will. They crowded in rivalry round the palace of King Latinus. He stood firm like an unmovable rock in the sea, some ocean-rock where loud breakers crash, holding firm by its own mass however many the waves which yelp around, while crags and foam-splashed reefs roar vainly, and seaweed, smashed against its flank, swirls back again. But the aged chieftain, finding no means to overcome their blind resolve since events were moving at ruthless Juno's will, could only cry long, helpless appeals to the gods and the heedless winds: 'Woe! We are shipwrecked by fate, we are driven before the storm! My poor people, you will pay retribution for this sacrilege in your own blood. Ah, Turnus, the wrongfulness of your deed and its grim punishment will overtake you, and when at last you offer vows to the gods in veneration you will be too late. For me, my rest is won, and I am only deprived, right at the haven's mouth, of serenity in burial.' He said no more, but barred himself within his palace, and resigned the reins of government.

There was a sacred custom in Latium, Land of the West, which the Alban Cities continuously observed, and Rome, supreme in all the world, observes today when Romans first stir Mars to engage battle, alike if they prepare to launch war's miseries with might and main on Getae, Hyrcanians, or Arabs, or to journey to India, in the track of the dawn, and to bid the Parthians hand our standards back. There are twin Gates of War, for by that name men call them; and they are hallowed by men's awe and the dread presence of heartless Mars. A hundred bars of bronze, and iron's tough, everlasting strength, close them, and Janus, never moving from that threshold, is their guard. When the Fathers of the City have irrevocably decided for battle, the Consul himself, a figure conspicuous in Quirine toga of State and Gabine cincture, unbolts these gates, and their hinge-posts groan; it is he who calls the fighting forth, then the rest of their manhood follows, and the bronze horns, in hoarse assent, add their breath.

By this ritual Latinus was now asked to declare war on Aeneas and his men, and to throw open the grim gates. But the old father could not bear to touch them. He turned away and recoiled from the repellent duty; and he hid from sight among the shadows. Then the Saturnian Queen of the Gods herself descended from the sky and with her own hand drove in the obstructing doors; the hinge-posts turned; and she burst apart the iron-bound Gates of War.

Italy, the quiet land which no alarm could rouse before, was ablaze. Some of her men made ready to march on foot across her plains. Some galloped madly in clouds of dust, riding high on tall horses. All were clamouring for weapons. Some using rich grease were polishing shields till they were smooth and burnishing spearheads, or grinding down axes on whetstones. Delightedly they raised their standards and listened to trumpet-calls. Five great cities all erected new anvils and started to renew their armouries: powerful Atina, haughty Tibur, Ardea, Crustumerium, and towered Antemnae. They hollowed protective head-coverings, and bent willow-frames to fit shield-bosses. Others forged bronze corslets, or beat out smooth quivers from the resisting silver. All their respect for share and sickle, all their love of the plough, had given way to this. They refashioned their fathers' swords in furnaces. Now battle-trumpets began to sound. The watchword which meant war went forth. One man seized a helmet with trembling hands and ran from his house; another backed his neighing team into its chariot-harness, donning shield and corslet of three-leash gold, and girding on his trusty sword.

Muses, the time has come for you to throw Helicon wide open and inspire me to tell who were the kings who were then rallied for war, what manner of soldiers followed each of them in their ranks to throng the plains, who were the men who even in those far days were the flower of Italy's fertile land, and what arms expressed her spirit's fire. For you, you are divine, and you have the gifts of memory and story; but only the faintest echo of the great tale has come down to me.

The first to enter the war and march his armed men forth was the furious Mezentius, scorner of gods, coming from Etruria's frontiers. Close by him marched his son Lausus, exceeded in beauty by none but the stalwart Laurentine Turnus. Lausus, the horse-tamer, the vanquisher of wild beasts in fight, led a thousand warriors from the city of Agylla, who followed him all in vain; he deserved more happiness than could be his under his father's tyranny, and merited a better father than Mezentius.

After them came Aventinus, a son of Hercules, handsome as his father was handsome. He vauntingly drove over the grassland a chariot decorated with a palm of victory which his horses had won, and bore on his shield his father's blazon, the Hydra with its fringe of a hundred snakes. Aventinus had been secretly born into the realm of day in Mount Aventine's wood; his mother was Rhea a priestess, a mortal woman who had union with a god when, in triumph after slaying Geryon, the Tirynthian Hercules came to the Laurentine farmlands and let his Spanish cows bathe in the Etruscan river. His soldiers carried in their hands for warfare javelins and sword-sticks, but they also fought with smooth sword-blades and Sabellian spits. Their captain himself moved up to the palace on foot, swinging a gigantic lion-skin, with the frightening bristles uncombed, which he wore fastened about his shoulders and drawn over his head with the white teeth grinning; and ferocious he looked in this garb of Hercules.

Next came two brothers from Tibur's battlements where the people are named after a third brother Tiburtus; they were Catillus and vigorous Coras, young and of Argive blood, who would charge ahead of a front line through showers of missiles like two centaurs, sons of the clouds, galloping down from the height of a mountain-crest and descending in swift career from snow-covered Othrys and from Homole, while vast forests yield to their passage and loudly snapping underwoods give them place.

Caeculus who founded the city of Praeneste joined them also. He was one whom every generation since has believed a son of Vulcan, born for royalty among cattle of the farm, and discovered, new-born, near the hearth-fire. With him came a levy of country men, summoned from far afield, men whose homes were on Praeneste's height, on Juno's farmlands at Gabii, by the cool Anio and amid porous Hernican rocks which rivulets bedew, with others who drew life from Anagnia's rich soil or from the river of Father Amasenus. Not all of them had weapons, or clattering shields, or rumbling chariots. Most of them would scatter sling-bolts of grey lead; but some brandished pairs of spears in their hands. They wore brown skull-caps of wolf-skin to shield their heads, and trod their footprints with the left foot bare, the right foot being shod with raw hide.

But meanwhile Messapus, Neptune's own son, Messapus the horse-tamer, whom Heaven's law permitted none to bring low by fire or by steel, handled the sword again, suddenly rallying to arms tribes which had long since lost the habit of marching in ranks of war, and had grown content with a life of ease. Of them some had their homes in Fescennium's citadel, or were Faliscans, plain-dwellers now; and others lived below Soracte's jagged crest-line, on farm-lands of Flavinium, by Mount Ciminus with its lake or in Capena's sacred groves. They moved in regular rhythm with marching songs in celebration of their king, like snow-white swans which sometimes, as they return from pasture through yielding clouds, extend their necks and chant their measured music, as the river and the Asian Marsh ring afar with the impact of the sound. No one would have thought that this moving multitude was indeed an army's bronze-clad ranks, but rather a cloud of strong-voiced birds in the air, driving to land from deep waters of the main.

And, see! Clausus, of ancient Sabine blood, was hastening a strong company forwards on the march; but he was like a great host in himself; and he is the ancestor of all the Claudian clan and the Claudian family which have spread over Latium since Sabines were given their share in Rome. With Clausus came an immense contingent, some of them the old Quirites, others from Amiternum, and all the band from Eretum and Mutusca where the olives grow; and also they who live in the City of Nomentum, the region of Rosea by Lake Velinus, on Tetrica's knife-edge crag, or Mount Severus, in Casperia, and Foruli and by Himella's river; they who drink Tiber and Fabaris, others sent by chill Nursia, and then too companies of Horta and the Latin folk, and also others whose land is divided, and washed, by Allia with its ill-fortuned name. They were as many as the billows which roll on Libya's whitening sea when pitiless Orion is hiding under winter's waves; or as thick as the ears of corn which are scorched when the sun shines with new strength in the Plain of Hermus or in Lycia's yellow cornfields. Shields clattered; and earth was alarmed by the tread of their feet.

It was Halaesus next, Agamemnon's man and foe to the name of Troy, who yoked horses to chariot; and he hurried the march of a thousand proud clans to the aid of Turnus. Of them some turned with the hoe the Massic soil most fertile for Bacchus, others had been sent by Auruncan elders down from their high hills or from the neighbouring level lands of the Sidicinians, and some marched from Cales; some lived by the Volturnus, the river of shoals, and there were the fierce folk of Saticula besides, and a band of Oscans also. Their missiles were rounded throwing-clubs, which it was their habit to fix to flexible leashes. Leather bucklers shielded their left arms, and they used scimitars for close fighting. Nor shall Oebalus go without mention in this story. It is said that Telon, while he reigned over the Teleboae in Capreae, being then of advancing age, begot by the nymph Sebethis a son who was not content with his inheritance, but was already seeking to subject to his rule extensive lands of Sarrastian tribes where Sarnus waters the plains, and the men whose homes were at Rufrae and Batulum and in Celemna's farmlands, or dwelling where amid apple orchards Abella's ramparts look down; and they were trained to fling the boomerang as do the Teutons; their head-coverings were of bark torn off the cork-tree, and they had glittering bronze-plated bucklers and glittering swords of bronze.

And mountainous Nersae sent Ufens to the battles, a prince famed in story for his good fortune in arms. His clansmen the Aequiculans were wild beyond other men, living on a hard soil and hunting constantly in forests. They are armed when they till the land, and ever they delight in driving home freshly won spoils and living by pillage.

There came also a priest of Marruvian race, who wore over his helmet a decoration of flourishing olive-leaves. This was the most valiant Umbro, and he had been sent by King Archippus. Umbro could even, with his hand and his music, sprinkle sleep on all the viper-kind and on water-snakes of poisonous breath, mollifying their anger and giving relief against their bites by his skill. But he had not power enough to heal a stroke from a Dardan lance; for his sleep-bringing charms and his herbs gathered in Marsian mountains were of no avail to cure his own wounds. Angitia's grove and the

Fucine Lake of the glassy wave wept for him; and the clear pools mourned.

Virbius, a son of Hippolytus, also came marching, most splendid, to war. Aricia was the mother who sent forth this distinguished son, and he had been reared in Egeria's forest beside the marsh at her lake's verge where at the altar of Diana rich sacrifices win favour. In the story they tell how Hippolytus, who had died by his step-mother's cunning and, torn asunder by stampeding horses, had fully paid in his blood the debt due to his father, afterwards rose again to the airs beneath the sky, to see heaven's stars once more, recalled to life by Apollo's herbs and Diana's love. But then the Almighty Father, who resented that a mortal man should rise from the nether shadows to the light of living, cast Apollo's son Aesculapius, the inventor of such a healing power, down to the waters of Styx by his own thunder-stroke. But Diana the Kindly hid Hippolytus safely away in a home apart, confining him to the nymph Egeria's wood, under her care, where he was to pass all his life alone in obscurity amid Italy's forests as Virbius, called by a different name. And this is in fact why horn-foot horses are not allowed in Diana's temple or her hallowed wood, because it was horses, taking fright at a monster out of the sea, which had thrown the chariot and the young prince to earth on the sea-shore. But none the less his son came driving his own fiery horses headlong over the level plain, as he dashed in his chariot to war.

Turnus himself moved to and fro among the foremost, splendid to see, weapons in hand, and towering by a full head above the rest. His tall helmet was crowned by a triple plume and supported a Chimaera breathing Etna's fires from its jaws; and ever louder it roared, and madder grew the menace of its flames as grimmer grew the battle amid streaming blood. To his polished shield Io gave distinction by her presence there in gold; she was shown as already a cow, already covered with bristles and raising her horns – a portentous device – ; and with her was shown Argus, guarding Io's maidenhood, and Father Inachus, who poured his river from a chased silver urn. Turnus was closely followed by a cloud of foot-soldiers, whose bucklered columns clustered thick over all the plain; the manhood of Argos, bands of Auruncans, Rutulians, Old Sicanians, embattled Sacranians and Labicans of the paint-splashed shields; with others who ploughed vales beside Tiber and Numicus' holy banks, or worked with their plough-shares Rutulian hills, Circeii's promontory, farmlands where Jupiter of Anxur presides, and Feronia, in her green wood-land's delight; and others who had homes where lies Satura's black marsh and where chill Ufens seeks out his course low in the valleys till he hides within the sea.

With these, Camilla came. She was of Volscian race, and led her cavalcade of squadrons a-flower with bronze. She was a warrior; her girl's hands had never been trained to Minerva's distaff and her baskets of wool, but rather, though a maiden, she was one to face out grim fights and in speed of foot to out-distance the winds. She might have skimmed over the tops of uncut corn-stalks without ever harming their delicate ears as she ran, or upheld her way through the midst of the sea supported on heaving waves without once wetting her swift foot-soles in its surface. A gathering of mothers and all the young men who were streaming from houses and fields looked forth admiringly at her as she passed, in open-mouthed astonishment to see how regal splendour clothed her smooth shoulders in purple, how her brooch clasped her hair in its gold, and how she wore on her a Lycian quiver and carried a shepherd's myrtle-staff with a lance's head.

BOOK EIGHT

THE SITE OF THE FUTURE ROME

TURNUS hoisted the war flag on the Laurentine Citadel, roused the mettle of his horses, and clashed his arms. Trumpets blared out their harsh music. At once all mental balance was lost. The whole of Latium was caught up in a fever of armed resistance; the younger men became riotously mad for blood. Their captains, Messapus, Ufens, and Mezentius, scorner of the gods, were the first to muster their levies from all around, stripping fields of their cultivators over a wide area. Venulus was even sent to mighty Diomede's city to ask help; he was to explain how Trojans already had a foothold in Latium, how Aeneas had sailed thither with the vanquished gods of his old home claiming that destiny required him to become its king, how numerous peoples were joining the Dardan prince, and his name was gathering repute far across Latium. What exactly was this prince's purpose in these initial actions, and what outcome of the fighting he desired should fortune go his way, were more clearly evident to Diomede himself than to King Turnus or even to King Latinus.

So went matters in Latium. And the hero of Laomedon's line, seeing all that passed, was tossed on a heaving tide of anxieties. Rapidly his mind leapt this way and that, in the hurried search for different viewpoints to help him think out all his problems: like the quivering light from water, swaying in a basin, struck by the sunlight or reflecting the moon's rays from its surface, and flitting everywhere and ranging far, till at last it leaps into the air and hits the panels in the ceiling overhead. It was night, and all over the world profound sleep held tired creatures, all tribes of flying things and all animals of the farm, when Aeneas, Troy's chieftain, his whole heart distracted by the horror of the war, sank down on the river bank under heaven's chill height, and only at a late hour allowed rest to spread over his limbs. And there appeared to him the God of the place, old Tiber himself, who arose from his pleasant stream amid his poplar-leaves. A fine linen clothed him in grey raiment, and shady reeds covered his hair. Then he spoke to Aeneas, and assuaged all his care with his words: 'O seed of the divine blood, who convey Troy's city back to us out of the hands of the foe and preserve for eternity the centre of her defence, you for whom this Laurentine earth and these Latin lands have long been waiting, here is your home assured and here for the Gods of Home is their sure place. Shrink not back. And be not frightened by the threats of war, for the high anger of the Gods and all their malignity have now died away. And since you must not think that all this is fancy, created by your sleep, here is a sign. Lying under holm-oak trees near the sea shore you shall find a huge white sow, stretched on the ground with her thirty young which she has just farrowed, all white like her, gathered round her teats. This spot shall be the place for your city, and there shall you find sure rest from your toils. Within thirty circling years from this time, Ascanius shall found a city of illustrious name, Alba. My prophecy cannot fail. Attend now, for I shall explain shortly by what means you may make your way victoriously through the tangle of problems in front of you. Here in this territory dwell Arcadians, of a family descended from Pallas. As comrades of King Evander they have followed him and his standard, and on a chosen site among the hills they have founded a city called Pallanteum after their ancestor's name. These Arcadians have long been at ceaseless war with the Latin nation. Join with them in treaty, and attach them as allies to your forces. I shall myself lead you along the banks of my course and enable you to row upstream against the current. Therefore come, Son of the Goddess; arise, and when the stars begin to set offer prayers in due form to Juno, and prevail over the threats of her wrath by vows of supplication. When you have your victory you shall pay me honour in full return. I am he whom you see scouring these banks and cutting through rich farmlands with this brimming stream, Tiber the water-blue, of all rivers the most loved by Heaven. And in this place is the outflow from my great hall, which is the source of life for proud cities.'

So spoke the River-God, and plunged into the deep pool, diving to its floor. Sleep and the night together left Aeneas. He arose, and, fixing his eyes on the sun's light dawning in the heaven, formally held aloft water from the river in hollowed palms, and cried from his heart to the sky: 'Nymphs, Laurentine Nymphs, whose birth is of the rivers, and, Father Tiber, you, and your hallowed stream, receive me, Aeneas, and grant me at long last a defence against my perils. You take pity on our distress; therefore, whatever spring may fill the pools which are your home, and wherever you yourself emerge in grandeur from the soil, always shall you be celebrated by me with honour and with offerings, O Horned River, who govern all waters of the Western Land. Only may you be at my side and in very presence confirm your revelations.' So saying Aeneas chose a pair of bireme ships from his fleet, manned them with rowing-crews, and as he did so he marshalled his comrades under arms.

Suddenly a remarkable and imposing sight came to view. On the green river-bank was a shining-white sow with her white litter of the same colour as herself, which had lain down on the ground in a wood. Aeneas the True brought implements, and stationed both sow and litter at an altar. And he sacrificed all to Juno, to Juno only, to Juno herself, the Supreme. Then did Tiber make smooth his heaving flood for the whole length of that night and withdrew the flow of his now voiceless waves, becoming so still as he levelled the ripples on his surface that it seemed like a kindly pool or peaceful marsh, on which no oar need strain. So then the Trojans began their journey and made good speed, encouraged by what Aeneas had been told. Greased pine-timbers slid by over shallow water. The very waves wondered, and the woods, strangers to such a sight, were surprised to see floating in the river the brightly painted ships with the warriors' far-gleaming shields. The Trojans rowed tirelessly till a night and a day were spent. They passed round long bends, and shaded by trees of many kinds they cut between green forests on the friendly river-surface. The fiery sun had climbed to the midpoint of the sky's circle when ahead of them they saw walls, a citadel, and scattered house-roofs; all this Roman might has now exalted to Heaven, but at that time Evander lived there in poverty. Quickly they turned prows shorewards, and drew near to the city.

It happened that on that very day the Arcadian king was paying anniversary honours to Amphitryon's mighty son Hercules and the other gods in a wood before his city. Together with him his son Pallas, the leading young Arcadians, and his Senate, all men of little wealth, were offering incense to the Deities and warm blood was steaming on the altar. When they first noticed the ships and saw them gliding between the shady woods with crews silently bending to the oars, they were alarmed at the sudden sight; and as one man they arose, leaving their banquet. But Pallas in an adventurous mood bade them not to interrupt the rite, and then seizing a weapon dashed alone to meet the strangers. While he was still far off, he shouted from some rising ground: 'Warriors, what motive has impelled you to explore this strange route? What is your destination? Of what race are you, where is the home which you leave behind you, and do you bring us peace, or war?' The chieftain Aeneas then answered from high on his ship's stern, stretching out in his hand before him an olive-spray in token of peace: 'You see before you men of Trojan birth, whose arms are hostile only to those men of Latium who, when we sought refuge with them, contemptuously repelled us, and made war. Now we seek Evander. Take our message to him; say that chosen leaders of Dardania have come asking an armed alliance.' At the sound of the tremendous name Pallas stood stock-still astounded. Then he answered: 'Pray, whoever you are, disembark, and address my father in person; come as our guest straight into our home.' He took him by the hand, and his handshake was firm and long. They walked forward and leaving the river came into the wood.

Aeneas then spoke friendly words to the king: 'Sir, of all who have Greek blood you are the best; and it is to you that by will of Fortune I hold forth in entreaty a spray graced with wool. Nor did my knowledge that you are an Arcadian, a leader of Greeks, and kin by birth to the two sons of Atreus, inspire me with any dread of you. Instead, my own valour, holy oracles from gods, the kinship between your father and mine, and your own renown throughout the world have all joined me to you and brought me here in willing obedience to my destiny. Dardanus, who sailed away to the Teucrian people and who was first father to our city Ilium and made her strong, was, as the Greeks relate, sprung from Electra the daughter of Atlas; for Atlas the mighty, who sustains the spheres of heaven on his shoulder, begot Electra. The father of your family is Mercury; he was conceived and borne by fair Maia on Cyllene's cold mountain-peak. Now, if we put faith in what we are told, Maia was begotten by Atlas, the same Atlas who supports the constellations of the sky. Thus our two families are both branches springing from the same original stock. Trusting to these ties, I have used neither envoys nor craft in my first approach to you, but instead have exposed my own life to risk, and come myself with my petition to your doors. We are menaced in pitiless warfare by the same Daunian Race which persecutes you. They believe that, if they expel us, there will be nothing to prevent them from bringing all the Western Land wholly under their yoke, and controlling the seas which wash its western and eastern coasts. Accept our pledge and give us yours. We have hearts valiant in war, we have spirit, and a manhood which has proved itself by deed.'

So Aeneas spoke. While he was speaking, Evander had been gazing for some time at his face and his eyes, and surveying his whole figure. Then, shortly, he answered: 'Most valiant of Trojans, how gladly I recognize you and welcome you! And how well I recall the words, the voice, and the face of great Anchises! For I remember how Priam, Laomedon's son, who was travelling to Salamis on a visit to the kingdom of his sister Hesione, continued onwards to pay another visit within the cold frontiers of Arcadia. At that time youth was just gracing my cheeks with their first bloom. I admired all the Trojan chiefs, and among them I admired Laomedon's own son; but as he walked Anchises towered high above all the rest. My young heart was full of a burning desire to go and speak to the prince, and clasp his hand in mine. So I went up to him, and in my keen interest I escorted him within the city of Pheneos. When he left he presented me with a magnificent quiver containing arrows from Lycia, a mantle with gold threads woven into it, and a pair of golden bits which are now in the possession of Pallas my son. That is why not only has my right hand joined yours in the compact which was the purpose of your visit, but in addition, when, at tomorrow's dawn, light is restored to the world, and I let you depart, you will be well satisfied with my assistance, and the material aid which I shall give. But meanwhile you must lend us your favour, and, since you have come as our friends, join us in celebrating this annual rite, which it would be a sin to postpone, and begin now to feel at home at your allies' board.'

This said, Evander gave command for the food and the drink, which had been removed, to be set out again, and found places for his guests on seats of turf. He had a special welcome for Aeneas, placing him on a maple-wood chair covered by a shaggy lion's skin. Then the Priest of the Altar, with the eager and attentive help of selected young servers, brought roast meat from the bulls, piled up baskets of those gifts which Ceres gives to the toil of man, and served the wine of Bacchus. Aeneas and the men from Troy feasted on a whole chine of beef and the sacrificial entrails.

When their hunger was banished and their appetite for food checked, King Evander spoke: 'This regular observance, with its ritual banquet, and this altar in honour of a mighty Power were by no means forced on us by some fanciful superstition or any disregard for the old gods. Trojan guest, we are in duty bound to discharge the obligations of this new worship; for we are men who have been saved from perils cruel indeed. Now look first at this rock-face, with its overhanging crag, and see how beyond it there still remains a mountain lair, now abandoned, with its massive structure shattered asunder and a trail of mighty havoc left by falling rocks. Here there was once a cavern, of a depth receding to a vast distance beyond the reach of any ray of sunlight. In this cavern Cacus, a man-monster of hideous aspect, had a home.

The ground was always reeking with newly spilt blood; men's faces, in the pallid horror of decay, hung suspended in defiance at the entry. This monster's father was Vulcan, and as he moved in giant bulk he belched his father's pitchy fires out of his mouth.

'But time at last brought to us, as it has to others, an answer to our prayers for aid in the arrival of a god. For Hercules himself, the supreme avenger, came; and came at his time of exultation, when he had lately slain and despoiled three-bodied Geryon. He travelled this way, driving some gigantic bulls which he had won by his conquest; and the cattle occupied the valley, and the river too. Cacus, who in his insane ingenuity wished to leave no act of crime or fraud undared or unattempted, carried off four large and splendid bulls and four exceptionally fine heifers from their stalls. And he dragged them all to his cave by their tails, so reversing their footprints to prevent their hooves from leaving any revealing tracks. He was now holding his stolen animals hidden in darkness within his rock; and there were no clues leading to the cave which could direct anyone who might search for them. Meanwhile Hercules the Amphitryonid had begun to move his well-fed herd from the stalls in preparation for leaving. While they were moving off, the cattle lowed; the woods were full of their plaintive calls and the hills were loud with their noise as they departed. A single cow, lowing deep down in the immense cavern, returned an answering cry; and well guarded though she was she cheated the hopes of Cacus.

'Then indeed Hercules' indignation blazed forth in one flash of venomous black rage. Seizing in his hands some weapons, including his heavily knotted club, he dashed for the steep cliffs of the lofty mountain. Till then, not one of us had ever seen Cacus afraid, with panic in his eyes. But now he fled without a thought, swifter than the east wind, making for his cave; and fear lent wings to his feet. He shut himself in by breaking a chain and so letting fall an enormous rock, which, through his father's skill, hung suspended by the iron; thus making the doorposts impassable by jamming this obstacle hard against them on either side.

'But look! The Tirynthian was already at the entrance in a fury of passion. He examined all possible approaches, peering now this way and now that, and grinding his teeth. In a boiling rage he circled the Aventine Mount three times. Three times he tried the stone-blocked entrance-way, but in vain. Three times down in the valley he sank back in weariness. Now there was a pinnacle of flint-rock which stood sheer, as if the stone had been cut away all round it, soaring to a dizzy height on the ridge above the cave; an impressive sight and a fit nesting-place for sinister birds of prey. It was inclined towards the downward slope, leaning towards the river on the left. Hercules now strained at it from the right side, pressing it forwards. He shook it, wrenched it from its roots, and then gave it a sudden thrust. At that thrust the great sky thundered, the river-banks leapt apart, and even the river flowed backwards in alarm. At once all Cacus' den, his monstrous castle, was uncovered and clear to view, and its shadowy recesses stood exposed; as if the earth through some convulsion had gaped apart, unlocking the deepest dwellings of the infernal world, and had flung wide open the pallid Empire hated of the gods, till the horrifying abyss comes into view from above and ghosts shudder at the inrush of light. So now Hercules having caught Cacus in this sudden unexpected daylight, trapped in his own hollow rock and howling as never before, pressed him hard with a shower of missiles from above, calling into play every means of attack, and driving at him with tree-branches and giant blocks of stone. On his side, Cacus, who had no retreat from his peril left open, choked forth thick smoke from his jaws, an astonishing sight; he filled his den with opaque and blinding darkness, and massed a night of spouting fumes with fire mingling in the murk. This the proud spirit of Hercules could not brook. With a headlong leap he flung himself through the fire just where the densest concentration of smoke rolled its waves, at the blackest part of the fog which churned through the vast cave. And seizing Cacus, who still vomited his ineffectual flames through the darkness, he twined him into a knot; and clung to him, choking him till his eyes started from his head and his throat went bloodless and dry. Then quickly he tore down the doors and the murky den was thrown open. The stolen cattle, the plunder which Cacus had been forced to renounce, were displayed to the heaven's view. The shapeless carcass was dragged forth by the feet. The onlookers could not have enough of gazing at the horrifying eyes, the face, and the shaggy bristling chest of the man-beast; or at the jaws, where the flames were dead.

'Ever since that time this rite has been observed, and they who came after have joyously kept the day. At first the responsibility fell to Potitius, and then to the Pinarian House, guardians of the worship of Hercules. Potitius erected this altar here in the wood. Our 'Greatest Altar' we shall always call it, and our 'Greatest' it shall always be. Therefore come, young warriors, garland your hair with leaves, and holding forth your cups of wine in your right hands, present them in reverence for that glorious deed. Call on the God, for god he is for us and for you, and offer the wine with good will.' Even as he finished speaking, he took a spray of poplar, Hercules' own shady tree, and entwined in his hair a wreath and pendant of its silver-green leaves. The wooden cup of the rite engaged his hands. Then they all quickly and joyfully poured libations onto their tables and said prayers to the Deities.

Meanwhile, evening drew near the lower slopes of Olympus. Now came the priests, led by Potitius, girt according to custom with skins, and carrying torches. All started the feasting again; they brought their own contributions for the second course, and piled loaded dishes on the altars. Next, Salii appeared with poplar-sprays wreathing their foreheads, to sing around the kindled altar-fires. There were two bands of them, one of younger and one of older men, and they celebrated in hymns the glorious acts of Hercules, how in the beginning he crushed and strangled by his own strength two snakes, those monsters which his stepmother had sent; how he shattered two cities of rare power for war, Troy and Oechalia; and how he completed a thousand hard labours because Juno hated him and imposed them on him as his destiny in the service of King Eurystheus. 'Oh, unconquerable! You are the slayer by your own might of those cloud-born creatures of two shapes in one, Hylaeus and Pholus, and also the monstrous Cretan Bull, and the gigantic lion under Nemea's rock. You shocked the lake of Styx into trembling, and the Watch-Dog of Orcus too, where he lies above gnawed bones in his blood-drenched cave. No apparition could frighten you, not even towering Typhoeus himself, standing, weapons in hand. Nor were you found without resource when the snake of Lerna enveloped you with its crowding heads. Hail, true son of Jupiter, who by your presence among the gods lend more brightness to their glory! Draw near to us and to your own holy rite, and visit us with your favour.'

So did they celebrate his deeds in their hymns. And then to crown their story they sang of the Cave of Cacus, and the fire-breathing monster himself. All the woodland rang in harmony with the gay sound and the hills echoed it back. Then, after they had completed their devotions, the whole gathering walked back to the city. The king, moving stiffly because of his years, kept Aeneas and his own son beside him for company as he walked, and lightened the journey with many topics of conversation. Wonderingly, Aeneas turned his alert eyes all about him, attracted by what he saw, and with much enjoyment asked questions about the relics of earlier generations, and listened to the explanations which King Evander, founder of the citadel at Rome, gave him: 'These woods used to be the home of native Fauns and Nymphs, and a race of men who were born from tree-trunks of tough wood. These men had no civilized way of life. They knew neither how to yoke oxen nor how to produce and garner food, storing a reserve, but lived off fruit from the bough and the hard fare that hunting yielded. The first to arrive among them was Saturn, from heavenly Olympus, an exile who had lost his throne and was retreating before Jupiter's weapons. He unified the folk, who had been living scattered among hill-tops and were slow to learn, giving them laws and choosing 'Latium' for the land's name, because he had been safe in hiding, 'latent', within its boundaries. Under Saturn's reign passed those centuries which are famed as 'golden', so gentle and peaceful was his rule, until gradually an inferior and tarnished age succeeded, mad for war and lusting to possess. Next there came a band of Ausonians and tribes of Sicanians; and Saturn's Land now began to forget its name. There followed kings, and among them a fierce giant, Thybris, after whom we who live in Italy named our river Tiber, so that it lost its true name, which had been Albula in ancient times. I myself had been banished from my homeland, and journeyed towards the extremity of the ocean until all-powerful Fortune and inescapable Destiny set me to live here, whither I had been forced to come by dread warnings from my mother, the Nymph Carmentis, and by the authority of the God Apollo.'

Scarcely were the words spoken when he straightway stepped forward and showed Aeneas first an altar and then the gate which Romans call the Carmental Gate, commemorating by this name the ancient honour conferred on the Nymph Carmentis, the prophetic seeress who was the first to foretell greatness for the sons of Aeneas and renown for Pallanteum. Next Evander showed Aeneas a thick wood which the forceful Romulus was to adopt as his 'sanctuary' and, under a dank crag, the Lupercal, the Wolf's Cave, which is named in the Arcadian fashion after the wolf-god, Lycaean Pan. He showed him also the hallowed grove of the Argiletum, and citing the spot in witness explained how Argus, though a guest, met his death. From there he conducted him to Tarpeia's Place and the Capitol, which is now all gold, but was once wild and ragged, covered with woodland undergrowth. Even in those old days that spot held a sinister awe of its own, which used to inspire fear and alarm into the country folk who then as now trembled at the trees there and the rocks. Evander continued: 'This wooded hill with its leaf-clad crest is the habitation of some god, but it is not known which god he is. The Arcadians believe that here they have often seen Jupiter himself shaking the dark aegis in his right hand to awake the clouds of storm. And here, now, you can also see two hill-towers whose walls have been shattered. They are relics and memorials of ancient men. Of these two citadels Father Janus founded the one, and Saturn the other; accordingly the one was long since given the name of Janiculum and the other Saturnia.' Conversing so, they approached Evander's home, the house of a poor man, and they saw herds of cattle lowing everywhere about the sites of the present-day Roman Forum and the smart Carinae. When they had arrived at the house, Evander said: 'Hercules himself in the hour of victory bowed his head to enter this door. This royal dwelling was not too small to contain even him. Guest of mine, be strong to scorn wealth and so mould yourself that you also may be fit for a God's converse. Be not exacting as you enter a poor home.' Having spoken so, he led the mighty Aeneas under the humble building's sloping roof, and showed him his bed, a couch of strewn leaves on which was spread the skin of an African bear. Night fell, and embraced the earth in her dark wings.

But meanwhile Venus, with a mother's deep and justified dismay at the resolute uprising and threats of the Laurentines, was speaking to Vulcan. She was in her husband's golden marriage-room, and as she began her plea she added a breath of divine love to her words: 'All the time that the Argive princes were bringing devastation on Troy's defence which was doomed by fate to destruction in war, and on her citadel which was bound to fall by the fires of hatred, never once did I ask of you weapons, or any other aid within the power of your skill, for my poor people: for I did not wish, dearest Husband, to drive you to exert your efforts in vain, even though I owed many a debt to Priam's sons and had often wept for the cruel sufferings of Aeneas. But now, since Jove has so commanded it, Aeneas has found a foothold within the country of the Rutulians. Therefore this time I do indeed come to you in humble entreaty, and of your revered divinity I ask arms for him, as a mother appealing for her son. The daughter of Nereus and the bride of Tithonus both prevailed on you by their tears. And see what nations gather, what walled cities have shut their gates and sharpen against me the blade which is to destroy my people!' So divine Venus spoke. Her husband was hesitant; but she passed her snow-white arms about him on this side and on that, and coaxed him with her caressing embrace. And suddenly, as always, he caught the flame; the familiar glow penetrated into his marrow and sped down his quivering bones; like the lightning-crack which will sometimes dart gleaming and sparkling through storm-clouds burst apart by the thunder-flash. His partner knew it. She was well aware of her own loveliness, and pleased at her trick. Then the old father, in the chains of that love which could never die, answered her: 'Why do you go so far back to find a plea? What has become of your trust in me, Lady Divine? Even in the old days, had your anxiety been so great as now, I could without wrong have armed your Trojans, for neither the Father Almighty nor Destiny forbade Troy to stand and Priam to live on for ten years more. So now, if you are making ready for war and such is your will, why, then, for any service which my craft can offer, for anything which can be made from iron or molten silver-gold, and for all might of the fires and the bellows-blast – , give over begging, and doubting your own powers!' And as he spoke he gave her the desired embrace; and then, relaxing upon the breast of his wife, he let the sleep of pleasure steal over his limbs.

But after, when night was already receding from the mid-point of her course, and first repose had dispelled sleep from him, the same hour when some housewife, whose burden it is to endure life in dependence on her distaff and Minerva's slight aid, will awake the fire asleep in the ashes, and adding the night-hours to her working-time, set her maids a long task, and keep them at it by lamplight, to enable her to guard her marriage in purity and bring up her little sons; at this same hour, and with a will as active, the God whose Might is Fire arose from his soft bed to work at his forge. By Aeolian Lipara an island rises steeply on spray-steaming rocks in the sea near Sicily's flank, where an underground cavern and galleries leading from Etna, originally excavated by the smithying Cyclopes, roar thunderously; for in them strong blows are heard resounding on anvils and re-echoing their growl. Chalybean ingots hiss within chambers of rock and in the furnaces pants the fire. The island is Vulcan's home; and Vulcania is its name.

To this place at that hour the God whose Might is Fire came down from high Heaven. Cyclopes were working iron in a vast gallery; they were Thunderer, Lightener, and the bare-limbed Fire-Anvil. They had in hand a roughly-shaped thunderbolt, of which a part was already shining-perfect but the rest remained unfinished; it was of the kind which the Father flings in great numbers down on the world from every quarter of the sky. They had fixed onto it three skeins of twisted rain, three belts of rain-charged cloud, and three of red fire and three of winged south wind. And now they were blending within their creation the flashes which bring the terror, the crashing, and the dread, with darting wrath wrapped in vindictive flames. Others elsewhere were urgently building for Mars one of those chariots with the flying wheels which he uses to enflame warriors and whole cities, and also a horror-inspiring aegis, to arm Pallas when her serenity is disturbed, to which, in mutual rivalry, the Cyclopes were giving the sparkle of golden serpent-scales, with snakes twining from either side, and for the Goddess's breast the Gorgon's head itself, shorn from the neck but still rolling its eyes. 'Away with all of it!' said Vulcan. 'Lay aside whatever you have begun, you Cyclopes of Etna, and give me your attention. We have arms to make for a man, a mortal warrior of high spirit. Now you need all your strength, your swift, grasping hands, and all your master-skill. Delay not an instant!' He said no more. All together the Cyclopes shared out their tasks fairly and went swiftly to work. Bronze and pure gold-ore flowed along the conduits, and wounding steel melted in a great furnace. They shaped out an immense shield fit for standing alone against all the missiles of Latium and they fixed all its seven layers fast together. Other Cyclopes, using bellows with a blast like the winds, drew in and discharged the air. Some tempered hissing bronze in a circular pool of water. The cavern rumbled under the anvils planted on its floor. With all their energy they raised arms rhythmically together and kept the mass of metal turning by the grip of their tongs.

While the Father-God whom Lemnos reveres was hastening this work in the region of Aeolia, the strengthening light of dawn and the morning song of birds under the eaves roused

Evander to leave his lowly house. The old king arose, put on his tunic, and laced Etruscan sandals to the soles of his feet. Next he slung his Tegean sword from his shoulder to fall at his side, and swung a panther's skin about him, hanging over on his left arm. With him were his two watch-dogs which had jumped down from the front-door step ahead of him and now trotted beside their master as he walked ahead. He was going to the separate house which was occupied by his guest Aeneas, for, as a true man should, he remembered their talk and the favour which he had promised. Aeneas, no less than he, was up and about in the early morning. Evander's son Pallas accompanied his father, and Achates was with Aeneas. They met and shook hands. Then they sat at their ease in the centre of the hall and took advantage of this chance to converse freely.

The king began the talk: 'You are the greatest of all Troy's leaders; while you still live I could never myself admit that the Trojan Empire and the life of Troy had met utter defeat. In comparison with that illustrious name, what warlike aid we have the strength to give is little enough. On one side we are enclosed by the Etruscan River, and on the other we are pressed by the Rutulians, whose arms clash even round our walls. But I can nevertheless attach to your side powerful nations who are already in the field and are equipped from the resources of wealthy kingdoms.

'This hope of relief we owe to a lucky surprise; for you, by finding your way here, fulfilled a demand of Destiny. Now situated not far from here is the City of Agylla whose citizens still dwell on the ancient rock on which it was founded, when long ago a Lydian people, a nation of fine warriors, settled there amid the hills of Etruria. Agylla flourished for many years until one of its kings, Mezentius, oppressed it under a tyrannical rule based on a ferocious use of armed force. I need not relate this despot's insane and wicked acts of bloodshed. May the gods hold such sufferings as he inflicted in store for his own self and for his kin! Why, he would even bind together the living and the dead with hands tied to rotting hands and faces to rotting faces, a torture indeed; and so he destroyed many victims by protracted death in this harrowing embrace, all drenched in decomposing filth. So at last his subjects, wearied with his unutterable lust for blood, gathered in arms around his home, cut down his retainers, and hurled flaming torches onto his roof. But during the massacre Mezentius had escaped into Rutulian country and gained protection from the arms of Turnus who was his guest-friend. So now all Etruria has risen in a violent but just impulse for vengeance, and, under threat of immediate war, they are insisting on the surrender of their king for execution. Aeneas, I shall enable you to lead them in their thousands. For indeed their ships are ready massed along their shores and they are loudly and impatiently demanding the order to advance into action. But an aged Liver-Diviner has been restraining them with his predictions of destiny: "You, elect manhood of Lydia, the flower and the valour of the ancient race, you whose just indignation presses you to action against the foe, set aflame by a wrath which Mezentius most fully deserves, you must know that it is not granted to any man of Italy that he yoke so mighty a nation as yours to himself, and therefore must you choose a foreign leader." At this the Etruscan host, in dread of the divine warning, encamped as before on the plain. Tarchon himself sent ambassadors here, bearing his kingdom's crown and sceptre, for he wished to entrust the regalia to me, asking me to join his camp and accede to the Etruscan throne. But my old age is cold and slow, left by lapse of time with little now to give, and my strength which is past valiant deeds denies me high command. I should have urged my son to accept, if he had not been of mixed descent, drawing part of his nationality from a Sabine mother. But you are one to whose years and connexions destiny has not been harsh. It is you, most valiant commander of Trojans and of Italians also, whom the Powers require. March on your way. Besides, I shall attach to you Pallas who is my one hope and consolation. Let him under instruction from you grow used to enduring war-service in the grim work of Mars; let him watch your deeds; let him from his earliest years look up to you. I shall give to him two hundred mounted Arcadians, the selected strength of our young manhood, and Pallas shall give to you an equal number in his own name.'

He had scarcely spoken when, as Aeneas, Anchises' son, and the faithful Achates both stood with downcast faces, starting trains of troubled thoughts in a mood of lonely gloom, the Cytherean herself gave her sign out of a cloudless sky. For suddenly lightning flickered in the heavens and thunder crashed, the whole sky appeared suddenly to fall, and the clarion note of an Etruscan trumpet seemed to bray across its breadth. They looked up; again and again crashed the tremendous sound. And then they saw arms showing through a cloud in a clear part of the sky, glowing red through bright air and clanging thunderously as if under blows. The others stood aghast. But Troy's hero recognized in the sounds the promise which his Goddess Mother had made. Then he said: 'Ah, Stranger Friend, you need never, surely, enquire what is the event which these wonders portend. This is Olympus, calling for me. My Goddess-Mother foretold that she would send this sign if war should threaten, and would bring me arms made by Vulcan through the air for my aid. Oh, piteous, that such fearful massacre hangs over the poor Laurentine people! Terrible, Turnus, is the penalty which you shall pay to me! And, Father Tiber, how many the valiant men, how many their shields and helms, which shall be swept rolling down beneath your waves! Now, let them break our compact! Now let them insist on battle!'

Having spoken so, he arose from his raised chair. First he stirred the smouldering altar with its flame sacred to Hercules, and happily he made his approach to the hearth-fire of yesterday where dwelt the gods of the little home. Then Evander and the warriors of Troy, each taking equal part, formally sacrificed some selected two-year sheep. Afterwards, Aeneas walked away to his ships, revisiting his comrades. Of their number he chose certain men of outstanding gallantry to come with him on his mission of war. The remainder floated effortlessly down with the help of the stream, carried by the flow of the current, to return with news for Ascanius of his father and of all that had occurred. Next, horses were provided for the band of Trojans who were now to take the road for the Etruscan lands. For Aeneas they led forth a specially chosen horse, caparisoned all over by a red-brown lion-skin with gilded claws glittering at its edge.

Rumour now suddenly took wings and swiftly spread through the little town, telling how riders were marching to the palace-gate of the Etruscan king. Mothers in dread redoubled their prayers; the danger more nearly matched their fears; and taller than before loomed the vision of Mars. Then the father, Evander, clasped the right hand of his departing son and clung to him, weeping inconsolably, as he said: 'Oh, if only Jupiter would bring back to me the years which are gone and make me as I was when beneath Praeneste's wall I victoriously brought down their whole front rank, burned piles of enemy shields, and sent King Erulus with this very hand to death! To Erulus at his birth, for grotesque is his story, his mother Feronia had given three lives, so that he could handle three sets of weapons and must three times be laid low in death. Yet in those days this hand of mine took from him all three lives and three times stripped his arms from him. If I were now as I was then, I should never have been parted from your loved embrace, son of mine, and Mezentius would never have brought brutal death on so many by the sword and widowed his city of so many of her men, as defiantly as if I no longer lived just across his frontiers. But you, High Powers, and O Jupiter, Sovereign Supreme of all the Divine, take pity, I beg you, on a king of Arcadians and hear a father's prayer. If your divine wills, and Destiny too, have Pallas in your safe keeping, preserving him for me, and if I may live with the certainty of seeing him and meeting him again, then do I entreat you for my life, that only; for I freely consent to endure any suffering which may befall me. But if you, Fortune, are threatening some unspeakable disaster, then may I be allowed, ah, in this very minute, to break off a life which is too cruel, while my anxieties still hold a doubt, while my expectations of the future are yet uncertain, and while I still hold you in my embrace, dear son, my late, my only joy, and before any sterner news can wound my hearing.'

So prayed the father from his heart at the last moment before the departure. Then suddenly he fainted and fell, and his serving-men carried him into his house.

And by now the cavalcade had already passed through the opened gates. Among the first rode Aeneas and his faithful Achates, and behind them the others of Troy's nobility. In the centre of the column was Pallas, conspicuous in his gaily coloured mantle and arms; he was like the morning star, which Venus loves more than all other constellation-fires, when dripping from Ocean's wave he lifts his holy countenance in the sky and the darkness melts quickly away. Mothers stood on the city-walls in fear, following with their eyes the flash of bronze from the squadrons and the cloud of dust. The armed column rode on through undergrowth, taking the most direct way to their destination. A shout arose. They formed line, and hooves with four-footed thunder shook the crumbling plain. Now near Caere's cool river there is a large wood, held for far around in traditional reverence and awe, and enclosed by curving hills guarding the glades with dark pines. The ancient Pelasgians, who long ago were the earliest occupants of the Latin land, had consecrated this wood, and with it a festal day, to Silvanus, god of the farmland and its cattle. Not far from her Tarchon was encamped with his Etruscans in a position of natural defence, and from a high hill their whole host could be seen deployed over a wide expanse of country. The chieftain Aeneas and his selected warriors rode up to this camp. Tired by their march, they looked to their horses and attended to their own comfort.

But meanwhile Venus had descended, her divinity shining forth from the clouds of heaven about her, to bring her gifts. She could see Aeneas in the distance beyond the cool river in a secluded valley, where he had withdrawn. She went straight up and addressed her words directly to him: 'See! The gifts which my husband's skill promised to you are now completed, and so you need never hesitate to call out any arrogant Laurentine to battle, or even challenge fiery Turnus himself.' So spoke the Cytherean, and invited her son's embrace. And she laid the sparkling arms under an oak before him. He was delighted at the gifts and the high honour which they implied. His eyes rested on each of the pieces in admiration, and he could never gaze his fill. He held them between his hands, and in his arms, and turned them over every way; that helmet, spouting flames, with terror in its crests; that sword, loaded with doom; the corslet of bronze, stiff and blood-red, vast like a dark-grey cloud when caught by the sun's rays it begins to glow and reflects the blaze afar; then next, the polished greaves made of many-times-smelted gold and silver-gold; and the spear, and that shield with its texture beyond all telling.

On the shield the God whose Might is Fire had wrought Italy's story and the triumphs of Rome, for he had heard the prophets and knew of the times to come; he had included all the lineage of future descendants, from Ascanius onwards, with the wars which they would fight in their due order. He had also wrought there the tale of the wolf which after littering had stretched herself on the ground in the green cave of Mars, with twin baby boys playing round her and hanging about her teats, sucking at their foster-mother without fear, while she, bending her smooth neck round, caressed each in turn and licked their limbs into shape. Near them the God had pictured Rome herself and the Sabine women swiftly carried off in defiance of custom's law from among the throng seated in the theatre while the Great Games in the circus were in progress; and then the new war suddenly flaring up between the men of Romulus and old Tatius with his austere folk from Cures; but afterwards there stood the same two kings, who had now laid conflict aside, with their bowls in their hands before the altar of armed Jove as over a sacrificed sow they were uniting in treaty. Next to that scene was shown Mettus, torn asunder by the four horses of his galloping team; ah! man of Alba, but you should have kept your word! And Tullus was represented dragging the lying chieftain's remnants through a wood with sprinkled blood bedewing the brambles. Porsenna too was pictured commanding Rome to receive back the banished Tarquin, and pressing the city in a fearful siege; and on their side the descendants of Aeneas were seen dashing to death for freedom's sake. Porsenna was shown again, this time the very image of an outraged, threatening potentate, being angered because Cocles dared to tear down the bridge, and because the maiden Cloelia broke her captivity and swam the river.

At the top of the shield Manlius, Warden of the Tarpeian Citadel, was at his post before the temple, defending the towering Capitol; and below, newly thatched with stiff straw, stood the cottage of Romulus. And on the Capitol a silver goose took sudden flight in a golden colonnade to give warning that the Gauls were at the threshold. Protected by the darkness under the kindly cover of night they had crept through the bushes and were about to reach the citadel. Golden was their hair and golden too their garments; they gleamed in striped cloaks and their necks were shown milk-white encircled with necklaces of gold. Each man brandished two short Alpine spears in his hand, and to protect their limbs they carried long shields. Next, Vulcan had hammered out leaping Salii and unclothed Luperci; and there were the wool-crested bonnets and the targes which fell from heaven. And chaste mothers were there, parading holy objects of religion in cushioned carriages through Rome. At a distance from these scenes the God had also depicted Pluto's tall gateway and the habitations in Tartarus with the punishments for crime; there Catiline hung from a threatening rock, and trembled to see the Furies' faces; and in a place apart were the righteous, with Cato their law-giver. Between the scenes in a broad band ran a representation in gold of the swelling sea, but with the surface showing blue, and white wave-crests of foam. Around, circling dolphins, shining bright in silver, cut through the surge, sweeping the sea's surface with their tails.

In the centre could be seen the bronze-plated fleets battling at Actium. All Leucate, in a ferment of moving martial array, came into view; the waves shone out with gold. On one side was Augustus Caesar leading Italians into battle, having with him the senate and populace, the little Gods of Home and the Great Gods of the race. He stood on the high quarter-deck of his ship; gaily his brow discharged twin beams of light, and on his head dawned his father's Julian Star. Elsewhere

Agrippa, with the aid alike of winds and gods, led his towering line, and his forehead shone with war's haughty distinction, the ship-rams of the Naval Crown. Opposing them was Antony; with him, on board, he had Egyptians and the whole strength of the East even to most distant Bactria; on his side was the wealth of the Orient and arms of varied design, and he came victoriously from the nations of the Dawn and the Red Sea's shore, followed – the shame of it! – by an Egyptian wife. All ships were closing at full speed. Churned by the back-drawn oars and the trident stems, the whole sea was foaming. All steered for the open water. It was as if the Isles of the Cyclades had been uprooted and were afloat on the sea, or as if high mountains met mountains in shock, so massive were the towering sterns on which the attackers stood. Fire-bolts of blazing tow were showered by hand and everywhere iron points were carried by their flying shafts. Neptune's acres reddened with freshly spilt blood. The queen in the centre called up her columns by sounding the tambourine of her land; she had as yet no thought of the pair of asps which fate held in store for her. Her gods, monstrous shapes of every species, even to the barking Anubis, levelled weapons against Neptune, Venus, and Minerva herself. In the battle's midst raged Mars, moulded in iron, and from the sky scowling Furies let loose their savagery; Strife with her robe rent strode in joy, and Bellona followed with her blood-stained scourge. But Apollo of Actium saw; and high on his vantage-point he already bent his bow. In dread of it, every Egyptian, the Indians, every Arab, and all the host of Sheba were on the point of turning in flight. The queen herself could be seen calling on the winds and setting sail, pictured at the very moment when she shook the sail-sheets loose. The God whose Might is Fire had portrayed her amid the massacre, pale with the pallor of impending death, as she sped over the waves before a north-west gale. Before her the River Nile, with sorrow expressed throughout his great length, opened his full robe, and with all his raiment invited the vanquished to the bosom of his blue waters and the refuge of his streams.

Next appeared Augustus Caesar as he drove in a threefold

triumph past the buildings of Rome and made to the Gods of Italy his solemn, deathless vow to build three hundred mighty shrines throughout his City. The streets were roaring with joyful merry-making and applause. In every temple mothers were dancing and in every one were sacrifices at the altars, before which slain bullocks lay stretched on the ground. Augustus Caesar himself was seated at shining Apollo's snow-white threshold, inspecting gifts from the nations and fixing them to majestic columns. Conquered peoples walked in their long line, as various in their dress and weapons as in their speech. Vulcan had modelled them, a tribe of Numidians here and of loose-robed Africans there, here Lelegeians and Carians, and there Gelonians with their arrows. The River Euphrates could be seen, and now there was more humility in his current's flow. The Morini too were shown, the most remote of men, and the Rhine with his pair of horns; the hitherto unconquered Scythians were there, and the River Araxes, resentful of his new bridge.

Aeneas looked in wonder at the scenes such as these pictured about the shield which Vulcan had made and his mother had given to him. He had no knowledge of the events, but none the less he found pleasure in their representations, as he lifted onto his shoulder the glory and the destiny of his heirs.

Symbolic of the shield.

BOOK NINE

SIEGE OF THE TROJAN CAMP

While this was happening in a distant part of the country, Saturnian Juno sent Iris down from the sky to the fiery Turnus. It chanced that Turnus was sitting in a wood sacred to his ancestor Pilumnus and set within a consecrated glen. Out of her rosy lips the daughter of Thaumas spoke in his presence: 'See, Turnus, the onward roll of time alone has brought unforced to you a blessing which no god would have dared to promise you, however earnest your desire. Aeneas has left his settlement, his comrades and his fleet, and is on his way to Evander's home, the seat of his sovereignty on the Palatine Hill. And, not satisfied even with that, he has pressed right on to those farthest cities of Corythus, where he musters the country folk and has a host of Lydians under arms. Why then do you hesitate? Now is the moment to call for horses and for your chariots of war. Burst a way through every obstacle; surprise their camp into a panic and swiftly make it yours.' So Iris spoke; and she soared to the sky on wings evenly poised, cutting in her flight a great rainbow against the background of the clouds. The young prince recognized her. He raised his palms together towards the stars above and sent a cry after her as she sped away: 'Iris, glory of the heavens, who brought you speeding down to earth from the clouds with a message for me? What has caused this sudden brilliance in the daylight? I see the sky's veil split in its centre, and stars adrift in the zenith. Whoever you are who call me to arms, I follow your mighty sign.' Having spoken his thought he walked forward to the water, scooped a handful from an eddy's surface, and prayed long to the Gods, loading high heaven with his vows.

And now all his army, a wealth of horses, a wealth of embroidered cloaks and gold, was moving across the open plain. Messapus controlled the vanguard and the young sons of Tyrrhus the rear; Turnus, as supreme commander, had his post in the centre of the column [towering by a full head above the rest as, weapons in hand, he moved to and fro]. That march was like Ganges rising silently and deepening along all his seven placid streams, or Nile, when he has withdrawn his enriching current from the river-plains, and is settled in his own bed once more. And now the watching Trojans saw far off a cloud of black dust begin to mass, and darkness rise over the plains. The first shout came from Caicus who was on an embankment fronting the foe: 'My countrymen, what is that rolling mass of pitchy gloom? Come quickly, with your blades and a store of missiles. Mount the walls. Ho! The enemy is at the gate!' With loud shouts the Trojans retired under cover, passing through all their gateways, and manned the ramparts; for as he departed their wise general Aeneas had warned them, in case of an emergency in his absence, not to risk action in the open field or venture a marshalled battle-array, but to be content to keep within their walled camp protected by their earthworks. Accordingly, though shame and anger counselled them to close with the enemy, they obeyed orders, presented shut gates to the foe, and awaited them under arms in their hollow towers.

But Turnus rode ahead of the more slowly moving column and galloped forward with twenty selected riders at his side. With surprising speed he was at the encampment, riding a piebald horse from Thrace and wearing a golden helmet with a scarlet plume. 'Young warriors,' he cried, 'would one of you like to be first upon the foe with me? For, see!' And he sent his spear spinning into the air to open hostilities. High on his horse he rode out onto the field. Shouting, his comrades took up his challenge and followed him with terror-striking battle-cries. They were astonished at the apparent cowardice of the Trojans who would not take the risk of fair fight on the field and come forth like men with their arms in their hands, but hugged their camp. Turnus rode wildly round it now to the right and now to the left, surveying the walls and looking for an access but finding none. Like a wolf lying in wait outside a crowded sheep-fold, howling right up to the enclosure and facing any force of wind and rain at darkest midnight while the lambs continue incessantly bleating, safe underneath their mothers; he, fierce and persistent in his rage, vents his fury against a prey which is out of reach, for his dry, bloodless jaws and long-mounting, ravenous hunger will not let him rest; such were the Rutulian's spasms of fury, rising to a blaze as he glared at those walls and that camp, and indignation heated his hard bones as he wondered how to attempt an entry and what method of approach might shock the Trojans from their enclosing stockade and bring them streaming out onto the plain. Finally, he attacked the fleet which lay hidden close under the flank of the encampment, fenced on one side by an earth-pier built round it, but elsewhere by nothing but the river-waves. Turnus called to his exultant comrades for fire. In hot passion he held tight in his grasp a blazing pine-brand. Urged by his own powerful presence among them, his men set to work in earnest. Every soldier at once stole any fire near at hand and armed himself with a black-reeking torch. Smoking pine-boughs threw their pitchy glare, and Vulcan sent upwards to the stars a mixture of ashes and sparks.

Which god averted the furious blaze from the Trojans? Which one drove that fearful fire back from their ships? Tell me, you Spirits of Song. There is only ancient warrant for the event, but the memory of it never dies.

At the time when Aeneas was beginning to shape his fleet on Phrygian Ida, as he prepared to steer forth onto deep seas, the Lady of Berecyntus, the Mother of the Gods herself, is said to have made this appeal to supreme Jove: 'Son, you are now master of Olympus. Accede therefore to your mother's prayer and grant the request which she makes to you. Once I had a wood of pines which I loved for many years; it was a grove standing on the crest of my fastness, darkened by black pitch-trees and maple trunks; and men brought offerings there. But when the young Dardan had need of a fleet, I gladly gave my trees to him. Now however I am distressed by anxiety and fear. Dispel my alarm and allow your mother's prayers to have such force that those ships may never be overcome, shattered by any voyage or any violence of the wind. Let it profit them that it was in my mountains that they had their origin.' Her son, who turns the stars in the firmament, spoke to her in reply: 'Mother, to what task are you inviting destiny? What is this that you ask for your ships? Are keels made by mortal hand to own immortal privilege? Would you that Aeneas should pass unimperilled every perilous risk on his way? What god is permitted such powers? It may not be. But when one day, having reached their journey's end, they are safe in an Italian harbour, then from every ship which has weathered the waves and conveyed the Dardan prince to Laurentine farmlands, I will strip her mortal shape and command them all to live on as goddesses of the vast sea, like Nereid Doto and Galatea as they cut through the ocean and breast the foam.' So he spoke; and with a nod of his head he ratified his words by his Stygian Brother's streams, the pitchy torrents and the banks with the black abyss between. And at his nod he set all Olympus quaking.

So now, since the Fates had completed the destined time, the day of the promise had come. The intent of Turnus to harm the holy ships warned the Great Mother to defend them from his burning brands. And suddenly a strange new light shone before all eyes, and there appeared a huge cloud, and with it Mount Ida's dancing bands, racing across the sky from the east. Then a voice of dread burst through the air and rang through the lines of Trojans and Rutulians alike: 'Haste not, Trojans, in fear, to defend my ships, neither arm your hands. Turnus shall be given power to burn the very ocean before he may burn these sacred timbers of pine. And you, the ships, go free, go, Goddesses of the Sea. Your mother bids you.' And forthwith every stern broke hawsers from the quays, plunged each ram downwards like a dolphin, and dived to the bottom. And from it – miraculous sight! – maiden forms emerged returning in numbers the same as the bronze-sheathed prows which had rested at the beach; and they swam upon the sea.

At this the Rutulians felt their vigour paralysed. Messapus himself was struck with terror, and his horses were in panic. Even the River Tiber checked with a growling roar and flinched, withdrawing hastily from the deep. Yet the confidence of fiery Turnus never sank, but rather he appealed to his men, raising their spirits, and indeed scolding them:

'It is the Trojans who are threatened by this miracle. For Jupiter has himself taken from them the help on which they principally relied. Their ships have not even waited for Rutulian weapons and Rutulian fire. So the seas are barred to the Trojans, and they have no hope of escape. Half the world has been removed from their reach. The land is controlled by us, for in all their thousands the nations of Italy are now in arms. Phrygians may boast support from divine oracles of fate, but such things hold no fears for me. The demands of Venus and Destiny are well enough answered in the bare fact of the Trojans' arrival on the farmlands of fertile Italy. Besides, I have a destiny of my own; I am destined to hack out from the roots by my own blade the nation of criminals who have stolen my bride away. It is not only the sons of Atreus who have had that painful experience, and it is not only Mycenae which has had the right to take up arms. The Trojans may plead that a single destruction of their race is enough. I answer, was not then a single crime enough? They did not have to vent their implacable hatred on every woman in the world. And now they are emboldened by their trust in their protecting walls and defensive moats which so narrowly divide them from death. But have they not seen the ramparts of Troy built by Neptune's own hand settle into the fires? Now, my comrades, my chosen band, which of you is ready to tear down this stockade with steel? Who joins me in the assault on their terror-stricken camp? I need no arms of Vulcan and no thousand ships to fight these Trojans. Yes and let all the Etruscans straightway come and join forces with them and swell their numbers. And they need not fear any cowardly theft of a talisman in the night, with a massacre of the guards on the crest of their fortress. Nor shall we hide out of sight in any horse's belly. By daylight and openly I am resolved to envelop their walls with fire; and I shall soon make them admit that it is not with Danaans that they have to deal, not merely with the young men of Greece whom Hector could hold off into the tenth year. But for the moment, warriors, as the better part of the day is spent, in what remains of it see to your comfort, happy in the day's success, and be sure that I shall provide you with some fighting.'

Meanwhile Messapus was assigned the duty of posting pickets to watch, blocking the gates, and girding the walls with a circle of watch-fires. Fourteen Rutulians were next chosen to patrol and watch the walls, and to each were attached a hundred men-at-arms, wearing bright red plumes and glittering with gold. All hurried off to their duties, some relieving the posts by turns and some stretching out on the grass to enjoy their wine and tipping up their bronze mixing-bowls. The circle of camp-fires burned bright. The Watch remained awake, gaming, through the night.

The Trojans stood under arms on their higher level, observing all this from the stockade. But they also inspected their gates in anxious fear, and without laying their weapons down they went on completing their battlements and communication-bridges. Mnestheus and the vigorous Serestus, whom their chief Aeneas had appointed to have charge over the fighting men and the direction of strategy should they be faced with any unexpected threat in his absence, took active command. The whole company bivouacked along the walls, drawing lots for the posts of danger, and each man did his tour of duty, watching that part of their front which he was detailed to guard.

Nisus, a son of Hyrtacus and a fierce warrior, was warden of a gate. Ida, mountain of the chase, had sent him on his journey with Aeneas; and he was swift with his javelin and his light arrows. Close by him was his comrade Euryalus, and no one more beautiful then he ever served Aeneas or put on Trojan arms; he was a mere boy and his unshaven face declared his early youth. The two were united in a fast affection and they remained inseparable when they hastened into battle; and on this occasion they were naturally sharing a single sentry-post guarding a gate. Nisus now said: 'Is it the gods who have put into our hearts this ardour for battle? Or do we all attribute to a god what is really an overmastering impulse of our own? For myself, I am bored by this peaceful quiet and have long been pondering a dash into combat or some other high enterprise. You see how careless these Rutulians have become through their confidence in their own position. Only here and there is a light flickering. The wine has overpowered them; they have sunk to the earth asleep and silence spreads over their wide camping-ground. This may suggest to you what is in my mind and the plan which is taking shape there. Our countrymen, the elders and the rank and file alike, are all insisting that Aeneas must be recalled and that messengers must be sent to tell him what the position is. If to you they are prepared to grant the reward which I mean to demand – the fame of the deed is all that I ask for myself – , I believe that I could find a way by the foot of the hillock over there to reach the walls and the battlements of Pallanteum.'

Euryalus was surprised, and demurred. Being elated with a keen thirst for glory, he at once answered his fiery friend: 'Does this mean, Nisus, that you are not willing to let me go at your side as your comrade in heroism? Am I to let you go alone into this great peril? That is not how my father, war-seasoned Opheltes, instructed me, as he reared me amid the Argive terror during the ordeal of Troy, nor is that the spirit in which I have fought by your side as I followed Aeneas the high-hearted and faced all that fate could do. Mine is indeed a temper to scorn the light of life and count it a cheap price to pay for the honour for which you strive.' To this Nisus replied: 'Never have I myself had any such doubt concerning you; that would have been indeed a sin. I wish I could be equally sure that supreme Jupiter, or however we should name the one who looks on our deeds with impartial eyes, will bring me safe back to you in triumph. But should some accident or some god hasten me to a disaster, such as often enough is seen to happen when the danger is as grave as this, then I should desire you to survive, for you are of an age to have more right to life than I. Let there be one to rescue my body from the battle, or redeem it for a price, and commit it formally to the earth, or, if Fortune, for such is her way, forbids that, to honour me with a cenotaph and thither bring me offerings. Besides, I would not be the cause of so terrible a grief to your poor mother, who alone of many mothers has daringly followed her son through all our travels, with never a thought for the walled city of mighty Acestes.' But Euryalus answered: 'You weave groundless pretexts, to no end. And my purpose has not weakened or changed. Let us hasten to work.' As he spoke he awakened other sentries, who moved up and did their tour of duty for them. The pair left the picket, Euryalus walking at the side of Nisus, to go in search of their prince.

All other living creatures throughout the world were then relaxing their anxieties in sleep and resting their hearts in forgetfulness of toil. But the chief leaders of Troy, the elect of her manhood, were holding a council on gravest concerns of their state, debating what action they should take and who should now bear the news to Aeneas. They stood in the meeting-place at the centre of their camp, leaning on their long spears, with hands resting on their shields. Suddenly Nisus, and Euryalus with him, arrived. They came in eager haste, pleading to be admitted forthwith on business of importance which would prove well worth the while. Iulus took control, and welcomed the excited pair. He asked Nisus to speak.

Then Nisus, son of Hyrtacus, said: 'Men of Aeneas, listen, if it please you, with sympathy, and do not judge our proposal by our youth. The Rutulians, overcome by sleep and wine, are all silent. Now we have noticed by our own observation a good place for a surprise raid. The gap lies at the fork of the roads outside the gate nearest the sea. Here there is an interval in the ring of watch-fires where nothing but black smoke rises towards the stars. If you allow us to try our luck and go in quest of Aeneas to the ramparts of Pallanteum, you will see that we shall presently be back with our spoils, after wreaking a havoc of slaughter. We shall not lose our way as we go, for during our constant hunting we have caught a first glimpse of that city from down in the valleys where we ourselves were out of sight, and we are familiar with all the river's course.'

At this, Aletes, the ripeness of whose judgement matched the weight of his years, answered: 'Gods of our Land, under whose divine guidance Troy remains for ever, you cannot yet intend to erase us Trojans utterly, if you have produced young warriors with so fine a spirit and so resolute a will.' As he talked so, he clapped each in turn on the shoulder and then clasped their right hands, while floods of tears ran down over his face and cheeks. Then he continued: 'Young heroes, what possible reward, fit to be given to you in return for your glorious action, can I imagine? The gods, and your own characters, will reward you first, and most splendidly; but all else Aeneas the True will most promptly award to you and he will be joined by Ascanius, on whom age has not yet laid a hand, and who would never forget so distinguished a service.'

Ascanius interposed: 'No, indeed, but since my whole life depends on my father's safe return, I adjure you both, by the mighty Gods who sustain our homes, yes, Nisus, by the Familiar Spirit whom Assaracus revered, and by grey-haired Vesta's inner shrine; and I place in your safe-keeping all my fortune and all my trust. Only call my father home and give me back the sight of him. If he is restored to me, then nothing holds for me any dread; and to you I shall present two cups entirely of silver bearing figures in high relief, which my father captured when he overcame Arisba; and also a pair of tripods, two large-sized talents of gold, and an ancient wine-mixing bowl given by Sidonian Dido. But besides, should fortune allow my father to seize Italy, and by the victory to gain mastery over Italy's sceptre, and proclaim an assignment of the spoils, why! you have seen the horse which Turnus was riding and the arms which he carried, all in a blaze of gold. That horse I shall surely separate from the other plunder and with it his shield and his glowing scarlet-crested helmet; they, Nisus, are your reward and from this very moment they are yours. My father shall also give you twelve of their older women most carefully chosen and captive men besides, each with his own arms, and, in addition, all the royal domain which Latinus at present owns. And now you, Euryalus, whose age is not so far in advance of mine, you so young and so rightly dear, I take you to my very heart and embrace you as my comrade in every adventure to come. Never shall I desire to win in my career any fame which you do not share, whether I am at war or at peace, and in all that I say or do I shall above all rely on you.'

Euryalus spoke in reply to him: 'That day will never come which proves me untrue to my present bold enterprise, granted only that fortune fall in our favour, and not adversely. But besides all that you give to me, I entreat one kindness more: I have a mother, of Priam's ancient line. She came with me, poor Mother, when I left home, and neither the land of Ilium nor the walled city of King Acestes could detain her. I now leave her, quite unaware of my risk, whatever the risk may be, and without a farewell – may the night and your own right hand bear witness –, for I know that I could never hold out against a parent's tears. But you, I beg you, console and help her if she is left bereaved and resourceless. Allow me to receive assurance of your good will in this; I shall go the more boldly to meet whatever comes.'

The Dardanids wept in sorrow, for they were deeply touched, the beautiful Iulus more than any, as this reflection of his own faithful love for his father caught at his heart. Then he spoke his thoughts: 'Be sure that all will be as your heroic enterprise deserves. For your mother shall be my mother, lacking only Creusa's name. More than a little gratitude awaits her for a son such as you. Whatever luck may attend your deed, I swear my oath to you by my own life, as by my life my father used in the past to swear. What I have promised to give you if you are successful and return will, in your default, be for her to have and for her kin, exactly the same.' So he spoke, with tears at the tenor of his own words, and as he did so he unslung from his shoulder his gold-plated sword which Lycaon of Cnossos had made with wondrous skill and fitted in an ivory sheath for easy carrying. Next, Mnestheus gave to Nisus a pelt despoiled from a shaggy lion; and the faithful Aletes exchanged helmets with him. The pair armed forthwith and strode off. As they went, a gathering of all the chieftains, older and younger, stood at the gates and sent their prayers after them. And for his part the beautiful Iulus, who bore beyond his years the mind and responsibilities of a man, gave them many messages for his father. But the breezes were to scatter them all, and make of them an ineffectual gift to the clouds.

The pair made their way out, climbing over the moats, and marched through night's shadow for the camp and all the danger which it held for them; though before the end came they were themselves to bring destruction on many. And now they saw men spread everywhere over the grass in drunken sleep, chariots tilted up on the sea-shore with the drivers lying amid the wheels and the reins, and arms on the ground and wine-vessels scattered about among them. The son of Hyrtacus spoke first, saying: 'Euryalus, our strong right arms must take bold action; the occasion demands it now. This way lies our road. You must keep keen-eyed and cautious guard over our rear to ensure that no force is allowed to spring up and attack us from behind. I will make havoc of all who are here and lead you forward along a clear, broad lane.' So he spoke, and checked his speech. As he did so he attacked with his sword the haughty Rhamnes who chanced to lie raised high on a pile of coverlets, breathing out his sleep in deep-chested snores. He was himself a king, and also a seer, whom King Turnus loved, but his prophesying could not save him from destruction. Nisus next overpowered three of his retainers, sprawling near their master with their weapons on both sides of them, and also the armour-bearer of Remus and his charioteer whom he found close beside his horses. He cut their drooping necks with his blade, then hewed off their master's head also, and left his trunk to gulp with the flow of blood which drenched the earth, and the bedding too, in its streams. He killed also Lamyrus, Lamus, and the young and most handsome Serranus, who had played long during that night, and lay there, his limbs vanquished by plentiful Bacchus; he would have been more fortunate if he had continued his gaming as long as night lasted and carried it on into the day. Nisus was like a starving lion, mad from driving hunger, moving through a crowded sheep-pen, with havoc all about him as he gnaws and drags the soft creatures voiceless for fear, and roars out of a blood-smeared mouth.

Euryalus blazed likewise with a sustained fury, and dealt carnage no less freely. He crept up on many a man-at-arms of little fame, Fadus, Herbesus, Rhoetus, and Abaris, catching them unawares; except that Rhoetus was awake and saw all, but could only shield himself in his fear behind a large wine bowl; and then as he rose in close encounter Euryalus plunged the whole length of his sword full in his breast, and withdrew it, with a stream of death. Rhoetus choked out his spirit in the dark red flood, bringing up as he died wine mixed in his gore. Euryalus pressed hotly forward in his stealthy onset. He was now hastening towards the company of Messapus and could see horses, tethered in order, cropping the grass, and the last of the camp-fires fading out, when Nisus, realizing that in his attack he was being carried away by his excessive passion for massacre, spoke shortly, saying: 'Let us desist, for daylight draws near and is dangerous. Our way through the foe is clear now; and we have drunk deep enough of vengeance.' They left behind many weapons of warriors all mounted in solid silver, and among them mixing-bowls and splendid coverlets. But Euryalus seized the trappings of Rhamnes and his gold-riveted sword-belt, and fitted them on his strong shoulder, vainly enough as it proved. They had been sent long since as a gift to Remulus of Tiber by the prosperous Caedicus, to pledge his deep friendship in absence, and later they had been given by Remulus at his death to his grandson to wear; when he died they were captured during warfare by Rutulians in battle. Euryalus next put on the helmet of Messapus with its handsome plumes; it fitted him well. The two then left the camp and started for safe country.

But meanwhile riders, who had been sent forward from the Latin city while the remainder of their army waited ready formed for battle on the plain, were now on the march and carrying an answer from the Latins to Prince Turnus' demands. There were three hundred of them, all bearing shields, under the command of Volcens. They had already nearly reached the camp and were in fact approaching its walls when they observed the Trojan pair just as they were turning off on a new line towards their left; the captured helmet betrayed

Euryalus, gleaming in the night-shadows, and reflecting rays of light, for he had forgotten that danger. The sight was not lost on the enemy. Volcens shouted from the head of the column: 'Stand, strangers! What is the purpose of your journey? You go armed; who are you? Where are you marching?'

They attempted no reply, but fled quickly into the forest, trusting to the night. The riders took positions on either hand to intercept them at track-junctions which they knew, and posted guards at every point of escape to encircle them. The wood stretched away mysteriously with its clustering thickets, the black darkness of the holm-oaks, and the dense brambles everywhere covering the ground. Euryalus was hampered both by the shadows cast by the boughs and by the weight of his plunder, and was deluded by his own fears and by the many ways leading in wrong directions, for only here and there could the right path be seen where there was a clearing in the tangled growth. Nisus however darted forward, and, running with never a thought, he had soon left the enemy behind and was clear of the danger. He passed the spot later called Alban after Alba Longa, but at that time used by King Latinus as a fenced cattle-station. Then he halted and looked round for his lost comrade, but in vain. 'Oh! Poor Euryalus,' he exclaimed, 'whereabouts did I leave you? Which way should I go to search for you – and unwind all my twisting path through this deceptive forest?' As he spoke he looked closely for his backward-leading tracks, and groped among the silent thickets trying to pick them out. Then he heard horses and the sound of pursuers and their signal-calls; nor had he long to wait before shouts reached his ears and he could see Euryalus, who, overcome at last by the treacherous ground and the darkness and unnerved by the sudden uproar, had been seized by the whole band, and was even then being hustled away, still hopelessly struggling with all his strength.

What was Nisus to do? What force or what daring feat of arms within his power could enable him to rescue the boy? Should he fling himself on the swords to certain death and hasten a glorious end by choosing the way of wounds? He drew back his arm, sharply, to spin his spear-shaft, and looking up to the moon on high he prayed aloud: 'Goddess, glory of all the stars, Latona's daughter, Guardian of the Woods, be with us now and aid us in our distress. If ever my father Hyrtacus brought any offerings to your altars with prayers on my behalf, and if I ever myself enriched them from my own successes in the hunt, or ever hung trophies from your dome or fixed them on your holy eaves, then guide my weapon's flight through the air and let me bring confusion on their band.' He ended his prayer and, straining with all his might, he discharged the steel. The flying spear lashed night's shadows asunder, struck full in the back of Sulmo, lodged there, and snapped, piercing his heart with its wood-splinters. Sulmo rolled on the ground vomiting a warm stream from his chest, his flanks quaked to a long-drawn gasping, and he went cold. The rest turned this way and that and looked around them. And see! Nisus, encouraged by the hit, was already poising another spear, holding it high to his ear. Before the enemy recovered from their shock, the weapon passed hissing through both temples of Tagus, pierced his brain, and clung, all warm, within it. Volcens was wild with savage fury, but could see no one there who could have cast a spear, or whom he could assail in his hot rage. So he shouted at Euryalus: 'But you, meanwhile, shall repay me with your warm young blood, and give me my vengeance for both'; and with the words dashed on him, drawn sword in hand. At the sight Nisus went mad with horror. The anguish of it was more than he could endure, and he could no longer remain in the darkness. 'Look,' he shouted, 'I did it! Here I am, I! Turn your steel on me, you Rutulians. All the fault is mine; the boy there ventured nothing, indeed could have done nothing. I appeal for witness to this sky above and those stars which know the truth. He only loved too well a luckless friend.' But even as he spoke the sword, forced strongly home, pressed through the ribs of Euryalus and burst his white breast; he rolled writhing in death, the blood spread over the lovely limbs, and his neck, relaxing, sank on his shoulders. He was like a bright flower shorn by the plough, languishing and dying, or poppies, weighted by a sudden shower of rain, drooping their heads on tired necks. Nisus immediately dashed into the midst of the foe, and passed them all by, seeking Volcens only and having no thought for anyone but him. The enemy massed around and would have forced him back in close combat from either hand. But none the less he pressed forward, whirling his thunderbolt of a sword, till he buried it full in the shouting face of the Rutulian and took life from his enemy even as he lost his own. Then, pierced through, he cast himself down on his lifeless friend and there at last found peace in a welcoming death.

Fortunate pair! If there is any power in my poetry, no day shall ever steal you from the memory of time, so long as sons of Aeneas dwell by the Capitol's immovable stone, and a Roman Father holds dominion yet.

The victorious Rutulians, masters now of new plunder and also recaptured spoils, bore the lifeless Volcens back to their camp, weeping. There the lamentation was already equally bitter because Rhamnes had been found massacred and with him all those other chieftains killed together in a single slaughter, among them Serranus, and Numa too. A large crowd quickly gathered by the bodies of the dead, the wounded, and those near to death, where the blood-stained ground was still warm and brimming rivers of foaming gore still flowed. They recognized the spoils as they passed them round, the glittering helmet of Messapus and the trappings whose recovery had cost such sweat and toil.

But already Aurora was leaving the saffron bed of Tithonus and her first gleam was sprinkling a fresh light over the world. Therefore, now that the sun streamed down and daylight had revealed the land, Turnus first armed himself, and then roused his men to arms, and each of his commanders massed his bronze-clad troops for battle, spreading every report that might whet their fury. Indeed, some even fixed the heads of Euryalus and Nisus on spear-points, a pitiful sight; and others followed, shouting, behind. The men of Aeneas resolutely ranged their line for resistance along the wall on their left flank, since their right was girt by the river; and they were sadly lining their deep moats and taking up their posts on their tall towers, when with a shock they saw their own friends' faces on the spears, streaming with dark gore and known all too well to their unhappy comrades.

Meanwhile winged Rumour flew in haste through the settlement with her message, and flitted right to the ear of Euryalus' mother. Poor lady, all warmth at once left her. The shuttle leapt from her hands and her skein of wool untwined. She dashed forth in distraction and terrible distress; and, wailing as women do and tearing her hair, she ran with mind deranged to the wall where stood the foremost ranks; she took no thought for the danger from the spears, no thought for the presence of men. And then she filled all the sky with her lament: 'Euryalus, is the thing at which I look really you, you who have been my one repose as my old age draws to its end? Oh, cruel, had you then the heart to leave me all alone? And was your poor mother not to be given even the chance to speak her last to you as you went forth to face those terrible risks on your mission? Alas, you now lie in a strange land, flung out to be prey for the dogs and vultures of Latium. Your mother never escorted you forth in procession of death, pressed close your eyes, or washed your wounds, shrouding you with the garment which I was striving night and day in haste to finish for you, drawing comfort from its weaving to soothe an old woman's cares. Where can I go to find you? In what land does your torn body lie? Where are your broken members, your sundered limbs? Son, is this all that is left for you to bring back to me of yourself? Was I to have no more than this of the son whom I have followed through all our journeys over land and sea? Pierce me, you Rutulians, if you have any pity! Cast all your spears at me, me only, and choose me before any other to kill with the blade! If not, you, supreme Father of the Gods, have mercy, and drive this hated self of mine deep down to Tartarus with your stroke, if I can by no other means cut short the cruelty of living.' Her weeping shook them all. Sobs of grief spread through the whole army; their strength was broken for battle, and languished. Then, as the mother allowed her grief to blaze out still more, Idaeus and Actor, on a word from Ilioneus and the bitterly weeping

Iulus, quickly took her up, carried her between them to her home, and laid her down.

But now afar off the trumpet crashed out its dreadful note with the music of its bronze. Shouting followed, and the sky roared back the echo. The Italians locked shields in line together and quickened their march, intending to fill in the moats and tear down the stockade. One detachment sought a way of direct approach and the chance of climbing the walls with scaling-ladders, at a point where the defending ranks were sparse and their front showed daylight through it, being less densely manned. Against the attackers the Trojans poured weapons of every kind, and they forced them down again with stout siege-pikes, being well experienced in the defence of walls from the long war at Troy. They also sent stones of deadly weight rolling down, hoping to break through the armoured front, which nevertheless beneath its tough tortoise-shell formation readily endured whatever should fall on it. But presently they could stand firm no longer, for, where a powerful concentration threatened, the Trojans released, tearing and rolling it down, a rock of mighty mass which burst through the canopy of shields and crushed a whole section of the Rutulian attack. The Rutulians, becoming less venturesome, lost their zest for fighting blind under cover, and now strove only to force the defenders back from their stockade with missiles at long range. But elsewhere Mezentius, a sight to strike very terror, brandished an Etruscan pine-brand, carrying fire and streaming smoke against the defence. Meanwhile Messapus the horse-tamer, Neptune's own son, shouted for scaling-ladders to climb the ramparts, seeking to tear down the stockade.

O Calliope! Spirits of Song, I pray to you, add your inspiration to my story as I tell of the devastation which the blade of Turnus spread on that field, the deaths which he dealt, and whom each warrior dismissed to Pluto's world. Join me in rolling back the vast scroll of that war. For you are divine and know the tale, and yours is the power to tell.

There was a tower, well placed and a dizzy sight from below, with high-level communication-bridges. The whole

Italian host was striving to storm it with their utmost strength and overturn it by any means in their power. In reply the Trojans sought to defend it with stones, and crowded together to whirl their missiles through open ports at their assailants. Turnus was at their head and he flung a kindled fire-bolt, blazing fiercely, and planted his flame on the tower's flank. Winds fanned it; it caught the planks, burnt into the supports, and took a hold. In the tower all was confusion and alarm, and a helpless desire to escape from this horrible plight. The Trojans there drew back, huddling to a part of the floor not yet threatened; and at once, under their sudden weight, the tower fell. The whole sky thundered with its crash. The huge mass followed the dying downwards as they fell to the ground pierced by their own spears, and with their breasts transfixed by the hard wood splinters.

Only Helenor and with him Lycus managed to slip safely away. Of these, Helenor was a man in early youth. His mother Licymnia was a slave, but she raised him as a son to Lydia's king, keeping his birth a secret; and though he had been forbidden to go, she had seen him leave, bearing arms, for Troyland. He went lightly armed, with only a bare sword, and with no tale of glory on his still unblazoned shield. Helenor now found himself in the midst of Turnus' thousands, with the Latin ranks standing close to him on this side and on that. As a wild beast, trapped by a dense ring of hunters, faces their missiles with rage and then springs onto a death which she knows is certain, and her leap carries her full upon the hunting-spears, just so lightly the boy dashed to his death among the massed enemy, making for the place where he saw the weapons cluster thickest. But Lycus was a far better runner than Helenor. He darted straight through his foes and their arms, reached the wall, and strove to grip the parapet above with his fingers and grasp the hands of his friends. But Turnus pursued, casting his spear even as he ran, and triumphantly reviled him, crying: 'So you hoped, mad fool, that you could slip from my hands?' As he spoke he seized him dangling and wrenched him down, together with a large piece of the wall; like Jove's own armour-bearer, his eagle, when he has carried off a hare or a shining-white swan in his curved talons and soars with it into the sky, or a wolf, beast of Mars, when he has snatched a lamb from a pen, and the mother with much bleating seeks after it.

Shouts arose on every side. The Latins dashed in and began to fill in the moat with rubble, while others flung lighted brands onto the sloping roofs of the towers. Ilioneus cast back at them a stone like some huge crag from a mountain, and just as Lucetius, equipped for fire-raising, was advancing on a gate, he brought him down. And Liger slew Emathion and Asilas Corynaeus; Liger had a sure aim with the javelin and Asilas with the arrow flying from afar unseen. Next Caeneus slew Ortygius and Turnus Caeneus, in his moment of victory; and he slew Itys also, and Clonius, Dioxippus, Promolus, Sagaris, and Idas as he stood in defence on top of the turreted wall. Capys killed Privernus who had just before been grazed by a light spear from Themillas, and, like a fool, had thrown aside his shield to move his hand to the wound. So then the speeding arrow easily found its winged way to him; his hand was pinned to his left side and the arrow buried itself within and, mortally wounding, burst the channels of his life's breath. There too Arcens' son was standing, clad in magnificent arms and a mantle with pictured scenes in needlework, brilliant with the red dye from Spain, and very handsome to see. He had been reared in the holy wood of Mars by the River Symaethus where at the altar of Palicus rich sacrifices win favour, and his father had sent him to war. Mezentius laid aside his spear. He drew back a whistling sling-bolt on its thong, swung it round his head three times, hit the foeman full in front with the now molten lead, split apart his forehead in the centre, and stretched him out full-length upon the sand.

Now it is said that this was the first occasion on which Ascanius, whose experience until now had been limited to scaring wild beasts into rapid flight, aimed a swift arrow in an act of war. By his own strength he laid the brave Numanus low, whose surname was Remulus, and who had lately taken a younger sister of Turnus to wife. Numanus, his heart swelling in pride at his new royalty, swaggered forward beyond the front rank shouting and displaying his gigantic size, and he uttered abuse both fit and unfit to repeat, making himself seem grand by his very noise: 'Twice-captured Phrygians, are you not ashamed to be this second time besieged and imprisoned behind a stockade, relying once again on walls to fend death from you? And these are the men who would force our brides from us by war! Now what god impelled you to come to Italy, or rather what insanity? You will find here no sons of Atreus, no Ulysses, inventor of deceitful speeches. We are by our birth a hard race. We carry our baby sons down to a river as soon as born and toughen them by the water's icy cold. Our boys go sleepless for their hunting and never do they let the woodlands rest. Their play is wheeling horses on the rein and speeding the pointed arrow from the bow. And our young men work and endure and are trained to privation; constantly they harrow and master the land; or set towns quaking in warfare. At every age we are bruised by iron. To goad our bullocks' backs we use a spear reversed. Old age slows us but it never weakens the vigour of our spirit or alters our strength; we crush the grey hairs under a helm and still enjoy bringing home fresh spoils and living by pillage. But you, your garments are embroidered in saffron and ablaze with purple dye. You love best a life of idleness, and indulgence in the dance is your joy. Why, your tunics have sleeves and your bonnets strings to tie! You are women of Phrygia, not Phrygian men. Go running over Dindyma's height, to the music of a twin-bore pipe of reed, for which indeed you are trained. The Mother of Ida's Berecyntian tabors and boxwood flutes are the tools of your trade. But leave arms to men; lay not claim to steel.'

Such were his boastful words of ominous warning; and he was too much for the endurance of Ascanius, who stretched his bow, drawing its horse-gut firmly to him, and stood still with arms wide apart. But first he humbly prayed and made his vows to Jupiter: 'Almighty Jupiter, sanction my bold enterprise. And in return I shall each year bring offerings in person to your temple. I shall set before your altar a bullock of shining white with gilded horns, holding his head as high as his mother, and already at the age to butt and to paw and scatter the sand.' The Father heard. He thundered on the left and there was blue sky in the part where he thundered; and at the same instant the bow, bearer of fate, twanged. The backdrawn arrow leapt forth and terrible was the hiss; it passed through the head of Remulus and the iron tip pierced to the hollow behind his brow. Ascanius said: 'There! Now go and make fun of bravery, you boastful man! This is the answer which the twice-captured Phrygians make to Rutulians.' That was all. At his success the Trojans raised a shout, roaring with joy, and lifting their hearts to heaven.

Now it chanced that long-haired Apollo was then looking down from a tract of the sky at the Italian troops and at the settlement. From his seat on a cloud he spoke to the victorious Iulus: 'Blessings on your new manhood, young prince, descendant of gods and ancestor of gods to be! You have found the path to the stars! Rightfully shall every war, which Destiny shall bring to pass, settle again to peace under the dynasty of Assaracus. Troy contains you not.' With these clear words he forthwith dived down the steep of sky, parting the eddies of air, and made straight for Ascanius. Then he altered the features of his face to resemble the aged Butes who had been squire and faithful warden of the gate to Dardan Anchises, and had afterwards been appointed companion to Ascanius by Aeneas his father. And as he walked Apollo was like the aged retainer in all his features, in voice, complexion, white hair, and weapons grimly clanging. Straightway he spoke to Iulus, now on fire with excitement: 'Let it suffice, Son of Aeneas, that Numanus has fallen to your bow and is unavenged. Apollo Most High grants you this first glorious feat and is not envious because your weapons are like his own. But for the future, while you are young, abstain from the war.' With this short message, Apollo, even while he was still speaking, vanished from mortal vision and melted far from sight into thin air. But some Dardan chieftains recognized the God, for they heard the rattle of his quiver as he sped away and knew the divine weapons. Therefore at the expressed will of Phoebus they held Ascanius in check, eager though he was to fight;

instead they themselves advanced again into the fray, exposing their lives to stark peril. A shout ran down the battlements along the full length of the walls. In eagerness they bent their bows and whirled their slings; all the ground was strewn with missiles. And now shields and hollow helms clanged in collision, and the fighting swelled to a new bitterness, as fierce as a rain-storm from the west lashing the earth when the watery constellation of the Charioteer rises, or as the hailstones shot down by clouds onto shallow seas when in the wild murk of southerly winds Jupiter sets spinning his showery squalls and bursts the cloud-vessels of the sky.

Pandarus and Bitias, sons of Alcanor, from Ida, who had been reared by the forest-nymph Iaera in Jupiter's holy wood, two young warriors towering like pines on their father's mountain, flung open the gate entrusted to them by their commander's order; and depending entirely on their own weapons, and of their own accord, they invited the enemy within their defences. Armed with steel and with plumes dancing high on their heads, they took post in the gate, in front of the towers on the right side and on the left. They were like a pair of oak-trees soaring together high in the air by flowing rivers, on the banks of the Po or by pleasant Athesis, and rearing unshorn locks to heaven, their tall heads nodding. Seeing the entrance open the Rutulians burst inside. Immediately Quercens, Aquicolus, a handsome figure in his armour, Tmarus the impulsive, and Haemon, man of Mars, either turned in flight before the onrush of whole battalions or laid down their lives on the very threshold of the gate. At this the angry rage of conflict swelled fiercer in every heart. The Trojans had now rallied and massed at the point of danger, and they even took courage to advance right into the open and fight there hand to hand.

To Turnus, the chief commander, as he spent his rage and spread confusion in another part of the battle, a message was delivered that the enemy were flushed with the success of their recent bloodshed, and were offering an open entrance. Turnus abandoned the task in hand and impelled by a giant's fury dashed to the Dardan gate where stood the defiant brothers.

With a javelin-cast he at once brought down Antiphates who was the first to move into his path, a bastard son of princely Sarpedon by a Theban mother; the shaft of Italian cornel flew through the unresisting air, cut into his belly, and penetrated upwards into his chest. The wound's black cavern gave forth a foaming flood; the blade warmed inside a pierced lung. Then Turnus mightily felled Meropes and Erymas and next Aphidnus, and then Bitias, for all the fire in his eye and all his roaring pride: not with a spear, however, for he would never have surrendered his life to a spear-cast wound, but with a power-javelin discharged and driven on its loud-whining way like a thunderbolt. The two bull-hides and the trusty corslet with the double layer of golden scales could not resist it. The giant limbs collapsed and sank; earth groaned, and the huge shield thundered as it fell on its bearer. So falls sometimes a rock-like pile which, built beforehand of massive masonry, men launch into the deep at Cumae on the Bay of Baiae; plunging, it trails just such a havoc behind, smashes into shallow waters and settles on the sea-bed as the sea swirls in turmoil and the dark sand is stirred. The crash sets high Prochyta quaking, and Inarime too, the island laid upon Typhoeus by Jove's command to make his resting hard.

And now Mars, Lord of Arms, gave more heart and more strength to the Latins, sharply goading their spirit and twisting the goad, and on the Trojans he unleashed the demons, Rout and black Panic. From all parts of the field the Latins gathered where the chance for action offered. The Warrior God swooped down into their hearts. Now Pandarus, seeing his brother's body stretched full-length on the ground, and realizing the condition of their plight and the disastrous turn of events, placed broad shoulders against the gate and, straining with a mighty effort, wrenched back the hinge-post and swung the gate shut by main force. By doing so he left many of his friends shut out and exposed to pitiless combat; but he shut many others inside with him, rescued in full flight; he was a fool, however, for he did not see the Rutulian king himself in the midst of the streaming mass, and by his own free act he penned him within the settlement, like a monstrous tiger among helpless cattle. At once the vision of Turnus became a thing of unearthly terror as it blazed on Trojan eyes. Horrifying to them was the clashing of his arms; blood-red quivered the plumes on his crest, and lightning flashed and flared from his shield. With a sudden shock the men of Aeneas recognized that hated shape, that gigantic figure. But then huge Pandarus leapt forward and hot with rage at his brother's death spoke out: 'This is not Amata's palace, that gift freely given to you as part of your dowry; nor is it Ardea which now encloses Turnus in her midst, sheltered by a homeland's walls. No! The scene before you here is a foeman's camp, with no chance to escape from it.' Turnus smiled at him and serenely replied: 'Lay on then, if there is valour in your heart. Engage the fight. You will soon be telling Priam how you have found here a second Achilles.'

He finished. Pandarus strained with all his strength and cast at him, spinning, a rough unfinished spear which still had on it its green bark and knots. But the wind parried it, for Saturnian Juno deflected the speeding danger, and the spear flew on into the gate. 'You will not escape my weapon, as I yours; my right arm drives it, and with force. Not such as you is he who casts, and wounds you, now.' So said Turnus, and he lifted his sword and rose high to the blow; with the blade he dealt a ghastly wound, splitting his brow, midway between his temples, right down to his young, smooth jaws. Loud sounded the crash and earth shuddered under the mighty weight. Pandarus as he died lay on the ground in a crumpled heap, his arms bespattered with blood and brain; and his head, divided, lolled on his right shoulder and on his left. The Trojans turned to flee in frightened haste, and scattered; and, if the victor had then immediately conceived the idea of smashing the bolts with a blow from his hand and letting in his comrades through the gates, that day would have been the last day of the war, and the end of the Trojan nation. But Turnus was in a blazing passion, and the violence of his mad blood-lust forced him on to the attack. First he surprised Phalaris, and Gyges, whose knee he cut from behind. He seized their spears from them and showered them against the backs of the fugitives.

Juno gave him new spirit and new strength. He sent Halys to join the dead, and Phegeus also, piercing his shield, and next Alcander, Halius, Noemon, and Prytanis, who were all zealously doing the work of Mars on the wall, and were caught unawares. Lynceus came striving towards him, and calling on his comrades. Turnus lunged to the right where the rampart was, and forestalled him with a flickering sword-slash; and his head, struck off by the single close-quarter blow, lay with his helmet far from his body. Turnus next killed Amycus, the ravager of wild beasts, who was of all men most dexterous in tainting weapons and arming steel with poison. And he killed Clytius the Aeolid, and Cretheus, the Muses' own companion and friend, to whom songs and lyres and the setting of verses to stretched strings were ever dear, one who was singing always of horses and warriors in arms, and of the battles which they fought.

At length the Trojan commanders, Mnestheus and the fierce Serestus, heard of the carnage among their men; they arrived on the scene and saw their comrades in rout and the enemy within their gates. Mnestheus cried: 'Where, fellow-Trojans, do you attempt to go in your flight? What other walls and what other strong settlement have you besides this? Will it be said that a single man, penned in with your earthworks all round him, dealt this fearful slaughter all over your town, meeting no avenger, and that he sent to Death's world all these, the finest of your manhood? Do you not feel, with cowards' shame, a pity for your suffering homeland, your ancient gods, and great Aeneas?' In this appeal the Trojans found a new fire and new strength. They rallied and closed their ranks. Turnus gradually withdrew from the fight, making for the river in the direction of the water-front. The Trojans now laid on all the more vigorously, shouting loudly, and closed in massed battle; like a band of hunters with presented spears pressing a savage lion, which, alarmed and furious, with ferocious eyes, retreats backward, for neither do his anger and his valour allow him to turn in flight, nor do the weapons and the hunters permit him, for all his desiring, to strive against them. Like him, Turnus stepped back reluctantly and without haste, his spirit seething with rage. Indeed, even so he twice charged again into the midst of the foe and twice drove them in rout and disorder along their walls. But now a band hurriedly gathered from the camp, and closed its ranks. Nor did Saturnian Juno dare to supply to Turnus any renewal of his strength, for Jupiter had sent Iris down through the air from the sky bearing to his sister words of stern command and the warning that, should Turnus not withdraw from the high defence-walls of the Trojans, it would go hard with him. Accordingly the young warrior had not now the strength in his shield and in his hand even to stand his ground, so overwhelmingly from every quarter came the hail of weapons. His helmet rang about his throbbing brow with incessant noise; the solid bronze began to gape under the rain of stones; his plumes were smashed away from off his head; his shield-boss could not stand up to the blows; and the Trojans, among them Mnestheus most thunderous, redoubled their casting of spears. And now all over Turnus the sweat broke out and spread like a river of pitch, for he had no chance to breathe and rest; he was now exhausted, and he shook, and panted in pain. Only then, at last, did he leap headlong down, with all his armour on him, and plunge into the river. And as he plunged, the river welcomed him to its yellow stream and bore him up on gentle waves. It washed the blood away and carried him back, happy, to his comrades.

BOOK TEN

THE RELIEF AND PITCHED BATTLE

MEANWHILE the gateway to Olympus, the seat of supreme power, was flung open wide and he who is Father of Gods and King over men called a council to his starry home on high whence he would often glance down on the whole world, on the camp of the Dardans, and on the people of Latium. The gods took their seats in the double-entranced hall. Jupiter himself began to speak: 'Majestic dwellers in the skies, why has your decision been reversed? Why do you engage in so fierce a conflict of opposing wills? I had withheld my permission for Italy to meet Trojans in combat of war. Why is there this rebellion against my prohibition? What fears have induced one side or the other to follow the path of arms and to provoke the sword? The due time for battle will come; hasten it not. That day will be when fierce Carthage shall force an opening in the Alpine mass and release dreadful havoc on strongholds of Rome. Then will you have freedom to compete in rivalry of hatreds in a lawful use of force. But now, let be; and be glad to help me settle the compact which I have willed.'

So, shortly, Jupiter spoke. But not short was the reply of golden Venus: 'O Father, O eternal Sovereignty over men and over all the world! There is no other power whom we can now entreat. Do you observe how the Rutulians insolently triumph and how Turnus in his glory drives his charging horses right through our Trojan ranks, swelling with pride at the favour shown him by Mars? No longer now are the Trojans' own defences closed to protect them, for their enemy actually joins in turmoil of battle within their gates, fighting along the walled earthworks till the moats overflow with blood. Aeneas knows nothing of it, for he is away. Will you never grant them relief from siege? Once more an enemy and once more a hostile army threatens the walls of Troy just when she is to be born again; and Diomede starts forth a second time against the Trojans, coming now from Aetolian Arpi. For myself I might well believe that I must again be wounded in battle, and that even now, while I speak, I, your own daughter, am keeping some mortal warrior waiting for me. If it was without your consent and against your divine will that the Trojans steered for Italy, then let them atone for their offences, and you should cease to uphold them with your aid. If however they were in fact led here by all those oracles from the High Gods and the Nether Spirits, why should anyone now have power to annul your command, and start a quite different destiny for them? Surely I need not recall how their fleet was gutted by fire on the shore at Eryx, how the King of the Storms roused his raging winds to fly out from Aeolia, or how Iris was sent speeding down from the clouds. Now Juno even sets demons to work for her, having never previously exploited that part of creation; and Allecto, loosed suddenly upon the upper world, has already coursed in riot through cities of Italy. No longer have I any interest in dominion; that was our hope only so long as fortune was with us; now let either side, whichever you choose, prevail. If there exists nowhere any region which your pitiless queen can allow to the Trojans, then, Father, I adjure you, by the smoking devastation of demolished Troy, permit me to remove Ascanius from the warfare in safety. Let my grandson survive. By all means let Aeneas be storm-tossed on waves unknown, and follow whatever path fortune may have offered. Only may my strength be enough to protect Ascanius and steal him from the horrors of battle. I own Amathus, Cythera, and the height of Paphos, and I have my temple at Idalium. Let him lay arms aside and unrenowned live out his life in one of these. Rule that Carthage must hold Italy crushed under her iron sway. If so, Ascanius shall put no obstacle in the way of any Tyrian city. Of what advantage was it to him to escape the curse of war, flee safe through the midst of Argive flames, and face every danger of the sea and the broad tracts of land, while the Trojans quested for Latium, there to build Troy's citadel again? Would it not have been better to settle upon those cinders, the last remains of home on the soil where Troy once stood? Father, I beg you, if the

Trojans must suffer, give them back their Xanthus and their Simois, and grant them to trace once more the whole cycle of Troy's misfortunes.'

Then spoke royal Juno in the urgency of her frantic hate: 'Why do you force me to break my pent silence and publish my veiled bitterness in speech? Did any man or any god coerce Aeneas to choose the path of war and make his unprovoked assault on King Latinus? "The Fates encouraged him to sail for Italy." No, he was actuated by Cassandra's raving. Did I press him to leave his settlement and trust his life to the winds? Or to leave the supreme direction of the war and the defence of his walls in the hands of a lad? Or to disturb the Etruscan allegiance and the peace of nations? What god, what ruthless power on our side, impelled him to do wrong? What part in all this has been played by Juno, or by Iris, dropping down from the clouds? "It is an outrage that Italians should ring the infant Troy with flames and that Turnus, whose ancestor was Pilumnus and whose mother the goddess Venilia, should take a firm stand on the soil of his own home." What is it, then, when Trojans take up the pitchy firebrand and violently assault the Latins, lay a heavy yoke on farmlands not their own and drive off their plunder, choose whose daughters they will marry, and seduce betrothed brides from their lovers? – they who plead for peace with outstretched hands, but display arms hung from their ships' sterns? You are allowed the power to steal Aeneas from the grasp of the Greeks, spreading before their eyes in your hero's place a cloud of shifting air, and to transform his ships into so many nymphs. Is it then so monstrous if I, in return, have given some aid to the Rutulians? "Aeneas knows nothing of it, for he is away." Let him continue to be away, and know nothing. "You own Paphos, Idalium, and the heights of Cythera." Well, why then interfere with a city charged with war-power, where passions are fierce? Is it I who have been seeking to overthrow from their foundations your Phrygian fortunes which were in any case already crumbling? Is it I, rather than that one who flung the luckless Trojans in the path of the Greeks? What was the reason why Europe and Asia violated their pact of peace by an act of treachery and rose up in arms? Was I the guide when the adulterous Dardan broke into Sparta? Or did I provide his weapons and use lust to foment a war? That was the right time to be anxious for your people. It is too late now for you to challenge me with your inaccurate protests and fling your pointless abuse.'

Such was Juno's speech. All the Heaven-Dwellers murmured in agreement with one speaker or the other, like the murmuring first breaths of a storm caught in a forest and warning mariners of imminent gales, though no movement is seen.

But then the Father Almighty, who holds first authority over the world, began to speak; and as he spoke the Gods' high hall fell silent, the earth deep down was set trembling, the steep sky was soundless, and then too the west winds sank and the ocean hushed his surface: 'So therefore, receive these my words in your hearts and implant them there. Since it has not proved permissible for Ausonians to join in compact with Trojans, and since the dissension among you finds no end, whatever the fortune enjoyed by individual men today, and whatever the furrow of hope which each of them ploughs, I shall make no discrimination whether he be Trojan or Rutulian; whether it is through the destiny of the Italians that the Trojan settlement is held in siege, or through malign prophecies and the curse of wandering laid on Troy. Neither do I absolve the Rutulians. To each man shall his own free actions bring both his suffering and his good fortune. Jupiter is impartially king over all alike. The Fates will find the way.' And Jupiter nodded, ratifying his oath by the rivers of his own Stygian Brother and by their banks of scorching pitch with the black gulf between; and with his nod he set all Olympus quaking. This was the end of the speaking. Jupiter arose then from his throne of gold, and the Heaven-Dwellers gathered about him and escorted him to the threshold.

Meanwhile the Rutulians pressed around at every gate, intent to shed the defenders' blood and lay them low, and to gird their ramparts with flames. On their side the whole force of Aeneas' men was besieged and pent within their stockade without hope of escape. Pitifully helpless stood the Trojans on their high towers, manning their walls with a sparse ring of defenders. In the front line were Asius, son of Imbrasus, Thymoetes, son of Hicetaon, the two who bore the name Assaracus, and Thymbris, now advanced in years, with Castor at his side; they were accompanied by Sarpedon's two brothers, Clarus and Thaemon, from proud Lycia. Acmon of Lyrnessus was carrying an enormous boulder, a huge fragment from a crag, straining with all his strength; for he was no lesser a man than Clytius his father or Mnestheus his brother. So they strove to repel the enemy, some with javelins and others with stones, and some discharging fire, or fitting arrows to the string.

And see! In the thick of them was the young Dardan prince himself, fit indeed for Venus' especial love. His handsome head was uncovered, and he glittered like a jewel set against dark gold to be an ornament for neck or head, or like gleaming ivory skilfully inlaid in boxwood or in terebinth from Oricum; his hair was clasped by a circlet of pliant gold, and streamed down from it over his milk-white neck. And, there, the proud-hearted clans could see another, Ismarus, arming reed-arrows with poison and aiming to wound: a descendant of an illustrious house in Lydia where strong men work the rich cornland, and Pactolus irrigates it with gold. Mnestheus was there too, exalted high by the glory of his earlier feat when he had repulsed Turnus from the earthwork of the walls; and Capys also, from whom the Campanian city derives its name.

So had the two armies clashed in the close conflict of stubborn war; and meanwhile Aeneas was cutting the channels of the sea at midnight. After leaving Evander he had entered the Etruscan camp and approached the king. He had then told him his name and his lineage, and answered all his questions concerning his own needs and resources, explaining fully how large an army the behaviour of Mezentius had won over to their side, and how ferocious was the temper of Turnus; he had also reminded him how limited must be reliance on human power, and added his entreaties. There was no delay at all. Tarchon concluded a pact with him and joined forces. So now the nation from Lydia had paid its debt to fate. In accordance with divine command they trusted themselves to the care of a 'Foreign Leader', and they embarked on their fleet at last. Aeneas' ship headed the line; she had Phrygian lions linked at her ram with Mount Ida overhanging above, a scene very dear to the exiled Trojans. At the bows sat great Aeneas himself, pondering in his thoughts the various eventualities of the war. And Pallas stayed close to him on his left asking him now about the stars guiding their course through the night and now about his adventures on land and sea.

Goddesses of Song, now throw Helicon wide and inspire me to describe the force which followed Aeneas at this time from Etruscan shores, manning their ships and sailing on the ocean.

Massicus was the first of the captains, and he cut through the sea-surface on his bronze-plated ship, the Tigress. Under him sailed a band of a thousand young warriors who had marched forth from the battlements of Clusium and the city of Cosae; their weapons were death-dealing bows and arrows in light quivers slung from their shoulders. With Massicus was the grim Abas. His contingent all bore splendid arms, and his ship's stern shone with a golden figure of Apollo. Populonia was the mother-city which had given him six hundred of her sons, young warriors experienced in war; and Ilva, the island fertile in inexhaustible mines of Chalybean iron, had sent three hundred more. Third in the line was Asilas, the mighty seer who mediated between men and gods, and who knew the secrets held by the entrails of beasts, the stars in the sky, the voices of birds, and the flash of presaging thunderbolts; he hastened forwards his thousand men, their spears bristling in the serried ranks. Pisae, the city on Etruscan soil founded from Pisa, the Greek city on the banks of the Alpheus, had placed them under his command. Next after him came the handsome Astyr, placing high trust in his horse and his iridescent armour. Three hundred more, all with one will to follow in the army, were contributed by folk who dwell in Caere's homes and the farmlands by the Minio, and at ancient Pyrgi and unhealthy Graviscae.

I am not one to pass you over, Cunarus, valiant war-leader of Ligurians; or you, Cupavo, though your followers were few. From your crest there arose swan's feathers, emblem of your father's transformation, for which Cupid and his mother have the shame. For they tell how Cycnus, in grief for his adored Phaethon, consoled himself for love's tragedy with the muse's aid, singing amid the leaves of poplar trees which had once been Phaethon's own sisters, and beneath their shade; and as he did so he drew over him, not the white hair of age, but soft feathers, and so left the world and, singing still, pursued the stars. His son Cupavo now sailed with men of his own generation massed on board the fleet, forcing his enormous ship the Centaur onwards by the oars; the ship bore down on the waters, her figurehead holding high a fearsome rock to menace the waves, as her long keel cleft its furrow through the deep.

Another who called up a company from his homeland's borders was Ocnus, son of fate-telling Manto and the Etruscan river, who gave to Mantua her walls and his mother's name. Mantua has a wealth of ancestry, not all of one lineage. She comprises three clans, each composed of four communities. They all accept Mantua as their capital city; but it is from the Etruscan strain that she draws her strength. There were five hundred others from the same region whom Mezentius had driven to arms against himself; and a figure of Mincius, veiled in grey reeds, the son of Lake Benacus, led them forth in their pine-built warships onto the broad seas. Weightily Aulestes moved, rising to the stroke and lashing the waves with a hundred tree-trunk oars, till the sea-way whitened where the surface was churned. The ship which carried him was the monstrous Triton, whose figure affrighted the blue channels with his horn of shell; as he swam, his hairy forepart down to his flanks displayed human shape but his belly ended in a beast of the sea. Beneath the breast of this hybrid monster the water murmured and foamed.

Such is the tale of the elect chieftains who sailed with thrice ten ships to the aid of Troy, their bronzen rams cleaving the level brine.

And now day had withdrawn from the sky; and kindly Phoebe was trampling Mid-Olympus with her night-wandering team. But to the limbs of Aeneas care allowed no rest; and so he sat at the helm himself, steering in person and tending the sails. Then, see! Suddenly, in mid-course, he was met by a band of his own friends. These were the nymphs, whom life-giving Cybele had commanded to assume goddesses' power over the sea, and to be changed each one of them into a sea-nymph from the ship which she had been before, one of those bronze-plated hulls which had rested on the beach; and now they swam level with him, cutting through the waves. Afar off they had recognized their own king; and they danced around him in salute. The most expert in speech among them, Cymodoce, followed in his wake. She held onto the stern with her right hand, lifting the whole length of her back above the surface, and with her left she noiselessly paddled in the waters below. Then, while he was still perplexed, she addressed him: 'Do you wake, Aeneas Divinely-Born? Wake, then; ease off the sheets, and let your sails fill. We are your fleet, once pines of Ida from her holy crest, and now nymphs of ocean. When by the blade and by the flame the treacherous Rutulian would have forced us into headlong flight, we, against our will, broke your moorings; and we have been seeking for you over the seas. The Mother refashioned us in this shape, out of pity; she has granted us to become goddesses, living all our lives beneath the waves. But, meanwhile, Ascanius your young son is besieged within wall and moats, attacked by showers of weapons and surrounded by Latins, bristling with martial ardour. Already Arcadian horsemen, and among them some valiant Etruscans, are standing by for action. But it is the fixed purpose of Turnus to confront them squarely with his own main squadrons before they can join the Trojan camp. Come, therefore, arise. As soon as dawn is breaking you must order your comrades to be marshalled for action, and you must yourself take your invincible shield, with its rim-circle of gold, which the God whose Might is Fire himself gave to you. If you trust in the truth of my message, tomorrow's dawn shall see vast heaps of Rutulian slain.' She finished, and, departing, forced the high stern onwards by a thrust of her hand, knowing well what strength to use. And the ship sped over the waves swifter than a javelin, swifter than an arrow which keeps pace with the winds; and after her the other ships too hastened their course.

Anchises' son, the Man of Troy, was mystified, astounded; but in obedience to the sign given to him he lifted up his heart and then, looking to the vault above, he offered a short prayer: 'Mother of Ida, Mother of the Gods, life-giver, lover of Dindyma, of cities tower-crowned and of bridled lions paired under one yoke, you now are my divine leader in the fight; may you give a fit fulfilment to this prophecy, and with favour in your steps be at the Trojans' side.' Such was his earnest prayer; and meanwhile the day had routed the darkness and, swiftly circling, returned with a light now full. His first act was to command his comrades to parade behind their standards, attune their mood to fighting, and prepare for battle. And now, standing high on his quarterdeck, Aeneas could already see his camp and his Trojans; and immediately he raised aloft his flashing shield in his left hand. From their walls the Dardans lifted a shout to the sky. This new access of hope quickened their rage, and strongly they cast their spears, like the flight through the sky of cranes from Strymon, outlined against dark clouds and hurrying in rout before south winds, trumpeting their loud signal-cries and leaving a clamour to trail behind. To the Rutulian king and his Italian captains it was bewildering indeed, until they looked round and saw the fleet already turned inshore and the sea all one movement of gliding ships. Aeneas' crest blazed on his head and from his plumed crown streamed the flame; his gold shield-centre spouted forth its broad beam, like the sinister, blood-red glow of a comet on some clear night, or Sirius the star that brings thirst and disease to suffering humanity, as he rises and burns with sinister glare to spread a menace over all the sky.

But the daring of Turnus never quailed. He was firmly confident that he could seize the shore in time and drive the foe back from the beaches as they came into land. [He did not wait, but spoke to raise his men's spirit and indeed taunted them:] 'It has come, the very chance for which you yearned and prayed, a chance to break their line with your swords!

The issue of the fight is in your grasp – if you act like men. Now each of you must remember his wife and his home, and recall the great deeds which won your fathers fame. Let us take the initiative and hurry to confront them at the water's edge while they are still nervous and hesitant, and their first few steps after landing are insecure. Fortune helps those who dare.' So he spoke and meanwhile debated with himself whom he might lead against the foe and whom best entrust with the siege of the walls.

But Aeneas was already landing his comrades by gangways from the high-riding sterns. Many, watching for the waves to spend their force and ebb, leapt out, entrusting themselves to the shallow water, while others slid down the oars. Tarchon examined the shoreline, and then suddenly turned his prow towards a point where no shoals heaved and no wave broke to come roaring back, but the sea swept smoothly in with a swelling and unimpeded flood. He appealed to his comrades: 'Now, my Chosen Band, bend to your tough oars. Lift ho! Carry her with you! Let your rams cleave into this foeman's land. Let your keels of themselves cut their furrow there. I would willingly wreck my own ship to moor her so, if only we can seize a foothold on the shore.' So did Tarchon speak out; his comrades rose to the oars, and they drove their ships amid foam onto fields of Latium, until the rams gripped dry land and every keel settled, unharmed. But not, Tarchon, your own ship! She was smashed onto a shoal, and lodged on an uneven reef, hanging there for a long time in precarious balance and taxing the strength of the rollers, till finally she broke up, and flung her crew overboard among the breakers where they were hampered by fragments of oars and floating thwarts, while at the same time the ebb of the waves dragged their feet from under them.

But nothing could delay Turnus, cramp him, or hold him back. Vigorous and quick-acting, he moved the whole of his battle-front against the Trojans and posted men to meet them on the shore. Trumpets rang out, Aeneas was the first to charge against the levies of country-folk, a good augury for the fortune of the fight, and he was the first to strike Latins down.

He killed Theron, tallest of men, who was forward in attacking him; Aeneas cut through the jointed bronze and the tunic stiffened with gold, and the sword exposed his flank and drained it of its blood. Next he struck Lichas, who had been cut from his mother after she was dead, and had therefore been consecrated to Phoebus because in infancy he had been permitted to escape the hazard of the knife. Not long after, Aeneas cast down to their death hardy Cisseus and monstrous Gyas who were felling entire ranks with their clubs; it was of no help to them that they used the same weapons as Hercules and that their own hands were strong; or that they had for their father Melampus, who, as long as the earth offered grievous labours for Hercules, had ever been his comrade. Aeneas then spun a javelin at Pharus, who was boasting loudly but doing no deeds, and planted it in his shouting mouth. And, hapless Cydon, you might have fallen too. You were following after your latest passion, Clytius, whose cheeks were golden with their first down, and piteously would you have lain low, felled by the Dardan's arm and released from the anxious love of youth which was always yours, had not the whole massed company of your brothers, sons of Phorcus, all rallied against Aeneas. Seven in number, they discharged seven spears, of which some rebounded harmlessly from his helmet or his shield, and others merely grazed him, for protecting Venus turned them aside.

Aeneas spoke to his faithful Achates: 'Pile me a supply of those missiles which once were lodged in Greek bodies on plains of Ilium. As you will see, not one will fail to take effect when my hand casts it against a Rutulian.' With that he seized a large spear, and cast; it flew, and battered through the bronze of Maeon's shield, bursting in one instant his corslet and his chest. His brother Alcanor moved quickly up to support him and upheld him with his right hand as he fell. Another flying javelin pierced his arm and sped onwards, bloodied now but still keeping its course, while the arm hung lifeless by its tendons from the shoulder. And now Numitor seized the spear from his brother's body and aimed a cast at Aeneas; but this time he could not succeed in planting it in the target of its aim; for it could do no more than graze the flank of stalwart Achates. At this moment up came Clausus of Cures, confident in the strength of early youth, and by a long cast of his stiff spear struck Dryops under the chin with forceful impact; the spear pierced his throat and even while he was speaking stole from him in one moment voice and life. So he struck the earth with his forehead and choked from his mouth the thick gore. Clausus also laid low three Thracians of the most exalted line of Boreas and three others sent forth to war by their father Idas from their homeland Ismara; and each of these fell in a different fashion. Then Halaesus closed in with a band of Auruncans, followed by Messapus, Neptune's son, driving his magnificent team. One after another they strove to drive out the invaders; and there on the very threshold of Italy the conflict raged. Just as winds in quarrel across broad heaven rouse their battle with equally matched courage and strength, for neither do they yield one to the other nor do clouds nor sea ever yield, so that the fight is long in balance and the winds strain against all the world; likewise the battle-ranks of Troy and Latium met there in shock, foot locked to foot and man to man in the press.

Elsewhere on the field, where a torrent had set boulders rolling and torn up bushes from its banks, and had driven them over a wide extent of land, Pallas, seeing that his Arcadians, who were unused to charging in dismounted array, but had been induced by the rough ground to send back their horses, were turning in flight before the hotly pursuing Latins, found one thing only left for him to do in such straits. He sought to reawaken their courage, now by entreaties and now by bitter taunts: 'Comrades, where is your flight to take you? I beg you, by your own valiant deeds, by the name of Evander who commands you, by those wars which he gloriously won, and by my own ambition aspiring now to match my father's renown, oh, never put your faith in a runaway's speed! By steel must you burst your way through your enemy. There lies the path which your proud land requires you and me, Pallas your leader, to take, where the mass of warriors presses most thick. No divine powers beset us, for the enemy driving against us is mortal like ourselves, and our lives and our hands are as many as theirs. And, see, the ocean encloses us with the whole sea's barrier. There is no land left for our retreat. Is it into the sea that we must go – or straight to Troy?'

So he spoke and forthwith charged into the thick of the enemy. The first to meet him was Lagus, and an unkind fate led him thither. For as he endeavoured to tear from the ground a weighty boulder, Pallas flung his javelin and pierced him through the middle where his spine divided his ribs. He then tugged at the spear to withdraw it from the bones where it lodged. Hisbo now leapt on him, but failed to forestall him, as he had rashly hoped. For Pallas was there and ready for him in time, and as Hisbo came on charging madly, made reckless by the horrible sight of his dear friend's death, he buried his sword in his swelling lung. Pallas attacked Sthenius and Anchemolus also, of Rhoetus' ancient line, who once had shamelessly violated his own stepmother's bed. And two others there were who fell on that Rutulian field, twin sons of Daucus, Larides and Thymber, so exactly alike that their own parents, in their sweet bewilderment, could not distinguish them. But Pallas made them cruelly different; for with Evander's sword he severed Thymber's head and sheared away Larides' right hand, which now sought its owner, with the fingers, twitching as they died, still clutching at the sword.

The Arcadians, inspired by their hero's rebuke and seeing his magnificent feats, gained strength to face the enemy from their mingled remorse and shame. And now Pallas pierced Rhoeteus as he fled past him on his pair-horse chariot. While he did so, Ilus had a respite and breathing-space, but only for a moment. For it had been at Ilus afar off that Pallas had aimed his tough spear, and Rhoeteus, fleeing before noble Teuthras and his brother Tyres, had run straight into the path of its flight; he rolled from his chariot and with nerveless heels beat on Rutulian ground. And just as when in summer-time winds arise in answer to prayer, and some shepherd starts fires here and there about forest-land, so that suddenly the intervening woods catch alight as well, till Vulcan's ragged, menacing battle-line spreads continuous across broad plains, and the shepherd sits victorious, looking down on the triumphant flames; so likewise all the valour of his comrades united into a single blaze and gave aid to Pallas. But Halaesus, ever swift in war, dashed up to face the foe and braced himself behind his arms. And now he slew Ladon, Pheres, and Demodocus and whipped off with gleaming blade the right hand which Strymonius had raised to grasp his throat; then he smote with a stone the face of Thoas and shattered his skull to a mess of brains and blood. Halaesus had been hidden in the forests by his father, who foresaw what was destined to come; but when the father himself grew old and white-haired and at last relaxed his eyes in death, the Fates laid their hands on his son and dedicated him to die by Evander's weapons. As he made for him Pallas prayed: 'Father Tiber, grant now to the spear-head, which I poise for the cast, a fortunate path through the breast of the hardy Halaesus. Then shall your own oak-tree possess these arms which I see before me, the spoils of my foe.' And the God heard that prayer. As Halaesus sought to shield Imaon, he unluckily exposed his chest, leaving it defenceless before the Arcadian spear. But Lausus, a tower of strength in that war, would not let his ranks remain dismayed, even at the slaying of such a hero. He began by killing the first warrior to confront him, Abas, the very knot and stay of the battle. Felled were Arcadia's sons, and felled were Etruscans, and Trojans too, whose lives the Greeks had failed to destroy. The battle-fronts met in shock, well matched in leadership and in strength. Those in the rear forced the front lines together till the congestion allowed no play of weapons or hands. On one side Pallas pressed vigorously onwards, and on the other Lausus, of little difference in age, and both magnificent to see. To both Fortune had denied a return to their homeland. Yet he who reigns in high Olympus did not permit these two to meet in combat face to face; for each had his doom presently waiting, from the hand of a mightier foe.

Meanwhile Turnus was warned by his guardian-sister Juturna to move up to the aid of Lausus. He cut through the battle's centre in his flying chariot. When he saw his comrades he said to them: 'It is time to stand down from battle. It is for me alone to charge Pallas; for I alone have a right to him. I only wish his father himself had been here to watch.' This he said and at his order his comrades withdrew from their positions on the field. Now when the Rutulians had withdrawn, the young Pallas, surprised at the imperious tone of his command, looked in amazement at Turnus, his eyes roving all over his giant form. He surveyed him, part by part, with a hostile stare across the gap between, and then with a vaunt of his own countered the arrogant prince's words: 'Soon shall I have fame, either by seizing a commander's spoils, or by an illustrious death. My father is equally resigned to either lot. Away with your threats!' With these words he strode out onto the midst of the field; and the blood congealed in Arcadian hearts. Turnus leapt from his chariot and prepared to close on foot. Like a lion, which from some high vantage point sees a bull standing on a plain afar off practising for combat, and darts down upon him, such was the picture which the onset of Turnus made. When Pallas judged that Turnus would be within range of a spear-cast, he moved forward first, hoping that, though ill-matched in strength, if only he acted with daring, chance might somehow give aid, and he spoke towards broad heaven: 'By your guest-friendship with my father when you came as a stranger to him, I pray you, Hercules, to support my great intent. Let Turnus, at point of death, see me wrest his bloody arms from him, and let his dying eyes endure the sight of his conqueror.'

Hercules heard the young man's prayer. Deep in his heart he repressed a heavy sigh; and his tears streamed helplessly. Then the Father spoke to his son in kindly words: 'For each man his day stands fixed. For all mankind the days of life are few, and not to be restored. But to prolong fame by deeds, that is valour's task. Under Troy's high ramparts fell all those many sons of gods; yes, and with them fell my own son, Sarpedon. Turnus also has his doom calling him; he too has reached the goal of his allotted years.' So he spoke and then turned his eyes away from the farmlands of the Rutulians. But

Pallas with all his strength discharged his spear and then whipped his bright sword from its hollow sheath. The spear flew on. It forced its way through the rim of the shield, hit where the armour covering the shoulder rises highest, and finally passed on, leaving a graze on mighty Turnus' skin. Turnus now held poised for long a spear of hard oak pointed with steel, and hurled it at Pallas, crying: 'Look! See whether my weapon pierces better!' So he spoke; and the spear-head with its shuddering impact lashed through the centre of Pallas' shield, with all its layers of iron and bronze and the many dense-packed coverings of bull's hide, rent through the defences of his cuirass, and pierced his broad chest. Hastily he tore the hot weapon from his wound, but in vain; for after it, through that self-same gash, poured his life-blood and his life. He crashed down onto his wound; his arms clanged over him; and dying he bit the hostile earth with his blood-stained mouth. Standing close over him, Turnus called: 'Arcadians, remember! Take back this message to King Evander from me: I return to him such a Pallas as he deserves. I freely grant what honour a tomb may afford, what solace burial may bring. The welcome which he gave to Aeneas shall be of no small cost to Evander.' So saying he planted his left foot on the lifeless Pallas and tore from him his heavy, massive sword-belt with its scene of horror engraved on it: a band of young bridegrooms all foully murdered early on their wedding-night, with blood in the marriage-chambers; a scene chased on the belt in lavish gold by Clonus, son of Eurytus. Such was the trophy which Turnus rejoiced and gloried to have won. How blind are men to fate and futurity, and how little they know how to preserve moderation at the proud moment of success! For Turnus a time will come when he will wish that he could pay a great price for Pallas to be restored unharmed, and will hate this day and its spoils. Meanwhile a great company of Pallas' comrades, with much weeping and lamentation, had laid him on his shield, and were bearing him back. Oh, Pallas, the bitter pain, and the high pride, which you will bring to your father when you return to him! This day first gave you to war, and the same day stole you away;

yet even so you leave behind you vast piles of Rutulian slain.

And now there came flying up to Aeneas no mere rumour of this bitter blow but an informant hard to doubt, reporting that his soldiers were within a narrow margin of destruction, and that the Trojans were routed and in critical need of help. This news set Aeneas ablaze. Mowing down with his sword every enemy within his reach, he drove a broad lane through the mass. He was in search of none but Turnus who was still exulting in his latest act of bloodshed. Before his mind's eye rose Pallas, Evander, the hospitality which he had first encountered on that day when he came as a stranger, and the right hands then joined in compact. As he sped onwards he took alive four young sons of Sulmo and four others reared by Ufens, meaning to sacrifice them as death-offerings to Pallas' ghost, pouring streams of captive blood on the pyre's flames. He then discharged a deadly spear at Magus who was some way off; but Magus adroitly moved closer in, and the spear flew, quivering, over him. Magus clasped Aeneas' knees and appealed in supplication: 'I pray you by your father's spirit and by all your hopes for Iulus now growing to manhood, spare this life of mine to go safe for my son and for my father. I have a proud mansion and buried deep within it lie talents of chased silver, and I own heavy bars of wrought and unwrought gold. The victory of your Trojans depends little enough on me; one single life cannot make all that difference.' He finished, and Aeneas answered him with this reply: 'Spare for your sons all those talents of silver and gold of which you tell. It was Turnus who first swept away all courtesies of war at the very moment when he slew Pallas. The spirit of my father Anchises judges so, and so does Iulus.' As he spoke he held Magus' helmet in his left hand, and while he still pleaded bent his neck back, and up to the hilt drove home his sword.

Not far away was Haemonides, priest of Phoebus and Trivia, with the band tied by its sacred ribbons round his brow, clad all in shining white attire with emblems also white. Aeneas met him and drove him over the field. He tripped and fell. Aeneas stood over him darkening him with his tall shadow, and took him for his victim; and Serestus gathered up his armour and carried it off over his shoulders as a trophy for Mars, king of marching men. But now Caeculus, descendant of Vulcan's lineage, and Umbro from the Marsian mountains, rallied the battle-line. Enraged, the Dardan-born confronted them. With his blade he had just struck off Anxur's left arm and with it his rounded shield. Anxur had been uttering some arrogant boast, putting trust in the force of mere words; probably he assumed that he would live long and reach grey hairs, forgetting the limitations of the human lot in his presumption. Now Tarquitus proudly pranced before Aeneas in gleaming armour and moved to meet his burning anger; his mother had been the nymph Dryope and his father Faunus, dweller in the woods. Aeneas drew back his spear, pinned Tarquitus to his own cuirass and the heavy burden of his shield, and then, as he pleaded helplessly and thought of much that he might say, he struck his head off onto the earth, kicked the warm trunk rolling, and spoke over it from his vindictive heart: 'Lie where you are, you who expected us to fear you! Your mother shall never lay you fondly in the earth, or consign your remains to any stately family tomb. For you shall be left to the wild birds of prey, or plunged in waters where the wave shall toss you and hungry fishes mouth your wounds.'

Then, forthwith, Aeneas pursued Antaeus and Luca, of Turnus' front line, and Numa the brave, and auburn-haired Camers, son of Volcens the great of heart, who once reigned in silent Amyclae, and who of all Italians was richest in land. Like Aegaeon, said to have had a hundred arms and a hundred hands, and to have blazed forth fire out of fifty breasts through fifty mouths, clashing fifty similar shields and drawing fifty swords to face the thunder-strokes of Jupiter; even so Aeneas wreaked his victorious savagery over all the field when once his sword-point warmed. And see, now he was straining to reach the breasts of that four-horse team which Niphaeus drove. But suddenly the horses, catching sight of him as he advanced, pacing onwards with his long strides and roaring terror, turned in sudden fright, galloped back, flung out their master, and whirled the chariot to the sea-shore. Meanwhile Lucagus was advancing to the field behind his pair of greys.

His brother Liger was with him to handle the reins and control the horses, while Lucagus vigorously swung his naked sword in sweeping circles. Impatient of their fierce ardour, Aeneas charged; and his mighty figure loomed towards them, spear pointed. Liger spoke to him: 'You see here no horses of Diomede nor chariot of Achilles nor plains of Phrygia. Here in our land and at this very hour shall come the end of this war and the end of your life.' Such were mad Liger's words, and far they flew. But it was not words that Troy's hero devised in answer; for he cast a spear against his foe. Lucagus, bending forward to the lash, was urging his team with the flat of his sword, and, left foot advanced, prepared for battle. The spear drove on through the lower rim of his shining shield and pierced his left groin; he was flung from his chariot and rolled dying on the soil. Aeneas the True spoke to him in bitter taunt: 'Lucagus, no coward flight of horses has betrayed your chariot, nor have imagined shadows turned them from facing the foe. It is you who have decided to desert your team, for you leapt down from your chariot!' With this sneer Aeneas seized hold of the horses. The unhappy brother had also fallen from the chariot, and was stretching helpless palms towards Aeneas: 'Man of Troy! I adjure you by your own self and by the parents who begot you for greatness! Leave my life to me. Take pity on me, who plead with you.' He tried to say more, but Aeneas spoke: 'That is not how you were talking of late. Let brother forsake not brother. Now die.' And with his weapon's point he exposed the hidden source of life within the breast.

So it was that the Dardan war-chief dealt death across that field. His rage was the rage of a mountain torrent or black tornado. And at last the young prince Ascanius and the manhood of Troy broke out from their camp. The siege had failed.

During these events Jupiter addressed himself to Juno: 'My Sister and my Queen whom I so dearly love, it is as you supposed; your judgement does not deceive you. It is Venus who upholds the power of Troy, and not their manhood's vital valour in war or their own proud spirit, dauntless in peril.' Juno meekly answered: 'Why, my dearest Lord, do you disturb me, when I am already sick at heart and fearful of your grim command? Of course, if there were now in my love the influence which long since it held and rightfully held, you would not indeed, Almighty, have denied me the power to steal Turnus from the fight and guard him safe for his father Daunus. As it is, let him perish. Let him render satisfaction to the Trojans with his sinless blood. Yet he traces his name from an origin in our own divine stock. Pilumnus was his father's great-grandfather. And often, in generosity of hand, he has loaded your temple-steps with many gifts.' The king of celestial Olympus shortly answered her: 'If your plea is only for a reprieve from immediate death, and a mere respite for the young prince, though afterwards fall he must, and if you realize that I ordain it so, then let Turnus flee; remove him in this way, and wrest him from the oncoming doom. So far I am at liberty to indulge you. But if some profounder reprieve hides beneath your prayers, and you think that the whole war's course can be disturbed or changed, you harbour false hopes.' In tears Juno replied: 'Ah, but suppose you really mean to grant the favour which your lips withhold, and award the longer span of life to Turnus? If not, an agonizing end awaits him, innocent though he is, or else I am straying, far from the truth. But, oh, if only my dread might prove a false mockery and you, who alone have the power, would yet change the course of your designs to a better end!'

Having spoken so, Juno, girt with a cloud and driving a storm before her through the air, forthwith darted down from heaven's height and made her way to the battle-lines of Ilium and the camp of the Laurentines. Then, being divine, she took a wisp of a shadow, a strengthless fragment of yielding cloud, and she wrought it into the shape of Aeneas, a sight miraculous and weird. She decked it with Dardan arms, and matched the shield of the Goddess-Born, and the plumes on his head. She gave to it words never real, sound without thought, and perfectly moulded the gait for its walking; like those shapes which are said to flit when death is past, or dreams which delude perception in depth of sleep. So now the phantom pranced gaily before the foremost rank, infuriating proud

Turnus with its weapon-play, and offering a challenge to him. He dashed upon the wraith and made a long cast of his whistling spear. It turned its footsteps round to flee. And now Turnus, thinking that Aeneas had indeed fled from him and was retreating, drank deep of a confused and delusive hope. 'Aeneas,' he cried, 'whither are you fleeing? Never forsake your plighted marriage! This right hand of mine shall now give you the soil for which you came searching over the waves.' And shouting such taunts, and waving the naked edge of his sword, he pursued, without ever realizing that the cause of his delight drifted on the wind. There happened to be a ship standing moored to a raised ledge of rock, with ladders in position, and a companion-way ready placed. She was the ship on which King Osinius had sailed to Latium from the borders of Clusium. Into her the wraith of a nervous Aeneas in flight flung itself to hide. Turnus pressed on at a pace as rapid, over every obstacle, and leapt up the steep companion-way. But scarcely had he reached the prow when Saturnian Juno snapped the mooring, wrenched the ship clear, and swept her out to sea over the retreating waves.

So, while Aeneas continued to seek combat with an adversary who was nowhere to be found, and cast down to their death many strong men in his path, Turnus himself drifted onwards across the mid-sea at the mercy of a veering wind. And now the airy wraith ceased to look any longer for places in which to hide. It soared high in the air and melted into a dark cloud. Mystified by his plight and little grateful for his escape, Turnus looked about him, and then with a cry held out both hands to the heavens above: 'Father Almighty, do you indeed mean me to be so severely punished? Do you count me guilty of a fault so grave? Where am I drifting to? Where was I when I began to drift? Why am I in flight? How am I to return? Shall I ever again see our camp or the walls of the Laurentines? What of that host of men who followed my standard? The horror of it! I have forsaken them, with death unspeakable all around them; am I now to see them scattered and hear their groaning as they fall? But what am I about? Ah, cannot some profoundest chasm of earth yawn deep enough to engulf me? Winds, better that you take pity! Drive this ship onto reefs or against cliffs. I, Turnus, freely entreat it of you. Let her run upon Syrtes' cruel quicksands where no Rutulian, nor any rumour acquainted with my shame, can follow me.' Speaking so, he wavered now this way and now that in doubt whether, distraught at so terrible a disgrace, he should impale himself on his sword-point, driving the unfeeling blade straight through his ribs, or cast himself overboard amid the waves, strive to swim till he could reach the curving shores, and so return to face the Trojans' weapons. Three times he tried each way, but three times Juno mightily restrained him and in heartfelt pity for the young prince forced him back. So gently he drifted, cutting through the deep water with aid from waves and current, until at last he was carried to land at the ancient city of his father Daunus.

In the meantime, warned by Jupiter, Mezentius hotly took up the fight, and charged the exultant Trojans. The Etruscan ranks closed for combat with him, and against that one warrior alone they concentrated all their hatred and all their showering weapons. But he stood like a rock, projecting into a waste of waters, confronting the utmost violence of the winds and exposed to open sea, which for ever endures all the force, and every threat, of sky and ocean, but remains steadfast. First he stretched Dolichaon's son, Hebrus, on the ground and with him Latagus, and Palmus quick to flee. Latagus he forestalled, striking him full in the face on his mouth with a huge jagged boulder of mountain-rock; Palmus he left to writhe, hamstrung and helpless, and then presented his arms to Lausus, to wear them on his shoulders and set the crest on his helm. He also slew the Phrygian Evanthes, and Mimas, close friend and contemporary of Paris, for Theano bore him into the daylight to his father Amycus on the same night when Cisseus' daughter Queen Hecuba, pregnant with a brand of fire, gave Paris life. Paris fell in the city of his fathers; but the Laurentine coast retains Mimas in a foreign land. Mezentius was like a fearsome boar which after many years of safety in pine-clad Vesulus, or by the Laurentine marshes where a forest of reeds has been his pasture, is at last pursued by snapping hounds down from the mountain-heights, and, finally, with the nets all round him, standing at bay, he roars defiance, shoulders bristling, so that none has valour to vent his rage on him or draw near and offer battle, but they only harass him from a safe distance with javelin-casts and shouts. Just so, not one of those who were righteously enraged against Mezentius had spirit to close with drawn sword, but they could only provoke him with missiles at long range and an uproar of shouting. He, dauntless and assured, faced every way, grinding his teeth, and shaking the spears from the hide of his shield.

Now there had come from the ancient territory of Corythus a Greek named Acron; he had been banished and so forced to leave his wedding unfulfilled. He was dealing confusion in the battle-centre, clad in the crimson of his plumes and a purple robe which the promised bride had given to him, when Mezentius saw him afar off; as many a time some ravenous lion wandering among fenced cattle-farms urged by a frantic hunger, chancing to see a fleeting goat or a stag with towering antlers, rejoices, and, monstrously gaping, with bristling mane, he lies at his feast over his victim, clinging to its entrails, while gruesomely the blood bathes the unpitying jaws; such now was the agile onslaught of Mezentius against his serried foes. Unhappy Acron was brought low. Breathing out his life he hammered the dark earth with his heels and spread blood over his shattered arms. Yet Mezentius did not even deign to fell Orodes as he ran away, or wound him with an unseen thrust of his sharp spear. Instead he moved round to meet him face to face and closed man to man, to prove himself a better man not by trickery but by true valour, in combat. Orodes dropped. Mezentius planted a foot upon him, leaned on it and tugged at his spear and said: 'My comrades, Orodes the proud, a force to reckon with in this war, lies low.' His comrades raised their shouts echoing his exultant triumph-cry. But Orodes, with his last breath, answered: 'Conqueror, whoever you are, you shall not rejoice for long before I am avenged; a fate like mine keeps watch for you. After me, here on this same field you too shall find your place.' At this Mezentius smiled, and anger was in the smile: 'Now die. As for me, the so-called

Father of Gods and King of Men will decide.' Saying this, he withdrew the spear from his body; the hard repose of iron sleep bore down on his eyes, and their light was extinguished for the everlasting dark. Caedicus now cut down Alcathous, Sacrator Hydaspes, and Rapo Parthenius and also Orses, a warrior of toughest strength. Messapus killed Clonius and the son of Lycaon, Erichaetes; Clonius, already fallen from his unbridled horse, lay prone on the ground, but when Messapus fought Erichaetes both were on foot. Also on foot, Agis the Lycian had advanced; but Valerus, who shared his grandfather's prowess, struck him to earth. Meanwhile Thronius was felled by Salius, and Salius by Nealces, who was famed for his javelin-cast and his arrow-shot, sped from afar and never seen.

Now Mars pressed heavily on both sides and gave equal share of anguish and equal exchange of death to each; for in equal measure were they killing and falling, victors and vanquished alike; neither this army nor that had ever a thought of retreat. In Jupiter's palace the gods pitied the pointless fury of both sides, sad that men, doomed in any case to die, should suffer ordeals so terrible. On one side Venus, and on the other, opposing her, Saturnian Juno, kept watch, and in the midst between the warring thousands pale Tisiphone vented her rage. But now Mezentius advanced furiously onto the field, shaking a gigantic spear. Tall he was, like Orion, who paces on foot as he rends his way through Nereus' deepest pools in mid-ocean and yet stands with head and shoulders above the waves, or carries home an aged rowan-tree from a mountain height, walking on the ground but hiding his head amid clouds; and like him Mezentius strode on in his massive armour. Looking down the long line of battle, Aeneas espied him and prepared to meet him face to face. Mezentius, still undismayed, awaited his high-hearted foe and stood firm-planted, solid in his own great bulk. And quickly he judged with his eye the right range for a spear-cast, and prayed: 'Right hand of mine, for you are my god, and weapon which I poise to throw, aid me now. I vow, as my trophy over Aeneas, to array Lausus himself in the spoils which I shall tear from that pirate's body.' So he spoke and then at long range cast the hissing spear. It flew, but glanced from Aeneas' shield and pierced the handsome Antores, who stood near, between his waist and thigh. Antores had been a comrade of Hercules; but when he was expelled from Argos he clung to Evander, settling in a city of Italy. Unluckily was he felled by a wound not meant for him; and he looked at the sky, and, dying, remembered the Argos which he loved. Then Aeneas the True cast his spear. It passed through the shield's domed circle of triple bronze, the layers of linen and the texture of three bulls' hides, and came to rest low down in the groin; but failed to carry its strength with it to its flight's end. Aeneas, delighted at seeing Etruscan blood, swiftly drew the sword from his side and dashed hotly on his shaken enemy. At the sight Lausus groaned deeply from love of his dear father, and the tears rolled down his face. And now, for my own part, if antiquity can ever win belief for a deed so grand, never shall I, young hero, pass in silence the hard death which fell to your lot, your sublime feat of arms, and your own self, so richly deserving fame.

Mezentius was giving ground, retreating hampered and helpless, for he had to drag the deadly spear-shaft which was still fixed in his shield. But suddenly his young son leapt forward and threw himself into the fight. And just when Aeneas was drawing himself up with arm lifted ready to strike Mezentius down, Lausus caught Aeneas' sword-point and by this check stayed him. Their comrades rallied, shouting loudly, and casting spears they forced their enemy to keep his distance by their missiles, until under the protection of his son's shield the father could withdraw. Aeneas, though seething with rage, kept carefully under cover. And as when storm-clouds stream down in pouring hail, and every ploughman and every tiller of the soil scatters in haste from the open fields, while every traveller hides under a safe shelter, perhaps some river's bank or a high, arching rock, for as long as the rain descends on the world, postponing all the work of their day till the sunshine is restored; so Aeneas, with the weapons showering upon him from every side, held off this thunder-cloud of war till its last discharge was spent. Then he spoke, addressing Lausus alone, chiding him and threatening: 'What are you doing, advancing to certain death, and daring a deed beyond your strength? Loyalty to your father tricks you into imprudence.' But none the less Lausus persisted in his insane challenge. And now the deadly fury within the Trojan war-chief mounted higher, and the Fates were gathering up their last threads for Lausus; for Aeneas drove his tough sword straight through the boy's belly and buried it up to the hilt. The point passed through his buckler, too light an armament for his defiant temper, and through the tunic which his mother had woven for him from threads of gold; and his blood streamed into the fold of it. Then his life left the body and through the air it fled, sorrowing, to join the spirits. But at the sight of his dying face and the mysterious pallor of death on his countenance, Anchises' son sighed heavily in pity as he discerned this reflection of his own love for his father. He stretched forth his right hand and spoke: 'O piteous boy, what shall Aeneas the True give to you to match your high feat of arms and your great goodness? Keep for yourself the arms which gave you so much joy; and I release you to join the spirits and ashes of your ancestors, if such a freedom can concern you. But even in disaster you at least have some consolation for your grievous death in knowing that you died by the right hand of mighty Aeneas.' He then set to chiding Lausus' comrades who were hanging back; and it was he who lifted Lausus from the ground where he lay defiling with blood his well-trimmed hair.

The father, meanwhile, was staunching his wound with water beside the wave of the River Tiber, and leaning against a tree-trunk to rest himself. His bronze helmet was hanging from a near-by branch and on the meadow-grass his heavy arms lay still. Round him stood young soldiers of his choice. Sick and gasping he was easing his neck; his long combed beard flowed down to cover his chest. He continually asked after Lausus and often sent a messenger to carry the command of his sorrowing father to him, and call him back. But even then comrades of Lausus, in tears, were bringing him in lifeless on a shield, a mighty hero vanquished by a mighty wound. Struck with a presentiment of evil Mezentius recognized the sounds of grief afar off. He fouled his white hair with handfuls of dust, stretched both hands towards heaven, and then, clinging to his son's body, he said: 'O Son, was I possessed by so irresistible a desire for life that I could allow you, my son whom I begot, to take my place under the foeman's hand to save me? Is your own father preserved by the wound which you bear, living because you died? Most miserable am I; the true bitterness of my banishment has only now come home to me, and now indeed does my wound strike deep. And besides, Son, it is I who have defiled your name by my guilt, for through the hatred which I earned was I exiled from my throne and the sceptre which my father bore. Therefore I owed a debt of reparation to my fatherland and my people's hate, and should, of my own will, have surrendered my guilty soul to endure death in every form. Yet instead I live, and even now I leave not the day's light and humankind. But leave them I will.'

With these words he raised himself on his wounded thigh, and undismayed, although failing energy sapped by the deep wound made his movements slow, he ordered his horse to be brought. This horse was his pride and his consolation, and on him he had ridden home in triumph from all his wars. To him, companion in his sorrow, he spoke, beginning with these words: 'Rhaebus, our lives have been long – if that word can be used of anything possessed by mortal creatures. Today either you shall be joint-avenger with me of Lausus' agonies and in victory help me carry back Aeneas' head and spoils stained with his blood, or, if there is no force left to open up that way for us, you will die with me; for, valiant friend of mine, I know you will never deign to submit to a foreigner's commands or a Trojan master.' So he spoke. He sank into the saddle, adjusted his legs in their familiar posture, and loaded both hands with sharp javelins. His head flashed with the sheen of bronze beneath the shaggy horse-hair plume; and so he galloped swiftly into the press. In that one heart together there surged a mighty tide of shame, madness and misery blending, love tormented by passion for revenge, and valour which knew itself true. Three times he offered loud challenge to Aeneas. Aeneas surely recognized the call, and in joy he prayed: 'O may the supreme Father of Gods so grant it, and may

Apollo grant it so!... Lay on! And close!' So he spoke his wish and advanced to meet his enemy with presented spear. But Mezentius answered him: 'How, most brutal foe, having stolen my son from me, can you make me fear? You have already found the one way to ruin me. I have no horror of death, and set no value on any god. Cease therefore. For I come ready to die; and first I bring to you these gifts.' With the words he flung a missile against his enemy, and then another, and another besides, and as he galloped in a wide circle he planted them in Aeneas' shield; but the gold shield-centre sustained them all, and Aeneas stood firm. Three times Mezentius rode in left-wise circles round him, ever casting missiles; and three times Troy's hero carried round with him as he turned a grotesque forest of spears in the bronze of his protecting shield. At length, tired of tearing out all the weapon-heads, and feeling the strain of fighting in this unequal conflict, he took careful thought what he should do, leapt forward, and cast his spear between the temple-cavities of the warrior horse. The four-foot creature rose, rearing straight upwards, beating the air with his hooves, threw his rider, fell upon him pinning him to the ground, and plunging forward head-first lay there with his shoulder broken.

Both Trojans and Latins kindled the sky with their impassioned shouts. Aeneas flew to Mezentius, whipped sword from scabbard, and spoke over him: 'Where now is the old fiery Mezentius and all the fury of his madman's will?' The Etruscan looked up to heaven and drank in the air; and recovering consciousness he made answer: 'Pitiless enemy, why mock me, why threaten me with death? There is no wrong in slaying; with no such belief did I come to do battle, and Lausus my son made no such compact between you and me. But, if there can be indulgence for conquered enemies, I make you one request. Allow my body its covering of soil. I know that my people's bitter hatred pens me round. Keep, I entreat you, their mad fury away from me, and admit me to share a sepulchre with my son.' So he spoke, and deliberately gave his throat to the point; and in waves of blood he scattered his life upon his arms.

BOOK ELEVEN

COUNCILS OF WAR: PITCHED BATTLE AGAIN

THE morrow's rising dawn had emerged from the ocean. Aeneas, deeply burdened as he was by thoughts of death, would naturally have preferred to devote his time to giving his comrades burial. But instead at first light from the east he started to fulfil his vows to the gods in return for his victory. He lopped the boughs from around a mighty oak-tree, reared it on a mound of earth, and decked it with the shining arms which were his spoils from the chieftain Mezentius, as a trophy to the great God whose Might is in War. On it he fixed the blood-stained crest of Mezentius, his broken spears, and his battered, twelve-times pierced, cuirass. He lashed the shield of bronze on the trophy's left side; and, last, he slung the ivory-hilted sword from its neck. Then he spoke words of encouragement to his comrades, for all his captains were with him and pressed closely round him: 'My friends, a great success has been achieved. Put from you all fear for the tasks to follow. These spoils are from a haughty king, the first-fruits of victory; here before you stands Mezentius, fashioned by my hands. Now we must march to King Latinus and the Latins' city-wall. Look to your arms like soldiers, and be expectant for the renewal of fighting, so that, as soon as the High Powers give word that we may wrench our standards from the ground and march our men from camp, no ignorant hesitancy or timorously cautious counsel may hamper our speed. But meanwhile let us commit these unburied bodies, once our comrades, to the earth; for that is the only courtesy which can reach them in the depths by Acheron.' And then, 'Go,' he said, 'Pay your last tributes to honour those splendid spirits who have won this new homeland for us with their life-blood. And first let Pallas be conveyed to Evander's city, a city of mourning now; he was found to lack no valour, when the dark day came which stole him away and plunged him in a cruel death before his time.'

So he spoke; and he wept. Then he walked back to the tent before which the body of lifeless Pallas was laid, watched by the now ageing Acoetes who had once been squire to Evander in his Arcadian days, but had later assumed a far less auspicious duty when he set out with Pallas as the appointed companion of a cherished ward. All the company of his retainers, and the concourse of Trojans, gathered round, and with them ladies of Ilium, their hair thrown free for the ceremony. But when at last Aeneas strode to the tall entrance, all struck their breasts and loud was the lamentation which they raised to the heavens, while the royal pavilion echoed the deep-toned misery of grief. Aeneas looked on the pillowed head of Pallas, the face white as snow, and in the smooth breast the gaping wound dealt by the Italian lance. Tears welled, and he spoke: 'Ah, piteous boy, Fortune came smiling; was it in jealousy that she then cruelly denied you to me, not letting you see my kingdom established, or ride back in conquest to your parents' home? How different were the promises which on leaving I made to your father Evander for his son, when he embraced me and sent me forth to win a great empire, anxiously warning me that my foes were vigorous men, and that we must fight our battles against a tough race! And as for Evander, he may even now be offering vows and, quite deceived by false hope, be piling sacrifices on his altars, while we, with ineffectual honour, escort in sorrow his young son, lifeless and owning no longer a debt to any heavenly power. Oh, that poor father, fated to look on at the harrowing funeral of his boy! Is this, after all, to be the triumphant return on which our hopes had been set? Is this how my solemn promises have been fulfilled? Ah, but, Evander, you will look on no defeated soldier-son, bearing wounds of shame; you will never be that father who prays for an accursed death because his own son has come safe home. Ah, Italy! Mighty was the protector whose loss you mourn; and great is your loss too, Iulus.'

When his lament was finished Aeneas ordered the piteous body to be lifted. He chose a thousand men from his whole array, and these he sent to attend the last rite and to share in the father's tears, a consolation all too slight for so heavy a grief, but owed to a parent's distress. Others, with nimble hands, made a bier of flexible wickerwork plaited with wild-strawberry shoots and oak-twigs, building the couch on it high and shading it with a canopy of leafy branches. Here they laid their young hero down, to lie in state on this rustic bed. He was like a flower nipped between the finger and thumb of some young maiden, a soft violet or a drooping hyacinth, languishing, with no glow of life in it now, though its natural shape has not left it yet; but earth, its mother, feeds it no longer, and renews its vigour no more. Aeneas next fetched forth two garments, stiff with gold-embroidered purple, which Sidonian Dido in the delight of her artistry had once made for him with her own hands, picking out its warp-thread with a line of gold. Sorrowing, as his last act of respect, he wrapped the young form in one of these, and with the other garment veiled the head, and its hair soon to burn on the pyre; and he piled high many prizes which Pallas had won from the Laurentine battle and gave command for the long train of his spoils to be brought forth. He added horses, and weapons which Pallas had stripped from his foes. And he had ready besides, with hands bound behind their backs, the captives destined to be sent as death-offerings to the shade, the blood of whose slaying was to sprinkle the flames. He next ordered men to carry tree-trunks arrayed in enemy arms, with their hated names affixed, suggesting the very presence of the hostile captains. Acoetes, a tragic figure in the weakness of age, walked in the procession, marring now his breast with his clenched hands and now with his finger-nails his face; till he fell, stretched full-length on the ground. They also led along chariots drenched in Rutulian blood. Behind walked Pallas' charger, Aethon, his trappings laid aside, weeping and wetting his face with great tear-drops. There were men too carrying Pallas' spear and his helmet, for victorious Turnus had his other arms. Then followed the whole line of mourners, the Trojans, all the Etruscans, and the Arcadians with their arms reversed. After the whole procession had gone on far ahead, Aeneas halted, and with a heavy sigh spoke again: 'We are called hence to other tears by this same grim destiny of war. Pallas, great hero, I bid you for ever hail, and for ever farewell.' Saying no more he moved off towards his own high defence-works and walked back into his camp.

By now ambassadors had arrived from the Latin city. They carried wreaths of olive-spray, and they asked Aeneas to grant them a favour and return to them their dead brought low by the blade and lying about the plain, and allow them to find rest in a grave. They pleaded that there could no longer be any quarrel with the vanquished who had passed from the light of heaven's day, and besought Aeneas to be merciful to his hosts of former time whom he had once called the kinsmen of his bride to be. Aeneas could not spurn their request and with ready kindliness accorded his permission. He went further and said: 'Ah, Latins, how unjustly and unhappily you have been involved in this terrible war which leads you to shrink from friendship with us! So you beg from me indulgence for the lifeless who perished by the chance of Mars? Why, for myself, I should as willingly have granted it to the living! I only came hither because Fate had here allotted to me a place to be my home. Nor do I make war on your whole nation. It was your king alone who abandoned his guest-friendship with me and chose instead to rely on the arms of Turnus. It would have been fairer had Turnus himself faced the death which these have died. If he means to set the term to this war by might of arms, and to rout the Trojans, then it would have been more fitting if he had himself engaged in combat against me. Of us two, he would have lived, to whom God, or his own right hand, had granted life. But depart now, and lay fire below your piteous countrymen.'

When Aeneas had spoken, his hearers were struck silent. They turned to one another exchanging silent looks of speechless wonder, and said not a word. Then Drances, an older man, ever bitter against the youthful Turnus and always pursuing him with denunciations and hate, opened his lips for reply, and began: 'Man of Troy, whose mighty deeds in battle surpass even your fabulous repute, what praises am I to choose to exalt you to the sky? Am I to admire you chiefly for your justice, or for your hardihood in war? For our part, we are only too glad to deliver your answer to the city of our fathers and, if fortune offers us a way, we shall ally you to our king, Latinus. It is for Turnus to seek his own peace-treaty. Indeed, we shall even be happy to heave stones on our own shoulders to help build New Troy, and so raise high the massive walls appointed by Fate.' When he had so spoken, all with one loud shout agreed with him. They fixed a truce to last twelve days. Peace held the pledges; and Trojans and Latins mingled without hurt as they wandered through woods or on mountain slopes. Strokes of the two-edged axe of iron rang on tall ash-trees. They overthrew pines which towered towards the sky. Unwearyingly they wedged and split tough oak and scented cedar; and on groaning wagons they transported rowan-trees.

But by now Rumour, who had so recently been reporting Pallas' success in Latium, had taken wing to carry the first news of the terrible grief to beset the heart of Evander and his palace and all his city. The Arcadians hurried to their gates, seizing funeral brands in obedience to their ancient custom. Their torches lit up the road which, stretching in its long line, became a broad streak of light parting the country in two. The Trojan procession advanced to meet them and they formed one moving throng of mourners. As soon as the mothers saw them drawing near the houses, their shrieking set the city ablaze with sorrow. Then no restraint could hold Evander. He ran into the midst, and when the bier was lowered to the ground he flung himself down upon Pallas and clung to him weeping and sobbing. And only with difficulty at long last did grief allow his voice to find a free passage: 'O Pallas, not such was the promise which you once made to your father, assuring me that you would beware how you trusted yourself to the savagery of Mars. Yet I know well how strong is the youthful instinct of warrior-pride and how exquisitely sweet is honour won in a first encounter. Oh, sad first-fruits of a young life! Hard schooling in a war so close to home! And not a single god listened to my vows and prayers! And you, my Queen, sainted, revered, how blessed are you in your death, for you did not live to know this anguish! But I, not so; I have outlived my span, victor over my fate, merely to survive as a father without a son. If only I had been the one to follow the arms of my Trojan friends and to fall, overwhelmed by a rain of Rutulian missiles! If only of my own free will I had surrendered my breath, and then this procession had been bearing me, not Pallas, home! But I would find no fault in you, Trojans, nor in our treaty, nor in the hands which we plighted in guest-friendship. This disaster of which you bring me news was destined to fall on me in my old age and has been in store for me from the beginning. And, if it was always inevitable that my son must meet an early death, at least I may be consoled to remember that when he fell he was helping the Trojans to reach Latium and had first slain countless Volscians; nor, Pallas, could I ever allot you a more honourable funeral than this which Aeneas the True, the Lords of Phrygia, the Etruscan princes and all their army have chosen for you. They bring, for grand memorial of your victory, those whom your right arm cast to death; and you, Turnus, if his age had been equal to yours and the years had given him the like strength, you also would have been standing there now as a huge tree-trunk clad in your arms. But I must not let my private sorrow detain the Trojans from the fight. For now you must march; and carefully take my answer in this message to your King: "Your valour now owes the death of Turnus as a debt to both father and son. For that alone I prolong a life rendered hateful to me by the loss of Pallas; and it is both your own one chance of success and the one good deed which you can do for me. I seek for myself no joy in life; that would be sin; but only to bring some joy to my son among the shades." '

Meanwhile Aurora had lifted her strengthening light for pitiful humanity, bringing back to them their tasks and their toils. The chieftain Aeneas and King Tarchon had erected pyres along the sweep of the shore. Hither men carried the bodies of their dead, all following the fashion of their forebears. Black-smoking brands were applied to the base of the pyres, and the height of heaven was shrouded in darkness by the murk. Then, girt with their shining arms, they circled thrice the kindled pyres; thrice ceremonially they rode on horseback round the sad fire of death, and their lips cried forth with lament. The earth and the weapons too were all sprinkled with their tears. The shouting of men and the braying of trumpets rose to the sky. And then some cast upon the fires spoils ripped from slain Latins, helmets and handsome swords, bridles, and wheels which had warmed on the axle; and others threw as offerings favourite things belonging to the dead, their shields and the weapons which had availed them nothing. And there many a strong bull was killed as a sacrifice to Death. They cut the throats of bristle-haired boars and of flocks which they had seized from every field to spout their blood into the flame. And now all along the shore they watched their comrades burning, stood guard over pyres half-consumed, and could not be torn away from the funeral-place until moist night swung round the sky, inset with blazing stars.

Elsewhere the unhappy Latins also built pyres without number. Of the bodies of their dead, some, and many they were, they buried in the earth, and others they removed, taking them to ground near by, to send home to their own city. The rest they cremated without ritual or count, a huge, chaotic heap of carnage. Widespread across the country gleamed everywhere the clusters of eager fires. Not till the third dawn had drawn aside the chill shadow from the sky did they begin in sorrow to pull down the piled ashes, where the fire had been and the bones lay in confusion; and then they heaped onto them a mound of the still-warm earth.

But meanwhile it was within the houses in the city of wealthy Latinus that the clamour was loudest, and there the long-drawn wails of lamentation reached their height. Here were mothers and their sons' unhappy brides, sisters' loving hearts in grief, and children orphaned of their fathers. They cursed the untoward war, and Turnus' wedding-plan. They demanded that Turnus should himself find a decision by single combat, since it was he who claimed the supreme honour of Italy's throne. Furiously Drances added weight to the demand, assuring them that Aeneas' challenge was to Turnus alone, and for him only that summons to combat. At the same time many various arguments were adduced in opposing speeches which favoured Turnus. Besides, he was under the protecting shadow of the queen's majestic authority; and his own great reputation and the trophies which he had won supported his claim.

Amid these disturbances, and when the blaze of dissension was at its hottest, just then, to crown all, the ambassadors returned from Diomede's mighty city, arriving in sad mood with his answer. Nothing had been achieved by all the expenditure of effort; the gifts, the gold and the earnest prayers had had no effect; the Latins must look for other war-aid, or sue for peace with the Trojan king. Under this great disappointment even King Latinus sank crushed. The anger of the Gods, witnessed by the freshly made grave-mounds before their eyes, already warned them that Aeneas was clearly by divine warrant a man of destiny. Therefore King Latinus gathered within his tall gates a high council of the first in the land, summoned by his command. The councillors came streaming to the palace along the crowded streets and assembled. Latinus, whose age was the greatest and whose sceptre was supreme, sat in the midst, with little gladness on his brow. Forthwith he commanded the ambassadors who had been sent back from the Aetolian city to deliver their messages, requiring of them the detailed answers to all that he had asked. All talk was quickly silenced in the hall. Obedient to command, Venulus opened the debate and spoke:

'Countrymen, we have seen Diomede and his camp of Argives. We completed our journey, surviving all its chances; and we have touched that very hand by which the land of Ilium perished. Diomede, his victory won, was busy founding his city Argyripa, named after his ancestors' race, in Iapygian lands by Garganus. We were admitted to his presence and made free to speak before him. We presented our gifts. And we recounted our name and our fatherland, explained who had made war upon us, and disclosed our motive for coming to Arpi. He heard us and with serene countenance replied: "Ah, fortunate nations, realms of Saturn, you ancient folk of Ausonia! What unusual event disturbs your peace and persuades you to provoke war, of which you know so little? All of us, who outraged the land of Ilium with the sword, have paid the full toll of our sinning in unutterable punishments throughout the world, a band whom Priam himself might pity, to say nothing of all the deep tribulations which we suffered warring under Troy's towering battlements, or of those heroes whom far-off Simois hides beneath his waters. Minerva's lowering star, and that Euboean headland, the avenging Caphereus, know the tale. After that campaign we were dispersed to distant shores; the son of Atreus, Menelaus, was exiled even to the Pillars of Proteus, and Ulysses saw the Cyclopes of Etna. I could tell how fared the kingdom of Neoptolemus; how the home of Idomeneus was wrecked, and how Locrians now dwell on an African coast. The Mycenean himself, the Emperor of mighty Achaeans, fell stricken, as he entered his own gate, by the hand of his wicked queen; his victory over Asia was complete, but the adulterer lay in wait. And to think how divine jealousy denied me my return to my father's altars, never more to see the wife for whom I yearned nor lovely Calydon! And now followed a miracle, in very truth an ominous and horrifying sight, for my comrades are lost, having flown on wings to the high air, ah, ghastly visitation on my people! Now are they birds, wandering along our rivers, and their tearful calling sounds everywhere among the rocks. Yet surely I should have expected all of it, even from that fatal hour when in my madness I attacked with my sword the divine flesh of Venus herself, committing the outrage of wounding her in the hand. Oh, never seek to force me into another such fray! There has never been any war between me and the Trojans since their citadel was uprooted; and there is no joy for me in the memory of those old, unhappy things. Therefore, give not to me but to Aeneas those gifts which you bring for me from your homeland's territory. I have faced his vicious javelins and closed with him hand to hand; trust my experience when I tell how mightily he springs up behind his high-held shield, and what is the cyclone-force of his spinning spear. If Ida's land had borne two other such heroes, the Trojans would actually have crossed to attack cities of Inachus, destiny would have been reversed, and Greece would now have been the land of mourning. During all the time lost before the ramparts of obdurate Troy, it was only by the hands of Hector and Aeneas that victory was withheld from the Greeks, so that it escaped their grasp till the tenth year. Both shone in distinction of valour and excelling power of weapons, but in righteousness Aeneas led. Let your right hands join in compact on whatever terms are offered; but take care to avoid the clash of arms on arms." So now in one report, most excellent Majesty, you have heard the terms of the prince's answer and also the view which he takes of this terrible war.'

Hardly had the ambassador so spoken when a loud murmur of conflicting opinion passed swiftly along the lines of the Italians from face to anxious face; as when boulders obstruct swift rivers, and water rumbles in the pent eddies, while the banks near by echo the slap of waves. But as soon as their thoughts were steadied and the anxious lips again at rest, the king on his raised throne first made his address to the gods and then began his speech:

'Latins, I could have wished, and better it had been, to reach decision on our main issue sooner, and not to assemble a council at such an hour, when the foe camps before our walls. We wage untimely war, my countrymen, against sons of gods and unconquered men whom battles never weary and who even when defeated can never lay down the sword. If you had any expectation of allying Aetolian arms to yourselves, put it from you. We may indeed hope, each one of us, for anything we choose; but you see how slender every possible hope has now become. The rest you know from the direct evidence of your eyes, if not indeed the touch of your fingers, how our affairs lie shattered in utter ruin. Nor would I blame any man. What boundless valour can do, it has done; the conflict has been waged with the whole strength of the realm. But even now let me reveal to you a hesitant proposal which I have been pondering, and explain it shortly, if you will attend. I own an ancient domain adjacent to our Tuscan river, its length stretching westward to the Sicanian frontier and beyond; it is sown by Auruncans and Rutulians who work with the ploughshare the hard surfaces of the hills, and use the roughest of them for pasture. Let this whole tract, with the high, mountainous district of the pines, pass to the Trojans in friendship; let us prescribe fair conditions for a treaty, and invite them into our realm as our allies. Let them settle here if they desire it so ardently, and build their walled city. If, however, they prefer to approach some other nation, with a view to some different territory – and there is no reason why they should not, if they wish, withdraw from our soil – then let us construct twenty ships for them, or as many as they have the strength to man, of tough Italian oak. All the timber lies near the sea. The Trojans can specify the number and design of the ships. We should provide the bronze, the labour, and the shipyards for them. Furthermore, it is my will that a hundred ambassadors from the noblest Latin familes should go forth to carry our message to them and conclude a secure agreement; they should go holding out the olive-spray of peace in their hands, conveying talents of gold and of ivory as gifts, and also carrying to them the throne and the robe which are the emblems of our sovereignty. Take open counsel, therefore, how to mend our stricken fortunes.'

Then arose Drances, antagonistic as before, and tormented by the fame of Turnus, which goaded him to a perverse bitterness and malice. Drances was a man of considerable wealth, whose strength lay in his speech; his arm never warmed to battle, but in matters of policy he was held to be an adviser deserving respect, drawing power from the very instinct to rebel. His mother's nobility had given him an arrogant pride of birth, but on his father's side his ancestry remained a mystery. Drances now used his oratory to add weight and substance to his spite:

'Your proposal, excellent Majesty, is clear to everyone and has no need of eloquence from me. Every one of us knows in his heart what our nation's fortune imposes on us, but we all mutter in fear and decline to speak out. Yet shall I speak out, though one whom you all know may threaten me with violence and even death for it. But let him give over blustering, and grant freedom of speech; and I mean that one, through whose unblessed leadership and ominous temper we see so many of our splendid leaders fallen and our whole city sunk in grief, while he skirmishes against the Trojan camp, menacing the very sky with his brandishings, but relying for his safety on flight. Most excellent King, pray add just one more gift to all those many which you so generously bid us send or promise to the Trojans. Let no man's violence prevail on you against giving your daughter away, as is a father's right, to her splendid suitor in a marriage worthy of her, and thus binding this peace firmly by an enduring sanction. If however the terror which grips our minds and hearts is indeed so intense, then let us make our appeal direct to him, and address our plea for tolerance to the man himself. Let him give way. Let him waive his personal right in deference to King and Fatherland. Yes, you who are the very source and origin of all these sufferings imposed on Latium, why do you again and again fling your helpless countrymen into obvious danger? War can never save us. Turnus, all of us require peace of you, and, with peace, the only inviolable warrant of peace. See, I am the first to come to you and on bended knee – I whom you make out to be your enemy, and who may be your enemy, for all that I care. Pity your own folk, lay down your pride, and accept defeat. We have looked enough on retreat and death; we have gone far enough in stripping broad lands of their inhabitants. Or else, if your motive is glory, if your will is so obstinate and remorseless, and if you have set your heart on receiving a palace as a dowry, then dare; and march confidently breast to breast against your enemy. Are we to think that, simply to gain the good fortune of a royal bride for Turnus, we, since our own lives are apparently worthless, are to lie scattered over the plains, a multitude unburied and unwept? Surely you yourself, if you are a man of spirit and have any of your father's warlike mettle in you, must wish to look your challenger in the face.'

At such a speech as that, Turnus exploded with characteristic violence. He gasped; and let fly all his heart's deep bitterness at Drances:

'Yes, Drances, you have a great deal, as always, to say – and just when the state of the war demands strength of hand. You are always the first to arrive when the Council is called. But so long as the earthworks of our walls still hold the enemy back and the moats are not yet brimming with blood, you have little right to fill the Council-House with the big words which come flowing from your mouth so glibly with no danger whatever to you. The time, Drances, for the thunders of your eloquence – your usual style – and for charging me with cowardice, will not come till your right arm has piled as many heaps of Trojan carnage as mine has, and, like mine, has left field on field splendid with trophies of victory. You are allowed the freedom to try for yourself what vital valour can do; and you have not, I imagine, far to go to find enemies, for they stand all around our walls. Well? Do we march against our adversaries? Why are you dallying? Or will your war-spirit always exist only in the hot air of your verbosity and in your feet, so quick to flee? And you say I am routed, I? Foul villain! Shall anyone fairly claim that I am routed when all the time he sees Tiber flowing swollen with Trojan blood, and observes how all Evander's house is fallen low, his heir dead, and his Arcadians stripped of their arms in defeat? That is not the impression I gave to Pandarus and gigantic Bitias or those other thousands, either, whom in one day on my victorious course I plunged to Tartarus, though I was shut within their walls and penned inside the enemy's ramparts. "War can never save us." Madman, make that prophecy to the Trojan's chance of life, and to your own. Go on clouding all things in a confused murk of fear, extolling the strength of that twice-conquered race, and meanwhile disparaging the arms of Latinus! Why, now even the chiefs of the Myrmidons shudder at Trojan prowess; yes, Tydeus' own son Diomede, and Larissaean Achilles! The river Aufidus flows backwards pursued by Adriatic waves! And then – when he pretends that he is afraid to face me in a quarrel, the cunning rogue! – he only means to use this pretence of fearfulness to sharpen the point of his accusations against me. Well, the life of such as you is safe enough from this right arm; so never shrink away! You are welcome to your life; you can keep it in your breast.

'But now, Sire, I return to you, and to your weighty proposal. If you rest no hope now in our arms, if we are indeed as forsaken as this and if, after but one repulse of our army, we are utterly fallen and fortune can never again retrace her steps, then let us stretch out unresisting hands and beg for peace. But yet – if only we still had with us some trace of our old valour! Him I count as beyond all other men happy in his success and of peerless temper, who, rather than see such shame, has fallen and once for all bitten the dust in death. On the other hand, if we still have some resource, if our manhood is not yet all engaged, if there are cities and nations of Italy left to aid us, and if the Trojans themselves have won their glory at the cost of blood – for the hurricane swept over all alike and they too have had their losses – , why then do we accept inglorious failure on the very threshold of our task? Why, before even the trumpet sounds, do our limbs start to tremble? Time, and the changeful stress of passing days, have often enough brought improvements with them. Fortune has tripped many; but, turn and turn about, she always comes back and sets them on solid ground again. Well, the Aetolian and his city Arpi will not aid us. Yet Messapus will, and Tolumnius, too, with his happy auguries, and so will other chieftains whom these many nations have sent. No little glory shall fall to those who have been chosen as the finest in Latium and Laurentine lands. And there is Camilla also, of noblest Volscian breed, with all her array of riders in squadrons a-flower with bronze. If however the Trojans require me alone for single combat, and that is acceptable to you, and if therefore I alone am obstructing the good of all, why, Victory has not so far shown so bitter a hatred for these hands of mine, and has not hitherto held off so far from them, that I should refuse to make any trial in the service of a hope so fair. I shall go in high heart to meet him, even if he excels the might of Achilles himself and dons arms, the equal of his, made by Vulcan's hands. I, Turnus, in valour second to none of the heroes of old, have vowed this my life as my offering to you all, and to Latinus, father of my bride. Does Aeneas challenge me alone? I accept and welcome his challenge. And if in this challenge the anger of the Gods is revealed, I would not have Drances make atonement by dying in my stead; nor, if valour and glory alone are at stake, would I let him take them for his.'

So they, in sharp opposition, debated their anxious plight; but already Aeneas was moving his camp and his battle-front. And, see, the news now darted swiftly through the palace buildings, spreading intense excitement and striking keen alarm into the city: the Trojans, marshalled for battle, and with them the Etruscan contingent, were bearing down on them all over the plain from the river Tiber. At once the nation was shaken to the heart and thrown into confusion. The violent shock aroused their angry passions. In their feverish haste, they were insistent for taking arms, all the younger men shouting for weapons, though their elders whispered and wept. And then all around a great clamour rose into the air, a mixture of many discordant intents, like the noise from flocks of birds which have chanced to settle in some hill-forest, or when swans send their harsh notes along echoing pools where the fishes live in Padusa's stream.

Turnus seized this moment and said, 'Ah, no, Citizens! Had you not better assemble a Council, and sit praising the blessings of peace? It is only the enemy charging us, their arms in their hands, to capture the kingdom.' Saying no more, he sprang up and strode rapidly from the lofty palace. 'You, Volusus,' he said, 'give orders to the Volscian companies to arm. Take the Rutulians also. Messapus and Coras with his brother will deploy the cavalry, armed for battle, on a broad front across the plain. Let a detachment secure the approaches to the city and take over the towers. The remainder of our force will attack with me along a route which I shall direct.' There was no arguing with the orders. Troops came hurrying from every part of the city and manned each sector on the walls. The chieftain Latinus himself abandoned the Council and his own momentous plans, postponing them in the stress of this grim hour and reproaching himself continually for not having freely received Dardan Aeneas and willingly made him his city's ally as bridegroom to his own daughter.

Meanwhile men were everywhere digging trenches before

the gates, and carrying stakes and stones up onto the defences. Harshly a trumpet sounded the bloody call to war. Mothers and children stood on the walls forming a motley ring around the city, for need was desperate and the supreme trial made its demands on all. The Queen too, attended by a large retinue of matrons, drove up with offerings to the temple on the crest of Minerva's citadel, and by her walked the maiden Lavinia, the cause of all the terrible calamity, with beautiful eyes downcast. The matrons climbed to the temple, and filled it with incense-fumes; and from the tall gateway poured out in sorrow their prayer: 'Goddess of Armed Might, Maid Tritonian presiding over war, break the Phrygian pirate's weapon with your hand, and fell him prone on the earth. Bring him low, beneath your own high gates.'

In feverish zeal Turnus armed himself for battle. He was already clad in his corslet redly glowing and stiff with its scales of bronze, and he had enclosed his lower legs in golden greaves. His head was as yet bare, but he had girded his sword to his side. All golden he glittered as he hurried down from the citadel's height, exultant in his high spirit and in his hope of finding his foe at hand; like some stallion which has broken his tether and, free at last, gallops from his stall with all the open plains before him, hastening towards the pastures where herds of mares are feeding, or perhaps goes to bathe once again in the water of some favourite river, and afterwards leaps ahead, lifts his neck, and neighs in delight, his mane dancing over withers and shoulders. Here quickly Camilla rode up to meet Turnus, her Volscian regiment with her, and hard by the gates the princess leapt from her horse; and all her band, following her lead, dismounted, slipping deftly to the ground. Camilla spoke to Turnus: 'Turnus, if the brave have a right to self-confidence, then I, having the courage, offer to meet the Horse of Aeneas' army and to advance alone against the Etruscan cavaliers. Let me set my hand to the opening perils of war. You take your stand dismounted near the walls and keep watch over our ramparts.' Turnus, fixing his eyes on the dread marvel of this girl, answered her offer: 'Maid, Italy's glory, what thanks and what repayment can I conceive as fit for you?

But as it is, since your spirit rises far above all recognition, why, then, share the toil with me. Aeneas, as rumour says, and as scouts, sent forward and now returned, confirm, has resolutely despatched his light cavalry divisions in advance of him to reconnoitre all the plains, while he himself takes the route over the steep unguarded hill-country, and may appear at any moment, swooping down the slopes onto the city. I have in hand a ruse of war. There is a sunken track within the forest where I plan to block the jaws at each end by posting armed soldiers there. You must take position and prepare to receive the charge of the Etruscan Horse. You will have with you, eager to aid you, Messapus, the squadrons of Latium, and also the contingents of Tiburtus. You must share with me the responsibility of command.' So he spoke, and with like words he also cheered on Messapus and the captains of his allies to battle; and then moved forward against the foe.

There is a glen, with winding curves, apt for concealment and the ruses of war. The slopes crowd down on it from both sides, shadowed by clustering leaves; the path leading into it is ill-defined, its jaws are narrow, and the entrances close and forbidding. Above the glen among the vantage-points right up among the hill-tops lies unfrequented level ground which affords safe cover out of sight, whether the plan is to engage by charging from the left or from the right or to remain in position high up on the slopes and roll great boulders down. Hither the young leader hurried by tracks whose direction he well knew. He seized the position and settled down to wait in the confined space of the woods.

Now meanwhile Latona's daughter in the Dwellings on High was addressing swift Opis, one of the band of holy maidens who companioned her. The words which she spoke to her were grave: 'O Maiden, Camilla advances to murderous war, and all in vain girds on my own favourite weapons, she who beyond all others is dear to me. For indeed this love which I, Diana, bear to her is nothing new, or lately come to me; it is not only now that my soul is stirred by its sudden, sweet awakening. Camilla's father Metabus had been banished from his throne on account of the hatred which his arrogant use of his strength had drawn upon him. Being forced to leave Privernum, his ancient city, he carried with him his baby daughter to be his companion in exile, and fled with her right through the midst of the war's fighting. He named her Camilla after her mother's name Casmilla, changing one syllable. He carried her himself wrapped close before him within his garment's fold as he journeyed to the lonely forests on the long mountain-ridges. The relentless threat of armed force assailed him from every side, for the Volscians had deployed their troops and were all round him ranging everywhere. But see! Directly across his flight lay the river Amasenus, which had overflowed and was foaming above its banks, so copious had been the storm of rain which a cloudburst had discharged. As Metabus prepared to swim it, his love for his baby made him pause, for he feared for the dear burden which he carried. Rapidly he reviewed each expedient in turn, and though doubts remained he made a sudden, firm, decision. By good fortune he was carrying in his stout hand a mighty war-spear of fire-toughened oak with knots in the sturdy wood. He took his daughter and first wrapped her closely in the pith and bark from a cork-tree in the forest. Then he lashed her to the spear-shaft in the middle to preserve balance. And now, poising the spear in his strong right hand, he raised his voice to heaven: "Kindly Maid, Latona's daughter, dweller in the woodlands, I, her own father, vow this my daughter to you to be your handmaid. Holding your weapon, the first which she has ever held, she flees from her foes and is your suppliant. Goddess, I implore you, accept for your own her who is now entrusted to the uncertainty of a gust of wind." As he spoke, he drew back his arm, and he cast the spinning spear-shaft; the waters roared; and over that tearing river flew Camilla, helpless on the whistling spear. Metabus, with the enemy in great numbers now almost upon him, flung himself into the stream, and soon, having won his way across, he wrested from the grassy turf the spear with the little girl tied to it: the gift which he had now given to Diana.

'No city would admit Metabus within its buildings or even its walls; and since his wild temper would never allow him willingly to give himself up, he passed all his life among the shepherds' lonely mountains. Here, amid the thickets of these savage haunts, he reared his daughter at the udders of a brood mare of the herd and on the milk of wild animals, pressing their teats for her delicate lips. And when the little one had for the first time planted footprints with the soles of her own young feet, Metabus armed her hand with a sharp javelin and slung from the infant shoulder sharp-pointed arrows and a bow. Instead of a gold band for her hair or a mantle's long drape, a skin stripped from a tigress hung down from her head and over her back. Even at that age she used to cast baby spears from her soft little hand; and she would whirl a sling on a smooth leather thong round her head, and with it bring down some crane from Strymon or a white swan. Many were the mothers in all the Etruscan towns who longed to have her for a son's bride, but in vain; for she found complete happiness in Diana alone, and cherished unendingly her love for her weapons and her maidenhood, touched by none. I would that she had never sought to challenge the Trojans and had never been caught up in such a war, for then she could have been one of my companions still, and still dear to me.

'But come, Nymph; since Destiny now bears heartlessly against her, go, skimming on your downward path from the skies, and visit the Latin land where, ominous of doom, stern battle is joined. Take these; and from this quiver draw an arrow for my vengeance. Let it exact my price in blood from any man who wounds her, outraging her hallowed flesh, whoever he may be, whether Trojan or Italian. Afterwards I shall wrap her piteous body in a mist and convey it, undespoiled and with all her arms still about her, to her tomb, and lay it to rest in her homeland.' So Diana spoke; and Opis, her form shrouded with a black whirlwind, dropped lightly through the airs of the sky, and the weapons clattered at her side as she sped.

Meanwhile, a division of Trojans drew near to the city walls, and thither came also Etruria's chieftains and all the cavalry, disposed in squadrons of equal strength. All over the plain pranced horses with ringing feet, and they fretted against tight reins, neighing and cavorting now this way and now that.

Far and wide over the field stood a bristling iron crop of spears, and the plains blazed with uplifted weapons. But against them Messapus, the cavalry of Latium, Coras and with him his brother, and the maid Camilla's regiment of horse advanced to confront them on the plain. Firmly they drew their right hands far back, they thrust the spear-shafts forward, and the spear-points quivered. On marched the warriors, horses neighed, and excitement quickened. The two oncoming armies had now halted, within a spear-cast's range. Then, with a sudden shout, they leapt forward, cheering on their horses till they were battle-mad, and pouring as they galloped a shower of shafts from every side, thick as snow-flakes, till their shadow veiled the sky. Forthwith Tyrrhenus and Aconteus the fierce gathered their strength and charged with levelled spears. They were the first to fall, and loud was the crash as they fell; for they shattered and burst, in collision together, the breasts of their four-foot steeds. Aconteus was shot forward like a thunderbolt, or some heavy missile discharged by artillery, fell headlong, and scattered his life into the air. The ranks panicked and broke. The Latins turned, slung their shields on their backs, and rode for the city walls, pursued by the Trojans, with Asilas, at the head of his own squadrons, in the lead. But when they were nearing the gates the Latins again raised a cry and reined round the supple necks of their horses. Now the Trojans fled, gave rein, and retired far off. They moved like the ocean when it advances by flow and ebb, now surging landwards, flinging its waves high upon the cliffs with bursts of spray and drenching the farthest edge of the sand with its enveloping flood, and now suddenly in swift retreat, rolling boulders with it in the suction of its backwash, till the water grows shallow and slides away, and its withdrawal leaves the shore dry. Twice the Etruscans routed the Rutulians and drove them back towards the ramparts, and twice they were beaten off, and had to cast anxious glances over their shoulders and sling shields behind to protect their backs. But when they met for a third action they engaged all their battle-fronts and interlocked tightly. Each soldier chose his man; loud waxed the groans of the dying; and in the pools of blood weltered bodies and weapons, and horses too in their death-throes mingled with human carnage; and violent grew the battle. Orsilochus spun a javelin at Remulus' horse, for he shrank from closing with his rider; and he left the iron point embedded under the horse's ear. Maddened by this blow and the unendurable pain of the wound, the charger stamped and reared, thrashing the air with his forelegs and heaving up his chest; and Remulus, unhorsed, rolled on the ground. Catillus flung Iollas down, and also Herminius, mighty of spirit and mighty of stature and arms; his head was bare and his hair deep gold; bare were his shoulders, and he had no dread of wounds, so powerful was the frame which he presented to any attack. Yet now the spear was driven right between those broad shoulders and stayed there, quivering; it made the strong man double up in pain. Everywhere dark blood was spilling as in battle's rivalry they dealt out the death of the steel and sought by the way of wounds a glorious end.

Meanwhile Camilla rode armed with her quiver, exulting like an Amazon, through the midst of the slaughter, having one breast exposed for freedom in the fight. Sometimes with all her strength she would be casting her tough spear-shafts in dense showers, and sometimes without pause for rest her hand would wield a stout battle-axe. From her shoulder's level twanged the golden bow, the weapon which Diana uses. And sometimes too, when compelled to fall back, she would aim sharp arrows in her retreat, turning her bow to shoot behind her. Meanwhile around her were the comrades of her choice, the maiden Larina, and Tulla, and Tarpeia wielding her bronze axe, daughters of Italy whom Camilla, Diana's handmaiden, had chosen for her train of honour to be her faithful attendants for peace or for war. They were like Amazons of Thrace who, warring in their brilliant accoutrements, make Thermodon's streams echo to the hoof-beats, as they ride, it may be with Hippolyta, or else when martial Penthesilea drives back in her chariot from war, and her soldier-women, shrieking wild battle-cries, exult as they wave their crescent shields.

Oh! furious Maid, whom first and whom last did your spear unhorse? And how many were the strong men whose bodies you stretched dying on the ground? The first was Euneus, son of Clytius, as he faced up to her; and she battered through his unguarded breast with her long firwood-shafted spear. He fell, choking forth rivers of blood, chewed the gory earth, and as he died writhed about the wound on which he lay. Then she slew Liris and also Pagasus: Liris as he rolled backwards off his horse which had stumbled, and sought to recover his reins, and Pagasus as he came up to the aid of Liris and stretched a weaponless hand to his falling friend; both alike fell headlong. To them she added Amastrus, Hippotas' son; and, leaning forward to the throw, pursued with long-range javelin-casts Tereus, Harpalycus, Demophoon and Chromis. For every sharp-pointed spear which the Maid released spinning from her hand, a Phrygian warrior fell. Some way off, Ornytus, a hunter, in the arms of war to which he was not used, was riding on his Iapygian horse. When he became a warrior he donned a skin ripped from a bullock to cover his broad shoulders, and protected his head with a wolf's face, the jaws gaping wide and the white teeth grinning; and he carried as his weapon a countryman's hunting-spear. As he moved through the midst of the battalions he towered by a whole head above them all. During a rout of his comrades it needed no great effort for Camilla to cut off his escape and pierce him through; and then, as she stood over him, she spoke from the hate in her heart: 'Etruscan, did you imagine that you were chasing wild beasts in a forest? Well, the day has come which will prove that you and your fellows imagined wrongly; and it will be proved through a woman's weapons. Yet you shall carry to the spirits of your fathers no mean fame – the fame of falling by Camilla's spear.'

Directly afterwards she killed Orsilochus and Butes, two Trojans of massive strength. Butes had his back turned, and she pierced him with her lance between corslet and helmet where as he rode his neck showed white and his buckler hung below from his left arm. From Orsilochus, who pursued her in a wide circling course, she fled – at first. Then she foiled him by swinging into a narrower orbit and wheeling round behind him, so that the pursued became the pursuer. Next, rising high in the saddle, she dealt blow after blow with her stout battle-axe, smashing through armour and bones, even while he still cried out many a plea for mercy; the wounding spattered his face with the still-warm brains. And now there met her the warrior son of Aunus, dweller on the Apennines, and, as long as fate allowed him the use of guile, not the meanest of the Ligurians. He stood still, alarmed at the sudden sight of her. Seeing that he could not now slip from the fight however fast he ran, nor turn the princess aside from her onset, he decided to try an ingenious trick, and began to speak to her: 'What is so marvellous about being a woman warrior when you have so powerful a horse on which to rely? Set aside your means of flight, depend on nothing but the resources of dismounted combat, and dare to meet me hand to hand on level ground. You will soon see whose conceited vanity it is which is bringing disaster on her.' So he spoke; and Camilla, in a hot fury of smarting resentment, handed her horse to a comrade, and fearlessly took her stand on foot, armed like her foe with bared sword and plain buckler. So the young Ligurian supposed that he had succeeded in his ruse. For his part, without an instant's delay, he took to flight; he reined round his four-foot steed, and, forcing him into a gallop with his iron-spurred heels, away he flew. 'Silly Ligurian!' cried the Maid. 'It is you who are being deceived by a stupid and arrogant conceit. You were slippery! But it has done you no good to try your native tricks, for your cunning will never bring you safe home to Aunus your father, who is a cheat like yourself.' Hardly had the Maid said this when with all her fleetness she darted forward on foot like a flash, passed the horse, and facing him from in front grasped the reins, engaged the Ligurian, and took her vengeance from his hated blood; as easily as the sacred falcon, taking wing from some high rock, will overtake a dove far up in the clouds, grasp it, hold it, and with hooked talons disembowel it, while blood and out-torn feathers float down from the sky.

But meanwhile the Father of Men and Gods, enthroned high on Olympus, had eyes to observe such a deed. The Sire stirred the Etruscan Tarchon to furious battling, goaded him fiercely on, and inspired him with rage. Accordingly, Tarchon charged on horse-back amid the carnage where the ranks were in retreat. Using every resource of appeal he urged the regiments of his cavalry forward, calling on each man by name, and rallying the routed to face the battle once more: 'Etruscans, spineless as always, are you for ever incapable even of shame? What is your fear? Has the cowardice in your hearts reached such new depths? To think that a mere woman has routed all this host and driven you back in straggling disarray! Why then do we wear swords? Why do we hold these spears in our hands if we cannot use them? Oh, you are quick enough to answer the call of love, and love's engagements in the night! And yes, when the curved pipe summons you to the Bacchic revel, you may look forward greedily enough to a feast laid with the wine-vessels in place on loaded tables, only waiting for your seer to report his happy omens and for the sacrifice of a fat victim to invite you to assemble in some stately grove. This is your real interest; here your passion lies.' Having thus spoken frankly, Tarchon at the risk of his life spurred his horse into the thick of the fight, and recklessly charged straight at Venulus; he dragged him down off his horse, clasped him under his right arm, and with a violent effort carried off his enemy, holding him in front of his chest. A shout rose to the sky and every Latin turned to look. Carrying both the man and his arms, Tarchon flew like a streak of fire across the level ground. Then from the end of his foe's spear he broke off the iron head and groped for an unprotected place where he could deliver a mortal wound. Venulus fought back against him and tried to keep the hand away from his throat, parrying force with force. As a golden eagle flying high will carry a snake which it has seized, with feet entwined and talons tightly gripping, and the snake, though wounded, continues to writhe in coils, lifts stiffening scales, and holds itself erect, its mouth still hissing, but the eagle, none the less, uses its hooked beak to harass it while it struggles, and all the time beats the high air with its wings; so Tarchon bore his prey in triumph from the Tiburtine lines. Following their leader's example and emulating his success, the Etruscans charged.

And now Arruns, a man whom fate would soon claim, galloped round Camilla, javelin in hand, cleverly anticipating her moves for all her speed, and on the alert for the easiest opportunity to strike. Wherever in her furious career the Maid dashed through the battle's centre, there Arruns moved nearer and silently kept close on her tracks; and wherever she went, either in victorious return from combat or withdrawing from the foe, there the young fighter swiftly and unobtrusively guided his reins. Always he sought an opening for an attack, now here and now there; and circled persistently round and round, holding his quivering spear intent and relentless in his hand. Now Chloreus, sacred to Cybelus and once his priest, chanced to appear, shining and conspicuous from afar in Phrygian armour; and the foam-flecked horse, which he rode so hard, was protected by a horse-cloth of clustering bronze scales like plumage, linked together with gold. He himself was a brilliant figure in the glow of red dye, besides his foreign purple, as he sped sharp Cretan arrows from his Lycian bow, a bow plated with gold, which he carried slung from his shoulder. He was a seer; and golden, too, was his helm, and of red-gold was the brooch which knotted his mantle of saffron, with its rustling linen folds, and a needle-thread of gold tricking out his tunic and the oriental leg-coverings which he wore. The Maid, huntress that she was, had eyes for no other, but followed only him in all the battle's conflicting mass, either hoping to fasten arms from Troy as an offering on a temple-wall, or wishing to parade herself in captured gold. In a girl's hot passion for plundering those spoils she was ranging heedlessly about the battle-lines, when at last Arruns finally chose his moment and unobserved set flying his spear, lifting his voice in prayer to Heaven above: 'God most high, Apollo, guardian of Soracte the holy, God whom we Etruscans worship more than all other men, feeding from heaped fuel the pinewood blaze, and, to worship you, tread firmly upon deep embers as we pass through the centre of the fire in full confidence of righteousness, grant, All-Powerful Father, that our dishonour may be wiped clean by arms of mine. I seek not the Maid's spoils, nor a trophy of her defeat, nor any plunder;

I shall leave it to my other deeds to bring me fame, and indeed I shall gladly enough return to the cities of my fatherland without renown, if only this intolerable scourge may fall by a wound from me.' Phoebus heard him, and decided to grant fulfilment to a part of his prayer, but the rest he scattered into the fleeting winds. He granted the prayer that he might bring Camilla down in the dismay of sudden death; but he did not grant that his proud land should see him return, and the gusts bore those words away into the southerly gales. So, then, the spear which his hand discharged hissed through the air; and in fierce concentration the Volscians, to a man, turned towards their princess and every eye was on her. But Camilla herself was quite oblivious to the whistling sound as the javelin came flying out of the sky, until the shaft found its mark under her bared breast, and there stayed fixed, forced deeply home to drink of a maiden's blood. Her comrades gathered in quick alarm and upheld their falling mistress. And Arruns fled on, more moved than any, for fear blended with his joy, and no more did he dare to trust his spear, or face the weapons of the Maid; like some wolf which, even before any threatening weapons can pursue him, when he has killed a shepherd or a large bullock, at once hastens to hide himself high in trackless mountain fastnesses, well aware of his reckless deed; he slackens his tail and tucks it between his legs, quivering and stroking his belly, as he makes for the woods. Like such a wolf did Arruns in his confusion withdraw from sight, mingling amid the armed men and wishing only to escape. The dying Camilla with one hand dragged at the spear; but the iron point had reached the ribs and was fast, deep within the wound between the bones. The blood left her and she sank to the ground; her eyes chilled, and began to droop in death; the once rosy colour left her face. And now with her last breath she spoke to Acca, a companion of her own age faithful to her beyond the rest, and the one confidante with whom she shared her troubles. To her she spoke these words: 'Acca, my sister, here my endeavour ends. An agonizing wound destroys me; and around me the world grows dim and black. Make your escape. And deliver this my last message direct to

Turnus: let him move up into battle and fend the Trojans from the city. And now fare you well.' Even as she spoke she was letting fall the reins, and limp and helpless slipping to the earth. She was already cold, and slowly her spirit took its release from her body's every part, and she laid down her now nerveless neck and her head vanquished by death; and her weapons forsook her. Sobbing, and bitter, her life fled down to the Shades. At her death, overpowering indeed was the shout which arose and smote the sky, with its golden stars. And with Camilla unhorsed, the battle hardened, and the whole host of Trojans, the Etruscan chieftains, and Evander's Arcadian squadrons charged together in massed array.

Meanwhile Diana's sentinel Opis had long been at her post high among the mountain-peaks, and undismayed had observed the fighting. Far off, amid the yelling, battle-mad warriors, she saw Camilla stricken by death's bitter stroke, and gave a sigh; and thus from the very depths of her heart she spoke her lament: 'Ah, Maiden, too hard and too heavy was the requital which you paid for attempting to challenge Trojans in war! Nor was it any help at all to you that you worshipped Diana in the wild wood's solitude and wore slung from your shoulder the quiver which is our token. Yet your queen has not left you honourless in death's extremity. Your passing shall not be without fame throughout the nations of the world; and never shall you bear the slight of dying unavenged. For he who has desecrated your flesh by dealing you this wound, whoever he may be, shall repay you by dying as he has deserved.' Now a high mound of earth stood near the foot of the lofty mountain. It was the tomb of an ancient Laurentine king, Dercennus; and it was built of piled-up soil and screened by the shadow of holm-oak trees. To the barrow quickly the goddess came, and there was a great beauty in her swift and powerful motion. And here forthwith she took her stand; and from the height of the mound she observed Arruns. Seeing him there in his gleaming arms and swollen with vanity, she spoke to him: 'Why do you turn as if to depart? Guide your steps this way; come here, to die, and receive a fit repayment for Camilla. But to think that one so mean as you should perish by Diana's own weapons!' So spoke the Thracian goddess, and took a winged arrow from her gold-plated quiver. With deadly aim she stretched the bow. She drew the string back till the curving bow-ends nearly met, and strained evenly with her hands till the left touched the iron arrowhead and the right brought the bow-string hard against her breast. And then, in the same instant of time, Arruns heard the rush of air as the arrow hissed, and the iron already stood fixed in his breast. His comrades recked nothing of him; they left him, groaning his last and breathing his life away, in an unnoticed place amid the dust of the plain. Opis winged her way back to Olympus.

The first to flee at the loss of their mistress were Camilla's own light squadrons. The Rutulians fled in utter disarray, and vigorous Atinas fled too; captains, separated from their companies, and leaderless squadrons sought safety, turning away and riding fast for the ramparts. None had strength to check the Trojans by missiles or to make a stand against them as they came on in hot pursuit, their hands ready to deal death. Instead, they slung their loosely strung bows over their drooping shoulders. The plain quaked and crumbled under the horses' four-hoof beat. Dust rolled towards the city walls in a confusion of black murk. Mothers stood on watch-towers, smote their breasts, and raised their women's wailing to the stars of heaven. The first of the defeated to burst running into the open gates were followed closely by the crowding enemy, intermingling with the stream of fugitives who could not elude their miserable end; for even in their own gateway, within their own city's ramparts, and with the refuge of their buildings round them, they were pierced, and breathed their last. Some of the defenders then shut the gates, daring neither to leave an entry for their friends nor, despite their entreaties, to admit them within the walls and there arose a most piteous massacre of those who maintained an armed defence of the entrance or rushed right onto the weapons. Of those who were shut out before the very gaze of their weeping parents, some in the pressure of the rout rolled headlong down into the moat, while others spurred onwards with loose rein, and blindly battered at the hinge-posts of the gates which stubbornly barred their way. Even mothers on the walls, inspired by true love of their homeland and zealous to emulate the example which they had seen Camilla set, cast weapons with their own hands in nervous haste, using instead of steel hard-oak cudgels and stakes pointed in the fire. They burned to defend the walls to the death, in the forefront of the fight.

Meanwhile, out in the forests the bitter message reached Turnus and obsessed his thoughts; for Acca, to the violent distress of the young prince, had now brought him tidings of the desperate crisis, reporting that the Volscian ranks were all destroyed, and Camilla had fallen; that the enemy had swept all before them in triumphant victory and were moving on the city in deadly onslaught; and that panic was already reaching the city walls. Feverishly obeying Jupiter's cruel and imperious will, he descended from the hills which he had been occupying and left the wild woodland slopes. He had scarcely moved forward out of sight and reached level ground when Aeneas, Troy's chieftain, entered the undefended pass, surmounted the hill-crest, and emerged from the forest-shade. Thus both commanders swept on in all haste to the city walls, each with his whole army, and distant not many paces from each other. As he looked ahead across the dust-smoking plain, Aeneas saw the Laurentine column, and simultaneously Turnus, hearing the onward tramp of feet and the snorting of horses, recognized the presence of Aeneas in deadly readiness for action. They would then at once have engaged in combat and put themselves to the test of battle, if the crimson sun had not been already bathing his weary horses in the Spanish Sea, and bringing back the night, as day declined. So the armies settled in camps before the city, and built stockades for their defences.

BOOK TWELVE

DECISION: THE DEATH OF TURNUS

TURNUS could see that the Latins, broken by the malice of Mars, had no strength left, and that every eye singled out him alone, demanding that his spontaneous offer should now be made good. His heart beat high for war and he blazed with an implacable fire which needed no kindling; as some strong lion of the African desert, gravely wounded in the breast by huntsmen, gives battle at last; and, joyously tossing his luxuriant mane from his neck, snaps off, undaunted, the spear which some stalker has planted in him, opens a blood-smeared mouth, and roars. Such was the hot-headed ardour of Turnus, and his obdurate passion mounted. In turbulence of spirit he began to address the King: 'I, Turnus, offer no hindrance. There is no reason why those cowards who follow Aeneas should withdraw their challenge or renounce their compact. I go to do battle. Father, as our Chief, bring implements of sacrifice and prescribe terms of truce. While you Latins sit and look on, either with this right arm shall I send the Dardan, that Asiatic runaway, down to Tartarus, and by my sword shall I alone fling back the shame which rests on us all, or else let him hold us vanquished in his hand and let the maiden Lavinia pass to him to be his bride.'

Mastering his emotions Latinus answered Turnus: 'Ah, young prince of peerless spirit, the more keenly you excel in your impetuous valour, so much the more intently must I, in fairness, take counsel and weigh anxiously every danger. You yourself already possess the kingdom left to you by your father Daunus, and many other cities, captured by your own right arm. And besides, I, Latinus, have gold, and a generous spirit. There are other unwed maidens, of no mean descent, in Latium and Laurentine lands. Let me then speak plainly and tell you my thoughts, however painful they may be to express; and do you take my meaning earnestly to heart. I could not, without sin, unite my daughter to any one of her former suitors; every prediction, divine and human, warned me against doing so. And yet my love for you, our kinship, and the grief and tears of my queen prevailed over me, so that I broke every restraint, stole the promised bride from her betrothed, and wickedly went to war. You see for yourself, Turnus, what military disasters have hounded me ever since, and you know what tribulations you, beyond all others, have had to undergo. Vanquished in two great battles, we can now scarcely preserve any hope for the future of Italy, even within our city. Tiber's streams are yet warm with our blood, and our broad plains are white with our bones. Now why must I return again and again to this same point? And why am I so mad as to keep changing my purpose? I should be ready enough to accept the Trojans as allies if death had first removed Turnus. If so, why do I not instead put an end to all the strife while Turnus is still unharmed? What will your own kindred, the Rutulians, say, and indeed what will be the judgement of all Italy, if – and may fortune give the lie to my fear – I prove to have sent you to your death solely because you sought my daughter in a marriage-union with our house? Think of war's shifting chances. Pity your aged father who in Ardea, your distant home, is sorrowing for his far-off son.'

But not one whit could the fierce resolution of Turnus be deflected by words. His passion mounted higher yet; the malady grew sharper with the cure. As soon as he could speak, he began to say: 'Sire, for my sake, I pray you, lay aside this care which you feel on my account, and let me bargain death for honour. My hand can shower missiles of strong steel as well as another's; and, no less, when I inflict a wound, does the life-blood flow. His goddess mother will certainly not be at his side to cover his flight in mist – fit ruse for a woman – ; and if he tries to hide in shadows, it will be in vain.'

But the Queen was terrified at the renewed risk of battle, and in tears, like one about to die, she clasped her daughter's fiery lover: 'Turnus, I entreat you, by these tears of mine, by any regard for Amata which can still touch your heart! You are now my one hope; you are my only repose in the unhappiness of my old age; on you rests all the majesty and power of Latinus, for our whole house totters and leans precariously on your support. One thing alone I beg: avoid close combat with the Trojans. Whatever fortune awaits you in the fight which you plan, that same fortune, Turnus, is also in store for me; and, if you die, I too shall leave the hated light of day. For never shall I survive to see, from captivity, Aeneas made my son.'

Lavinia heard her mother's appeal. The tears streamed down her cheeks, aflame and feverish from the deep flush spreading quickly over her heated countenance; as when some craftsman has painted a stain of blood-red dye on Indian ivory, or when white lilies are blended with many roses and reflect their glow, such were the colours shown on the maiden's face. Turnus fixed his eyes on her in a distraction of love; and all the hotter grew his passion for arms. His answer to Amata was short: 'Do not, I beg you, Mother, send me forth on my way to the pitiless conflict of Mars with so ominous a presage as these tears. Not for Turnus is the freedom to postpone his death. Now, Idmon! Be my messenger and deliver to the Phrygian potentate these words of mine, which he will not like. As soon as tomorrow's dawn, riding on wheels of crimson, first blushes in the heavens, he is to send no Trojans into battle against Rutulians, but both Trojan and Rutulian arms are to be at rest. By his blood and mine alone are we to settle this war. On that field must Lavinia's hand be won.'

With these words he quickly withdrew into the palace. He called for his horses and joyfully watched their restive excitement. These horses had been given to Pilumnus by Orithyia herself – a proud possession, for they could outmatch snow in their white brilliance and the winds in their speed. About them stood their active charioteers, clapping cupped hands on their chests to rouse their mettle and combing the manes which fell about their necks. Then Turnus drew over his shoulders a corslet stiff with gold and pale golden-bronze. He also fitted on and adjusted his sword and shield and his helm with the red-plumed horns. The God whose Might is Fire had himself made that sword for Turnus' father, Daunus, and tempered it while still white-hot in waters of Styx. Then firmly Turnus grasped his stout spear which stood ready leaning against a tall pillar in the centre of the hall; a spoil won from the Auruncan, Actor. Turnus shook it till it quivered, and cried aloud: 'Spear of mine, which never yet failed me at my call, now has the time come. The heroic Actor carried you once; and now you are in the right hand of Turnus. Grant me to bring him low, that half-man of a Phrygian, and with main strength to rend and rip his corslet from him. Let me foul in the dust that hair crimped with curling-tongs and oiled with myrrh!' The mad mood swept him on. Fire glittered in his flashing eyes, and all his face showed the fierce heat within, a heat to send sparks flying; like some bull he was, which, preluding battle, starts to bellow and strike dread, and seeks to charge his horns with rage; which spars with a tree-trunk, challenging the air with his strokes, or scatters the sand, skirmishing before the fight.

Meanwhile Aeneas was glad that there was at last a prospect of settling the war through the new agreement now being offered. In grim mood, clad in the arms which his mother had brought to him, he, no less than Turnus, whetted the edge of his valour and whipped up a passionate anger. He spoke reassuringly to his comrades and to the anxious and downcast Iulus, explaining the hand of Destiny in these events. Then he instructed officers to take his answer back to King Latinus, indicating his decision and declaring his conditions for peace.

The dawn of a new day was barely beginning to sprinkle its glow on mountain-crests and the horses of the sun had just begun to arise out of ocean's depth, breathing light from their high-held muzzles. Marshals, Rutulian and Trojan, had already measured out a duelling-ground close by the ramparts of the mighty city, and were preparing it, setting in the centre of it braziers and altars of turf to the gods whom both sides honoured; and priests clad in long ritual aprons and wearing wreaths of holy herbs on their brows were bringing the water and the fire. The host of the Italians marched out, their serried columns streaming through the crowded gateways. From the other side all the army of Troy and Etruria, in their differing accoutrements, came hastening, armed with steel as fully as if war's bitter fighting called them thither. And there too were the captains, hurrying through the midst of their thousands in their haughty purple and gold, Mnestheus of Assaracus' line, and valiant Asilas, and Messapus the horse-tamer, Neptune's own son. At a given signal all withdrew, each to his allotted place; they planted their spears in the ground, and against them leant their shields. Then, streaming from their homes in high excitement, came the mothers, the weaponless multitude, and the old and feeble; and they gathered on towers and roof-tops, or took their stand upon the tall gates.

Juno meanwhile looked forth from a high crest, a hill known now as Alban, but in those times a nameless eminence without regard or fame; and she watched the plain, the Laurentine and Trojan hosts, and Latinus' city. Forthwith she spoke to Turnus' sister, a goddess like herself, who presided over the pools and the roaring rivers, an office assigned to her by Jupiter, high King of Heaven, in recompense for a stolen maidenhood: 'Nymph, pride of the rivers, and very dear to my heart, you know how I have preferred you in my favour beyond all other maids of Latium who have been forced to mount the thankless bed of strong-hearted Jupiter, and I have gladly given you your place in your own part of the sky. Learn, Juturna, a grief which must be yours; and do not reproach me, for wherever fortune seemed to permit me, and the Fates allowed success to Latium, I have protected Turnus and your walled city. But now I see the young prince engage battle with a destiny weaker than his foe's. The day of the Fates and malevolent force draw near. I cannot look with my own eyes on this truce and on this combat. But you, if you have the daring to give your brother some more potent aid, go forward; for it is meet. It may be that some brighter issue may attend you both – unhappy pair!' She had scarcely spoken so, when the tears started from Juturna's eyes, and thrice, and yet again, she struck her hand upon her beautiful breast. 'This is no time for tears,' said Saturnian Juno. 'Hasten; and, if you can find the means, steal your brother from death; or else, shatter this treaty which they have now devised, and reawaken the war. It is with my sanction that you will dare.' With this exhortation she left her sorely stricken to the heart, and uncertain and perplexed.

While they spoke the kings themselves came forth, Latinus driving in a huge and massive four-horse chariot, wearing twice six gilded rays around his glittering brows, in token of his ancestor the sun. Turnus rode behind a pair of white horses, with two broad-headed spear-shafts quivering in his grip. Then from the Trojan camp came the chieftain Aeneas, the founder of the Roman breed, shining in a blaze of light, with his shield like a star, and arms of Heaven's making; and close by him came forth Ascanius, the second hope of Roman greatness. A priest in a toga of pure white brought the young of a bristled boar, and a two-year sheep never shorn; and he drove the victims up to altars already blazing. The princes turned their eyes to the rising sun, offered handfuls of salt meal, made the mark of their blades on the animals' brows and poured drink-offerings on the altars from their bowls. Then Aeneas the True bared his sword and prayed: 'Sun, be now my witness, and Earth of Italy, on whom I call, since for your sake have I been given strength to support my heavy trials until now; and to you, Father Almighty, and to you, his Saturnian Queen – ah, Goddess, now at last, as I hope, kindlier towards us – I pray; and to you Mars, Father, Glorious, who divinely sway every war; and I call on you, Springs and Rivers, and on every Majesty in Heaven's height, and on every Power in the blue ocean; if it should chance that victory pass to Ausonian Turnus it is hereby agreed that the vanquished shall depart to Evander's city, that Iulus shall resign his claim to these lands, and that never afterwards shall men of Aeneas renew war or reappear in arms to challenge this realm with their sword. But if instead Victory should grant us proof that the favour of Mars is ours – and this I think is the more likely, and may it be the divine purpose of the gods to bring it to pass! – then I shall never command Italians to obey Trojans, nor do I seek any royalty for myself. Let the two nations, each still unsubjected, enter upon an everlasting compact under equal terms. I will introduce our

Trojan rituals and our gods. But Latinus, as father of our united families, shall retain all power of the sword and all majesty of civil authority. The Trojans shall build for me my own walled city, and Lavinia shall give to that city her name.'

Aeneas spoke first, and Latinus followed him. Looking upwards to the sky and stretching his right hand out towards the heavens he prayed: 'I also, Aeneas, swear by Earth, Sea, and Stars, by Latona's twin children, by Janus the two-browed and by the might of Gods Infernal and by the shrines of implacable Dis. May the Father, whose thunder-stroke is every treaty's sanction, hear my oath. I touch this altar; and I call as my witnesses the Divinities who are here and these fires which burn between us. Never shall come the day which sunders this pact of Italian concord, however fortune may fall. No force shall ever bend my will – no, not though it confound the earth in a deluge and plunge it into the waves, shatter the sky, and cast it down into Hell. My will shall stand as surely as this sceptre' – for he chanced to be holding a sceptre in his right hand – 'can never more sprout new leaves or cast any shade from boughs, since it was first cut from low on the parent-stem in its woodland home, and laid down limbs and tresses at the stroke of the blade, having no mother now. Once it was a tree; but now a craftsman's hand has sheathed it in graceful bronze, and given it for elders of Latium to bear.'

Such were the speeches which they made as they ratified the compact between them in full view of all the captains. They then formally slaughtered their consecrated victims over the flame; they tore out their inner parts while they were yet breathing, and piled laden dishes on the altars.

But in spite of all, the Rutulians had long been judging this duel unfair. Their hearts were already torn by many discordant impulses; but now they grew still more disturbed when they gained a closer view of the contestants, and noted their unequal strength. The sight of Turnus himself increased their anxiety yet further when he stepped out in front without a word, and in humble piety paid reverence at the altar with downcast eyes and the down of young manhood showing on his cheeks, where the youthful colour had paled. Now as soon as his sister Juturna had noticed that such talk was beginning to spread and that the feelings of the multitude were changeful and insecure, she disguised herself in the form of Camers. Camers was descended from exalted ancestors; his father's valour had bequeathed him brilliant fame, and he was himself most active in arms. Disguised as Camers, Juturna darted amidst the ranks, well knowing what to say. She spread a crop of different rumours, and said: 'Are you not ashamed, Rutulians, to expose one single man's life to destruction to save all your fine army? Are we not their equals in numbers and in strength? See! It is their whole force here before you, these Trojans and Arcadians, and that omen-ridden contingent of Etruscans hostile to Turnus. Why, even if only every second man among us were to close with them, it would still be hard to find an opponent for each. Turnus himself, no doubt, will mount in glory to the High Gods at whose altars he now dedicates his life, and his fame will survive deathless on the lips of men; but we, who today sit passively in our fields, shall lose our homeland and be forced to obey arrogant overlords.'

So spoke Juturna, and at her words the spirits of the young fighting men caught fire, and hotter now and yet hotter they burned. A murmur crept from rank to rank and a change of heart came over Laurentines and Latins alike. Men who had lately been hoping for a rest from battle and rescue from their plight now wanted weapons, pitying the unfair lot of Turnus, and ardently wishing that the compact had never been made. Juturna then acted again and even more impressively. She displayed, aloft in the sky, a sign peculiarly calculated to confuse Italian minds and lead them astray by its meaning.

For Jupiter's bird, an eagle, showing golden, with a glint of red as he flew, had been harrying some birds of the seashore, chasing flocks which winged their noisy way before him, when suddenly he swooped towards the waves and seized the leading swan in his talons' ruthless grip. At this the Italians became alert and attentive, and beheld a marvellous sight. For now all the birds ceased to flee, but instead with loud cries they wheeled round, formed into a flock like a cloud darkening the sky with their wings, and drove their enemy in retreat through the air till their pressure, and the weight of his burden, overcame him. He faltered in mid-flight, and from his talons he dropped his prey into the river. Then he fled away, far off into the clouds. At that the Rutulians shouted in high fervour, greeting the presage, and prepared for action. The first to speak was their prophet, Tolumnius: 'This is the very sign for which I have often prayed. I accept it, and I see in it the action of the Gods. It is I who will lead you! Seize the sword, therefore, my hapless countrymen, whom this ruthless newcomer intimidates with his warring, and whose coastlands he ravages with his violence just as if you had been poor, strengthless birds. For he too will take to flight; he will set sail, and flee far away over the deep. But you, you must be all of one heart and close your ranks. Fight to save your Prince from the battle which would steal him from you.'

So speaking, he dashed forward and hurled a spear full against the enemy. Surely aimed, the cornel-wood shaft whistled as it cut through the air; and in the same single instant with the spear's sound a tremendous shout was heard, for all the rows of onlookers were immediately in uproar and every heart swelled with excitement. The spear flew on. Directly in its path there chanced to be standing nine stalwart brothers, sons of a single mother, the faithful Etruscan wife of Arcadian Gylippus to whom she had borne them. The spear struck one of the brothers, in his middle where the sewn belt chafed against his belly and the buckle bit the ends joining from either side. He was a young warrior splendid to see in his glittering arms; but the spear drove through his ribs and stretched him on the yellow sand. His spirited brothers stood solid together, burning with grief. Some laid hands on hilts and drew their swords, and some seized missiles of iron; and all charged, blindly. Against them the Laurentine ranks advanced; and then, once again, Trojans, Etruscans, and Arcadians in their highly coloured armour massed and came on like a flood; so much were they all alike dominated by one passionate desire to settle the issue with the sword. In a flash they dismantled the altars. A confused storm of weapons darkened the sky, and down fell the iron rain. Wine-bowls and braziers were scattered. Latinus himself fled; the treaty was void, and back he carried his insulted gods. Some bridled chariot-teams, or leapt onto their horses and stood ready with drawn swords. Messapus, thirsting to wreck the treaty, rode his horse against Aulestes, an Etruscan king wearing a kingly crown, and scared him into retreat. As he stumbled hastily back, he had the ill-luck to become entangled in the altars directly behind and was pitched onto his head and shoulders. Up rode Messapus, flying furiously at him spear in hand, and, rising in the saddle with that weapon large as a beam, even as he attempted a long plea for mercy, dealt him a violent thrust. 'He has it now!' Messapus cried. 'A far finer victim, this, for sacrifice to the Great Gods.' Italians gathered quickly and despoiled the still warm limbs. Corynaeus snatched up a smouldering brand from the altar, and as Ebysus closed in to strike he beat him to the stroke and dashed the flames in his face. His thick beard blazed up and gave off a smell of singeing. Corynaeus followed up his blow, and with his left hand seized his distracted opponent by the hair; he pressed his knee into him with his weight behind it, and forced him down to the ground, and then stabbed him in the side with his rigid blade. Podalirius with drawn sword was chasing Alsus, a shepherd who was moving swiftly among the flying weapons along the battle-front. But as Podalirius towered over him Alsus drew back his axe, aimed directly at his attacker, and cleft through the centre of his brow and his chin; and his armour was drenched in spouting gore. The hard repose of iron sleep bore down on his eyes; and their light was extinguished for the everlasting dark.

Meanwhile Aeneas the True, bare-headed and stretching out an unarmed hand, called loudly to his men: 'Where are you going in such haste? Why this sudden outburst of strife? Oh, restrain your anger! The truce is already made, and its terms agreed. The right of combat is mine alone. Leave all to me and have no fear for the outcome, for it is I who must confirm the compact which has been made, and it was to me alone that Turnus was promised at the ritual sacrifice.' But even as he was speaking and calling loudly to his men, see, an arrow, hissing on its winged journey, flew straight at him. No one ever knew what hand sped it, whose driving force started it on its way, or what accident, or what god, brought the Rutulians so proud a distinction, for all the credit for this notable feat was kept a secret; no one ever boasted that he had wounded Aeneas. Turnus, seeing Aeneas retiring from the lines and his captains in dismay, burned anew with the sudden fire of hope, called for horses, called for arms, and like a flash leapt exultantly into his chariot and took a firm grip of the reins.

Soon he was galloping over the field, sending many valiant warriors to their doom, and leaving others writhing near to death; he rode down the ranks beneath his chariot and quickly gathered more spears to shower them on the fleeing. He was like blood-red Mars himself when, aroused near the cold streams of Hebrus, he clashes his shield and gives rein to his battle-mad horses to herald war; they fly over the open plain outstripping the winds of south and west till farthest Thrace groans under their hoof-beats; and all about him the figures of black Dread, Wrath and Treachery, the God's own retinue, drive trampling on. Like Mars, and as vital as he, Turnus lashed his horses, steaming, sweating, through the battle's throng. They pranced on enemies pitiably slain, flying hooves sprinkled a bloody dew, and the sand which they kicked up was blent with gore. Turnus cast to their death Sthenelus, Thamyrus, and Pholus, these last two in hand-to-hand fight, the first by striking him from afar; and from afar also he struck down the two sons of Imbrasus, Glaucus and Lades. Imbrasus himself reared them in Lycia, training them both to fight in close combat and to ride their horses faster than the wind, and had fitted them out with matching arms. And there, some way off and charging into the battle's centre, was the illustrious warrior Eumedes, son of Dolon famous of old; he recalled his grandfather by his name and his father by his daring spirit and skill of hand. For Dolon had once dared to demand for himself, as his prize for adventuring as a spy into the camp of the Greeks, the team of Peleus' son; but Diomede rewarded him very differently for so audacious a deed, and he ceased to covet the horses of Achilles. Turnus saw Eumedes in the distance on the open plain. First he sent a light javelin in pursuit of him over the long space between, and then he halted his chariot-pair and leapt down from his car; and at once he was on him, bestrode the fallen, gasping enemy, pressed his foot hard down on his neck, wrenched the sword from his right hand, and with a flashing stroke bathed it deep in his throat. He added a spoken taunt: 'See, Trojan! Lie there, and measure your length in the fields of our Western Land which you sought to gain by war. This is the prize which they win who dare to make test of me by the blade; this is how they establish their walled city.' And next with a cast of the spear he sent Asbytes to bear him company, and Chloreus too, and Sybaris, Dares, Thersilochus, and Thymoetes, whose horse had unseated him and thrown him over its withers. And as when the blast of north winds from Edonia roars across the dark Aegean driving the rollers to the shore, and the storm-clouds flee from the sky before the winds' assault, so did the ranks retreat before Turnus wherever he carved his way; their lines turned about, and ran. Turnus came on, swept forward by the force of his charge, and as he drove his chariot into the wind it tossed his flying plume. But Phegeus could not brook his onset nor his proud battle-cry. He thrust himself full in the path of the chariot, and with his strong right arm caught the galloping horses and swung to one side their mouths, foaming on the bits. Phegeus was dragged, clinging to the yoke, with flank exposed. Turnus' broad-headed lance drove home and burst through his two-leashed cuirass, but barely tasted his flesh in a surface-wound. Even so Phegeus turned to face his foe; he held up his shield before him, and attempting self-defence drew his pointed sword. But before he could attack, the chariot-wheel, spinning on its axle in its violent onrush, drove him headlong down and stretched him on the earth. Instantly Turnus followed up with a slash of his blade between the lower rim of his helmet and his corslet's upper edge, severed his head, and left the trunk on the sand.

Now while Turnus was thus triumphantly dealing death about the plain, Mnestheus, the faithful Achates, and Ascanius brought Aeneas, blood-stained and leaning at every second step on a long lance, back into their camp. Furiously he struggled to draw out the head of the broken arrow, and insisted that they must adopt the quickest means of relief by widening the wound with a cut from a broad-bladed sword to lay right open the place where the arrow-head lodged hidden, and let him return to the fray. And now there stood beside him Iapyx, Iasus' son. Him Phoebus had loved beyond all others, and long since, overcome by his sharp passion, had freely offered him his own arts and his own powers, prophecy, the lyre, and his swift archery. But Iapyx wished to prolong the life of his father, then sick to the point of death; and he preferred to know the potencies of herbs, and the practice of healing, and to ply this quiet art, resigning fame. Savagely growling, Aeneas stood there leaning on his long spear, with a throng of his warriors around him, and Iulus among them in great distress; but he was unmoved by their tears. The old Iapyx, his garment girt up and twisted back in the fashion of the Physician God, anxiously tried every means, using the healing hand and Apollo's potent herbs, but all in vain; and in vain he worked the arrow-head with his fingers, or seized the iron piece in the forceps' grip. But no good fortune attended him and Apollo his patron helped him not at all. And all the time, horrifying across the plain, louder and thicker came the battle-roar, and disaster drew nearer. Now they could see the dust-cloud solid in the sky. Horsemen closed in towards them; showers of darts fell right in the midst of the camp. Grim shouting rose to heaven from young men warring and falling beneath the hard hand of Mars.

But now, shaken by her son's undeserved suffering, Aeneas' mother Venus picked from Cretan Ida the plant dictamnus, whose stalk is tressed with luxuriant leaves, and whose flower is bright red; it is a fodder well known indeed to the wild goats when the flying arrows stay clinging in their backs. With her form shrouded in a mantle of mist, Venus carried this plant down to them, and with its healing power she secretly tinctured the water which they had poured into a sparkling cauldron; and finally sprinkled in it health-giving juices of ambrosia and fragrant panacea. Such was the water in which the old Iapyx bathed the wound, not knowing its virtue. And suddenly all the pain which Aeneas had felt vanished, and from deep down in the wound the flow of blood quite ceased; then the arrow-head came away readily in Iapyx's hand, dropping out of its own accord, and forced by no one. Aeneas' strength, fresh as of old, returned to him. Iapyx shouted: 'Quick! Bring our hero his arms! Why stand you still?' He was the first to rekindle their spirits to face the foe: 'No human powers produced this glad result, nor any guidance of human skill; nor is it my hand, Aeneas, which brings you healing. A mightier than I, some Deity, is at work. He sends you back, to do yet greater deeds.'

Athirst for battle, Aeneas had already enclosed his calves, the right and then the left, in gold, and in scorn of delay brandished his flashing spear. And now his shield was fitted to his side and his cuirass to his back; and, in armour as he was, he enfolded Ascanius in a close embrace and lightly kissed his lips through his helmet's visor. 'From me, my son,' he said, 'you may learn what is valour and what is strenuous toil: as for what good fortune is, others must teach you that. Today my right arm will keep you safe in warfare and will lead you where rich prizes may be won. But when in due time your own age ripens to maturity, it will be for you to see to it that you do not forget, but recall in your thoughts the examples set you by your kindred. Your father is Aeneas and your uncle was Hector. Let that be your inspiration.'

With these words he strode, a mighty figure, from the gates, waving his monstrous spear. As he did so, Antheus and Mnestheus also hurried out at the head of a massed column. The whole army now left the camp and streamed forward. Soon all the plain was a confusion of blinding dust, and the earth quaked and shuddered under their trampling feet. From the earthwork opposite, Turnus saw them coming; so did his Ausonians, and a chill tremor ran through the very marrow of their bones. But first, before any of the Latins, Juturna heard the noise and recognized its meaning; she trembled, and recoiled. Aeneas came swiftly on, and hastened the march of his army, a streak of dark menace moving across the open plain. Like some storm-cloud he came, which, at the sky's discharge, travels landwards over mid-sea, while far inland hearts of poor farming-folk shudder in foreboding, for the storm will bring down their trees, flatten their crops, and spread general ruin over wide lands; the winds fly ahead, and carry the sound to the shores. Such was the war-leader of Troyland, as he drove his host onwards against his foes; and each man in his army pressed into tight formation and phalanx closed on phalanx, till the ranks were a single mass. And now Thymbraeus had already smitten the huge Osiris with his sword. Mnestheus massacred Arcetius, Achates Epulo, and Gyas Ufens. Tolumnius, the seer, who had been the first to discharge a spear against their adversaries, himself fell. A shout was raised to the sky. The Rutulians in their turn now wheeled about and fled, showing their heels to the enemy and running to escape in clouds of dust. But Aeneas did not deign to send these runaways to their death, nor did he press on to engage those who offered to confront him foot to foot or levelled their missiles at him. For he was on the track only of Turnus, searching for him everywhere in the dense murk and claiming him alone for combat.

In dread of that conflict the brave maiden Juturna was shaken to the heart. She therefore flung Metiscus, Turnus' charioteer, from his post where he stood with the reins about him, and left him far behind where he had slipped down over his yoke-shaft. Quickly she took his place and handled and guided the rippling reins, being now in every feature like Metiscus, with his voice, his figure, and his arms. Like a swallow, which darts, a black speck, through the spacious farm-buildings of some wealthy landowner, passing in her wheeling flight back and forth about high barns, as she gathers tiny scraps of food, morsels to feed her twittering nestlings, while her call is heard now in empty sheds and now about the ponds – so Juturna herself darted behind the horses through the enemy's midst, and flew with the chariot's violent onrush, ranging the whole plain. Now here and now there she flaunted her still exultant brother, and yet would never allow him to close in combat, but instead swerved aside and galloped far afield. But none the less Aeneas followed the twisted circles of her course, striving to encounter Turnus; and he tracked him, and along the shattered ranks with loud voice he called on him. But each time that his eyes fell on his enemy and he tried to match the flight of the wing-footed horses by his own fleetness of foot, Juturna at once reined the chariot round, and swung it away. Ah, what was Aeneas to do? At a loss, he wavered as in a shifting current, torn in purpose this way and that by conflicting calls. But now Messapus, running lightly, pointed at Aeneas one of the two tough, iron-headed spear-shafts which he chanced to be carrying in his left hand, and he sent it, spinning, surely aimed to strike. Aeneas stopped, and gathered himself behind his armour, dropping down on one knee; nevertheless, the strongly driven spear caught the crown of his helmet and dashed from his head the tops of the plumes. At this his anger rose to a fury indeed. This treacherous attack had altered his design. Realizing that the retreating horses and chariot were galloping far afield, he first called long on Jupiter and on the altars of the violated truce to bear him witness, and then, at last, charged into the midst of the foe. Dreadful, with the God of Battle giving him aid, he awoke a massacre, ruthless, indiscriminate, and opened all the floodgates of his wrath.

What god can now set forth for me in story all the horrors, all the various deeds of death, and tell how the chieftains perished, when all over the field of battle first Turnus, and then Troy's hero in his turn, drove them fleeing? Jupiter!— Did you indeed ordain that nations who were to live together afterwards in everlasting peace should clash in such violence? With a blow in the side Aeneas met the Rutulian Sucro. The encounter with Sucro was the first to bring the charging Trojans to a standstill. But he did not long delay Aeneas, who drove his pitiless sword, where doom comes quickest, through the ribs which encased the heart. Turnus struck Amycus, engaging him on foot – for he was unhorsed – and also his brother, Diores; he smote Amycus as he charged, with a long lance, and Diores with the point of his sword. He tore away the heads of both of them, and hung them from his chariot where he carried them to sprinkle their bloody dew. Aeneas sent to their death Talos, Tanais, and valiant Cethegus. He engaged all three at once, and also Onites, man of gloom, who drew his name from Echion's city and his life from Peridia's motherhood. Turnus on his side killed some brothers who had come from Apollo's lands in Lycia, and also Menoetes, a young Arcadian, who had hated war – in vain. He had had his poor house, and plied his trade, about the channels at Lerna, where fish are plentiful, knowing nothing of attendance on men of power; and in the same place his father had sown crops on rented land. Like fires released from different directions upon a parched forest, where thickets of bay-trees crackle, or like foaming rivers roaring in violent descent from mountain-heights, and each devastating its own track in its haste to reach the plains, were Aeneas and Turnus, as, swift and eager, they tore through the battle. Then, if never before, the rage within them grew tempestuous. Their unconquerable hearts swelled to bursting, and all their might was behind their every blow.

Murranus was loudly crying names with an ancient ring, the names of his own grandsires, and their sires before them, and all his lineage, the whole of it traced down through kings of Latium. Aeneas brought him low, shattered by a stone – a whirlwind-cast of a mighty piece of rock –, and stretched him on the ground. He lay with the reins and yoke above him, and the wheels rolled him forward, and the flying hoofs of his horses, all unaware of their master, beat and beat on him, trampling him down. Turnus met Hyllus as he charged roaring in most arrogant pride, and cast his spear full on the gold helmet guarding his brow; the spear went clean through the helmet, piercing the brain, and there it lodged. And, O Cretheus, bravest of the Greeks, even your right arm could not rescue you from Turnus. Neither did Cupencus' gods protect him at the approach of Aeneas; his bronze shield failed to stay the blow, and in pitiable plight he took the weapon full in the chest. Those Laurentine plains also saw Aeolus fall, and lie stretched on his broad back, sprawling over the ground. Yes, now you fell, though Greeks in their ranks and even

Achilles who was too strong for Priam's empire could never bring you low; here now you met your life's end. You had your proud mansion at Ida's foot where at Lyrnessus stood your splendid home; but your grave is in Laurentine soil. The whole of each line of battle now turned to engage, every man among them, all the Latins, all the Dardanids, Mnestheus, fierce Serestus, Messapus the horse-tamer, valiant Asilas, the whole armed mass of Etruscans, and Evander's Arcadian squadrons, each soldier relying on himself alone, and putting every ounce of his strength into the striving, with never a respite, never any rest, but only the extreme of effort for the fight.

But then the mother of Aeneas, goddess of rarest beauty, prompted him to move against the defence-walls and wheel his army quickly towards the city, to alarm the Latins by threat of sudden disaster. For Aeneas, turning his eyes this way and that as he tracked Turnus in different parts of the fighting, caught sight of the city which, just as if it were at peace, was still quite unmolested, and playing no part in the great war. Forthwith his imagination kindled at the thought of a yet more terrible stroke of battle. He called to him his captains, Mnestheus, Sergestus, and valiant Serestus, and then took his stand on some rising ground. Thither assembled all the rest of the Trojan army, in closed ranks and without laying down their sharp weapons or their shields. Aeneas, standing in their midst on a mound of earth, spoke: 'Let my commands be obeyed without delay. Jupiter is with us. And I would have none move the more slowly because my change of plan comes without warning. Today I shall tear up this city, the cause of the fighting, the very capital of Latinus' kingdom, and lay its smoking rooftops level with the soil, unless they acknowledge their defeat and obediently accept our sway. Do you think that I shall wait until it pleases Turnus to face me in combat – until, after being vanquished once already, he consents to turn and engage with me again? Here, my countrymen, is the fountain-head, the source of this wicked war. Now quickly fetch fire-brands, and then exact the restoration of your truce by the argument of flames.'

When Aeneas had spoken, his troops adopted the wedge-formation, every spirit among them striving with equal ardour, and in a dense mass charged against the wall. With surprising speed, scaling-ladders and fire were suddenly on the scene. Some of the Trojans dispersed to the gates and cut down the pickets before them. Others sent the iron spinning, and shadowed the sky with their weapons. Aeneas himself, standing amid the foremost, pointed with outstretched hand towards the ramparts and loudly accused Latinus, calling the Gods to witness that once again he was being forced into battle, that twice over the Italians had become his enemies, and that this was the second violation of a truce. And now panic and dissension arose among the citizens. Some advised unbarring the city, throwing the gates wide to the Dardanids, and dragging the king himself onto the battlements. But others paraded with their arms and insisted on defending the walls: as when a shepherd has tracked bees to their home in some volcanic rock containing many a hiding place, and fills it with acrid smoke; the bees inside, in desperation, hurry everywhere about the waxen fortress, hissing loudly as they whet their anger, while the reeking smoke rolls black about their home; the rock resounds darkly murmuring within, and fumes escape to the open air.

A new misfortune now befell the exhausted Latins, so grave that it shook the whole city to its foundations. The Queen had looked forth from her apartments and seen the enemy approaching, the walls under threat of attack, and flames flying up to the roofs, but nowhere any Rutulian battle-line to confront the attackers, and no sign of the army which Turnus led. The poor queen believed that the young prince had lost his life in the battle's conflict; and, with her mind distraught, in sudden agony she cried out that she was herself the culprit, the whole cause and source of the calamity. Frantic, demented, she poured out her heart in words of grief; and, intent on ending her life, violently rent her purple robes and attached a noose of rope to a beam on high in preparation for an ugly death. As soon as the unhappy ladies of Latium heard of the disaster which had befallen their queen, the princess

Lavinia was the first to tear her flower-bright tresses and her rosy cheeks with her own hands; and after her all the others around her went wild with grief, till the whole palace echoed afar with the mourning, and from there the tidings of gloom were spread throughout the city. Hearts sank. Latinus walked in rent garments, dazed by the fate of his queen and his city's fall, defiling his white hair with handfuls of foul dust, and incessantly blaming himself for not having from the first willingly received Dardan Aeneas and freely accepted him as his daughter's bridegroom.

Meanwhile, Turnus, warring on the farther boundary of the plain, was pursuing some stragglers; but he moved less fiercely and his exultant joy in his horses' charge was flagging more and more. On the breeze there now came to him a clamour of grief, with an undertone of dread; the loud turmoil of the city struck his hearing, alert for every sound, as a murmur with never a hint of joy. 'Ah me,' he said, 'why are the ramparts loud with these sounds of confusion and mourning? What means this noise of outcry streaming here from the city, so far away?' Thus he spoke, and in great agitation grasped and drew in his reins, and halted. Then suddenly, his sister, who in the shape of Metiscus had been guiding the chariot and the team, reins in hand, confronted him with this reply: 'Turnus, we had better continue our pursuit of these Trojans, here where we are, and where our success proves what is our right course of action. There are others who can manfully defend our homes. Aeneas drives against the Italians, and awakes a turmoil of battle. Let us also use our strength, and loose death, with no quarter, on the Trojans. You will not leave the field inferior to him in your record of enemies slain or in honour of combat.' Turnus answered her words: 'Sister mine, long since I knew you, even from the first moment when you committed yourself to this warfare by so cunningly wrecking the truce; and equally now is it in vain that you disguise your divinity. But who willed that you should descend from Olympus to endure our heavy toil? Was it simply to allow you to look on your poor brother's death-agony? For what chances have I, now? What fortune can any longer promise me life? Myself have I seen, before my very eyes, Murranus, dearer than all whom I now have left to me, fall like a giant, vanquished by a giant's wound, and heard his own voice calling on my name as he died. The luckless Ufens has fallen, to be spared the sight of my dishonour, and Trojans hold his body and his arms. Am I to endure to see our homes demolished, which is the one shame still wanting to my bitter plight, without refuting the insults of Drances by my sword? Or shall I turn my back on the foe and let this land of Italy see Turnus in retreat? But is it then so very pitiable to die? O you Spirits below, be good to me, since the High Powers above have withdrawn their favour, I shall come down to you a guiltless soul with never a taint of the coward's sin, for never will I bring disgrace on my exalted forefathers.'

Scarcely had he spoken when, flying through the midst of the foe, came Saces, riding a foam-drenched horse, and wounded full in the face by an arrow. He galloped up to Turnus and entreated him, calling him by name: 'Turnus, it is on you at the last that all our lives depend. Take pity on your people. Thunderous in arms, Aeneas threatens to cast down our Italian fortress from its height and give it over to be uprooted from the earth. Even now firebrands fly upwards to our roofs. It is to you that every Latin face, each Latin eye, now turns. Our King, Latinus, can only mutter to himself, in doubt whom he should call his daughter's bridegroom and to whose terms he should incline. And the Queen herself, so devoted to you, has fled in the extremity of her terror from the light of day and found death by her own hand. Messapus and the vigorous Atinas alone uphold our line of battle before the gates. About them on both sides stand enemies densely massed, whose naked swords stand bristling like a crop of iron corn. Yet you spend the time manoeuvring your chariot out here on deserted grassland.'

Turnus was struck silent in bewilderment at this picture of manifold calamity. He stood still and speechless with eyes fixed. In that one heart together there surged a mighty tide of shame, madness and misery blending, love tormented by passion for revenge, and valour which knew itself true. As soon as the shadows dispersed from his mind and the light was restored, he turned distractedly his burning eyes to the battlements, and looked from the chariot towards the great city. And, yes! A whirlwind-crest of flame rolled billowing towards the sky; already, leaping from floor to floor, it had a whole tower in its grip – the very tower which he had himself built to a great height with a firm structure of beams, setting it on wheels and fitting it with drawbridges on high. 'Sister,' he said, 'at this very moment Fate is prevailing over us. Think not to cause delay. Let us follow where God and our own hard fortune call. I am resolved to meet Aeneas hand to hand, and bear whatever bitterness death may hold for me. Sister, never again shall you see me forget my honour. But first, I entreat you, let me do this one mad deed before I die.' Having spoken he leapt from his chariot to the ground, left his sister sorrowing, and darted on through the missiles of the foe. With one violent rush he burst through the battle's centre. He came like a rock crashing headlong down from a mountain-crest, wrenched out perhaps by a wind after floods of rain have washed it free, or else time has crept beneath it with the years and worked it loose; sheer downwards the great crag charges with a mighty impulse, self-willed, bounding upwards off the ground, and rolling before it in its path forests, and herds, and men; so Turnus charged to the city's wall through shattered ranks where the ground was soaked deepest in streams of blood and the air whistled with the shafts of spears. He made a gesture with his hand and as he did so he shouted: 'Rutulians, now desist. Latins, restrain your spears. Whatever fortune holds in store, it is for me. Right requires none but me to atone for the truce on your behalf and find decision by the sword.' All drew apart and left a space in the midst.

Then Troy's chieftain, Aeneas, hearing the name of Turnus called, left the high fortress-walls. Thrusting aside all impediment, he broke off the operations in hand, and rejoiced exultantly, striking a dread thunder from his arms. He towered like Athos or like Eryx, or like old Father Apennine himself, with his rustle of shimmering holm-oak trees, joyously lifting his snow-covered head to the sky. At this terrible moment all strove hard for the best view of the fight. Rutulians, Trojans, and every Italian, some of them standing on the tall battlements, and others who had been battering the foot of the wall with their rams, removed their arms from their shoulders and laid them down. Even Latinus stared in amazement at the sight of these two great heroes, born in distant parts of the world, now met together at last and seeking decision by the sword.

As soon as the two saw a level stretch of ground clear and open for their use, they ran swiftly forward, and, while still far apart, cast their spears. Then they clashed in close combat and their bronze shields clanged as they met. Earth groaned beneath them. They redoubled their sword-strokes and smote again. It was hard to distinguish chance and prowess in the fight's confusion. As when on massive Sila or high on Taburnus two bulls charge brow to brow for bitterest battle, while herdsmen in alarm draw back and all the other cattle stand silent in dread, though the heifers, lowing, wonder which bull is to be emperor of the pastures and obeyed by all the herd; and most violently they exchange blows, each straining to drive his horns home, and bathing heads and shoulders in streams of blood, while all the woodland echoes their bellowing; so did the Trojan Aeneas and the Daunian hero meet shield to shield, and so did their mighty clash resound through heaven. Jupiter himself held up a pair of scales, carefully centring the tongue of the balance; and then he placed in the pans the differing destinies of the two champions, to decide which one should come happy from the ordeal, and whose weight should bring death swinging down.

But then Turnus, thinking that he saw a safe opening, flashed out; he raised his sword with all his strength and reach, drew himself up for the blow, and struck. The Trojans, and the nervous Latins, cried out; all down their lines both armies were tense. But the sword itself proved treacherous and broke, and in mid-stroke it would have left the hot-headed striker defenceless, had not instant flight given him a respite; for as soon as he saw his hand without its sword and holding only a hilt which he did not recognize as his own, Turnus fled, swifter than the easterly wind.

It is said that, when he first mounted his newly harnessed chariot in headlong haste to begin battle, Turnus had left his father's sword behind, and seized instead the weapon of his charioteer Metiscus; and that had sufficed so long as he had only Trojans in straggling rout to fight; but as soon as he faced instead divine weapons forged by Vulcan himself, the mortal blade as it struck flew in splinters like brittle ice, and now its fragments gleamed back at him from the yellow sand. The sight caused a panic in Turnus, and he fled, striving to reach the open plain now at this point and now at that; and this way and that he plaited a course of aimless curves, for all about him the Trojans hemmed him in, closely ringing him round, while on one side a broad marsh and on the other the city's steep battlements blocked his way.

Aeneas was no less vigorous in pursuit, though sometimes his knees, slowed by the arrow-wound, delayed him and denied him speed as he pressed hot-foot on the traces of his terror-stricken foe. He was like a hound at a time when, knowing that he has a stag entrapped by a river or hemmed in by dread of the red-feather scares, he presses on him, running and barking; the stag darts to and fro a thousand ways, in fear of ambush and the river's high bank; but the untiring Umbrian hound hangs on to him, mouth wide open, and at every moment about to grip, snapping his jaws as if he already had him, but biting nothing and eluded still.

And now the shouting rose to a roar. The lakes and river-banks around echoed and echoed it again. The whole sky thundered with the clamour. Turnus fled on, and as he fled he continued to upbraid all the Rutulians, calling to each by name and insistently demanding his own familiar sword. Aeneas in turn threatened destruction and immediate death to any who came near, and he had them trembling, frightened the more by his further threat to tear up their city by the roots; and despite his wound he pressed on. They had now run until they had five times completed a circular course and had five times retraced their steps circling in the opposite direction; for in very truth they strove to gain no trivial prize in sport, but it was for the life-blood of Turnus that they vied.

It happened that once there had stood in that place a bitter-leaved wild olive tree, sacred to Faunus; it was now a tough wooden stump, but had been revered in the past by mariners, who, when rescued from the waves, would often fix on it offerings to their Laurentine God, and suspend on it the garments which they had vowed. But the Trojans had not recognized the sanctity of this stock, and had removed it to enable them to join battle on clear ground. In this wild olive stood the spear of Aeneas, carried there by its own impact, and held fast in the root's stubborn grip. The Dardanid bent over it, working it to wrench the blade out by his strength, and meaning to send the missile in pursuit of an enemy whom he could not reach by his speed alone. Turnus, now mad with fear, prayed: 'Faunus, I beg you, take pity on me. And, soil of my own dear land, if I have always upheld your honour, whereas these men of Aeneas have profaned it by their warring, hold fast the steel of this spear.' So he spoke, and the prayers which he called on the god to answer with his aid were not in vain. For Aeneas, though he stayed wrestling long at the stubborn stock, could not by any effort find the strength to prise open the tough timber's bite. And as he strove and strained at his task, Juturna the Daunian goddess, once more transformed into the shape of Metiscus the charioteer, ran forward and gave back to her brother his own sword. But Venus, resentful that such freedom of action should have been permitted to this daring nymph, now drew near, and tore the spear from the deep root. And so the champions in high heart, their weapons and their spirits restored to them, one relying on his sword and the other fierce with spear held high, stood facing each other again, panting, but ready for combat under the rule of Mars.

Meanwhile, however, the King of All-Powerful Olympus spoke to Juno who was gazing at the fight from a glowing cloud: 'What, my Queen, shall now be the end? What at this final hour is still left for you to do? You yourself know, and you admit that you know, that it is the right of Aeneas to be raised to Heaven as a God of Italy, and that Destiny has allotted to him an exalted place among the stars. What, therefore, is your purpose? Or what do you hope to gain by lingering among the chill clouds? Was it fitting that a deity should be outraged by a wound from a mortal man, or that Turnus should have had restored to him the sword of which he had been deprived – for Juturna could have done nothing without your help –, so that the conquered champion was given a new lease of energy? But now, at the last, desist, and let my entreaty sway you. Let not this deep resentment silently devour you; nor let rancour so often speak back from your sweet lips. This is the moment of final decision. You had sufficient power to drive the Trojans in torment over lands or over waves, and to kindle a horrible war, to bring ugly shame on a home, and infect a wedding with grief. Further effort I forbid.'

So Jupiter spoke; and with submissive countenance the Saturnian goddess replied: 'Jupiter Supreme, yes. It is because this your desire is known to me that against my own will I have forsaken Turnus, and departed from Earth. Else, never had you seen me here alone on my airy seat, enduring all things outrageous or no, but girt with flames I should have been standing close to the battle-front, dragging the Trojans on into bitterest fight. I did indeed persuade Juturna to aid her brother in his helplessness; I confess it; and I approved her daring still bolder deeds to save his life. But I never intended that she should indeed draw the bow and send her arrows flying. I swear it by the inexorable source of Styx' Fountain, that only sanction which High Gods hold in awe. And now for my part I withdraw, and I leave the battle, for I hate it now. But one petition, not covered by any law of Destiny, I address to you, for the sake of Latium and the grandeur of a people who are yours. So be it; let them conclude a peace, sealed with a marriage of fair hope, and bind themselves by a treaty's terms. But command not Latins, in a land which is their own, to change their ancient name, to become Trojans, or to be called Teucrians; command none to speak a different tongue or wear another garb. Let there be Latium still, and, down the centuries, Alban kings; let there be the Roman breed drawing power from Italian manliness. Troy has fallen, and fallen permit her, and her name, to stay.'

Smiling, the Creator of the world and all mankind answered her: 'You are true sister of Jupiter, and Saturn's other child, such strength is in those waves of bitterness which you set rolling in your heart's depth! But now, come, allay this violence of spirit, to which you need never have yielded. That which you wish, I give. You prevail, and I will it; my own wishes I waive. The ancient folk of Italy shall retain the speech of their forefathers and their way of life; and their name shall be as now it is. The Trojans shall only blend, absorbed, in the Italian breed. Custom and ritual of sacrifice I shall impose. I shall make all to be Latins of a single speech. From the union you shall see a race of mixed Italian blood arise, exceeding in religious duty all other men and even gods, nor shall any nation celebrate your rites so devoutly as they.' To this Juno nodded her assent, made happy now, and reversed her will; and in this same moment she left the cloud, and departed from the sky.

This done, the Father pondered within himself a further plan; for he prepared to detach Juturna from her brother in the fight. There are said to be two demons, by name the Dread Ones, born by Dead of Night in one birth, they and Tartarean Megaera with them; and their Mother bound all alike in serpent coils and gave them wings with the speed of the wind. These two demons attend near Jupiter's throne by his royal threshold, in readiness to serve his wrath. They sharpen the edge of fear for suffering humanity whenever the Father of Gods wreaks death's horror or pestilences, or strikes an alarm of war into cities which have sinned. Jupiter now sent swiftly down from heaven's height one of these two demons, with command to meet Juturna, and be to her a sign. She flew, and swooped to earth with tornado-speed, like an arrow shot from a bow-string through cloud by Parthian or Cretan, and sped on its way to dart through the half-light, hissing but never seen, and armed with a cruel poison's venom, a weapon for which there is no healing. So darted the Daughter of Night as she made her way to earth. When she saw the Trojan lines and the army of Turnus, at once she shrank to the form of that small bird which in the night-time perches on tombstones or deserted roof-tops and eerily sings her late song among the shadows. Changed into this shape, the demon noisily passing and passing again flew into the face of Turnus and beat his shield aside with her wings. Every limb of Turnus went limp, numbed by a strange dread. His hair stiffened in horror; his voice was clogged in his throat. And when Juturna recognized afar off the hiss of the demon's wings, with a sister's agony she loosened and tore her hair, and marred her cheeks with her finger-nails and bruised her breast with clenched hands. 'Turnus,' she cried, 'what help can your sister bring you now? Or what is now left for me, after all my enduring? By what craft could I now prolong your days of light? Can I pit myself against a horror such as this? Even now, at this moment, I leave the field of battle. Foul birds, seek not to affright me, for already I fear. Well do I recognize the beating of those wings, with their note of death; clear to me now is the imperious command of strong-hearted Jupiter. Is this the return which he makes for my maidenhood? To what end did he grant me everlasting life, and why did he cancel mortality's law for me? Else could I at least have set a term to this grim anguish and passed through the shadows by my poor brother's side. Is this my immortality? And shall my life know any joy when you are gone, Brother mine? Oh that somewhere earth might yawn to depths deep enough for me, to let me, divine though I am, descend to the ghosts far below!' So much she said. And she covered her head in a grey veil, and sobbing she dived and hid herself and her divine power to aid in the depths of her stream.

Aeneas, on his side, pressed ahead shaking his huge tree of a spear, and spoke from his relentless heart: 'Now, what new delay can you expect? Turnus, there is no drawing back now. It is no longer a trial of speed; this time you must match me, hand to hand, in the stern test of arms. Take whatever shape you will, and call up whatever strength is yours, of courage or guile. Wing your way, if you so choose, to the stars on high, or lock yourself away in hiding within caverns of earth.' With a toss of his head Turnus replied: 'Arrogant foe, it is not your heated words which affright me. I fear only Gods, and especially the hostility of Jove.' No more he said; but, looking about, he saw a stone of great size, ancient and huge, which chanced to lie at hand on the plain where it had been placed to mark a field's boundary, and save the farmlands from disputes of ownership. Scarcely could twelve selected men of such physique as earth produces now have borne on their shoulders that stone; but heroic Turnus snatched it up with his hand in impetuous haste, and was about to hurl it on his foe, raising himself to greater height for the action and running at high speed. But he had no sense of running or moving, or lifting his hands, or giving its impulse to the monstrous stone. His knees gave way. His blood froze hard and chill. And then the stone too which he had cast whirled across empty space, delivered no blow nor even traversed the whole distance. As sometimes in our sleeping, when at night a languor of stillness lies heavy on our eyes, we dream that we strive desperately to run ever onwards, and we fail, and sink down fainting at the very moment of our greatest effort; our tongue is strengthless, the body's powers will give no normal response, and neither words nor even voice will come: so was it with Turnus, for wherever he exerted his valour to find an opening, the weird goddess denied him progress. Through his mind flashed changing images. His eyes rested on the Rutulians, and on the city; he faltered in fear, and started to shudder at the spear-point's imminence. He could find no place of refuge, nor any strength to press home an attack on his foe; nor could he anywhere see his chariot or his sister at the reins.

While Turnus hesitated, Aeneas poised at him the quivering spear which was his doom. He marked with a careful eye the chance which he sought; and then at full range, with all his strength behind the spear, he cast. Never do stones, shot swiftly from siege artillery, so crash; never so loud are the explosions which burst from a bolt of thunder. The spear, charged with its ghastly death, flew as strongly as a black hurricane; it passed through the outer circle of the sevenfold shield and the lower hem of the cuirass; and, whistling, pierced the middle of Turnus' thigh. Stricken, the mighty hero sank to the ground with his knee bent under him. The Rutulians leapt to their feet and groaned; all around the hills echoed, and far and wide the upland forests answered the cries. Turnus, brought low, raised his eyes and an outstretched right hand in humble entreaty, and said: 'This is my own desert; I make no appeal. Enjoy the fortune which falls to you. And if a poor father's sorrow can affect you – and you yourself had in Anchises such a father as mine – I beg of you, take pity on Daunus in his old age, and restore me, or, if you so prefer it, my dead body despoiled of life, to my own people. You have conquered; and Ausonian men have seen me hold forth hands uplifted in defeat. Lavinia is yours to wed. Stretch not your hatred farther.'

Aeneas stood motionless, a fierce figure in his armour; but his eyes were restless, and he checked the fall of his right arm. And now at any moment the plea of Turnus, already working in his mind, might have prevailed on his hesitation, when suddenly, there before him, he saw slung over his shoulder the accursed baldric of Pallas and his belt, inset with the glittering rivets, which he had known of old when they had belonged to his young friend whom Turnus had brought low with a wound, and overcome. This baldric Turnus was wearing now over his own shoulder, and the trophy was fatal to him. Aeneas' eyes drank in the sight of the spoils which revived the memory of his own vengeful bitterness. His fury kindled and, terrible in his rage, he said: 'Are you to be stolen hence out of my grasp, you who wear spoils taken from one whom I loved? It is Pallas, only Pallas, who by this wound which I now deal makes sacrifice of you; he exacts this retribution, you criminal, from your blood.' Saying this and boiling with rage he buried his blade full in Turnus' breast. His limbs relaxed and chilled; and the life fled, moaning, resentful, to the Shades.

LIST OF VARIATIONS FROM THE OXFORD TEXT

FOR those readers who may wish to follow the original Latin along with this translation, there follows a list of all the passages in which the Latin reading adopted by the translator differs from that of the Oxford Classical Text (edited by Hirtzel, 1900). *All* lines bracketed in that text have been translated; where there are strong reasons for supposing that lines are spurious or misplaced, brackets are used in the translation. The first version given below is in each case the Latin rendered in the translation; it is followed by the Oxford Text reading (OCT). Variations in the spelling of proper names, and variations which make little or no difference to the translation, are not listed.

[In twenty-five of the passages cited below, the text of the new OCT (edited by Mynors, 1969) is the same as that followed (against Hirtzel) in the translation. J.D.C.]

Book One

l. 224 *des*piciens mare velivolum (OCT dispiciens)
365 ubi nunc ingentia cern*is* / moenia (OCT cernes)
455 manus int*er* se (OCT intra)
599 omnibus exhaust*os* iam casibus (OCT exhaustis)
636 munera laetitiamque *dei* (OCT dii)
664 nate, meae vires, mea magna potentia solus, / nate, patris summi qui tela . . . (OCT has comma after potentia)

Book Two

101 sed quid ego haec autem nequiquam ingrata revolvo? / quidve moror, si omnis uno ordine . . . (OCT ends question after moror)
294–5 hos cape fatorum comites, his moenia quaere, / magna pererrato statues quae denique ponto. (OCT places the comma after magna)
398 *di*mittimus Orco (OCT demittimus)
445 turris ac *tecta* domorum / culmina (OCT tota)
579 domumque, patr*es* natosque videbit (OCT domumque patris, genitive)
616 insedit *nimbo* effulgens (OCT limbo)

Book Two – contd

739 erravitne via seu lassa resedit? / incertum: nec post ... (OCT has comma, not question-mark, after resedit)

Book Three

111 hinc mater cultrix Cybel*e* (OCT Cybeli) – See note on VII, 543.
127 et crebris legimus freta con*cita* terris. (OCT consita)
372 multo suspen*sus* numine (OCT suspensum)
433 si qua est Heleno prudentia, vati / si qua fides ... (OCT has comma after vati, not before)

Book Four

54 *incensum* animum *in*flammavit amore (OCT impenso, flammavit)
94 memorabile n*o*men (OCT numen)
217 Maeonia mentum mitra ... sub*nixus* (OCT subnexus)
573 'praecipit*es* vigilate, viri, ...' (OCT sociosque fatigat / praecipitis: 'vigilate, viri, ...')
646 conscendit furibunda *rogos* (OCT gradus)
683 date vulnera, lymphis / abluam ... (OCT date, vulnera lymphis ...)

Book Five

80 salve, sancte parens iterum; salvete recepti ... (OCT has comma after parens, and no stop after iterum)
512 *atra* in nubila (OCT alta)
573 Trinacr*ii* (OCT Trinacriis)
786 nec poenam traxe per omnem: / reliquias Troiae, cineres atque ossa ... (OCT traxe per omnem / reliquias Troiae: cineres atque ossa. ...)

Book Six

203 gemin*a* super arbore sidunt (OCT geminae)
427 animae flentes in limine primo, / quos ... (OCT has comma after flentes, not after primo)
561 quis tantus *plangor* ad *auras*? (OCT clangor, auris)
586 flammas Iovis (OCT flammam)
630 Cyclopum *ducta* caminis (OCT educta)

Book Six – contd

724 caelum ac terr*as* (OCT terram)

725 lucentemque globum lunae, *Titanaque et* astra .. (OCT Titaniaque)

852 (hae tibi erunt artes) pac*i*que imponere morem (OCT pacisque)

Book Seven

4 ossaque nomen . . . sign*ant* (OCT signat)

412 magnum *tenet* Ardea nomen (OCT manet)

543 et caeli convexa per auras (OCT reading, obelized). This reading is retained; for a discussion, see *The Classical Quarterly*, Vol. 34 (1940), page 129; this also concerns Book III, line 111.

695–6 hi Fescenninas *arces*, A*e*quosque Faliscos, / hi Soractis habent *acies* . . . (OCT acies . . . arces . . .)

Book Eight

90 ergo iter inceptum celerant rumore secundo; / labitur . . . (OCT inceptum celerant. rumore secundo / labitur . . .)

205 at *furiis* Caci mens effera . . . (OCT furis)

533 . . . quem casum portenta ferant: ego poscor Olympo. (OCT ego poscor. Olympo / hoc signum cecinit . . .)

Book Nine

11 Lydorumque manum collectos armat agrestis. (OCT manum, collectos)

66 ossibus ardet, / qua temptet (OCT has full stop after ardet, and a question-mark later)

348 . . . et multa morte recepit. / purpur*eam* vomit ille animam . . . (OCT . . et multa morte recepit / purpureum: vomit ille animam. . .)

391–2 '. . . quave sequar, rursus perplexum iter omne revolvens / fallacis silvae?' simul et vestigia retro . . . (OCT . . . quave sequar?' rursus perplexum iter . . .)

412 *ad*versi (OCT aversi)

429 '. . . sidera testor; / tantum infelicem nimium dilexit amicum.' (OCT . . . sidera testor'; / – tantum infelicem. . . .)

810 discussaeque iubae capiti, nec sufficit umbo . . . (OCT iubae, capiti nec sufficit umbo)

Book Ten

24 inundant sanguine foss*ae* (OCT fossas)
49 et qu*am*cumque viam dederit . . . (OCT quacumque)
237 *horrentis* Marte Latinos (OCT ardentis)
280 in manibus Mars ipse *viris*. (OCT ipse, viri.)
291 qua vada non *spirant* (OCT sperat)

316–17 et tibi, Phoebe, sacrum, casus evadere ferri / *quod* licuit parvo. (OCT sacrum: casus evadere ferri / quo licuit parvo?)
660 ff. The lines are translated in the following order:
(661) illum autem Aeneas absentem in proelia poscit,
(662) obvia multa virum demittit corpora morti,
(665) cum Turnum medio interea fert aequore turbo.
(663) tum levis haud ultra latebras iam quaerit imago,
(664) sed sublime volans nubi se inmiscuit atrae.
678 saevisque vadis inmittite *Sy*rtis (OCT syrtis)
850 nunc misero mihi demum / ex*il*ium infelix . . . (OCT exitium)

Book Eleven

152 promissa parenti, / cautius . . . (OCT has a full stop after parenti)
613 primique ruinam / dant sonitu ingen*ti* (OCT ingentem)
737 indixit tibia Bacchi, / exspectate (OCT Bacchi. exspectate . . .)
892 (monstrat amor verus patriae) ut videre Camillam . . . (OCT ends brackets after Camillam)

Book Twelve

221 *pubentes*que genae (OCT tabentesque)
423 secuta manum, *nullo* cogente, sagitta (OCT nulla)
916 *telum*que instare tremescit (OCT letumque)

GLOSSARY OF NAMES

THERE are nearly nine hundred names in the *Aeneid*, most of them the names of human beings or of divinities. Some need no explanation beyond what Virgil himself says, others are place-names marked on one of the maps and needing no further comment, and of the rest rather less than half will be found in this Glossary.

The information given here is only the bare minimum. More can be found in many easily accessible books, such as classical dictionaries of Greek and Roman names, histories of Greece and Rome, and some other Penguin books such as Robert Graves' *The Greek Myths*, and of course the other translations, especially the translations of Homer, Sophocles, Lucretius, and Ovid.

ACESTES, a chieftain of Trojan descent, settled in Sicily before Aeneas arrived.

ACHAEANS, Homer's name for the Greeks in general.

ACHERON, a river in Hades; the name means 'River of Grief'.

ACHILLES, a Greek warrior, principal character in the *Iliad*.

ACRISIUS, very ancient mythical king of Argos, in South Greece.

ACTIUM, a promontory on the north-west coast of Greece where Augustus (at that time called Octavius) defeated Antony and Cleopatra in a sea-battle, 31 B.C.

ADRASTUS, a mythical king of Argos; his pallor was due to the sight of his two sons-in-law dead on the battlefields at Thebes.

AEACID, any descendant of Aeacus, ancestor of Achilles and the kings of Macedon.

AEAEA, island home of Circe in the *Odyssey*.

AEGAEON, mythical giant who made war on the Gods.

AENEAS, son of Venus and Anchises, member of the Trojan royal family; took a fairly prominent part in the Trojan war, and became leader of the survivors after the sack of Troy; the principal character in this book.

AETOLIA, original home of Diomede in north-west Greece.

AGAMEMNON, brother of Menelaus and commander-in-chief of the Greek forces at Troy.

AGATHYRSANS, a tribe in Thrace, to the north of Greece.

AGENOR, ancient king of Tyre.

AGRIPPA, admiral under Augustus, in command at Actium.

AGYLLA, another, older, name for Caere, an Etruscan town about 20 miles north-west of Rome.

AJAX, a Greek warrior; this is *not*, however, the one prominent in the *Iliad*, who committed suicide before the sack of Troy; this one offended

Minerva during the sack by doing violence to Cassandra, and was punished with shipwreck and death on the way home.

ALBA LONGA, the Latin city founded by Ascanius on the Alban hills.

ALCIDES, another name for Hercules, grandson of Alceus.

ALLIA, tributary of the Tiber, scene of a disastrous Roman defeat in 390 B.C.

ALOEUS, mythical giant, whose giant sons, Otus and Ephialtes, made war on the Gods.

ALPHEUS, river in south-west Greece, flowing past Olympia.

AMATHUS, a city in Cyprus where Venus was worshipped.

AMAZONS, mythical women-warriors of Thrace and Asia Minor.

AMMON, the Egyptian god Amoun, identified with Jupiter.

ANCHISES, a member of the Trojan royal family, rewarded for his piety by union with Venus, by whom he became the father of Aeneas.

ANCUS, the fourth king of Rome.

ANDROGEOS, the name of two men (a), in Book 2, a Greek warrior, and (b), in Book 6, son of Minos the king of Crete, supposed to have been killed by the Athenians.

ANDROMACHE, wife of Hector, principal Trojan warrior in the *Iliad*.

ANTENOR, a Trojan prince, said to have escaped to Italy before Aeneas came.

ANTONY, 'Mark Antony', the rival of Augustus, defeated by him at Actium.

ANUBIS, an Egyptian god in the form of a dog.

APOLLO (also called PHOEBUS, as in Greek), son of Jupiter and Latona, a god concerned with prophecy, medicine, and archery.

ARAXES, a river in Armenia, flowing into the Caspian Sea.

ARCADIA, a mountainous district in south Greece.

ARCTURUS, a bright star in the constellation Boötes near the Pole Star.

ARDEA, a city south of Rome on the west coast of Italy, capital city of the Rutulians, the modern Terracina.

ARETHUSA, a river or river-goddess of south Greece, believed to have flowed, or travelled, under the sea to Sicily, pursued by the river or river-god Alpheus.

ARGILETUM, a crowded quarter of Rome near the Forum; the name was supposed to mean 'the death of Argus'.

ARGOS, city in the north of south Greece, believed by some to have been the home and capital city of Agamemnon, instead of Mycenae.

ARGUS, (a), in Book 7, a keen-sighted guardian set to watch over Io, and killed by Mercury, (b) in Book 8, the mysterious 'stranger' killed at Argiletum.

ARGYRIPA, another name for Arpi, the city founded by Diomede in Apulia in Italy.

ARIADNE, daughter of Minos, king of Crete; she helped Theseus to escape from the Labyrinth.

ARICIA, a town south of Alba Longa where Diana was worshipped.

ARISBA, a city not far from Troy.

ARPI, the city founded after the Trojan war by Diomede on the east coast of south Italy in Apulia near the modern Foggia.

ASCANIUS, also called Iulus, young son of Aeneas and Creusa.

ASIA, in Virgil's time this means only Asia Minor, or a region on the west coast of Asia Minor.

ASTYANAX, baby son of Hector and Andromache, killed by the Greeks when Troy fell.

ATHOS, easternmost of three promontories near the modern Salonika.

ATLAS, a mountain in north-west Africa, sometimes imagined as a giant holding earth and sky apart.

ATREUS, king of Mycenae, father of Agamemnon and Menelaus.

AUFIDUS, a river in south-east Italy, flowing into the Adriatic.

AUGUSTUS, the adopted son of Julius Caesar; the founder of the Roman imperial system and first Emperor, reigning from 27 B.C. to A.D. 14. One of his prominent ministers was Maecenas, Virgil's patron.

AULIS, the port at which the Greek forces mustered to sail for Troy.

AURORA, the goddess of dawn, or (often) the dawn itself.

AURUNCAN, the name of some early inhabitants of central Italy.

AUSONIAN, probably another name for Auruncan; Virgil often uses it to mean just 'Italian'.

AVENTINE, one of the seven hills of Rome.

AVERNUS, a lake near Naples, thought to be an entrance to the world of the dead: the modern Lago di Averno.

BACCHUS, the Greek Dionysus, a god of vegetation and wine, worshipped with somewhat wild 'Bacchic' rites by women 'Bacchanals', especially on Mount Cithaeron, near Thebes.

BACTRIA, a country in Asia beyond the Caspian Sea.

BAIAE, a seaside resort near Naples, the modern Baia.

BARCA, a city in north Africa, near Cyrene.

BEBRYCIAN, of or from Bebrycia or Bithynia, in north Asia Minor.

BELLONA, 'War's Goddess', a female counterpart of Mars.

BERECYNTUS, a mountain near Troy sacred to Cybele.

BOREAS, the North Wind, sometimes imagined in human form.

BRIAREUS, another name for Aegaeon, a giant with a hundred hands.

BRUTUS, a Roman aristocrat, supposed to have expelled the last king of Rome, 'Tarquin the Tyrant', in 510 B.C.

BUTHROTUM, a port on the west coast of Greece, near the modern Corfu.

CAENEUS, (a) in Book 6, a mythical character: originally a nymph Caenis who was changed into an invulnerable man by Poseidon (Neptune), and, according to Virgil, back again into a woman; (b), in Book 9, an Italian warrior.

CAERE, an Etruscan city north-west of Rome.

CAIETA, the name of a headland on the west coast of Italy, the modern Gaeta.

CALCHAS, a prophet with the Greek forces at Troy.

CALLIOPE, one of the Muses, goddesses who inspire poets.

CALYDON, a city in north-west Greece, the original home of Diomede; it was punished by Diana, who sent a ferocious boar to ravage the country.

CAMARINA, a city in Sicily. The oracle said 'Do not move Camarina'; in defiance of this, the inhabitants drained a marsh called Camarina, and this enabled their enemies to approach and capture the city.

CAMILLA, a warrior-maiden, Italian version of an Amazon.

CAMILLUS, a Roman general who rescued Rome after its capture by the Gauls in 390 B.C.; he was later instrumental in recovering standards from them.

CAPITOL, the crest of one of the 'seven hills of Rome', where Jupiter's temple eventually stood.

CARIANS, a people of south-west Asia Minor.

CARPATHIAN sea, the Aegean Sea near Rhodes and Crete.

CARTHAGE, a Phoenician colony in North Africa, which fought three bitter wars (the 'Punic' wars) with Rome, from 264 B.C. onwards; the second was organized by Hannibal. Carthage was finally destroyed in 146 B.C.

CASSANDRA, daughter of Priam, loved by Apollo and given the gift of true prophecy by him; but he rendered it useless by making everyone distrust her.

CATILINE, a Roman revolutionary whose plot Cicero suppressed in 63 B.C.

CATO, a conservative Roman statesman, famous as a rigid moralist.

CENTAUR, a mythical creature, half man and half horse.

CERAUNIA, 'Thunderbolt Headland', on the west coast of Greece.

CERES, the Greek Demeter, the 'Earth-Mother', associated with grain crops.

CHALYBEAN, as used by the Chalybes, mythical inventors of iron-working thought to have lived in north Asia Minor.

CHARON, a ferryman who took the dead across the river Styx as in Greek myths; among the Etruscans Charon counted as more generally a death-god.

CHARYBDIS, mythical monster (or whirlpool?) in the Straits of Messina.

CHIMAERA, (a) in Book 5, the name of a ship called after: (b) in Books 6 and 7, a mythical monster, a mixture of lion, goat, and snake.

CIRCE, a sorceress who changed men into animals by magic (see *Odyssey*, Book 10).

CIRCEII, in Homer, Circe lives on an island called Aeaea, but Virgil seems to imagine her living at Circeii (thought to be named after her) on the Italian coast, near the modern Terracina.

CISSEUS, (a) a Trojan warrior; (b) the father of Hecuba, Priam's wife. Before Paris was born, she dreamed that she was giving birth to a firebrand.

CITHAERON, a mountain near Thebes where Bacchus was worshipped.

CLAROS, a town near Colophon in Asia Minor, with an oracle of Apollo.

CLAUDIAN, the name of a distinguished Roman aristocratic family.

CLAUSUS, a Sabine aristocrat, supposed to have migrated to Rome in 514 B.C. and there founded the Claudian family.

CLOELIA, a Roman girl, held as hostage by Porsenna until she boldly escaped and swam back to Rome across the Tiber.

CNOSSOS, the chief city of Crete, home of Minos and the labyrinth.

COCLES, nickname, supposed to mean 'one-eyed', of the famous Horatius, who 'kept the bridge' across the Tiber, while his comrades broke it down.

COCYTUS, the 'River of Wailing', one of the rivers of Hades.

COEUS, one of the Titans, sons of Earth.

CORINTH, a prosperous city near the isthmus in central Greece, captured and destroyed by the Romans under Mummius in 146 B.C.

CORYBANTES, dancing priests who performed wild rites in honour of Cybele in Asia Minor and her counterpart in Crete.

CORYTHUS, a city in Italy (perhaps Cortona, near the modern Arezzo) where Dardanus was said to have lived before migrating to Asia Minor; in other versions, Corythus is the name of Dardanus' father.

COSSUS, a Roman general who captured Fidenae in 428 B.C. and killed the enemy general in single combat, thus winning 'commander's spoils'.

CREUSA, daughter of Priam, first wife of Aeneas and mother of Ascanius.

CUMAE, a city near the modern Pozzuoli, just north of Naples, with an oracle and an entry to the world of the dead. 'Cumaean' means 'at Cumae'.

CUPID (the Greek Eros), the God of Love, imagined as a boy, son of Venus.

CURES, a small Sabine town, the home of Numa, second king of Rome.

CURETES, dancing priests, like the Corybantes; associated in legend with the birth of Jupiter (Zeus), in Crete.

CYBELE, also called the Phrygian Mother; an important goddess of Asia Minor, worshipped with orgiastic rites, particularly near two mountains Berecyntus and Cybelus; her devotees were often eunuchs.

CYCLOPS, a Sicilian giant with one eye, blinded by Ulysses (Odysseus) (see *Odyssey*, Book 9).

CYCNUS (the name means 'swan'), a mythical king of Liguria, who loved Phaethon and was transformed into a swan.

CYLLENE, a mountain in south Greece, birthplace of Mercury.

CYNTHUS, a hill on the island of Delos.

CYPRIAN, a name, or title, of Venus, who had several shrines in Cyprus.

CYTHERA, an island near the south-east coast of Greece where Venus was especially worshipped; hence she is called 'the Cytherean'.

DAEDALUS, an architect who built the Cretan labyrinth and helped Theseus and Ariadne to escape from it. Being forced to leave Crete, he made wings for himself and his son Icarus; he himself reached Cumae and built a temple to Apollo, but Icarus 'crashed' on the way.

DANAANS, a general name for the Greeks.

DANAE, a mythical princess of Argos, said to have been set adrift on the sea in a box with her baby son Perseus; in other versions they drifted ashore on the island of Seriphos, but Virgil makes them come to Ardea on the west coast of Italy.

DARDANUS, mythical founder of Troy and ancestor of the Trojans, said to have migrated there from Italy. The Trojans are therefore called Dardans, Dardanians, or Dardanids.

DAUNUS, father of Turnus; hence 'Daunian' means Rutulian.

DECII, a Roman family; two members were said to have saved their armies by sacrificing their own lives during Italian wars in the fourth century B.C.

DEIPHOBUS, a Trojan prince, son of Priam and married to Helen after the death of Paris; killed by the Greeks, perhaps with her help, when Troy fell.

DELOS, a small island in the Aegean Sea, said to be the birthplace of Apollo, and sacred to him. He is therefore called 'the Delian God'.

DIANA, the Greek Artemis, sister of Apollo. She has 'three forms': in the sky Phoebe (the moon), on earth Diana, a huntress-maiden, and in the underworld Hecate or Trivia ('Goddess of the Three Ways'), concerned with magic rites.

DIDO, also called Elissa, a Phoenician princess who founded and ruled Carthage.

DINDYMA, a mountain in Asia Minor, where Cybele was especially worshipped.

DIOMEDE, a Greek warrior, prominent in the *Iliad*; he wounded Mars (Ares) and Venus (Aphrodite) in battle, and in punishment was exiled from his home in Aetolia; he settled at Arpi, in south-east Italy.

DRUSI, a Roman family; several members were important in politics.

EDONIA, a district in Thrace, north of Greece.

ELIS, a city in south-west Greece.

ELISSA, Dido's other name.

EPIRUS, a district of north-west Greece, roughly the modern Albania.

ERATO, one of the Muses, associated with love-poetry.

EREBOS, a part of the world of the dead, usually a deep chasm.

ERIDANUS, a mythical river, with its source in the underworld; later thought to be the Po or the Rhine.

ERIPHYLE, a mythical heroine who betrayed her husband Amphiaraus and was killed by her own son Alcmaeon.

ERYMANTHUS, a mountain in south Greece, where Hercules killed a boar.

ERYX, (a) a mythical Sicilian hero, son of Venus, and a famous boxer; (b) a mountain in Sicily, near the modern Trapani, named after him, where Venus was especially worshipped; (c) a city near this mountain.

ETRUSCANS, a nation, perhaps from Asia Minor, who settled in north-west Italy (Etruria) roughly between the modern Florence and Naples.

EUBOEA, large island close to the east of north Greece.

EUMENIDES, the 'Kindly Ones', a polite name for the Furies, spirits who avenged bloodshed or 'Spirits of the Curse'.

EUROTAS, a river in south Greece, flowing near Sparta.

EURYSTHEUS, mythical king of Tiryns, a city in the north of south Greece, said to have set Hercules his 'twelve labours'.

EVADNE, a mythical heroine who killed herself in sorrow for the death of her husband Capaneus.

EVANDER, a mythical Greek king from Arcadia who settled on the future site of Rome.

FABII, a Roman family; the most famous member saved the Roman army in the second Punic War (216 B.C.) by skirmishing and avoiding a major battle with Hannibal; hence he was called the Cunctator, 'the inactive'.

FABRICIUS, a Roman general in the war against Pyrrhus of Macedon (282–279 B.C.) noted as being poor but incorruptible.

FAUNUS, an ancient Italian god of woods and wild animals, sometimes regarded as one deity, and sometimes as many 'fauns'.

FUCINE (English spelling), a lake about 50 miles east of Rome.

FURIES, spirits who avenged bloodshed; also called the Eumenides, or 'Spirits of the Curse'.

GAETULIANS, a savage tribe, variously placed in north Africa.

GANYMEDE (semi-English spelling), son of Tros, a young Trojan prince, carried up to heaven by Jupiter to be his cup-bearer.

GARAMANTIANS, a tribe in north Africa.

GARGANUS, a promontory on the east coast of Italy, the modern Gargano.

GAULS, Celtic people who occupied France and north Italy; they came south and captured Rome in 390 B.C., but were driven back and conquered during the next two centuries.

GELA, the name of a river and a Greek city in Sicily, the modern Terranova; the name means 'laughter', but the city had an unhappy history.

GELONIANS, a tribe in south Russia.

GERYON, a mythical giant with three bodies, killed by Hercules.

GETAE, a tribe living near the mouth of the Danube.

GLAUCUS, (a) in Book 5, an 'Old Man of the Sea'; (b) in Book 12, a Trojan warrior; and (c) in Book 6, the dead warrior is the one mentioned in the *Iliad*, Book 6, and elsewhere, or an ancestor of his.

GRACCHUS, the name of two brothers who introduced reforms of the Roman constitution, 133–122 B.C.

GRAVISCAE, a port on the west coast of Italy, north of Rome, probably the port of the Etruscan city Tarquinii; its name means 'heavy', apparently from an unhealthy climate.

GRYNIUM, a city on the west coast of Asia Minor, with an oracle of Apollo.

HARPALYCE, a mythical Thracian princess, warrior and huntress.

HARPY, a mythical monster, a bird with a human head.

HEBRUS, (a) a river in Thrace; (b) a Trojan warrior.

HECATE, a goddess of the underworld, associated with magic; see DIANA.

HECTOR, a son of Priam; the principal Trojan warrior in the *Iliad*.

HELEN ('Helen of Troy'), wife of Menelaus, king of Sparta; her abduction by Paris was the cause of the Trojan War.

HELICON, a mountain in Boeotia, north of Athens; the home of the Muses.

HERCULES (in Greek, Heracles), a mythical hero, persecuted by Juno (Hera) and set to perform twelve labours, most of which involved killing monsters; he was thus often regarded as the saviour of humanity.

HERMIONE, a Greek princess, daughter of Menelaus and Helen.

HERMUS, a river in Asia Minor.

HERNICAN, in the region of the Hernici, in central Italy south-east of Rome.

HESIONE, daughter of Laomedon, an early king of Troy; saved from a sea-monster by Hercules.

HESPERIA, 'Land of the Evening' (that is, the west); a Greek name for Italy and Sicily.

HESPERIDES, 'Daughters of the West' – mythical maidens who lived in a garden 'far away to the west', containing a tree which bore golden fruit.

HIPPOLYTA, queen of the Amazons, wife of Theseus.

HIPPOLYTUS, a mythical hero, son of Theseus and Hippolyta; the victim of false accusations by his stepmother Phaedra. Neptune (Poseidon) was under an obligation to his son Theseus, and caused Hippolytus' death when asked to do so by Theseus.

HOMOLE, a mountain in Thessaly (north Greece).

HYADS, 'Rain-Stars', a part of the constellation Taurus; they rise at midnight during rainy seasons.

HYDASPES, a river in India, tributary of the Indus; perhaps the modern Jhelum, near Rawalpindi.

HYDRA, 'Water-snake', a mythical monster killed by Hercules.

HYRCANIAN, of Hyrcania, a region north-east of modern Persia.

ICARUS, son of Daedalus.

IDA, the name of several mountains, notably one near Troy and another in Crete.

IDALIUM, a city in Cyprus, where Venus was especially worshipped.

IDOMENEUS, leader of the Greeks from Crete in the Trojan War.

ILIA, a priestess of Vesta at Rome, also called Rhea Silvia; the mother of Romulus and Remus, founders of Rome.

ILIONEUS, an old and respected Trojan, travelling with Aeneas.

ILIUM, another name for Troy.

ILUS, (a) an early name of Ascanius later changed to Iulus; (b) son of Tros and father of Laomedon; (c) a Trojan warrior with Aeneas.

INACHUS, a very ancient mythical king of Argos, father of Io.

IO, a princess of Argos, loved by Jupiter; Juno changed her into a cow, and spitefully tormented her.

ISMARA, a mountain (and also a city) in Thrace.

ITHACA, island home of Ulysses (Odysseus) on the west coast of Greece.

IULUS, another name for Ascanius; intended to indicate the descent of the Julian family, including Augustus, from Aeneas.

IXION, a mythical hero, guilty of assaulting Juno (Hera).

JANICULUM, a hill just across the Tiber from Rome, to the north-west.

JANUS, a god with two faces, associated with doorways and beginnings.

JOVE, another name for Jupiter.

JULIUS, the family name of Julius Caesar and his adopted son Augustus.

JUNO, the Greek Hera, wife of Jupiter; hostile towards the Trojans, particularly because Paris judged her inferior to Venus in beauty.

JUPITER, the Greek Zeus; father and ruler of the gods; also called Jove.

JUTURNA, an Italian goddess of springs and streams; sister of Turnus.

KID-STARS, part of the constellation Auriga, associated with the rainy season.

LAERTES, father of Ulysses (Odysseus).

LAODAMIA, the young bride of Protesilaus, the first Greek to land at Troy; she killed herself on hearing of his death.

LAOMEDON, former king of Troy, father of Priam; noted for his dishonesty in withholding rewards promised to Apollo, Neptune, and Hercules for services rendered.

LAPITHS or LAPITHAE, a tribe in north Greece, noted for a mythical battle with the Centaurs.

LARISSA, a city in Thessaly, near the modern Volos; the home of Achilles, who is therefore called Larissaean.

LATIUM, coastal district and nearer mountain-ranges of Italy, south of Rome; the people are called Latins, and their king Latinus.

LATONA, a goddess, mother of Apollo and Diana.

LAURENTINE, the name of an ancient people living on the coast of Latium; their city Laurentum has been supposed identical with Lavinium.

LAVINIA, young daughter of king Latinus; betrothed to Turnus, but later married to Aeneas.

LAVINIAN, in the region of Lavinium, the city founded by Aeneas near the coast of Latium, between the modern Ostia and Anzio.

LEDA, the wife of Tyndareus, king of Sparta; mother of Helen.

LELEGEIANS, an ancient people of Asia Minor.

LEMNOS, an island in the Aegean Sea where Vulcan (Hephaestus) was especially worshipped.

LETHE, 'forgetfulness', a river in the underworld; all who drank of its waters lost their memory.

LEUCATE, a promontory on an island, Leucas, near Ithaca, and west of Greece.

LIBURNIAN, from a district north of the Adriatic, famous for its fast ships.

LIGURIAN, from Liguria, a district in the extreme north-west of Italy, near the modern Genoa.

LIPARA, a small volcanic island in a group north-east of Sicily near Stromboli.

LOCRIANS, a people from north Greece, who migrated to the 'toe' of Italy and to the coast of north Africa.

LUPERCI, young men dressed only in wolf-skins, who performed a ceremony of 'beating the bounds', perhaps in honour of Faunus; the ceremony (called the Lupercalia) also included fertility-magic.

LYCAEAN, native of Mt Lycaeus in Arcadia.

LYCIA, a district in south-west Asia Minor; the natives are Lycians.

LYDIA, a district in western Asia Minor.

LYRNESSUS, a city near Troy, sacked by Achilles.

MAEOTIS, the Sea of Azov, near the Crimea.

MAIA, a goddess, mother of Mercury.

MALEA, a promontory at the south-east extremity of Greece; just east of the modern Cape Matapan.

MANLIUS, a Roman officer, on guard on the citadel of Rome during the Gallic invasion in 390 B.C. Warned by the sacred geese, he saved the position.

MARCELLUS, (a) at the end of Book 6, a Roman general who defeated the Gauls in north Italy in 222 B.C. and won the 'commander's spoils' by killing their leader in single combat; (b) also at the end of Book 6, immediately after, a young nephew of Augustus who was expected to succeed him as emperor, but died in 23 B.C. when only twenty years old.

MARS, the Greek Ares, god of war.

MASSYLIAN, a member of a tribe in north Africa.

MEGARA, a port on the east coast of Sicily.

MELAMPUS, an ancient mythical poet and seer.

MELIBOEA, a town in Thessaly, north of the modern Volos.

MEMNON, an Aethiopian hero, son of the Dawn (Aurora), who helped the Trojans against the Greeks; he had divinely-made armour.

MENELAUS, king of Sparta, brother of Agamemnon and husband of Helen.

MERCURY, the Greek Hermes, messenger of the Gods, and 'escort' of the dead.

METTUS, Latin general of Alba Longa who broke his word during a war with Rome.

MINCIUS, a river in north Italy, near Mantua and Virgil's birthplace.

MINERVA, a Roman goddess associated mainly with the home and domestic arts such as weaving; she is regularly identified with the Greek Pallas Athena, goddess of the home and the city and a warrior-maiden, daughter of Zeus (Jupiter) and patroness of Odysseus.

MINIO, a river in Etruria, north of Rome.

MINOS, a mythical king of Crete, for whom Daedalus built the labyrinth; after his death he became, like Rhadamanthus, a judge of the dead.

MINOTAUR, a mythical monster, usually a man with a bull's head; the offspring of Pasiphae; lived in the Labyrinth and devoured prisoners sent there.

MISENUS, a follower of Aeneas; supposed to have given his name to a headland, the modern Capo Miseno between Naples and Ischia.

MONOECUS, 'lone dweller'; Hercules was supposed to have lived for a time in solitude at a place near the modern Monaco where Monte Carlo is.

MORINI, a Gallic tribe from the region of modern Belgium.

MUSAEUS, an ancient mythical poet, 'successor' to the first poet, Orpheus.

MYCENAE, an ancient city south of the isthmus of Corinth; in Homer, the capital city of Agamemnon.

MYRMIDONS, a Greek tribe from Thessaly furnishing Achilles' contingent at Troy.

NEMEA, a city near the isthmus in central Greece, where Hercules killed a monstrous lion.

NEOPTOLEMUS, also called Pyrrhus, Achilles' son.

NEPTUNE, the Greek Poseidon, the most important of the sea-gods.

NEREUS, an ancient sea-god; his daughters (Nereids) are sea-nymphs.

NUMA, (a) the second king of Rome, devoted to religion and peace; (b) in Book 9 an Italian warrior, killed during the night raid; (c) another Italian warrior (unless Virgil has forgotten) appears in Book x.

NUMICUS, a small but very sacred river in Latium between Lavinium and Ardea.

NUMIDIAN, member of a nomadic tribe in north Africa, brilliant horsemen, who rode their horses without bridles.

NUMITOR, (a) grandfather of Romulus and Remus; (b) an Italian warrior.

NYSA, a mountain somewhere in Asia (or perhaps mythical); the birthplace of Bacchus (Dionysus).

OCEAN (*the* Ocean), imagined as a river, flowing right round the world.

OECHALIA, a city on Euboea (off the east coast of Greece) sacked by Hercules.

OENOTRIA, ancient name for a region of Italy; the inhabitants are 'Oenotrians'.

OLYMPUS, a high mountain in north-east Greece (towards the modern Salonika) where, according to Homer, Jupiter and most of the gods live; often, however, the name means the sky.

ORCUS, another name for Pluto, ruler of the dead; it is also used to mean the *land* of the dead.

ORESTES, son of Agamemnon and Clytaemnestra, who murdered her husband on his return from Troy; Orestes, at the command of Apollo, avenged this murder by killing his mother, and was tormented by the Furies for doing so.

ORICUM, a city in west Greece, opposite the 'heel' of Italy.

ORION, a mythical giant, noted as a huntsman; he was changed by Diana into a constellation which rises with the sun about the autumnal equinox.

ORITHYIA, a mythical heroine, loved by Boreas (the North Wind) and herself changed into a wind.

ORPHEUS, mythical poet, believed the earliest.

ORTYGIA, 'quails' home', the name for (a) Delos, (b) part of Syracuse in Sicily.

OSCANS, a tribe who lived in very early times in Campania, a district south of Latium.

OTHRYS, the name of (a), in Book 2, the father of Panthus; (b), in Book 7, a mountain in Thessaly.

PACHYNUS, a headland on the south coast of Sicily, towards Malta.

PACTOLUS, a river of Asia Minor which carried down deposits of gold dust.

PADUA, a city near Venice in north Italy.

PALAMEDES, a Greek hero, executed on a false charge of treason at the suggestion of Ulysses during the siege of Troy.

PALATINE, one of the 'seven hills of Rome', site of Augustus' 'palace'.

PALICUS, an obscure god or mythical hero worshipped in Sicily.

PALINURUS ('Wind astern'), the helmsman of Aeneas, supposed to have given his name to a promontory on the west coast of Italy, some distance south of Salerno.

PALLANTEUM, (a) a city in Arcadia, named after Pallas; (b) the name given to the settlement of Evander on the Palatine Hill at the future site of Rome.

PALLAS, (a) another name for Minerva; (b) an ancestor of Evander; (c) the young son of Evander, who goes to fight for Aeneas.

PAN, a Greek god of the wild country and of herds, partly a goat-god, who inspired 'panic' in the country folk; his 'home' is in Arcadia.

PANDARUS, (a) in Book 9, a Trojan warrior serving with Aeneas; (b) in Book 11, a previous Trojan warrior who violated a truce by shooting at the Greeks; see *Iliad*, Book 4.

PAPHOS, a city in Cyprus where Venus was especially worshipped.

PARIS, son of Priam and brother of Hector; he abducted Helen from Sparta.

PARTHENOPAEUS, a mythical hero, one of the 'Seven against Thebes'.

PARTHIANS, a tribe of famous archers from the Middle East who severely defeated the Romans at Carrhae, 53 B.C. Augustus recovered the lost standards by treaty in 19 B.C.

PASIPHAE, wife of Minos (king of Crete) and mother of the Minotaur.

PELASGIANS, very ancient people in Greece, Italy and elsewhere, sometimes regarded as aboriginals.

PELEUS, a mythical Greek hero, father of Achilles.

PELOPS, founder of the ancient dynasty of Mycenae and ancestor of Agamemnon and Menelaus; he gave his name to the Peloponnese ('Pelops' island').

PELORUS, a promontory on the north-east coast of Sicily.

PENTHESILEA, mythical queen of the Amazons.

PENTHEUS, a mythical king of Thebes, driven mad by Bacchus.

PHAEACIA, a mythical land (perhaps Corfu); see *Odyssey*, Books 6–8.

PHAEDRA, second wife of Theseus, and stepmother of Hippolytus; she fell in love with him, and later occasioned his death.

PHAETHON ('shining'), mythical hero who was allowed to drive the chariot of his father the sun, but lost control of it, and was killed with a thunderbolt by Jupiter.

PHENEOS, a city of Arcadia in south Greece.

PHILOCTETES, a Greek hero who owned the bow once used by Hercules, and with it helped the Greeks to capture Troy.

PHLEGYAS, a mythical king of the Lapiths, said to have burnt Apollo's temple at Delphi, and to have been punished in the underworld by being made to sit under a rock which threatened to fall at any moment.

PHOEBE, see DIANA; in Book 4 Phoebe is the moon.

PHOEBUS, see APOLLO; sometimes confused with Helios, the Sun.

PHORCUS, a sea-god.

PHRYGIA, a district in central and northern Asia Minor; 'Phrygian' often means 'Trojan', an impolite name, as Phrygians came to be considered effeminate. The 'Phrygian Mother' is Cybele.

PHTHIA, older name for Thessaly in north Greece, home of Achilles.

PICUS ('woodpecker'), an ancient Italian god, imagined in the form of a woodpecker.

PILUMNUS ('spearman'), ancient Italian god.

PIRITHOUS, companion of Theseus in his attempt to abduct Proserpine from the underworld.

PISA, (a) a city in south Greece; (b) a city in north-west Italy.

PLEMMYRIUM ('flood'), a promontory on the east coast of Sicily near Syracuse.

PLUTO, also called Orcus, and in Greek Hades, king of the dead, brother of Jupiter.

POLYBOETES ('owning many cattle'), perhaps to be identified with Polyphetes, a Trojan warrior mentioned in the *Iliad*, Book 13. The spelling varies.

POLYPHEMUS, the Cyclops blinded by Ulysses; see *Odyssey*, Book 9.

PORSENNA ('Lars Porsena of Clusium'), an Etruscan king who marched against Rome in an attempt to restore King Tarquin, banished in 510 B.C.

PORTUNUS, a sea-god, associated with harbours.

PRIAM, the last king of Troy, husband of Hecuba and father of Hector, Paris, Cassandra, Helenus, Deiphobus, and many others.

PRISTIS, 'whale' or 'shark', the name of a ship.

PROCRIS, a mythical heroine who doubted the fidelity of her husband Cephalus and was accidentally killed by him.

PROSERPINE, semi-English spelling for Proserpina, the Greek Persephone, daughter of Ceres (Demeter), carried off by Pluto to be Queen of the dead.

PROTEUS, a prophetic sea-god, liable to change into various shapes; the 'Pillars of Proteus' are imagined near Egypt.

PYRRHUS, another name for Neoptolemus, son of Achilles.

QUIRINUS, a very ancient Italian god, later thought to be Romulus deified, and an important Roman national deity. Anything associated with him is 'Quirine' or 'Quirinal', and the title 'Quirites', often given to the Romans, seems to mean either 'Men of Quirinus' or possibly 'Spearmen' (if from 'quirus' a spear).

REMUS, brother of Romulus and co-founder of Rome; Romulus was given more favourable signs of augury and inauguration, and started to build on the Palatine; Remus derisively jumped over the wall, and Romulus, in a fit of jealousy, killed him.

RHADAMANTHUS, a mythical king of Cnossos in Crete; after his death he was appointed to be judge of the dead.

RHEA, (a) a very ancient Greek goddess, wife of Saturn and mother of Jupiter, Juno, Neptune, and others; (b) a Roman priestess of Vesta also called Ilia or Rhea Silvia, who became the mother of Romulus and Remus.

RHESUS, a Thracian king who came to the aid of the Trojans during the siege; Ulysses and Diomede raided his camp and killed him; see *Iliad*, Book 10.

RHOETEUM, a port near Troy; 'Rhoetean' often means just 'Trojan'.

ROMULUS, son of Mars and Ilia; founded Rome in 753 B.C.

RUTULIAN, belonging to the Rutuli, the nation of Turnus, living south of Rome near the modern Anzio.

SABELLIANS, an Italian tribe, the same as, or including, the Sabines, who lived in a district to the east of Rome; their influence on early Roman history and religion was considerable.

SABINUS, a mythical ancient king of the Sabines.

SALAMIS, (a) an island near Athens; (b) a city in Cyprus named after it, to which Teucer, half-brother of Ajax, migrated after the Trojan War.

SALII ('jumpers'), priests who danced at Rome in honour of Mars, carrying sacred shields.

SAME, an island near Ithaca.

SAMOS, an island off the west coast of Asia Minor.

SAMOTHRACE, an island to the west of Troy, near the Dardanelles.

SARPEDON, a Lycian prince, son of Jupiter and ally of Priam; killed at Troy; see *Iliad*, Book xvi.

SATURN, the Greek Kronos, father of Jupiter and Juno; supposed to have been driven out of Olympus by Jupiter, after which he came to Italy and ruled there during a mythical 'Golden Age'.

SCAEAN, 'left-hand', the name of a gate in the walls of Troy.

SCIPIO, a family name of the Cornelii, several of whom were prominent generals during the Punic Wars; one especially (Scipio Africanus) commanded at the battle of Zama (202 B.C.) at which the Carthaginians were decisively defeated.

SCYLLA, (a) in Book 3, a sea monster, living in a cave in the Straits of Messina; she devoured the crews of passing ships, and called after her (b) in Book 5, the name of a ship.

SCYROS, an island in the Aegean where Achilles' contingent mustered on the way to Troy; the birthplace of Neoptolemus.

SCYTHIANS, a tribe of horsemen in south Russia.

SELINUS ('parsley'), a city in west Sicily.

SERRANUS, (a) in Book 6, the name of Regulus, a Roman who was called from his farm to command in the first Punic War, and was captured by the enemy in Africa in 255 B.C.; (b) in Book 9, an Italian warrior opposing Aeneas.

SIBYL, a priestess and clairvoyant at Cumae, near Naples; other 'Sibyls' are mentioned elsewhere, mainly on the fringe of the Greek world.

SICANIANS, a tribe of warriors whose history is obscure; they lived in central Italy before moving, eventually, to Sicily, but may have come from north Africa a long time before. The 'Sicanian Bay' is the east coast of Sicily.

SIDON, a Phoenician city near Tyre.

SIGEUM, a port near Troy; the 'Straits of Sigeum' are the Dardanelles.

SILA, a mountain-chain in the 'toe' of Italy.

SILVANUS, an ancient Italian god of uncultivated land.

SIMOIS, a river on the plain of Troy.

SIRENS, maidens who sang beautifully, and lured sailors onto a reef; see *Odyssey*, Book 12.

SIRIUS, the Dog-Star, which rises with the sun in late summer at a dry and unhealthy season.

SPARTA, a city inland in south Greece, home of Menelaus and Helen.

STHENELUS, (a) a Greek warrior mentioned in the *Iliad*; (b) a Trojan warrior with Aeneas.

STROPHADES, two small islands off the south-west coast of Greece.

STRYMON, a river in Thrace, the home of cranes.

STYX, 'Hate', one of the rivers of the underworld, imagined as flowing several times around the perimeter; the adjective STYGIAN means 'deathly' or 'of the underworld'.

SYMAETHUS, a river and town in east Sicily.

SYRTES, the name of two bays on the north coast of Africa, one between modern Tripoli and Benghazi, the other between Tripoli and Tunis; noted for quicksands and the absence of harbours.

TABURNUS, mountainous region in south Italy, east of modern Caserta.

TARCHON, the leader of the Etruscan forces allied to Aeneas; the name is perhaps connected with Tarquin.

TARENTUM, a port on the 'instep' of Italy, the modern Taranto.

TARPEIA, (a) in Book 8, a Roman girl, supposed to have betrayed Rome to the Sabines; (b) in Book 11, a companion of Camilla.

TARQUIN, the name of two Etruscan kings of Rome, the second of whom, 'Tarquin the Tyrant', was expelled from Rome in a rising led by Brutus in 510 B.C.

TARTARUS, the ancient Hell, in the deepest part of the underworld.

TATIUS, a king of the Sabines who fought against the early Romans, but later made peace, and ruled jointly with Romulus.

TENEDOS, a small island near Troy, to the south-west.

TEREUS, a mythical king of Thrace, who violated Philomela, the sister of his wife Procne; in revenge for this Procne killed their son Itys, and all three were later changed into birds.

TEUCER, (a) frequently an ancestor of the kings of Troy; hence the Trojans are often called 'Teucrians'; (b) in Book 1, half-brother of the greater Ajax from Salamis, who migrated to Cyprus and was known to Dido, according to Virgil.

THALIA, one of the Muses, goddesses of song and story.

THEBES, a city in north Greece, the home of Pentheus.

THERMODON, a small river in east Asia Minor.

THERSILOCHUS, (a) in Book 6, a Trojan warrior mentioned in the *Iliad*; (b) a warrior with Aeneas.

THESEUS, a mythical king of Athens, who killed the Minotaur and carried off Ariadne from Crete; later he attempted with Pirithous to carry off Proserpine from the underworld.

THETIS, a sea-goddess, mother of Achilles.

THOAS, (a) in Book 2, a Greek warrior at Troy; (b) in Book 9, an Italian warrior opposing Aeneas.

THRACE, a country to the north-east of Greece, including much of the coastline between the modern Salonika and the Dardanelles.

TIBER or TIBERIS, a river in central Italy, flowing south-west; Rome was built on the south bank, about twelve miles from the mouth, and about four centuries after the events of the *Aeneid*; the first Trojan settlement was at the mouth on the south bank on the site of the later Ostia. The river is sometimes imagined as a god, Tiberinus. Other forms of its name are Thybris and Thymbris.

TIBUR, a small town about 15 miles north-east of Rome, the modern Tivoli; the people are called 'Tiburtine'.

TIMAVUS, a river north of the Po in north-west Italy.

TIRYNTHIAN, native of Tiryns, a city near Argos in south Greece; the home of Hercules.

TISIPHONE, 'Avenger of Blood', a female fiend of the underworld.

TITANS, a family of mythical giants, a generation older than Jupiter and Juno; they included Hyperion and Phoebe, later identified with the sun and moon, hence the sun is called 'Titanic'.

TITHONUS, a mythical human hero married to Aurora (Dawn) and granted immortal life but not immortal youth.

TITYOS, a mythical giant who assaulted Latona, mother of Apollo and Diana; he was punished for this in the underworld.

TMARUS, a mountain in Epirus; Tmarian, native of the region.

TORQUATUS, a Roman general in the Samnite Wars, famous as a stern disciplinarian.

TRITON, a sea-god, or 'merman', who played music on a horn made from a sea-shell; Pallas Athena is sometimes called 'Tritonian' owing to an obscure connexion with the sea, or perhaps Lake Tritonis on the north coast of Africa.

TRIVIA, 'Goddess of the Three Ways', a title of Hecate; see DIANA.

TROILUS, a young son of Priam, killed by Achilles. The story of his romance with Cressida is not found until the Middle Ages.

TROY, a very ancient city in Asia Minor, near the Dardanelles, the scene of the *Iliad*. The traditional date for its sack is about 1200 B.C. 'Homer's Troy' is thought by the archaeologists to be the seventh of many cities built at various dates on this site.

TULLUS, the third king of Rome, who conquered Alba Longa and put Mettus to death.

TURNUS, young king of the Rutulians, an Italian people with a capital at Ardea, south of Rome, not far from the modern Anzio.

TYDEUS, father of Diomede.

TYNDAREUS, father, or supposed father, of Helen, who is thus called 'Tyndarid'.

TYPHOEUS, a mythical fire-breathing giant, thought to be imprisoned under a volcano.

UCALEGON ('Not caring'), a Trojan warrior mentioned in the *Iliad*.

UFENS, (a) in Book 7, a river in west Italy; (b) in Book 12, an Italian warrior.

ULYSSES, the Latin form of Odysseus, a Greek warrior at Troy, and the central figure of the *Odyssey*. He is the 'Man from Ithaca'.

UMBRIAN, native of north central Italy; the name is used for a breed of dog used for hunting, just as we talk of a 'Labrador' or 'Skye terrier'.

VELIA, seaside resort on the west coast of Italy, about 50 miles south of Salerno.

VELINE (English spelling), a lake and river in central Italy, about 40 miles north-east of Rome, near modern Riete.

VENUS, the Greek Aphrodite, Goddess of Love and mother of Aeneas; she had shrines at many places in Cyprus and at Eryx in Sicily; such place-names helped to shape the legends about Aeneas and fix his route.

VESTA, a Roman goddess of great antiquity, associated with the hearth and deeply venerated by the Romans.

VIRBIUS, a mythical Italian hero, supposed to be Hippolytus come to life again; it is also, apparently, the name of his son.

VOLSCIANS, a tribe of Italians living near Rome, to the south-east, occupying the mountains now called Monti Lepini.

VOLTURNUS, a river in south-west Italy, the modern Volturno, flowing past Casilinum, the modern Capena.

VULCAN, the Greek Hephaestus, god of fire and metal-working; the word 'volcano' is derived from his name, and Vulcania is a volcanic district of Sicily, near Mt Etna; he was especially worshipped at Lemnos, an island in the Aegean Sea.

XANTHUS, a river on the plain of Troy.

ZACYNTHUS, an island near Ithaca on the west coast of Greece.

ZEUS, the supreme god of the Greeks, identified with the Roman Jupiter.

SELECT BIBLIOGRAPHY

A full bibliography, including articles in English, for Virgil and his works, compiled by R. G. Austin, is available in *The Joint Association of Classical Teachers, Paper No. 1*, revised in 1968.

Greece and Rome, New Surveys in the Classics, No. 1, by R. D. Williams (Oxford, 1967) is devoted to Virgil and lists many important books and articles.

The following books are particularly important for the *Aeneid*:

C. M. Bowra, *From Virgil to Milton*, London, 1945.

Steele Commager (ed.), *Twentieth Century Views*: *Virgil*, New Jersey, 1966.

T. A. Dorey and D. R. Dudley, *Studies in Latin Literature and its Influence*: *Virgil*, London, 1969.

T. S. Eliot, *Poetry and Poets*, London, 1957.

T. R. Glover, *Virgil*, London, 1904, 7th ed. 1942.

W. F. Jackson Knight, *Accentual Symmetry in Vergil*, Oxford, 1939. *Roman Vergil*, London, 1944; revised edition Peregrine Books, 1966. 'Vergil and Homer' in *Many-Minded Homer*, London, 1968. *Vergil*: *Epic and Anthropology*, London, 1967.

J. W. Mackail, *The Aeneid of Virgil* (introduction and commentary), Oxford, 1930.

Brooks Otis, *Virgil*: *a Study in Civilized Poetry*, Oxford, 1963.

H. W. Prescott, *The Development of Virgil's Art*, Chicago, 1927.

M. C. J. Putnam, *The Poetry of the Aeneid*, Harvard, 1965.

K. Quinn, *Latin Explorations*, London, 1963. *Virgil's Aeneid*: *a Critical Description*, London, 1968.

E. K. Rand, *The Magical Art of Virgil*, Harvard, 1931.

M. R. Ridley, *Studies in Three Literatures*, London, 1962.

W. Y. Sellar, *The Roman Poets of the Augustan Age*: *Virgil*, Oxford, 1877, 3rd ed. 1897.

L. P. Wilkinson, *Golden Latin Artistry*, Cambridge, 1963.

G. W. Williams, *Tradition and Originality in Roman Poetry*, Oxford, 1968.

W. A. Camps, *An Introduction to Virgil's Aeneid*, Oxford, 1969.

The War in Latium
L.Vulsiniensis
Marta
Graviscae
Minio
L.Sabatinus
Agylla [Caere]
Pallanteum [Roma]
Ostia
Lavinium
? Laurentum
Tiberis
Nar
Nursia
Amiternum
Nersae
Himella
Lacus Fucinus
? Fescennium
Fidenae
Anio
Tibur
Praeneste
Alba Longa
Liris
Ardea
Privernum
? Ufens
Amasenus
Anxur
Circeii
Caieta
Volturnus
Capua
Cumae
Neapolis
Inarime
Baiae
Sarnus
Capreae
Miles
0
50
SW
The Site of Rome
Janiculum
Tiber
Citadel
Capitoline
Altar to Hercules
Forum
Palatine
Argiletum
Aventine
Quirinal
Viminal
Esquiline
Carinae
Caelian

Padua
Mantua
Timavus
R. Po
Arx Monoeci [Monaco]
ETRURIA
UMBRIA
Ilva
[Elba]
CORSICA
Tiberis
Pallanteum [Roma]
C. Garganus
Trojan Camp
LATIUM
Argyripa [Arpi]
Lavinium
Antium
Caieta
APULIA
CAMPANIA
Cumae
SARDINIA
Neapolis [Napoli. Naples]
Capreae
Tarentum
Petelia
Lacinium
Aeolian Is.
Scylaceum
Lipara
Eryx
Acesta
Pelorus
Caulonia
Drepanum
Lilybaeum
Selinus
Cyclops' Harbour
Acragas
Megara
Thapsus
Carthage
Gela
Ortygia
Camarina
Helorus
Pachynus
Melita [Malta]
MEDITERRANEAN

The Voyages of Aeneas
Miles
0
50
100
THRACE
?Aeneadae
Thasos
Samothrace
Athos
Imbros
Rhoeteum
Troy
MYSIA
Mt Olympus
Lemnos
Tenedos
Mt Ida
Antandros
Ceraunia
?Phaeacia
[Corfu]
Buthrotum
EPIRUS
THESSALY
AEGEAN
Lesbos
LYDIA
Smyrna
Leucas
Actium
Leucate
Calydon
Thebes
Euboea
Chios
Erythrae
Claros
Same
Ithaca
ATTICA
SEA
Samos
Athens
Mycenae
ARCADIA
Zacynthos
Argos
Myconos
Delos
Paros
Donusa
Strophades Is.
Sparta
Naxos
Oleandros
Rhodes
Malea
Cythera
?Pergamea
Cnossus
Mt Ida
Mt Dicte
CRETA
SEA

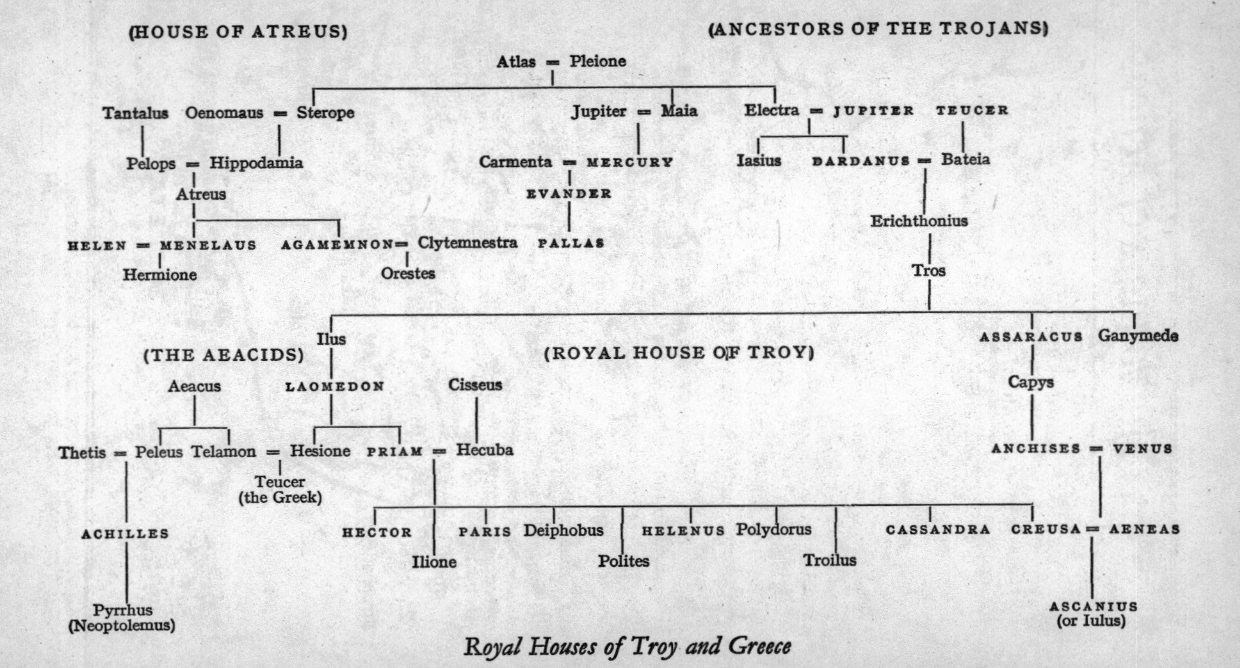

Royal Houses of Troy and Greece

MORE ABOUT PENGUINS AND PELICANS

Penguinews, which appears every month, contains details of all the new books issued by Penguins as they are published. From time to time it is supplemented by our stocklist, which is our complete list of almost 5,000 titles.

A specimen copy of *Penguinews* will be sent to you free on request. Please write to Dept EP, Penguin Books Ltd, Harmondsworth, Middlesex, for your copy.

In the U.S.A.: For a complete list of books available from Penguins in the United States write to Dept CS, Penguin Books, 625 Madison Avenue, New York, New York 10022.

In Canada: For a complete list of books available from Penguins in Canada write to Penguin Books Canada Ltd, 2801 John Street, Markham, Ontario L3R 1B4.